Sketches of the Life and Character of Patrick Henry

Sully Pinxt

PATRICK HENRY.

THE LIFE AND CHARACTER

OF

PATRICK HENRY.

BY WILLIAM WIRT
OF RICHMOND, VIRGINIA.

"In quo hoc maximum est, quod neque ante illum, quem ille imitarateur neque post illum qui eum imitari poosset. inventus est." *Paterc.* lib. i. cap. v.

"His distinguishing characteristic is this, that he was preceded by none whom he imitated, nor did any come after who could imitate him."

REVISED EDITION,

WITH HEADINGS TO EACH CHAPTER, AND SUCH AN ARRANGEMENT OF THE NOTES CONTAINED IN THE FORMER EDITIONS, AS TO RENDER THE WORK SUITABLE FOR A CLASS BOOK IN ACADEMIES AND SCHOOLS.

ITHACA, N. Y.:
PUBLISHED BY ANDRUS, GAUNTLETT, & CO.,
No. 69 OWEGO STREET.

1850.

PREFACE

The reader has a right to know what degree of credit is due to the following narrative; and it is the object of this preface to give him that satisfaction.

It was in the summer of eighteen hundred and five, that the design of writing this biography was first conceived. It was produced by an incident of feeling, which, however it affected the author at the time, might now be thought light and trivial by the reader; and he shall not, therefore, be detained by the recital of it. The author knew nothing of Mr. Henry, personally. He had never seen him, and was of course compelled to rely wholly on the information of others. As soon, therefore, as the design was formed of writing his life, aware of the necessity of losing no time in collecting, from the few remaining coevals of Mr. Henry, that personal knowledge of the subject which might ere long be expected to die with them, the author despatched letters to every quarter of the state in which it occurred to him as probable that interesting matter might be found; and he was gratified by the prompt attention which was paid to his inquiries.

There were, at that time, living in the county of Hanover, three gentlemen of the first respectability, who had been the companions of Mr. Henry's childhood and youth; these were, Col. Charles Dabney, Capt. George Dabney, and Col. William O. Winston; the two first of whom are still living. Not having the pleasure of a personal acquaintance with these gentlemen, the author interested the late Mr. Nathaniel Pope in his object, and, by his instrumentality, procured all the useful information which was in their possession. Mr. Pope is well known to have been a gentleman of uncommonly vigorous and discriminating mind; a sacred observer of truth, and a man of the purest sense of honour. The author cannot recall the memory of this most amiable and excellent man, to whom (if there be any merit in this work) the friends of Mr. Henry and the state of Virginia owe so many obligations, without paying to that revered memory the tribute of his respect and affection. Mr. Pope was one of those ardent young Virginians, who embarked before they had attained their maturity, in the cause of the American revolution: he joined an animated and active corps of horse, and signalized himself by an impetuous gallantry, which drew upon him the eyes and the applause of his commander. In peace, he was as mild as he had been brave in war; his bosom was replete with the kindest affections; he was in truth, one of the best of companions, and one of the warmest of friends. The fact that he was the acknowledged head of the several bars at which he practised in the country, may assure the reader of his capacity for the commission which he so cheerfully undertook, in regard to Mr. Henry; and the unblemished integrity of his life may assure him also of the fidelity with which that commission was executed. So many important anecdotes in the following work depend on the credit of this gentleman as a witness, that the slight sketch which has been given of his character, will not, it is hoped, be thought foreign to the purpose of this preface. Mr. Pope did not confine his inquiries to the county of Hanover: he was indefatigable in collecting information from every quarter; which he never accepted, however, but from the purest sources; and his authority for every incident was given with the most scrupulous accuracy. The author had hoped to have had it in his power to gratify this gentleman, by submitting to his view the joint result of their labours, and obtaining the benefit of his last corrections; but he was disappointed by his untimely and melancholy death. He fell a victim to that savage practice, which, under the false name of honour, continued to prevail too long; and his death is believed to have been highly instrumental in hastening that system of legislation in restraint of this practice, which now exists in Virginia.

Besides the contributions furnished by Mr. Pope, the writer derived material aid from various other quarters. The widow of Mr. Henry was still living, and had intermarried with Judge Winston; from this gentleman (who was also related to Mr. Henry by blood, and had been intimately acquainted with him through the far greater part of his life,) the author received a succinct, but extremely accurate and comprehensive memoir.

Col. Meredith, of Amherst, was a few years older than Mr. Henry, had been raised in the same neighbourhood, and had finally married one of his sisters. Having known Mr. Henry from his birth to his death, he had it in his power to supply very copious details, which were taken down from his narration by the present Judge Cabell, and forwarded to the author.

One of the most intimate and confidential friends of Mr. Henry was the late Judge Tyler. The judge had a kind of Roman frankness, and even bluntness, in his manners, together with a decision of character and a benevolence of spirit, which had attached Mr. Henry to him, from his first appearance on the public stage. They were, for a long time, members of the House of Delegates together, and their friendship continued until it was severed by death. From Judge Tyler the author received a very minute and interesting communication of incidents, the whole of which had either passed in his own presence, or had been related to him by Mr. Henry himself.

The writer is indebted to Judge Tucker for two or three of his best incidents; one of them will probably be pronounced the most interesting passage of the work. He owes to the same gentleman, too, the fullest and liveliest description of the person of Mr. Henry, which has been furnished from any quarter; and he stands further indebted to him for a rare and (to the purpose of this work) a very important book—the Journals of the House of Burgesses for the years seventeen hundred and sixty-three, four, five, six, and seven.

From Judge Roane the author has received one of the fairest and most satisfactory communications that has been made to him; and the vigour and elegance with which that gentleman writes, has frequently enabled the author to relieve the dulness of his own narrative, by extracts from his statements.

Mr. Jefferson, too, has exercised his well-known kindness and candour on this occasion; having not only favoured the author with a very full communication in the first instance; but assisted him, subsequently and repeatedly, with his able counsel, in reconciling apparent contradictions, and clearing away difficulties of fact.

Besides these statements, drawn from the memory of his correspondents, the writer was favoured, by the late Governor Page, with the reading of a pretty extended sketch, which he had himself prepared, of the life of Mr. Henry; and he has, furthermore, availed himself of the kind permission of Mr. Peyton Randolph, to examine an extremely valuable manuscript history of Virginia, written by his father, the late Mr. Edmund Randolph; which embraces the whole period of Mr. Henry's public life.

In addition to these stores of information the author has had the good fortune to procure complete files of the public newspapers, reaching from the year seventeen hundred and sixty-five down to the close of the American revolution; by these he has been enabled to correct, in some important instances, the memory of his correspondents, in relation not only to dates, but to facts themselves.

He has been fortunate, too, in having procured several original letters, which shed much light on important and hitherto disputed facts, in the life of Mr. Henry.

The records of the General Court, and the archives of the state, having been convenient to the author, and always open to him, he has endeavoured assiduously and carefully to avail himself of that certain and permanent evidence which they afford; and has been enabled, by this means, as the reader will discover, to correct some strange mistakes in historical facts.

The author's correspondents will find, that he has departed, in some instances, from their respective statements; and he owes them an explanation for having done so: the explanation is this—their statements were, in several instances, diametrically opposed to each other; and were sometimes all contradicted by the public prints, or the records of the state. It ought not to be matter of surprise, that these contradictions should exist, even among those most respectable gentlemen, relying, as they did, upon human memory merely; and speaking of events so very remote, without a previous opportunity of communicating with each other. It will be seen by them, that the author has been obliged in several instances, to contradict even the several histories of the times, concerning which he writes; but this he has never done, without the most decisive proofs of his own correctness, which he has always cited, nor has he ever departed from the narratives of his several correspondents, except under the direction of preponderating evidence. As among those contradictory statements, *all* could not be true, he has sought the correction by public documnets, when such correction was attainable; and when it was not, he has selected, among his narrators, those whose opportunities to know the fact in question seemed to be the best. This he has done, without the slightest intention to throw a shadow of suspicion on the credit of any gentleman who has been so obliging as to answer his inquiries; but merely from the necessity which he was under, either of making *some selection*, or abandoning the work altogether; and because he knew of no better rule of selection, than that which he has adopted.

Although it has been so long since the collection of these materials was begun, it was not until the summer of eighteen hundred and fourteen that the last communication was received. Even then, when the author sat down to the task of imbodying his materials, there were so many intricacies to disentangle, and so many inconsistencies, from time to time, to explain and settle, and that, too, through the tedious agency of cross-mails, that his progress was continually impeded, and has been, to him, most painfully retarded.

Other causes, too, have contributed to delay the publication. The author is a practising lawyer; and the courts which he attends, keep him perpetually and exclusively occupied in that attendance, through ten months of the year; nor does the summer recess of two months afford a remission from professional labour. In Virginia, the duties of attorney, counsellor, conveyancer, and advocate, are all performed by the same individual; hence, the summer vacation, instead of being a time of leisure, is not only the season of preparation for the approaching courts, but is subject, moreover, to a perpetual recurrence of what are here called *office* duties, which renders a steady application to any other subject impossible.

These sketches are now submitted to the public, with unaffected diffidence; not of the facts which they detail, for on them the author has the firmest reliance; but of the manner in which he has been able to accomplish his undertaking. For, (to say nothing of his inexperience and want of ability for such a work) he has been compelled to write (when he was suffered to write at all) amidst that incessant professional annoyance which has been mentioned, and which is known by every man who has ever made the trial, to forbid the hope of success in any composition of this extent. Conld the writer have looked forward, with any reasonable calculation, to a period of greater ease, his respect for the memory of Mr. Henry, as well as his regard for himself, would have induced him to suspend this undertaking until that period should have arrived. But having no ground for any hope of this kind, he has thought it better to hazard even these crude sketches, than to suffer the materials, which he had accumulated with so much toil, and for an object which he thought so laudable, to perish on his hands.

These remarks are not made with the view of deprecating the censures of critics by profession; but merely to bespeak the candour of that larger portion of readers, who are willing to be pleased with the best efforts that can be reasonably expected from the circumstances of the case. The author, however, is well satisfied that the most indulgent reader (although benevolently disposed to overlook defects of execution) will be certainly disappointed *in the matter itself* of this work; for, notwithstanding all his exertions, he is entirely conscious that the materials, which he has been able to collect are scanty and meager, and utterly disproportionate to the great fame of Mr. Henry. It is probable, that much of what was once known of him had perished, before the author commenced his researches; and, it is very possible, that much may still be known, which he has not been able to discover; because it lies in unsuspected sources, or with persons unwilling, for some reason or other, to communicate their information. It is the conviction, that he has not been able to inform himself of the whole events of Mr. Henry's life, and that his collection can be considered only as so many detached SKETCHES. If, in this humble and unassuming character, it shall give any pleasure to the numerous admirers of Mr. Henry, in Virginia, the author will have attained all that he has a right to expect.

RICHMOND, Va. Sept. 5th, 1817.

NOTE A.

IT appears by the journals of the house of burgesses, of the 14th November, seventeen hundred and sixty-four, (page 38,) that a committee was appointed to draw up the following address, memorial, and remonstrance; which committee was composed of the following persons, to wit: Mr. Attorney, (Peyton Randolph,) Mr. Richard Henry Lee, Mr. Landon Carter, Mr. Wythe, Mr. Edmund Pendleton, Mr. Benjamin Harrison Mr. Cary, and Mr. Fleming, to whom, afterward, Mr. Bland was added. The address to the king is from the pen of the attorney.*

* On the authority of Mr. Jefferson.

"*To the king's most excellent Majesty.*

"Most Gracious Sovereign,

"We, your majesty's dutiful and loyal subjects, the council and burgesses of yonr ancient colony and dominion of *Virginia*, now met in general assembly, beg leave to assure your majesty of our firm and inviolable attachment to yous sacred person and government; and as your faithful subjects here have at all times been zealous to demonstrate this truth, by a ready compliance with the royal requisttion during the late war, by which a heavy and oppressive debt of near half a million had been incurred, so at this time they implore permission to approach the throne with humble confidence, and to entreat that your majesty will be graciously pleased to ptotect our people of this colony in the enjoyment of their ancient and inestimable right of being governed by such laws, respecting their internal polity and taxation, as are derived from their own consen(, with the approbation of their sovereign or his substitute: a right which, as men, and descendants of *Britons*, they have ever quietly possessed, since, first by royal permission and encouragement, they left the mother kingdom to extend its commerce and dominion.

ADVERTISEMENT.

THE appearance of a duodecimo edition of Marshall's Life of Washington, suggested to the proprietors of *The Life of Patrick Henry*, the desirableness and utility of the present edition. As that masterly sketch of the heroic deeds and character of the Father of his country, furnishes to the youth of our land the most impressive lessons of patriotism and manly energy, so it was presumed that this graphic delineation of the genius of the "*forest-born Demosthenes*," was admirably calculated to elicit in the youthful mind, feelings of emulation which time might develop into action and honourable usefulness. It was not, however, alone for youth, or for the use of the *School Libraries* of our several states, that this work has assumed its present form—it was equally designed for those who would have purchased the former edition, had it been less expensive, who will find under a less commanding appearance, the same as is contained in the octavo edition—the only alteration being in a more convenient arrangement of some of the notes.

WIRT'S

LIFE OF PATRICK HENRY.

CHAPTER I.

Birth of Patrick Henry—Family Reminiscences—Early Propensities—Is placed under the Care of a Merchant—Engages in Business with his Brother—Becomes bankrupt—Is married—Commences farming—Abandons Agriculture and recommences mercantile Business—Is again unfortunate—Becomes acquainted with Mr. Jefferson—Determines to study Law—Is licensed—Contest on the Subject of the Tobacco Law—Mr. Henry retained as Counsel—Success of his first Effort.

Patrick Henry, the second son of John and Sarah Henry, and one of nine children, was born on the twenty-ninth of May, seventeen hundred and thirty-six, at the family-seat, called Studley, in the county of Hanover and colony of Virginia. In his early childhood, his parents removed to another seat, in the same county, then called Mount Brilliant, now the Retreat; at which latter place Patrick Henry was raised and educated. His parents, though not rich, were in easy circumstances; and, in point of personal character, were among the most respectable inhabitants of the colony.

His father, Col. John Henry, was a native of Aberdeen in Scotland. He was, it is said, a first cousin to David Henry, who was the brother-in-law and successor of Edward Cave, in the publication of that celebrated work, "The Gentleman's Magazine," and himself the author of several literary tracts: John Henry is also said to have been a nephew, in the maternal line, to the great historian Dr. William Robertson. He came over to Virginia, in quest of fortune, some time prior to the year seventeen hundred and thirty, and the tradition is, that he enjoyed the friendship and patronage of Mr. Dinwiddie, afterward the governor of the colony. By this gentleman, it is reported, that he was introduced to the elder Col. Syme of Hanover, in whose family, it is certain, that he became domesticated during the life of that gentleman; after whose death he intermarried with his widow, and resided on the estate which he had left.

It is considered as a fair proof of the personal merit of Mr. John Henry, that, in those days, when offices were bestowed with peculiar caution, he was the colonel of his regiment, the principal surveyor of the county, and, for many years, the presiding magistrate of the county court. His surviving acquaintances concur in stating, that he was a man of liberal education; that he possessed a plain, yet solid understanding; and lived long a life of the most irreproachable integrity and exemplary piety.

His brother Patrick, a clergyman of the church of England, followed him to this country some years afterward; and became, by *his* influence, the minister of St. Paul's parish in Hanover, the functions of which office he sustained throughout life with great respectability. Both the brothers were zealous members of the established church, and warmly attached to the reigning family. Col. John Henry was conspicuously so. "There are those yet alive," says a correspondent, (Mr. Pope. in eighteen hundred and five,) "who have seen him at the head of his regiment, celebrating the birth-day, of George III. with as much enthusiasm as his son Patrick afterward displayed in resisting the encroachments of that monarch."*

Mrs. Henry, the widow of Col. Syme, as we have seen, and the mother of Patrick Henry, was a native of Hanover county, and of the family of Winstons. She possessed, in an eminent degree, the mild and benevolent disposition, the undeviating probity, the correct understanding, and easy elocution, by which that ancient family has been so long distinguished. Her brother William, the father of the present Judge Winston, is said to have been highly endowed with that peculiar cast of eloquence, for which Mr. Henry became, afterward, so justly celebrated. Of this gentleman, I have an anecdote from a correspondent, (Mr. Pope,) which I shall give in his own words:—

"I have often heard my father, who was intimately acquainted with this William Winston, say, that he was the greatest orator whom he ever heard, Patrick Henry excepted; that during the last French and Indian war, and soon after Braddock's defeat, when the militia were marched to the frontiers of Virginia, against the enemy, this William Winston was the lieutenant of a company; that the men, who were indifferently clothed, without tents, and exposed to the rigour and inclemency of the weather, discovered great aversion to the service, and were anxious and even clamorous to return to their families;

* Mr. Burk's account of Mr. Henry is extremely careless and full of errors. He begins by making him the son of his uncle:—"*Patrick Henry*, the son of a Scotch gentleman of *the same name*," &c.—3d vol. of the History of Virginia, page 300.

when this William Winston, mounting a stump, (the common *rostrum*, you know, of the field-orator of Virginia,) addressed them with such keenness of invective, and declaimed with such force of eloquence, on liberty and patriotism, that when he concluded, the general cry was, 'Let us march on; lead us against the enemy!' and they were now willing, nay, anxious to encounter all those difficulties and dangers which, but a few moments before, had almost produced a mutiny.

Thus much I have been able to collect of the parentage and family of Mr. Henry; and this, I presume, will be thought quite sufficient, in relation to a man, who owed no part of his greatness to the lustre of his pedigree, but was, in truth, the soul founder of his own fortunes.

Until ten years of age, Patrick Henry was sent to a school in the neighbourhood, where he learned to read and write, and made some small progress in arithmetic. He was then taken home, and under the direction of his father, who had opened a grammar-school in his own house, he acquired a superficial knowledge of the Latin language, and learned to read the character, but never to translate Greek. At the same time, he made a considerable proficiency in the mathematics, the only branch of education for which, it seems, he discovered in his youth, the slightest predilection.

But he was too idle to gain any solid advantage from the opportunities which were thrown in his way. He was passionately addicted to the sports of the field, and could not support the confinement and toil which education required. Hence, instead of system, or any semblance of regularity in his studies, his efforts were always desultory, and became more and more rare; until at length, when the hour of his school exercises arrived, Patrick was scarcely ever to be found. He was in the forest with his gun, or over the brook with his angle-rod; and, in these frivolous occupations, when not controlled by the authority of his father, (which was rarely exerted,) he would, it is said, spend whole days and weeks, with an appetite rather whetted than cloyed by enjoyment. His school-fellows, having observed his growing passion for these amusements, and having remarked that its progress was not checked either by the want of companions or the want of success, have frequently watched his movements to discover, if they could, the secret source of that delight which they seemed to afford him. But they made no discovery which led them to any other conclusion than (to use their own expression) that "he loved idleness for its own sake." They have frequently observed him lying along, under the shade of some tree that overhung the sequestered stream, watching, for hours, at the same spot, the motionless cork of his fishing line, without one encouraging symptom of success, and without any apparent source of enjoyment, unless he could find it in the ease of his posture, or in the illusions of hope, or, which is most probable, in the stillness of the scene and the silent workings of his own imagination.

This love of solitude, in his youth, was often observed. Even when hunting with a party, his choice was not to join the noisy band that drove the deer; he preferred to take his stand, alone, where he might wait for the passing game, and indulge himself, meanwhile, in the luxury of thinking. Not that he was averse to society; on the contrary, he had, at times, a very high zest for it. But even in society, his enjoyments while young, were of a very peculiar cast; he did not mix in the wild mirth of his equals in age; but sat, quiet and demure, taking no part in the conversation, giving no responsive smile to the circulating jest, but lost, to all appearance, in silence and abstraction. This abstraction, however, was only apparent; for on the dispersion of a company, when interrogated by his parents as to what had been passing, he was able, not only to detail the conversation, but to sketch, with strict fidelity, the character of every speaker. None of these early delineations of character are retained by his contemporaries; and, indeed, they are said to have been more remarkable for their justness, than for any peculiar felicity of execution.

I cannot learn that he gave, in his youth, any evidence of that precocity which sometimes distinguishes uncommon genius. His companions recollect no instance of premature wit, no striking sentiment, no flash of fancy, no remarkable beauty or strength of expression; and no indication, however slight, either of that impassioned love of liberty, or of that adventurous daring and intrepidity, which marked so strongly, his future character. So far was he, indeed, from exhibiting any one prognostic of this greatness, that every omen foretold a life, at best, of mediocrity, if not of insignificance.

His person is represented as having been coarse, his manners uncommonly awkward, his dress slovenly, his conversation very plain, his aversion to study invincible, and his faculties almost entirely benumbed by indolence. No persuasions could bring him either to read or to work. On the contrary, he ran wild in the forest, like one of the *aborigines* of the country, and divided his life between the dissipation and uproar of the chase and the languor of inaction.

His propensity to observe and comment upon the human character was, so far as I can learn, the only circumstance which distinguished him, advantageously, from his youthful companions. This propensity seems to have been born with him, and to have exerted itself, instinctively, the moment that a new subject was presented to his view. Its action was incessant, and it became, at length almost the only intellectual exercise in which he seemed to take delight. To this cause may be traced that consummate knowledge of the human heart which he finally attained, and which enabled him, when he came upon the public stage, to touch the springs of passion with a master-hand, and to control the resolutions and decisions of his hearers, with a power, almost more than mortal.

From what has been already stated, it will be seen how little education had to do with the formation of this great man's mind. He was, indeed, a mere child of nature, and nature seems to have been too proud and too jealous of her work, to permit it to be touched by the hand of art. She gave him Shakspeare's genius, and bid him, like Shakspeare, to depend on that alone.

Let not the youthful reader, however, deduce, from the example of Mr. Henry, an argument in favour of indolence and the contempt of study. Let him remember that the powers which surmounted the disadvantage of those early habits, were such as very rarely appear upon this earth. Let him remember, too, how long the genius, even of Mr. Henry, was kept down and hidden from the public view, by the sorcery of those pernicious habits; through what years of poverty and wretchedness they doomed him to struggle; and, let him re member, that, at length, when in the zenith of his glory, Mr. Henry himself had frequent occasion to deplore the consequences of his early neglect of literature, and to bewail "the ghosts of his departed hours."

His father, unable to sustain, with convenience, the expense of so large a family as was now multiplying on his hands, found it necessary to qualify his sons, at a very early age, to support themselves. With this view, Patrick was placed at the age of fifteen, behind the counter of a merchant in the country. How he conducted himself in this situation, I have not been able to learn. There could not, however, I presume, have been any flagrant impropriety in his conduct, since, in the next year, his father considered him qualified to carry on business on his own account. Under this impression, he purchased a small adventure of goods for his two sons, William and Patrick, and, according to the language of the country, "set them up in trade." William's habits of idleness were, if possible, still more unfortunate than Patrick's. The chief management of their concerns, devolved, therefore, on the younger brother, and that management seems to have been most wretched.

Left to himself, all the indolence of his character returned.

Those unfortunate habits which he had formed, and whose spell was already too strong to be broken, comported very poorly with that close attention, that accuracy and persevering vigour, which are essential to the merchant. The drudgery of retailing and of book-keeping soon became intolerable; yet he was obliged to preserve appearances by remaining continually at his stand. Besides these unpropitious habits, there was still another obstacle to his success, in the natural kindness of his temper. "He could not find it in his heart" to disappoint any one who came to him for *credit;* and he was very easily satisfied by apologies for non-payment. He condemned, in himself, this facility of temper, and foresaw the embarrassments with which it threatened him; but he was unable to overcome it. Even with the best prospects, the confinement of such a business would have been scarcely supportable; but with those which now threatened him, his store became a prison. To make the matter still worse, the joys of the chase, joys now to him forbidden, echoed around him every morning, and by their contrast, and the longings which they excited, contributed to deepen the disgust which he had taken to his employments.

From these painful reflections, and the gloomy forebodings which darkened the future, he sought, at first, a refuge in music, for which it seems he had a natural taste, and he learned to play well on the violin and on the flute. From music he passed to books, and, having procured a few light and elegant authors, acquired, for the first time, a relish for reading.

He found another relief, too, in the frequent opportunities now afforded him of pursuing his favourite study of the human character. The character of every customer underwent this scrutiny; and that, not with reference either to the integrity or solvency of the individual, in which one would suppose that Mr. Henry would feel himself most interested; but in relation to the structure of his mind, the general cast of his opinions, the motives and principles which influenced his actions, and what may be called the philosophy of character.

In pursuing these investigations, he is said to have resorted to arts, apparently so far above his years, and which looked so much like an afterthought, resulting from his future eminence, that I should hesitate to make the statement, were it not attested by so many witnesses, and by some who cannot be suspected of the capacity for having fabricated the fact. Their account of it, then, is this:—that whenever a company of his customers met in the store, (which frequently happened on the last day of the week,) and were themselves sufficiently gay and animated to talk and act as nature prompted, without concealment, without reserve, he would take no part in their discussions, but listen with a silence as deep and attentive as if under the influence of some potent charm. If, on the contrary, they were dull and silent, he would, without betraying his drift, task himself to set them in motion, and excite them to remark, collision, and exclamation. He was peculiarly delighted with comparing their characters, and ascertaining how they would severally act in given situations. With this view he would state a hypothetic case, and call for their opinions one by one, as to the conduct which would be proper in it. If they differed, he would demand their reasons, and enjoy highly the debates in which he would thus involve them. But multiplying and varying those imaginary cases at pleasure, he ascertained the general course of human opinion, and formed, for himself, as it were, a graduated scale of the motives and conduct which are natural to man. Sometimes he would entertain them with stories, gathered from his reading, or, as was more frequently the case, drawn from his own fancy, composed of heterogeneous circumstances, calculated to excite, by turns, pity, terror, resentment, indignation, contempt; pausing in the turns of his narrative, to observe the effect; to watch the different modes in which the passions expressed themselves, and learn the language of emotion from those children of nature.

In these exercises, Mr. Henry could have had nothing in view beyond the present gratification of a natural propensity. The advantages of them, however, were far more permanent, and gave the brightest colours to his future life. For those continual efforts to render himself intelligible to his plain and unlettered hearers, on subjects entirely new to them, taught him that clear and simple style which forms the best vehicle of thought to a popular assembly; while his attempts to interest and affect them, in order that he might hear from them the echo of nature's voice, instructed him in those topics of persuasion by which men were the most certainly to be moved, and in the kind of imagery and structure of language, which were the best fitted to strike and agitate their hearts. These constituted his excellences as an orator; and never was there a man, in any age, who possessed, in a more eminent degree, the lucid and nervous style of argument, the command of the most beautiful and striking imagery, or that language of passion which burns from soul to soul.

In the meantime, the business of the store was rushing headlong to its catastrophe. One year put an end to it. William was then thrown loose upon society,* to which he was

* I have seen an original letter from Col. John Henry to his son William, in which he remonstrates with him on his wild and dissipated course of life.

never afterward usefully attached; and Patrick was engaged for the two or three following years, in winding up this disastrous experiment as well as he could.

His misfortunes, however, seem not to have had the effect either of teaching him prudence or of chilling his affections. For, at the early age of eighteen, we find him married to a Miss Shelton, the daughter of an honest farmer in the neighbourhood, but in circumstances too poor to contribute effectually to her support. By the joint assistance of their parents, however, the young couple were settled on a small farm, and here, with the assistance of one or two slaves, Mr. Henry had to delve the earth, with his own hands, for subsistence. Such are the vicissitudes of human life! It is curious to contemplate this giant genius, destined in a few years to guide the councils of a mighty nation, but unconscious of the intellectual treasures which he possessed, encumbered, at the early age of eighteen, with the cares of a family; obscure, unknown, and almost unpitied; digging, with wearied limbs and with an aching heart, a small spot of barren earth, for bread, and blessing the hour of night which relieved him from toil.

Little could the wealthy and great of the land, as they rolled along the highway in splendour, and beheld the young rustic at work in the coarse garb of a labourer, covered with dust and melting in the sun, have suspected that this was the man who was destined not only to humble their pride, but to make the prince himself tremble on his distant throne, and to shake the brightest jewels from the British crown. Little, indeed, could he himself have suspected it; for amid the distresses which thickened around him at this time, and threatened him not only with obscurity but with famine, no hopes came to cheer the gloom, nor did there remain to him any earthly consolation, save that which he found in the bosom of his own family. Fortunately for him, there never was a heart which felt this consolation with greater force. No man ever possessed the domestic virtues in a higher degree, or enjoyed, more exquisitely, those pure delights which flow from the endearing relations of conjugal life.

Mr. Henry's want of agricultural skill, and his unconquerable aversion to every species of systematic labour, drove him, necessarily, after a trial of two years, to abandon this pursuit

There is reason to believe, however, that at a later period, he may have reformed, since a gentleman, to whom the manuscript of this work was submitted, notes on this passage, that when he was at college at Williamsburgh, he recollects to have seen William Henry a member of the assembly, from the county of Fluvanna; that he was called colonel, and was, he afterward understood, pretty well provided as to fortune.

altogether. His next step seems to have been dictated by absolute despair; for, selling off his little possessions, at a sacrifice for cash, he entered, a second time, on the inauspicious business of merchandise. Perhaps he flattered himself that he would be able to profit by his past experience, and conduct this experiment to a more successful issue. But if he did so, he deceived himself. He soon found that he had not changed his character, by changing his pursuits. His early habits still continued to haunt him. The same want of method, the same facility of temper, soon became apparent by their ruinous effects. He resumed his violin, his flute, his books, his curious inspection of human nature; and not unfrequently ventured to shut up his store, and indulge himself in the favourite sports of his youth.

His reading, however, began to assume a more serious character. He studied geography, in which it is said that he became an adept. He read, also, the charters and history of the colony. He became fond of historical works generally, particularly those of Greece and Rome; and, from the tenacity of his memory and the strength of his judgment, soon made himself a perfect master of their contents. Livy was his favourite; and having procured a translation, he became so much enamoured of the work, that he made it a standing rule to read it through, once at least, in every year, during the early part of his life.* The grandeur of the Roman character, so beautifully exhibited by Livy, filled him with surprise and admiration; and he was particularly enraptured with those vivid descriptions and eloquent harangues with which the work abounds. Fortune could scarcely have thrown in his way, a book better fitted to foster his republican spirit, and awaken the still dormant powers of his genius; and it seems not improbable, that the lofty strain in which he himself afterward both spoke and acted, was, if not originally inspired, at least highly raised, by the noble models set before him by this favourite author.

This second mercantile experiment was still more unfortunate than the first. In a few years it left him a bankrupt, and placed him in a situation than which it is difficult to conceive one more wretched. Every atom of his property was now gone, his friends were unable to assist him any further; he had tried every means of support, of which he could suppose himself capable, and every one had failed; ruin was behind him; poverty, debt, want, and famine, before; and, as if his cup of misery was not already full enough, here were a suffering wife and children to make it overflow.

* Judge Nelson had this statement from Mr. Henry himself

But with all his acuteness of feeling, Mr. Henry possessed great native firmness of character; and, let me add, great reliance, too, on that unseen arm which never long deserts the faithful. Thus supported, he was able to bear up under the heaviest pressure of misfortune, and even to be cheerful, under circumstances which would sink most other men into despair.

It was at this period of his fortunes, that Mr. Jefferson became acquainted with him; and the reader, I am persuaded, will be gratified with that gentleman's own account of it. These are his words:—"My acquaintance with Mr. Henry commenced in the winter of seventeen hundred and fifty-nine—sixty. On my way to the college I passed the Christmas-holydays at Col. Dandridge's, in Hanover, to whom Mr. Henry was a near neighbour. During the festivity of the season, I met him in society every day, and we became well acquainted, although I was much his junior, being then in my seventeenth year, and he a married man.

"His manners had something of coarseness in them; his passion was music, dancing, and pleasantry. He excelled in the last, and it attached every one to him. You ask some account of his mind and information at this period; but you will recollect that we were almost continually engaged in the usual revelries of the season. The occasion, perhaps, as much as his idle disposition, prevented his engaging in any conversation which might give the measure either of his mind or information. Opportunity was not, indeed, wholly wanting; because Mr. John Campbell was there, who had married Mrs. Spotswood, the sister of Col. Dandridge. He was a man of science, and often introduced conversation on scientific subjects. Mr. Henry had, a little before, broken up his store, or rather it had broken him up; but his misfortunes were not to be traced, either in his countenance or conduct."

This cheerfulness of spirit, under a reverse of fortune so severe, is certainly a very striking proof of the manliness of his character. It is not, indeed, easy to conceive that a mind like Mr. Henry's could finally sink under any pressure of adversity. Such a mind, although it may not immediately perceive whither to direct its efforts, must always possess a consciousness of power sufficient to buoy it above despondency. But, be this as it may, of Mr. Henry it was certainly true, as Dr. Johnson has observed of Swift, that "he was not one of those who, having lost one part of life in idleness, are tempted to throw away the remainder in despair."

It seems to be matter of surprise, that even yet, amid all those various struggles for subsistence, the powers of his mind had not so far developed themselves as to suggest to any friend the pursuit for which he was formed. He seems to have been a plant of slow growth; but, like other plants of that nature, formed for duration, and fitted to endure the buffetings of the rudest storm.

It was now, when all other experiments had failed, that, as a last effort, he determined, of his own accord, to make a tria of the law. No one expected him to succeed in any eminent degree. His unfortunate habits were, by no means, suited to so laborious a profession: and even if it were not too late in life for him to hope to master its learning, the situation of his affairs forbade an extensive course of reading. In addition to these obstacles, the business of the profession, in that quarter, was already in hands from which it was not easily to be taken; for (to mention no others) Judge Lyons, the late president of the court of appeals, was then at the bar of Hanover, and the adjacent counties, with an unrivalled reputation for legal learning; and Mr. John Lewis, a man, also, of very respectable legal attainments, occupied the whole field of forensic eloquence.

Mr. Henry himself seems to have hoped for nothing more from the profession than a scanty subsistence for himself and his family, and his preparation was suited to these humble expectations; for to the study of a profession, which is said to require the lucubrations of twenty years, Mr. Henry devoted not more than six weeks.* On this preparation, however, he obtained a license to practise the law. How he passed with two of the examiners, I have no intelligence; but he himself used to relate his interview with the third. This was no other than Mr. John Randolph, who was afterward the king's attorney-general for the colony; a gentleman of the most courtly elegance of person and manners, a polished wit, and a profound lawyer.

At first, he was so much shocked by Mr. Henry's very ungainly figure and address, that he refused to examine him: understanding, however, that he had already obtained two signatures, he entered with manifest reluctance, on the business. A very short time was sufficient to satisfy him of the erroneous conclusion which he had drawn from the exterior of the candidate. With evident marks of increasing surprise, (produced no doubt by the peculiar texture and strength of Mr. Henry's style, and the boldness and originality of his combinations,) he continued the examination for several hours: interrogating the

* So say Mr. Jefferson and Judge Winston. Mr. Pope says nine months Col. Meredith and Capt. Dabney, six or eight months. Judge Tyler, one month; and he adds: "This I had from his own lips. In this time, he read Coke upon Littleton, and the Virginia laws."

candidate, not on the principles of municipal law, in which he, no doubt, soon discovered his deficiency, but on the laws of nature and of nations, on the policy of the feudal system, and on general history, which last he found to be his stronghold.

During the very short portion of the examination which was devoted to the common law, Mr. Randolph dissented, or affected to dissent from one of Mr. Henry's answers, and called upon him to assign the reasons of his opinion. This produced an argument; and Mr. Randolph now played off on him the same arts which he himself had so often practised on his country customers; drawing him out by questions, endeavouring to puzzle him by subtleties, assailing him with declamation, and watching continually the defensive operations of his mind. After a considerable discussion, he said: "You defend your opinions well, sir; but now to the law and to the testimony." Hereupon, he carried him to his office, and opening the authorities, said to him: "Behold the face of natural reason; you have never seen these books, nor this principle of the law; yet you are right, and I am wrong; and from the lesson which you have given me (you must excuse me for saying it) I will never trust to appearances again. Mr. Henry, if your industry be only half equal to your genius, I augur that you will do well, and become an ornament and an honour to your profession." It was always Mr. Henry's belief that Mr. Randolph had affected this difference of opinion, merely to afford him the pleasure of a triumph, and to make some atonement for the wound which his first repulse had inflicted. Be this as it may, the interview was followed by the most marked and permanent respect on the part of Mr. Randolph, and the most sincere good-will and gratitude on that of Mr. Henry.*

It was at the age of four-and-twenty that Mr. Henry obtain-

* This account of Mr. Henry's examination is given by Judge Tyler, who states it as having come from Mr. Henry himself. It was written before I had received the following statement from Mr. Jefferson; and although there is some difference in the circumstances, it has not been thought important enough to make an alteration of the text necessary. This is Mr. Jefferson's statement:—"In the spring of seventeen hundred and sixty, he came to Williamsburgh to obtain a license as a lawyer, and he called on me at college. He told me he had been reading law only six weeks. Two of the examiners, however, Peyton and John Randolph, men of great facility of temper, signed his license with as much reluctance as their dispositions would permit them to show. Mr. Wythe absolutely refused. Robert C. Nicholas refused also at first; but, on repeated importunities and promises of future reading, he signed. These facts I had afterward from the gentlemen themselves; the two Randolphs acknowledging he was very ignorant of the law, but that they perceived him to be a young man of genius, and did not doubt that he would soon qualify himself."

ed his license. Of the science of law, he knew almost nothing: of the practical part he was so wholly ignorant, that he was not only unable to draw a declaration or a plea, but incapable, it is said, of the most common or simple business of his profession, even of the mode of ordering a suit, giving a notice, or making a motion in court. It is not at all wonderful, therefore, that such a novice, opposed as he was by veterans, covered with the whole armour of the law, should linger in the background for three years.*

During this time, the wants and distresses of his family were extreme. The profits of his practice could not have supplied them even with the necessaries of life; and he seems to have spent the greatest part of his time, both of his study of the law and the practice of the first two or three years, with his father-in-law, Mr. Shelton, who then kept the tavern at Hanover courthouse. Whenever Mr. Shelton was from home, Mr. Henry supplied his place in the tavern, received the guests, and attended to their entertainment. All this was very natural in Mr. Henry's situation, and seems to have been purely the voluntary movement of his naturally kind and obliging disposition.

Hence, however, a story has arisen, that in the early part of his life, he was a barkeeper by profession. The fact seems not to have been so: but if it had been, it would certainly have redounded much more to his honour than to his discredit; for as Mr. Henry owed no part of his distinction either to birth or fortune, but wholly to himself, the deeper the obscurity and poverty from which he emerged, the stronger is the evidence which it bears to his powers, and the greater glory does it shed around him.

About the time of Mr. Henry's coming to the bar, a controversy arose in Virginia, which gradually produced a very strong excitement, and called to it, at length, the attention of the whole state.

This was the famous controversy between the clergy on the one hand, and the legislature of the people of the colony on the other, touching the stipend claimed by the former; and as this was the occasion on which Mr. Henry's genius first broke forth, those who take an interest in his life, will not be displeased by a particular account of the nature and grounds of the dispute. It will be borne in mind, that the church of England was at this period the established church of Virginia;

* "He was not distinguished at tne bar for near four years."—Judge Winston: yet Mr. Burke intin [illegible] that he took the lead in his profession at once. Vol 3d, 301.

and by an act of assembly, passed so far back as the year sixteen hundred and ninety-six, each minister of a parish had been provided with an annual stipend of sixteen thousand pounds of tobacco. This act was re-enacted, with amendments, in seventeen hundred and forty-eight, and in this form had received the royal assent. The price of tobacco had long remained stationary at two pence in the pound, or sixteen shillings and eight pence *per* hundred. According to the provisions of the law, the clergy had the right to demand, and were in the practice of receiving, payment of their stipend in the specific tobacco; unless they chose, for convenience, to commute it for money at the market-price.

In the year seventeen hundred and fifty-five, however, the crop of tobacco having fallen short, the legislature passed "an act to enable the inhabitants of this colony to discharge their tobacco-debts in money for the present year:" by the provisions of which, "all persons, from whom any tobacco was due, were authorized to pay the same either in tobacco or in money, *after the rate of sixteen shillings and eight pence per hundred, at the option of the debtor.*" This act was to continue in force for ten months and no longer, and did not contain the usual clause of suspension, *until it should receive the royal assent.*

Whether the scarcity of tobacco was so general and so notorious, as to render this act a measure of obvious humanity and necessity, or whether the clergy were satisfied by its generality, since it embraced sheriffs, clerks, attorneys, and all other tobacco-creditors, as well as themselves, or whether they acquiesced in it as a temporary expedient, which they supposed not likely to be repeated, it is certain, that no objection was made to the law at that time. They could not, indeed, have helped observing the benefits which the rich planters derived from the act; for they were receiving from fifty to sixty shillings per hundred for their tobacco, while they paid off their debts, due in that article, at the old price of sixteen shillings and eight pence. Nothing, however, was then said in defence either of the royal prerogative or of the rights of the clergy, but the law was permitted to go peaceably through its ten months' operation.

The great tobacco-planters had not forgotten the fruits of this act, when, in the year seventeen hundred and fifty-eight, *upon a surmise* that another short crop was likely to occur, the provisions of the act of seventeen hundred and fifty-five were re-enacted, and the new law, like the former, contained no suspending clause. The crop, as had been anticipated, did fall short, and the price of tobacco rose immediately from sixteen and eight pence to fifty shillings per hundred. The clergy now took the alarm, and the act was assailed by an indignant, sarcastic, and vigorous pamphlet, entitled, "The Two-Penny Act," from the pen of the Reverend John Camm, the rector of York-Hampton parish, and the Episcopalian commissary for the colony.*

He was answered by two pamphlets written, the one by Colonel Richard Bland, and the other by Colonel Landon Carter, in both which the commissary was very roughly handled. He replied, in a still severer pamphlet, under the ludicrous title of "The Colonels Dismounted." The colonels rejoined; and this war of pamphlets, in which, with some sound argument, there was a great deal of what Dryden has called "the horse-play of raillery," was kept up, until the whole colony, which had at first looked on for amusement, kindled seriously in the contest from motives of interest. Such was the excitement produced by the discussion, and at length so strong the current against the clergy, that the printers found it expedient to shut their presses against them in this colony, and Mr. Camm had at last to resort to Maryland for publication.

These pamphlets are still extant, and it seems impossible to deny, at this day, that the clergy had much the best of the argument. The king in his council took up the subject, denounced the act of seventeen hundred and fifty-eight as a usurpation, and declared it utterly null and void. Thus supported, the clergy resolved to bring the question to a judicial test; and suits were accordingly brought by them, in the various county courts of the colony, to recover their stipends in the specific tobacco. They selected the county of Hanover as the place of the first experiment; and this was made in a suit instituted by the Reverend James Maury,† against the collector of that county and his sureties.

The record of this suit is now before me. The declaration is founded on the act of seventeen hundred and forty-eight, which gives the tobacco; the defendants pleaded specially the act of seventeen hundred and fifty eight, which authorizes the

* The governor of Virginia represented the king; the council, the house of lords; and the Episcopalian commissary (a member of the council) represented the spiritual part of that house; the house of burgesses was, of course the house of commons.

† Mr. Burk (vol. 3d, page 303) makes the Rev. Patrick Henry the plaintiff in this cause; in this he is corrected by the records of the county. Mr. Burk also sets down "The Two-Penny Act," to the speculations of a man by the name of Dickinson; in this he is confuted by the act itself; the preamble expressly founding it on the shortness of the crop.

commutation into money, at sixteen and eight pence; to this plea the plaintiff demurred, assigning for causes of demurrer, first, that the act of seventeen hundred and fifty-eight, not having received the royal assent, had not the force of a law; and, secondly, that the king, in council, had declared the act null and void. The case stood for argument on the demurrer to the November term, seventeen hundred and sixty-three, and was argued by Mr. Lyons for the plaintiff, and Mr. John Lewis for the defendants; when the court, very much to the credit of their candour and firmness, breasted the popular current by sustaining the demurrer.

Thus far, the clergy sailed before the wind, and concluded, with good reason, that their triumph was complete: for the act of seventeen hundred and fifty-eight having been declared void by the judgment on the demurrer, that of seventeen hundred and forty-eight was left in full force, and became, in law, the only standard for the finding of the jury. Mr. Lewis was so thoroughly convinced of this, that he retired from the cause; informing his clients that it had been, in effect, decided against them, and that there remained nothing more for him to do. In this desperate situation, they applied to Patrick Henry, and he undertook to argue it for them before a jury, at the ensuing term.

Accordingly, on the first day of the following December, he attended the court, and, on his arrival, found in the courtyard such a concourse as would have appalled any other man in his situation. They were not the people of the county merely who were there, but visiters from all the counties, to a considerable distance around. The decision upon the demurrer had produced a violent ferment among the people, and equal exultation on the part of the clergy; who attended the court in a large body, either to look down opposition, or to enjoy the final triumph of this hard-fought contest, which they now considered as perfectly secure.

Among many other clergymen, who attended on this occasion, came the Reverend Patrick Henry, who was the plaintiff in another cause of the same nature, then depending in court. When Mr. Henry saw his uncle approach, he walked up to his carriage, accompanied by Colonel Meredith, and expressed his regret at seeing him there. "Why so?" inquired the uncle. "Because, sir," said Mr. Henry, "you know that I have never yet spoken in public, and I fear that I shall be too much overawed by your presence, to be able to do my duty to my clients; besides, sir, I shall be obliged to say some *hard things* of the clergy, and I am very unwilling to give pain to your feelings." His uncle reproved him for having engaged in the cause; which Mr. Henry excused by saying, that the clergy had not thought him worthy of being retained on their side, and he knew of no moral principle by which he was bound to refuse a fee from their adversaries; besides, he confessed, that in this controversy, both his heart and judgment, as well as his professional duty, were on the side of the people; he then requested that his uncle would do him the favour to leave the ground.

"Why, Patrick," said the old gentleman, with a good-natured smile, "as to *your* saying hard things of the clergy, I advise you to let that alone: take my word for it, you will do yourself more harm than you will them; and as to my leaving the ground, I fear, my boy, that my presence could neither do you harm nor good in such a cause. However, since you seem to think otherwise, and desire it of me so earnestly, you shall be gratified." Whereupon, he entered his carriage again, and returned home.

Soon after the opening of the court, the cause was called. It stood on a writ of inquiry of damages, no plea having been entered by the defendants since the judgment on the demurrer. The array before Mr. Henry's eyes was now most fearful. On the bench sat more than twenty clergymen, the most learned men in the colony, and the most capable, as well as the severest critics, before whom it was possible for him to make his *debut*. The court-house was crowded with an overwhelming multitude, and surrounded with an immense and anxious throng, who, not finding room to enter, were endeavouring to listen without, in the deepest attention.

But there was something still more awfully disconcerting than all this; for in the chair of the presiding magistrate sat no other person than his own father. Mr. Lyons opened the cause very briefly: in the way of argument he did nothing more than explain to the jury, that the decision upon the demurrer had put the act of seventeen hundred and fifty-eight entirely out of the way, and left the law of seventeen hundred and forty-eight as the only standard of their damages; he then concluded with a highly-wrought eulogium on the benevolence of the clergy.

And now came on the first trial of Patrick Henry's strength. No one had ever heard him speak, and curiosity was on tiptoe. He rose very awkwardly, and faltered much in his exordium. The people hung their heads at so unpromising a commencement; the clergy were observed to exchange sly looks with each other; and his father is described as having almost sunk with confusion from his seat.

But these feelings were of short duration, and soon gave place to others, of a very different character. For now were those wonderful faculties which he possessed, for the first time, developed; and now was first witnessed that mysterious and almost supernatural transformation of appearance, which the fire of his own eloquence never failed to work in him. For as his mind rolled along, and began to glow from its own action, all the *exuviæ* of the clown seemed to shed themselves spontaneously.

His attitude, by degrees, became erect and lofty. The spirit of his genius awakened all his features. His countenance shone with a nobleness and grandeur which it never before exhibited. There was a lightning in his eyes which seemed to rive the spectator. His action became graceful, bold, and commanding; and in the tones of his voice, but more especially in his emphasis, there was a peculiar charm, a magic of which any one who ever heard him will speak as soon as he is named, but of which no one can give any adequate description. They can only say that it struck upon the ear and upon the heart, *in a manner which language cannot tell.* Add to all these, his wonder-working fancy, and the peculiar phraseology in which he clothed its images; for he painted to the heart with a force that almost petrified it. In the language of those who heard him on this occasion, "he made their blood run cold, and their hair to rise on end."

It will not be difficult for any one who ever heard this most extraordinary man, to believe the whole account of this transaction, which is given by his surviving hearers; and from their account, the courthouse of Hanover county must have exhibited on this occasion, a scene as picturesque, as has been ever witnessed in real life.

They say that the people, whose countenance had fallen as he arose, had heard but a very few sentences before they began to look up; then to look at each other with surprise, as if doubting the evidence of their own senses; then, attracted by some strong gesture, struck by some majestic attitude, fascinated by the spell of his eye, the charm of his emphasis, and the varied and commanding expression of his countenance, they could look away no more.

In less than twenty-minutes, they might be seen in every part of the house, on every bench, in every window, stooping forward from their stands, in deathlike silence; their features fixed in amazement and awe; all their senses listening and riveted upon the speaker, as if to catch the last strain of some heavenly visitant. The mockery of the clergy was soon turned into alarm; their triumph into confusion and despair; and at one burst of his rapid and overwhelming invective, they fled from the bench in precipitation and terror. As for the father, such was his surprise, such his amazement, such his rapture, that, forgetting where he was, and the character which he was filling, tears of ecstasy streamed down his cheeks, without the power or inclination to repress them.

The jury seem to have been so completely bewildered, that they lost sight, not only of the act of seventeen hundred and forty-eight, but that of seventeen hundred and fifty-eight also; for thoughtless even of the admitted right of the plaintiff, they had scarcely left the bar, when they returned with a verdict of *one penny damages*. A motion was made for a new trial; but the court, too, had now lost the equipoise of their judgment, and overruled the motion by a unanimous vote. The verdict and judgment overruling the motion, were followed by redoubled acclamations, from within and without the house.

The people, who had with difficulty kept their hands off their champion, from the moment of closing his harangue, no sooner saw the fate of the cause finally sealed, than they seized him at the bar, and in spite of his own exertions, and the continued cry of "order" from the sheriffs and the court, they bore him out of the courthouse, and raising him on their shoulders, carried him about the yard, in a kind of electioneering triumph.

O! what a scene was this for a father's heart! so sudden; so unlooked for; so delightfully overwhelming! At the time, he was not able to give utterance to any sentiment; but, a few days after, when speaking of it to Mr. Winston, (the present Judge Winston,) he said, with the most engaging modesty, and with a tremour of voice, which showed how much more he felt than he expressed, "Patrick spoke in this cause near an hour! and in a manner that surprised me! and showed himself well-informed on a subject, of which I did not think he had any knowledge!"

I have tried much to procure a sketch of this celebrated speech. But those of Mr. Henry's hearers who survive, seem to have been bereft of their senses. They can only tell you, in general, that they were taken captive; and so delighted with their captivity, that they followed implicitly, whithersoever he led them: that, at his bidding, their tears flowed from pity, and their cheeks flushed with indignation: that when it was over, they felt as if they had just awaked from some ecstatic dream, of which they were unable to recall or connect the particulars. It was such a speech as they believe had never before fallen from the lips of man; and to this day, the old people of that county cannot conceive that a higher compliment can be paid to a speaker, than to say of him, in their own homely phrase:—"*He is almost equal to Patrick, when he plead against the parsons.*"

The only topic of this speech of which any authentic account remains, is the order of the king in council, whereby the act of seventeen hundred and fifty-eight had been declared void. This subject had in truth been disposed of by the demurrer; and, in strictness of proceeding, neither Mr. Henry nor the jury had anything to do with it. The laxity of the county-court practice, however, indulged him in the widest career he chose to take, and he laid hold of this point, neither with a feeble nor hesitating hand; but boldly and vigorously pressed it upon the jury, and that, too, with very powerful effect.

He insisted on the connexion and reciprocal duties between the king and his subjects; maintained that government was a conditional compact, composed of mutual and dependant covenants, of which a violation by one party discharged the other; and intrepidly contended that the disregard which had been shown, in this particular, to the pressing wants of the colony, was an instance of royal misrule, which had thus far dissolved the political compact, and left the people at liberty to consult their own safety; that they had consulted it by the act of seventeen hundred and fifty-eight, which, therefore, notwithstanding the dissent of the king and his council, ought to be considered as the law of the land, and the only legitimate measure of the claims of the clergy.

The nature of this topic, and the earnest and undaunted manner in which Mr. Henry is said to have pursued and maintained it, proves that even at this period, which has been marked as the era of our greatest attachment and devotion to the parent country, *his* mind, at least, was disposed to pry into the course of the regal administration, and to speak forth his sentiments without any fear of the consequences. The reception which the people gave to the argument, proves that they also had no superstitious repugnance to the consideration of such topics, nor any very insuperable horror at the idea of a separation. Not that there is ground to suspect that any one had, at this time, realized such an event, or even contemplated it as desirable.

The suggestion, therefore, which I have sometimes heard, that Mr. Henry was already meditating the independence of the colonies, and sowing the seeds of those reflections which he wished to ripen into revolt, is, in my opinion, rather curious than just. I believe that he thought of nothing beyond success in his cause; and since the desperate posture in which he found it demanded a daring and eccentric course, he adopted that which has been already stated. The character of his argument proves that he was naturally a bold and intrepid inquirer, who was not to be overawed from his purpose by the name even of sovereignty itself; and of course that he was made of good revolutionary materials.

But an adequate provocation had not at this time been given: and it would be imputing to Mr. Henry a criminal ambition, of which there is no proof, to suppose that he was meditating the subversion of a government, against which the voice of serious complaint had not yet been heard. Besides, Mr. Henry's standing in society was at this period so humble, as to have rendered the meditation of such a purpose, on his part, presumptuous in the extreme; and equally inconsistent both with his unassuming modesty, and that natural good sense and accurate judgment which are, on all hands, assigned to him.

Immediately on the decision of this cause, he was retained in all the cases, within the range of his practice, which depended on the same question. But no other case was ever brought to trial. They were, all throughout the colony, dismissed by the plaintiffs; nor was any appeal ever prosecuted in the case of Mr. Maury. The reason assigned for this by Mr. Camm is, that the legislature had voted money to support the appeal on the part of the defendants, and that the clergy were not rich enough to contend against the whole wealth and strength of the colony.*

The clergy took their revenge in an angry pamphlet from the pen of Mr. Camm, in which a very contemptuous account is given both of the advocate and the court. Mr. Henry is stigmatized in it as *an obscure attorney:* and the epithet was true enough as to the time past, but it was now true no longer. His sun had risen with a splendour which had never before been witnessed in this colony; and never afterward did it disgrace this glorious rising.

* Mr. Camm is right as to the interference of the legislature. I have not been able, however, to find any resolution of the legislature to this effect, ear lier than the seventh of April, seventeen hundred and sixty-seven: where Mr. Maury's case was decided in Hanover, on the first of December, seventee hundred and sixty-three. The following is extracted from the journal of the day first mentioned:—

"On a motion made—Resolved, that the committee of correspondence be directed to write to the agent, to defend the parish-collectors from all appeals from judgments here given, in suits brought by the clergy, for recovering their salaries, payable on or before the last day of May, seventeen hundred and fifty-nine; and that this house will engage to defray the expense thereof."

CHAPTER II.

State of Society in Virginia—Mr. Henry's Popularity—His Appearance befor the House of Burgesses—The Stamp-Act—Mr. Henry is elected a Member of the House—Anecdote of Washington—Sketches of Public Characters: John Robinson, Peyton Randolph, Edmund Pendleton, George Wythe and Richard Henry Lee—He opposes the Aristocracy of the House on the Proposition for a Loan-Office—Introduces his celebrated Resolutions against the Stamp-Act—The Effect—Mr. Jefferson's Account of this Transaction—Anecdote of the Debate.

It is almost unnecessary to state, that the display which Mr. Henry had made in "*the parsons' cause*," as it was popularly called, placed him at once at the head of his profession, in that quarter of the colony in which he practised. He became the theme of every tongue. He had exhibited a degree of eloquence, which the people had never before witnessed; a species of eloquence, too, entirely new at the bar, and altogether his own. He had formed it on no living model, for there was none such in the country. He had not copied it from books, for they had described nothing of the kind; or if they had, he was a stranger to their contents.

Nor had he formed it himself, by solitary study and exercise; for he was far too indolent for any such process. It was so unexampled, so unexpected, so instantaneous, and so transcendent in its character, that it had, to the people, very much the appearance of supernatural inspiration. He was styled "*the orator of nature;*" and was, on that account, much more revered by the people than if he had been formed by the severest discipline of the schools; for they considered him as bringing his credentials directly from heaven, and owing no part of his greatness to human institutions.

There were other considerations, also, which drew him still more closely to the bosom of the people. The society of Virginia was at that time pretty strongly discriminated. A gentleman who lived in those days, and who had the best opportunities of judging on the subject, has furnished the following interesting picture of it:—

"To state the differences between the classes of society, and the lines of demarcation which separated them, would be difficult. The law, you know, admitted none, except as to the twelve counsellors. Yet, in a country insulated from the European world, insulated from its sister colonies, with whom there was scarcely any intercourse, little visited by foreigners, and having little matter to act upon within itself, certain families had risen to splendour by wealth, and by the preservation of it from generation to generation, under the law of entails; some had produced a series of men of talents; families in general had remained *stationary* on the grounds of their forefathers, for there was no emigration to the westward in those days; the Irish, who had gotten possession of the valley between the Blue Ridge and the North Mountain, formed a barrier over which none ventured to leap; and their manners presented no attraction to the lowlanders to settle among them.

"In such a state of things, scarcely admitting any change of station, society would settle itself down into several *strata*, separated by no marked lines, but shading off imperceptibly from top to bottom, nothing disturbing the order of their repose. There were, then, first, aristocrats, composed of the great land-holders, who had seated themselves below tidewater on the main rivers, and lived in a style of luxury and extravagance insupportable by the other inhabitants, and which indeed, ended in several instances in the ruin of their own fortunes. Next to these were what might be called *half-breeds;* the descendants of the younger sons and daughters of the aristocrats, who inherited the pride of their ancestors, without their wealth.

"Then came the pretenders, men, who, from vanity or the impulse of growing wealth, or from that enterprise which is natural to talents, sought to detach themselves from the plebeian ranks, to which they properly belonged, and imitated, at some distance, the manners and habits of the great. Next to these, were a solid and independent yeomanry, looking askance at those above, yet not venturing to jostle them. And last and lowest, a *feculum* of beings, called overseers, the most abject, degraded, unprincipled race; always cap in hand to the dons who employed them, and furnishing materials for the exercise of their pride, insolence and spirit of domination."

It was from the body of the yeomanry, whom my correspondent represents as "looking askance" at those above them, that Mr. Henry proceeded. He belonged to the body of the people. His birth, education, fortune, and manners, made him one of themselves. They regarded him, therefore, as their own property, and sent to them expressly for the very purpose of humbling the pride of the mighty, and exalting the honour of his own class.

Mr. Henry had too much sagacity not to see this advantage, and too much good sense not to keep and to improve it. He seems to have formed to himself, very early in life, just views of society, and to have acted upon them with the most laudable system and perseverance. He regarded government as instituted solely for the good of the people; and not for the benefit of those who had contrived to make a job of it. He looked upon the body of the people, therefore, as the *basis* of society, the fountair of all power, and, directly or indirectly, of all offices and honours, which had been instituted originally for *their* use. He made it no secret, therefore; nay, he made it his boast, that on every occasion, "he bowed to the majesty of the people."

With regard to himself, he saw very distinctly, that all his hopes rested on the people's favour. He therefore adhered to them with unshaken fidelity. He retained their manners, their customs, all their modes of life, with religious caution. He dressed as plainly as the plainest of them; ate only the homely fare, and drank the simple beverage of the country; mixed with them on a footing of the most entire and perfect equality, and conversed with them, even in their own vicious and depraved pronunciation.*

If this last were the effect of artful compliance, as has been strenuously affirmed, it was certainly carrying the system far ther than dignity would warrant. Mr. Henry should have been the instructer as well as the friend of the people, and, by his example, have corrected instead of adopting their errors. It is very certain, that by this course he disgusted many of those whom it was often his business to persuade; not because they considered it as a proof of vulgarity and ignorance, but because they regarded it as a premeditated artifice to catch the favour and affections of the people. That it was so, I am not disposed to believe. I think it much more probable, that those errors of pronunciation were the effect of early and inveterate habit, which had become incurable before he was informed of his mistake.

He had no occasion to resort to such petty artifices, either to gain or to hold the affections of the people. He held them by a much higher and a much firmer title: the simplicity of his manners; the benevolence of his disposition; the integrity of his life; his real devotion to their best interests; that uncommon sagacity, which enabled him to discern those interests in every situation; and the unshaken constancy with which he pursued them, in spite of every difficulty and danger that could threaten him. From the point of time, of which we are now speaking, it is very certain that he suffered no gale of fortune, however high or prosperous, to separate him from the people: nor did the people, on their part, ever desert him. He was

* Governor Page relates, that he once heard him express the following sentiments, in this vicious pronunciation:—"*Naiteral* parts *is* better than all the *larnin* upon *yearth*;" but the accuracy of Mr. Page's memory is questioned in this particular, by the acquaintances of Mr. Henry, who say, that he was too good a grammarian to have uttered such a sentence, although they admit the inaccuracy of his pronunciation, in some of the words imputed to him.

the man, to whom they looked in every crisis of difficulty, and the favourite on whom they were ever ready to lavish all the honours in their gift.

Middleton, in his life of Cicero, tells us, that the first great speech of that orator, his defence of Roscius of Ameria, was made at the age of twenty-seven; the same age, he adds, at which the learned have remarked, that Demosthenes distinguished himself in the assembly of the Athenians:—"as if this were the age," I quote his own words, "at which these great genios regularly bloomed toward maturity."

It is rather curious, than important, to observe, that Mr. Henry furnishes another instance in support of this theory; since it was precisely in the same year of his life, that *his* talents first became known to himself and to the world. Nor let the admirer of antiquity revolt at our coupling the name of Henry with those of Cicero and Demosthenes: it can be no degradation to the orator either of Greece or Rome, that his name stands enrolled on the same page with that of a man of whom such a judge of eloquence as Mr. Jefferson has said, that "*he was the greatest orator that ever lived.*"

But the taste of professional fame which Mr. Henry had derived from the "parsons' cause," exquisite as it must have been, was not sufficient to inspire him with a thirst for the learning of his profession. He had an insuperable aversion to *the old black-letter of the law-books*, (which was often a topic of raillery with him,) and he was never able to conquer it, except for preparation in some particular cause. No love of distinction, no necessity, however severe, were strong enough to bind him down to a regular course of reading.

He could not brook the confinement. The reasoning of the law was too artificial, and too much cramped for him. While unavoidably engaged in it, he felt as if manacled. His mind was perpetually struggling to break away. His genius delighted in liberty and space, in which it might roam at large, and feast on every variety of intellectual enjoyment. Hence, he was never profound in the learning of the law. On a question merely legal, his inferiors, in point of talents, frequently embarrassed and foiled him; and it required all the resources of his extraordinary mind to support the distinction which he had now gained.

The most successful practice in the county courts was, in those days, but a slender dependance for a family. Notwithstanding, therefore, the great addition to his business, which we have noticed, Mr. Henry seems still to have been pressed by want. With the hope of improving his situation, he removed, in the year seventeen hundred and sixty-four, to the county of Louisa, and resided at a place called the Round about. Here I have learned nothing remarkable of him, unless it may be thought so, that he pursued his favourite amusement of hunting with increased ardour.

"After his removal to Louisa," says my informant, "he has been known to hunt deer, frequently for several days together, carrying his provision with him, and at night encamping in the woods. After the hunt was over, he would go from the ground to Louisa court, clad in a coarse cloth coat, stained with all the trophies of the chase, greasy leather breeches, ornamented in the same way, leggings for boots, and a pair of saddle-bags on his arm. Thus accoutred, he would enter the courthouse, take up the first of his causes that chanced to be called; and if there was any scope for his peculiar talent, throw his adversary into the background, and astonish both court and jury, by the powerful effusions of his natural eloquence."

There must have been something irresistibly captivating in Mr. Henry's mode of speaking, even on the most trivial subjects. The late Judge Lyons has been heard to say of himself, while practising with Mr. Henry, that "he could write a letter, or draw a declaration or plea at the bar, with as much accuracy, as he could in his office, under all circumstances, *except when Patrick rose to speak;* but that whenever *he* rose, although it might be on so trifling a subject as a summons and petition for twenty shillings, he was obliged to lay down his pen, and could not write another word, until the speech was finished." Such was the charm of his voice and manner, and the interesting originality of his conceptions!

In the fall of seventeen hundred and sixty-four, Mr. Henry had an opportunity of exhibiting himself on a new theatre. A contest occurred in the house of burgesses, in the case of Mr. James Littlepage, the returned member for the county of Hanover. The rival candidate and petitioner was Nathaniel West Dandridge.* The charge against Mr. Littlepage was bribery and corruption. The parties were heard by their counsel, before the committee of privileges and elections, and Mr. Henry was on this occasion employed by Mr. Dandridge.

Williamsburgh, then the seat of government, was the *focus* of fashion and high life. The residence of the governor, (the immediate representative of the sovereign,) the royal state in

* Here is another mistake of Mr. Burk. He states the contest to have been between Col. Syme (Mr. Henry's half-brother) and Col. Richard Littlepage. The journal contradicts him, and supports the text. There was no such contest as that of which he speaks; at least, between the years seventeen hundred and sixty-two and seventeen hundred and sixty-eight.

which he lived, the polite and brilliant circle which he always had about him, diffused their influence through the city and the circumjacent county, and filled Williamsburgh with a degree of emulation, taste, and elegance, of which we can form no conception by the appearances of the present day. During the session of the house of burgesses, too, these stately modes of life assumed their richest forms; the town was filled with a concourse of visiters, as well as citizens, attired in their gayest colours; the streets exhibited a continual scene of animated and glittering tumult; the houses, of costly profusion.

Such was the scene in which Mr. Henry was now called upon, for the first time, to make his appearance. He made no preparation for it, but went down just in the kind of garb which he had been accustomed to exhibit all his life, and is said to have worn on this occasion particularly, a suit which had suffered very considerably in the service. The contrast which he exhibited with the general elegance of the place, was so striking, as to call upon him the eyes of all the curious and the mischievous; and, as he moved awkwardly about, in his coarse and threadbare dress, with a countenance of abstraction and total unconcern as to what was passing around him, (interesting as it seemed to every one else,) he was stared at by some as a prodigy, and regarded by others as an unfortunate being, whose senses were disordered.

When he went to attend the committee of privileges and elections, the matter was still worse. "The proud airs of aristocracy," says Judge Tyler, detailing this incident of Mr. Henry's life, "added to the dignified forms of that truly august body, were enough to have deterred any man possessing less firmness and independence of spirit than Mr. Henry. He was ushered with great state and ceremony into the room of the committee, whose chairman was Colonel Bland.*

"Mr. Henry was dressed in very coarse apparel; no one knew anything of him;† and scarcely was he treated with

* Mr. Tyler says, "that enlightened and amiable man, John Blair;" but in this he is corrected by the journal, which shows that Mr. Bland was the chairman of the committee of privileges and elections for that year. I should have thought, from the general accuracy of Mr. Tyler's statement, that Mr. Blair might have been officiating as chairman *pro tempore*, in the absence of Col. Bland; but that Mr. Blair does not appear, by the journal, to have belonged to the committee, or even to have been a member of the house in seventeen hundred and sixty-four. His name does not appear till seventeen hundred and sixty-six.

Mr. Tyler, reciting Mr. Henry's own narrative, after a lapse of several years, might very easily have confounded two names as similar as those of Bland and Blair.

† That is, I presume, of his person; for after the very splendid exhibition

decent respect by any one except the chairman, who could not do so much violence to his feelings and principles, as to depart, on any occasion, from the delicacy of the gentleman. But the general contempt was soon changed into as general admiration; for Mr. Henry distinguished himself by a copious and brilliant display on the great subject of the rights of suffrage, superior to anything that had been heard before within those walls. Such a burst of eloquence, from a man so very plain and ordinary in his appearance, struck the committee with amazement; so that a deep and perfect silence took place during the speech, and not a sound but from his lips was to be heard in the room."

So far, Judge Tyler. Judge Winston relating the same incident, says: "Some time after, a member of the house, speaking to me of this occurrence, said, he had, for a day or two, observed an ill-dressed young man sauntering in the lobby; that he seemed to be a stranger to everybody, and he had not the curiosity to inquire his name; but that, attending when the case of the contested election came on, he was surprised to find this same person counsel for one of the parties; and still more so when he delivered an argument superior to anything he had ever heard." The case, according to the report of the committee of privileges and elections, is not one which seems to present much scope for a very interesting discussion; but Mr. Henry's was one of those minds which impart interest to every subject they touch.

The same year, seventeen hundred and sixty-four, is memorable for the origination of that great question which led finally to the independence of the United States. It has been said by a gentleman, at least as well qualified to judge as any other now alive, (Mr. Jefferson,) that "Mr. Henry certainly gave the first impulse to the ball of the revolution." In order to show the correctness of this position, it is proper to ascertain the precise point to which the controversy with Great Britain had advanced, when Mr. Henry first presented himself in the character of a statesman.

In March, seventeen hundred and sixty-four, the British parliament had passed resolutions, preparatory to the levying a revenue on the colonies by a stamp-tax. These resolutions were communicated to the house of burgesses of Virginia, through their committee of correspondence, by the colonial agent; and having been maturely considered, resulted in the appointment of a special committee to prepare an address to

which he made, in the parsons' cause, his *name* could not have been wholly unknown: the text, however, gives the words of my correspondent faithfully.

the king, a memorial to the lords, and a remonstrance to the house of commons.

On the eighteenth of December, seventeen hundred and sixty-four, these papers were reported, and (after various amendments, which considerably diluted their spirit) received the concurrence of the council. The reader will perceive, on perusing them, (see Appendix, note A,) that while they affirm, in clear and strong terms, the constitutional exemption of the colony from taxation by the British parliament, they breathe, nevertheless, a tone so suppliant, and exhibit such a picture of anticipated suffering from the pressure of the tax on the exhausted resources of the colony, as to indicate that no opposition beyond remonstrance was, at this time, meditated. Remonstrance, however, was vain. In January, seventeen hundred and sixty-five, the famous stamp-act was passed, to take effect in the colonies on the first of November following.

The annunciation of this measure seems at first to have stunned the continent from one extremity to the other. The presses, which spread the intelligence among the people, were themselves manifestly confounded; and so far from inspiring the energy of resistance, they seemed rather disposed to have looked out for topics of consolation, under submission.* The truth is, that all ranks of society were confounded. No one knew what to hope, what more to fear, or what course was best to be taken. Some, indeed, were fond enough to entertain hopes that the united remonstrances of the colonial legislatures, the fate of which had not yet been heard, might induce the mother-country to change her policy; these hopes, however, were faint; and few there were that entertained them. Many, considered submission, in the present state of the colonies, as unavoidable; and that this was the opinion of Doctor Franklin himself, is apparent from the remark with which he took leave of Mr. Ingersol, on his departure for America.†

The idea of resistance, by force was nowhere glanced at in the most distant manner; no heart seems to have been bold enough, at first, to conceive it. Men, on other occasions marked for intrepidity and decision, now hung back, unwilling to submit, and yet afraid to speak out in the language of bold and

* Thus in the Pennsylvania Gazette of the thirtieth of May, seventeen hundred and sixty-five: "We hear the sums of money arising from the new stamp duties in North America, for the first five years, are chiefly to be applied toward making commodious post-roads from one province to another, erecting bridges where necessary, and other measures equally important to facilitate an extensive trade."

† "Go home and tell your countrymen to get children as fast as they can."—GORDON.

open defiance. It was just at this moment of despondency in some quarters, suspense in others, and surly and reluctant submission wherever submission appeared, that Patrick Henry stood forth to raise the drooping spirit of the people, and to unite all hearts and hands in the cause of his country.

With the view of making way for him, and placing him in the public councils of his country, Mr. William Johnson, who had been elected a member of the house of burgesses for the county of Louisa, vacated his seat by accepting the commission of coroner. The writ of election to supply his place was awarded on the first of May, seventeen hundred and sixty-five, and on the twentieth day of that month, it appears by the journals, that Mr. Henry was added to the committee for courts of justice.

Here, again, he was upon a new theatre, and personally unknown, except to those few who might have heard his argument on the contested election of Mr. Littlepage, the preceding winter. His dress and manners were still those of the plain planter, and, in his personal appearance, there was nothing to excite curiosity, or awaken expectation. The forms of the house, of which he was now for the first time a member, were, as has been stated, most awfully dignified; its active members were composed of the landed aristocracy and their adherents; and among them were men to whose superiority of talents, as well as influence and power, the yeomanry of the country had long been accustomed to bow with tacit and submissive deference.

John Robinson, the speaker of the house, was one of the most opulent men in the colony, and the acknowledged head of its landed aristocracy. He had now filled the chair of the house with great dignity, and without interruption, for five-and-twenty years. He was, also, the colonial treasurer; and from the high offices which he held, in connexion with the regal government, was as warmly attached to its authority by interest, as he was by taste and fashion to all the grandeur of its forms.

But, notwithstanding this close alliance with the court, his personal influence, in every class of society, was very great; and he held that influence by a tenure far superior to any that his own vast wealth or the power of the crown could confer. For he possessed a strong and well-informed mind, enlarged and corrected by great experience, and he united with it a benevolence of spirit and a courtesy of manners which never failed to attach every heart that approached him. The poor drew near to him without awe or embarrassment; they came, indeed, with filial confidence; for they never failed to find in him a sympathetic friend and an able counsellor. The rich enjoyed in him an easy, enlightened, and instructive companion; and, next to the governor, regarded him as the highest model of elegance and fashion.

An anecdote is related of this gentleman, which displays in a strong and amiable light, the exalted force of his feelings, and the truly noble cast of his manners. When Colonel Washington (the immortal saviour of his country) had closed his career in the French and Indian war, and had become a member of the house of burgesses, the speaker, Robinson, was directed, by a vote of the house, to return their thanks to that gentleman, on behalf of the colony, for the distinguished military services which he had rendered to his country. As soon as Colonel Washington took his seat, Mr. Robinson, in obedience to this order, and following the impulse of his own generous and grateful heart, discharged the duty with great dignity; but with such warmth of colouring and strength of expression, as entirely confounded the young hero.

He rose to express his acknowledgments for the honour; but such was his trepidation and confusion, that he could not give distinct utterance to a single syllable. He blushed, stammered, and trembled, for a second; when the speaker relieved him by a stroke of address that would have done honour to Louis XIV. in his proudest and happiest moment. "Sit down, Mr. Washington," said he, with a conciliating smile; "your modesty is equal to your valour; and that surpasses the power of any language that I possess."*

Peyton Randolph, the king's attorney-general, held the next rank to the speaker. He was not distinguished for eloquence; but he derived great weight from the solid powers of his understanding, and the no less solid virtues of his heart. He was well acquainted with all the forms of parliamentary proceeding; was an eminent lawyer, and a well-informed and practical statesman.

Richard Bland was one of the most enlightened men in the colony. He was a man of finished education, and of the most unbending habits of application. His perfect mastery of every fact connected with the settlement and progress of the colony, had given him the name of the Virginian antiquary.† He was a politician of the first class; a profound logician, and was also considered as the first writer in the colony.‡

Edmund Pendleton, the *protege* of the speaker Robinson, was also among the most prominent members in the house.

* On the authority of Edmund Randolph. † Edmund Randolph.

‡ "He was," says a correspondent, "the most learned and logical man of those who took a prominent lead in public affairs; profound in constitutional

He had, in a great measure, overcome the disadvantages of an extremely defective education, and by the force of good company and the study of correct authors, had attained to great accuracy and perspicuity of style. The patronage of the speaker had introduced him to the first circles, and his manners were elevated, graceful and insinuating. His person was spare, but well-proportioned; and his countenance one of the finest in the world; serene—contemplative—benignant—with that expression of unclouded intelligence and extensive research, which seemed to denote him capable of anything that could be effected by the power of the human mind.

His mind itself was of a very fine order. It was clear, comprehensive, sagacious and correct; with a most acute and subtle faculty of discrimination; a fertility of expedient which could never be exhausted; a dexterity of address which never lost an advantage and never gave one; and a capacity for continued and unremitting application, which was perfectly invincible.

As a lawyer and a statesman, he had few equals; no superiors. For parliamentary management, he was without a rival. With all these advantages of person, manners, address, and intellect, he was also a speaker of distinguished eminence.

He had that silver voice* of which Cicero makes such frequent and honourable mention—an articulation uncommonly distinct—a perennial stream of transparent, cool, and sweet elocution; and the power of presenting his arguments with great simplicity and striking effect. He was always graceful, argumentative, persuasive; never vehement, rapid, or abrupt. He could instruct and delight; but he had no pretensions to those high powers which are calculated to "shake the human soul."

George Wythe, also a member of the House, was confessedly among the first in point of abilities. There is a story circulated, as upon his own authority, that he was initiated by his

lore; but a most ungraceful speaker in debate. He wrote the first pamphlet on the nature of the connexion with Great Britain, which had any pretensions to accuracy of view on that subject; but it was a singular one: he would set out on sound principles, pursue them logically, till he found them leading to the precipice which we had to leap; start back, alarmed; then resume his ground, go over it in another direction, be led again, by the correctness of his reasoning, to the same place, and again tack about and try other processes to reconcile right and wrong; but left his reader and himself bewildered between the steady index of the compass in their hand, and the phantasm to which it seemed to point. Still, there was more sound matter in this pamphlet than in the celebrated Farmer's Letters, which were really but an *ignis fatuus*, misleading us from true principle."

* *Vox argentea.* See the Brutus, *passim.*

mother in the Latin classics.† Be this as it may, it is certain that he had raised upon the original foundation, whencesoever acquired, a superstructure of ancient literature which has been rarely equalled in this country. He was perfectly familiar with the authors of Greece and Rome; read them with the same ease, and quoted them with the same promptitude that he could the authors in his native tongue. He carried his love of antiquity rather too far; for he frequently subjected himself to the charge of pedantry; and his admiration of the gigantic writers of Queen Elizabeth's reign, had unfortunately betrayed him into an imitation of their quaintness.

Yet, with all this singularity of taste, he was a man of great capacity; powerful in argument; frequently pathetic; and elegantly keen and sarcastic in repartee. He was long the rival of Mr. Pendleton at the bar, whom he equalled as a common lawyer, and greatly surpassed as a civilian: but he was too open and direct in his conduct, and possessed too little management, either with regard to his own temper or those of other men, to cope with so cool and skilful an adversary. Though a full match for Mr. Pendleton in the powers of fair and solid reasoning, Mr. Pendleton could, whenever he pleased, and would, whenever it was necessary, tease him with quibbles, and vex him with sophistries, until he destroyed the composure of his mind, and robbed him of his strength.

No man was ever more entirely destitute of art than Mr. Wythe. He knew nothing, even in his profession, and never would know anything of "crooked and indirect by-ways." Whatever he had to do, was to be done openly, avowedly, and above-board. He would not, even at the bar, have accepted of success on any other terms.

This simplicity and integrity of character, although it sometimes exposed him to the arts and sneers of the less scrupulous, placed him before his countrymen on the ground which Cesar wished his wife to occupy; he was not only pure, but above all suspicion. The unaffected sanctity of his principles, united with his modesty and simple elegance of manners, his attic wit, his stores of rare knowledge, his capacity for business, and the real power of his intellect, not only raised him to great eminence in public, but rendered him a delightful companion, and a most valuable friend.

But Richard Henry Lee was the Cicero of the house. His face itself was on the Roman model; his nose Cesarean; the port and carriage of his head, leaning persuasively and gracefully forward; and the whole contour noble and fine. Mr. Lee was, by far, the most elegant scholar in the house. He had

* I heard it from the late Judge Nelson, his relation.

studied the classics in the true spirit of criticism. His taste had that delicate touch, which seized with intuitive certainty every beauty of an author, and his genius that native affinity which combined them without an effort. Into every walk of literature and science, he had carried this mind of exquisite selection, and brought it back to the business of life, crowned with every light of learning, and decked with every wreath, that all the muses and all the graces could entwine.

Nor did those light decorations constitute the whole value of its freight. He possessed a rich store of historical and political knowledge, with an activity of observation, and a certainty of judgment, that turned that knowledge to the very best account. He was not a lawyer by profession; but he understood thoroughly the constitution both of the mother-country and her colonies; and the elements also of the civil and municipal law. Thus, while his eloquence was free from those stiff and technical restraints which the habits of forensic speaking are so apt to generate, he had all the legal learning which is necessary to a statesman. He reasoned well, and declaimed freely and splendidly. The note of his voice was deeper and more melodious than that of Mr. Pendleton. It was the canorous voice* of Cicero.

He had lost the use of one of his hands, which he kept constantly covered with a black-silk bandage, neatly fitted to the palm of his hand, but leaving his thumb free; yet, notwithstanding this disadvantage, his gesture was so graceful and so highly finished, that it was said he had acquired it by practising before a mirror.† Such was his promptitude, that he required no preparation for debate. He was ready for any subject, as soon as it was announced; and his speech was so copious, so rich, so mellifluous, set off with such bewitching cadence of voice, and such captivating grace of action, that, while you listened to him, you desired to hear nothing superior, and indeed thought him perfect. He had a quick sensibility and a fervid imagination, which Mr. Pendleton wanted. Hence his orations were warmer and more delightfully interesting; yet still, to him those keys were not consigned which could unlock the sources either of the strong or tender passions.

His defect was, that he was too smooth and too sweet. His style bore a striking resemblance to that of Herodotus, as described by the Roman orator: "He flowed on, like a quiet and placid river, without a ripple."‡ He flowed, too, through banks covered with all the fresh verdure and variegated bloom

* *Vox canora.* See the Brutus, *passim.* † Edmund Randolph.

‡ *Sine ullis salebris, quasi sedatus amnis, fluit.* Orat. XII. 39.

of the spring; but his course was too subdued, and too beautifully regular. A cataract, like that of Niagara, crowned with overhanging rocks and mountains, in all the rude and awful grandeur of nature, would have brought him nearer to the standard of Homer and of Henry.

These were some of the stars of first magnitude that shone in the house of burgesses in the year seventeen hundred and sixty-five. There was yet a cluster of minor luminaries, which it were endless to delineate, but whose blended rays contributed to form that uncommon galaxy in which the plebeian Henry was now called upon to take his place. What had he to enable him to cope with all this lustre of talents and erudition? Very little more than the native strength of his character; a constancy of soul, which no array of power could shake; a genius that designed with all the boldness of Angelo, and an imagination that coloured with all the felicity of Titian.

It has been already stated, that Mr. Henry was elected with express reference to an opposition to the stamp-act. It was not, however, expected by his constituents, or meditated by himself, that he should lead the opposition. The addresses of the preceding year, made to the king, lords, and commons, in which so strong a truth had been stated, as that the stamp-act, if persisted in, would reduce the colony to a state of slavery, founded a hope that those who had commenced the opposition by remonstrance, would continue to give it the *eclat* of their high names, by resistance of a bolder character, if bolder should be necessary. Mr. Henry waited, therefore, to file in under the first champion that should raise the banner of colonial liberty. In the meantime, another subject unexpectedly occurred to call him up, and it was on this other that he made his *debut* in the house.

The incident has been stated to me in the following terms, by a gentleman (Mr. Jefferson) who heard the debate: "The gentlemen of this country had, at that time, become deeply involved in that state of indebtment which has since ended in so general a crush of their fortunes. Mr. Robinson, the speaker, was also the treasurer, an officer always chosen by the assembly. He was an excellent man, liberal, friendly, and rich. He had been drawn in to lend, on his own account, great sums of money to persons of this description; and especially those who were of the assembly.

"He used freely for this purpose the public money, confiding for its replacement in his own means, and the securities he had taken on those loans. About this time, however, he became sensible that his *deficit* to the public was become so enormous, as that a discovery must soon take place, for as yet the public had no suspicion of it. He devised, therefore, with his friends in the assembly, a plan for a public loan-office, to a certain amount, from which moneys might be lent on public account, and on good landed security to individuals.

"I find, in Royle's Virginia Gazette of the seventeenth of May, seventeen hundred and sixty-five, this proposition for a loan-office presented, its advantages detailed, and the plan explained. It seems to have been done by a borrowing member, from the feeling with which the motives are expressed, and to have been preparatory to the intended motion. Between the seventeenth and thirtieth, (the latter being the date of Mr. Henry's resolutions on the stamp-act,) the motion for a loan-office was accordingly brought forward in the house of burgesses; and had it succeeded, the debts due to Robinson on these loans would have been transferred to the public, and his *deficit* thus completely covered.

"This state of things, however, was not yet known: but Mr. Henry attacked the scheme on other general grounds, in that style of bold, grand, and overwhelming eloquence, for which he became so justly celebrated afterward. I had been intimate with him from the year seventeen hundred and fifty-nine and sixty, and felt an interest in what concerned him; and I can never forget a particular exclamation of his in the debate, which electrified his hearers. It had been urged, that, from certain unhappy circumstances of the colony, men of substantial property had contracted debts, which, if exacted suddenly, must ruin them and their families, but with a little indulgence of time, might be paid with ease.

"'What, sir!' exclaimed Mr. Henry, in animadverting on this, 'is it proposed then to reclaim the spendthrift from his dissipation and extravagance, by filling his pockets with money?' These expressions are indelibly impressed on my memory. He laid open with so much energy the spirit of favouritism, on which the proposition was founded, and the abuses to which it would lead, that it was crushed in its birth. He carried with him all the members of the upper counties, and left a minority composed merely of the aristocracy of the country. From this time his popularity swelled apace; and Mr. Robinson dying the year afterward, his *deficit* was brought to light, and discovered the true object of the proposition."*

* In reply to this communication, I stated my surprise that no evidence of this motion was to be found on the journals of the day, and begged my correspondent to explain it, which he does very satisfactorily in the following terms: "Abortive motions are not always entered on the journals, or rather they are rarely entered. It is the modern introduction of yeas and nays which has given the means of placing a rejected motion on the journals: and it is likely

The exclamation above quoted by my correspondent as having electrified Mr. Henry's hearers, is a striking specimen of one of his great excellences in speaking; which was, the power of condensing the substance of a long argument, into one short pithy question. The hearer was surprised, in finding himself brought so suddenly and so clearly to a just conclusion. He could scarcely conceive how it was effected; and could not fail to regard, with high admiration, the power of that intellect which could come at its ends by so short a course; and work out its purposes with the quickness and certainty of magic.

The aristocracy were startled at such a *phenomenon* from the plebeian ranks. They could not be otherwise than indignant at the presumption of an obscure and unpolished rustic, who, without asking the support or countenance of any patron among themselves, stood upon his own ground, and bearded them even in their den. That this rustic should have been able, too, by his single strength, to baffle their whole phalanx and put it to rout, was a mortification too humiliating to be easily borne. They affected to ridicule his vicious and depraved pronunciation, the homespun coarseness of his language, and his hypocritical canting in relation to his humility and ignorance.

But they could not help admiring and envying his wonderful gifts; that thorough knowledge of the human heart which he displayed; that power of throwing his reasoning into short and clear aphorisms; which, desultory as they were, supplied, in a great degree, the place of method and logic; that imagination so copious, poetic, and sublime; the irresistible power with which he caused every passion to rise at his bidding; and all the rugged might and majesty of his eloquence. From this moment, he had no friends on the aristocratic side of the house. They looked upon him with envy and with terror. They were forced at length to praise his genius; but that praise

that the speaker, who, as treasurer, was to be the loan-officer, and had the direction of the journals, would choose to omit an entry of the motion in this case. This accounts sufficiently for the absence of any trace of the motion on the journals. There was no suspicion then, (so far at least as I knew,) that Mr. Robinson had used the public money in private loans to his friends, and that the secret object of this scheme was to transfer those debtors to the public, and thus clear his accounts. I have diligently examined the names of the members on the journals of seventeen hundred and sixty-four, to see if any were still living, to whose memory we might recur on this subject; but I find not a single one now remaining in life." This debate must have been in seventeen hundred and sixty-five instead of seventeen hundred and sixty-four. The only surviving member of that year is Paul Carrington, sen., esq., who took his seat in the house after the debate in question.

was wrung from them, with painful reluctance. They would have denied it if they could. They would have overshadowed it; and did at first try to overshadow it, by magnifying his defects; but it would have been as easy for them to have eclipsed the splendour of the sun, by pointing to his spots.

If, however, he had lost one side of the house by his undaunted manner of blowing up this aristocratic project, he had made the other side his fast friends. *They* had listened with admiration, unmixed with envy. Their souls had been struck with amazement and rapture, and thrilled with unspeakable sensations which they had never felt before. The man, too, who had produced these effects, *was one of themselves*. This was balm to them; for there is a wide difference between that distant admiration, which we pay as a tax, due to long-standing merit, in superior rank, and that throbbing applause which rushes spontaneously and warm from the heart, toward a new man and an equal.

There is always something of latent repining, approaching to resentment, mingled with that respect which is exacted from us by rank; and we feel a secret gratification in seeing it humbled. In the same proportion, we love the man who has given us this gratification, and avenged, as it were, our own past indignities. Such was precisely the state of feeling which Mr. Henry produced, on the present occasion. The lower ranks of the house beheld and heard him with gratitude and veneration. They regarded him as a sturdy and wide-spreading oak, beneath whose cool and refreshing shade they might take refuge from those beams of aristocracy that had played upon them so long, with rather an unpleasant heat.

After this victorious sally upon their party, the former leaders of the house were not very well-disposed to look with a favourable eye on any proposition which he should make. They had less idea of contributing to foster the popularity and pamper the power of a man, who seemed born to be their scourge, and to drag down their ancient honours to the dust. It was in this unpropitious state of things, after having waited in vain for some step to be taken on the other side of the house, and when the session was within three days of its expected close, that Mr. Henry introduced his celebrated resolutions on the stamp-act.

I will not withhold from the reader a note of this transaction from the pen of Mr. Henry himself. It is a curiosity, and highly worthy of preservation. After his death, there was found among his papers one sealed, and thus endorsed: "Enclosed are the resolutions of the Virginia assembly in seventeen hundred and sixty-five, concerning the stamp-act. Let my executors open this paper." Within was found the following copy of the resolutions, in Mr. Henry's handwriting:—

"Resolved, That the first adventurers and settlers of this, his majesty's colony and dominion, brought with them, and transmitted to their posterity, and all other his majesty's subjects, since inhabiting in this, his majesty's said colony, all the privileges, franchises, and immunities, that have at any time been held, enjoyed, and possessed by the people of Great Britain.

"Resolved, That by two royal charters, granted by King James the first, the colonists, aforesaid, are declared entitled to all the privileges, liberties, and immunities of denizens and natural-born subjects, to all intents and purposes, as if they had been abiding and born within the realm of England.

"Resolved, That the taxation of the people by themselves, or by persons chosen by themselves to represent them, who can only know what taxes the people are able to bear, and the easiest mode of raising them, and are equally affected by such taxes themselves, is the distinguishing characteristic of British freedom, and without which the ancient constitution cannot subsist.

"Resolved, That his majesty's liege people of this most ancient colony, have uninterruptedly enjoyed the right of being thus governed by their own assembly, in the article of their taxes and internal police, and that the same hath never been forfeited, or any other way given up, but hath been constantly recognised by the king and people of Great Britain.

"Resolved, therefore, That the general assembly of this colony have the sole right and power to lay taxes and impositions upon the inhabitants of this colony; and that every attempt to vest such power in any person or persons whatsoever, other than the general assembly aforesaid, has a manifest tendency to destroy British as well as American freedom."

On the back of the paper containing those resolutions, is the following endorsement, which is also in the handwriting of Mr. Henry himself: "The within resolutions passed the house of burgesses in May, seventeen hundred and sixty-five. They formed the first opposition to the stamp-act, and the scheme of taxing America by the British parliament. All the colonies, either through fear, or want of opportunity to form an opposition, or from influence of some kind or other, had remained silent. I had been for the first time elected a burgess, a few days before, was young, inexperienced, unacquainted with the forms of the house, and the members that composed it. Finding the men of weight averse to opposition, and the commencement of the tax at hand, and that no person was likely to step forth, I determined to venture, and alone, unadvised, and unassisted, on a blank leaf of an old law-book* wrote the within.

"Upon offering them to the house, violent debates ensued. Many threats were uttered, and much abuse cast on me, by the party for submission. After a long and warm contest, the resolutions passed by a very small majority, perhaps of one or two only. The alarm spread throughout America with astonishing quickness, and the ministerial party were overwhelmned. The great point of resistance to British taxation was universally established in the colonies. This brought on the war, which finally separated the two countries, and gave independence to ours. Whether this will prove a blessing or a curse will depend upon the use our people make of the blessings which a gracious God hath bestowed on us. If they are wise, they will be great and happy. If they are of a contrary character, they will be miserable. Righteousness alone can exalt them as a nation.

"Reader! whoever thou art, remember this; and in thy sphere, practise virtue thyself, and encourage it in others.—P. Henry."

Such is the short, plain, and modest account which Mr. Henry has left of this transaction. But other interesting particulars have been handed down by tradition, and live still in the recollection of one, at least, now in life, as the reader will presently see by his own statement.

The resolutions having been prepared in the manner which has been mentioned, were shown by Mr. Henry to two members only, before they were offered to the house; these were John Fleming, a most respectable member for the county of Cumberland, and George Johnston, for that of Fairfax.†

The reader will remark that the first four resolutions, as left by Mr. Henry, do little more than reaffirm the principles advanced in the address, memorial, and remonstrance of the preceding year; that is, they deny the right assumed by the

* Judge Tyler says "an old Coke upon Littleton."

† Judge Winston, on the authority of Mr. Henry himself. The report of the day, that Mr. Johnston drew the resolutions, is certainly unfounded. Mr. Johnston, now only known from the circumstance of his having seconded Mr. Henry's resolutions, is one of those many friends of liberty who are sliding fast from the recollection of their country, and who deserve to be rescued from oblivion, by a more particular notice than it is in my power to bestow upon them. Of Mr. Johnston, I can learn only, that he was a lawyer in the Northern Neck, highly respectable in his profession; a scholar, distinguished for vigour of intellect, cogency of argument, firmness of character, love of order, and devotion to the cause of rational liberty—in short, exactly calculated by his love of the cause, and the broad and solid basis of his understanding, to uphold the magnificent structure of Henry's eloquence.

British parliament, and assert the exclusive right of the colony to tax itself. There is an important difference, however, between those state papers and the resolutions, in the point of time and the circumstances under which they were brought forward, for the address and other state papers were prepared before the stamp-act had passed; they do nothing more, therefore, than call in question, by a course of respectful and submissive reasoning, the propriety of exercising the right, before it had been exercised; and they are, moreover, addressed to the legislature of Great Britain, *by the way of prevention*, and in a strain of decent remonstrance and argument.

But at the time when Mr. Henry offered his resolutions, the stamp-act had passed; and the resolutions were intended for the people of the colonies. It will also be observed, that the fifth resolution, as given by Mr. Henry, contains the bold assertion, that every attempt to vest the power of taxation over the colonies in any person or persons whatsoever, other than the general assembly, had a manifest tendency to destroy British, as well as American freedom; which was asserting, in effect, that the act which had passed was an encroachment on the rights and liberties of the people, and amounted to a direct charge of tyranny and despotism against the British king, lords, and commons.

It is not wonderful that even the friends of colonial rights, who knew the feeble and defenceless situation of this country, should be startled at a step so bold and daring. That effect was produced; and the resolutions were resisted, not only by the aristocracy of the house, but by many of those who were afterward distinguished among the brightest champions of American liberty.

The following is Mr. Jefferson's account of this transaction: "Mr. Henry moved and Mr. Johnston seconded these resolutions successively. They were opposed by Messrs. Randolph, Bland, Pendleton, Wythe, and all the old members, whose influence in the house had, till then, been unbroken. They did it, not from any question of our rights, but on the ground that the same sentiments had been, at their preceding session, expressed in a more conciliatory form, to which the answers were not yet received. But torrents of sublime eloquence from Henry, backed by the solid reasoning of Johnston, prevailed. The last, however, and strongest resolution, was carried but by a single vote.

"The debate on it was most bloody. I was then but a student, and stood at the door of communication between the house and the lobby (for as yet there was no gallery) during the whole debate and vote; and I well remember that, after the numbers on the division were told and declared from the chair, Peyton Randolph (the attorney-general) came out at the door where I was standing, and said, as he entered the lobby: 'By God, I would have given 500 guineas for a single vote:' for one would have divided the house, and Robinson was in the chair, who he knew would have negatived the resolution.

"Mr. Henry left town that evening; and the next morning, before the meeting of the house, Colonel Peter Randolph, then of the council, came to the hall of burgesses, and sat at the clerk's table till the house-bell rang, thumbing over the volumes of journals, to find a precedent for expunging a vote of the house, which, he said, had taken place while he was a member or clerk of the house, I do not recollect which. I stood by him at the end of the table, a considerable part of the time, looking on, as he turned over the leaves; but I do not recollect whether he found the erasure. In the meantime, some of the timid members, who had voted for the strongest resolution, had become alarmed; and as soon as the house met, a motion was made and carried to expunge it from the journals.

"There being at that day but one printer, and he entirely under control of the governor, I do not know that this resolution ever appeared in print. I write this from memory: but the impression made on me at the time was such as to fix the facts indelibly in my mind. I suppose the original journal was among those destroyed by the British, or its obliterated face might be appealed to. And here I will state, that Burk's statement of Mr. Henry's consenting to withdraw two resolutions, by way of compromise with his opponents, is entirely erroneous."

The manuscript journal of the day is not to be found; whether it was suppressed, or casually lost, must remain a matter of uncertainty; it disappeared, however, shortly after the session,* and therefore could not have been among the documents destroyed by the British during the revolutionary war, as conjectured by Mr. Jefferson.

In the interesting fact of the erasure of the fifth resolution, Mr. Jefferson is supported by the distinct recollection of Mr. Paul Carrington, late a judge of the court of appeals of Virginia, and the only surviving member, it is believed, of the house of burgesses of seventeen hundred and sixty-five. The statement is also confirmed, if indeed further confirmation were necessary, by the circumstance, that instead of the five resolu-

* "The manuscript journal was missing ten years before hostilities between the two countries; therefore could not have been destroyed, as you supposed probable."—PAUL CARRINGTON, senr

tions, so solemnly recorded by Mr. Henry, as having passed the house, the journal of the day exhibits only the following four :—

"Resolved, That the first adventurers and settlers of this his majesty's colony and dominion of Virginia, brought with them and transmitted to their posterity, and all others his majesty's subjects, since inhabiting in this his majesty's said colony, all the liberties, privileges, franchises, and immunities, that have at any time been held, enjoyed, and possessed by the people of Great Britain.

"Resolved, That by two royal charters, granted by King James I., the colonists aforesaid are declared entitled to all liberties, privileges, and immunities of denizens and natural subjects to all intents and purposes, as if they had been abiding and born within the realm of England.

"Resolved, That the taxation of the people, by themselves, or by persons chosen by themselves to represent them, who can only know what taxes the people are able to bear, or the easiest method of raising them; and must, themselves, be affected by every tax laid on the people, is the only security against a burdensome taxation, and the distinguishing characteristic of British freedom, without which the ancient constitution cannot exist.

"Resolved, That his majesty's liege people of this his most ancient and loyal colony have, without interruption, enjoyed the inestimable right of being governed by such laws respecting their internal polity and taxation, as are derived from their own consent, with the approbation of their sovereign, or his substitute; and that the same hath never been forfeited or yielded up, but hath been constantly recognised by the kings and people of *Great Britain*."*

"By these resolutions," says Mr. Jefferson, "and his man-

* Such are the resolutions, as they were amended and passed by the house, with the exception of that which was rescinded on the next day.—Journals of seventeen hundred and sixty-five, page 150. Several historical mistakes have been committed in relation to these resolutions. Judge Marshall, in his Life of Washington, (vol. 2d, note 4th, of the appendix,) gives an erroneous copy of them, from the book called Prior Documents; in this, he is set right by the journals: he represents six as having been offered, and two rejected; his authority for this, again, is the Prior Documents: but he is contradicted by Mr. Henry, himself, who represents five only as having been offered and passed, and Mr. Henry's written statement accords with the clear and strong recollection both of Mr. Jefferson and Mr. Carrington.

Mr. Burk gives the same erroneous copy with Judge Marshall, and adds to them several mistakes of his own: he says the resolutions passed, by a large majority, *forty only having voted against them*. Mr. Burk did not know the number of the members, or he would have known that a vote of forty, in the negative, would not have left a large majority in favour of the resolutions. But we have the authority of Mr. Henry himself, (as we have seen,) of Mr.

ner of supporting them, Mr. Henry took the lead out of the hands of those who had, theretofore, guided the proceedings of the house; that is to say, of Pendleton, Wythe, Bland, Randolph." It was, indeed, the measure which raised him to the zenith of his glory. He had never before had a subject which entirely matched his genius, and was capable of drawing out all the powers of his mind. It was remarked of him throughout his life, that his talents never failed to rise with the occasion, and in proportion with the resistance which he had to encounter. The nicety of the vote, on his last resolution, proves that this was not a time to hold in reserve any part of his forces.

It was, indeed, an Alpine passage, under circumstances even more unpropitious than those of Hannibal; for he had not only to fight, hand to hand, the powerful party who were already in possession of the heights, but at the same instant to cheer and animate the timid band of followers, that were trembling, and fainting, and drawing back below him. It was an occasion that called upon him to put forth all his strength, and he did put it forth, in such a manner as man never did before.

The cords of argument with which his adversaries frequently flattered themselves that they had bound him fast, became packthreads in his hands. He burst them with as much ease as the unshorn Samson did the bands of the Philistines. He seized the pillars of the temple, shook them terribly, and seemed to threaten his opponents with ruin. It was an incessant storm of lightning and thunder, which struck them aghast. The faint-hearted gathered courage from his countenance, and cowards became heroes while they gazed upon his exploits.

Jefferson, and of Mr. Carrington, for saying that the resolutions were carried by a majority of *one only;* on what authority Mr. Burk speaks, we are not informed. His whole account of Mr. Henry's proposal on the next day, to secede, and of his finally giving up two resolutions, for the sake of unanimity, is contradicted again by Mr. Henry, Mr. Jefferson, and Mr. Carrington; there is no such statement in the papers of the day, and the author does not condescend to give us his authority. Mr. Burk's skeleton of Mr. Henry's speech, on that occasion, is believed to be equally apocryphal; the author of these sketches has not been able to procure a single authentic trace of that speech, except the anecdote presently given in the text.

Mr. Burk concludes his account of this affair thus: "Struck with the alarming tendency of these proceedings, the governor suddenly dissolved the assembly," &c.—Vol. 3d, page 310. In opposition to this statement, we are told by Mr. Henry himself, that when he offered his resolutions, the session was near its regular close; and the journals prove the fact to have been so. Mr. Henry left town for home on the evening of the day on which his resolutions were adopted; it was on the next day (consequently in his absence) that the motion to rescind was made; and the printed journals show that day and the day following to have been occupied with the usual business which closes a legislative session.

It was in the midst of this magnificent debate, while he was descanting on the tyranny of the obnoxious act, that he exclaimed in a voice of thunder, and with the look of a god:—"Cesar had his Brutus—Charles the First, his Cromwell—and George the Third"—("Treason," cried the speaker—"Treason, treason!" echoed from every part of the house. It was one of those trying moments which is decisive of character. Henry faltered not for an instant; but rising to a loftier attitude, and fixing on the speaker an eye of the most determined fire, he finished his sentence with the firmest emphasis)—"*may profit by their example.* If *this* be treason, make the most of it."*

This was the only expression of defiance which escaped him during the debate. He was, throughout life, one of the most perfectly and uniformly decorous speakers that ever took the floor of the house. He was respectful even to humility; and the provocation must be gross indeed which would induce him to notice it. Yet when he did notice it, better were it for the man never to have been born, than to fall into the hands of such an adversary. One lash from his scourge was infamy for life; his look of anger or contempt was almost death.

After this debate, there was no longer a question among the body of the people, as to Mr. Henry's being the first statesman and orator in Virginia. Those, indeed, whose ranks he had scattered, and whom he had thrown into the shade, still tried to brand him with the names of declaimer and demagogue. But this was obviously the effect of envy and mortified pride. A mere declaimer and demagogue could never have gained, much less have kept for more than thirty years, that ground which Mr. Henry held; with a people, too, so cool, judicious, firm, and virtuous, as those who achieved the American revolution.

From the period of which we have been speaking, Mr. Henry became the idol of the people of Virginia; nor was his name confined to his native state. His light and heat were seen and felt throughout the continent; and he was everywhere regarded as the great champion of colonial liberty.

The impulse thus given by Virginia, was caught by the other colonies. Her resolutions were everywhere adopted with progressive variations. The spirit of resistance became bolder

* I had frequently heard the above anecdote of the cry of treason, but with such variations of the concluding words, that I began to doubt whether the whole might not be fiction. With a view to ascertain the truth, therefore, I submitted it to Mr. Jefferson, as it had been given to me by Judge Tyler, and this is his answer: "I well remember the cry of treason, the pause of Mr. Henry at the name of George III., and the presence of mind with which he closed his sentence, and baffled the charge vociferated." The incident, therefore, becomes authentic history.

and bolder, until the whole continent was in a flame; and by the first of November, when the stamp act was, according to its provisions, to have taken effect, its execution had become utterly impracticable."*

CHAPTER III.

Repeal of the Stamp-Act—Session of 1766—Mr. Henry's Character as a Lawyer—Anecdote of Major Scott—State of Feeling in the British Parliament—Remonstrance of the Massachusetts Legislature—Obnoxious Character of the Soldiery stationed in America—Collision of the People in New York with the Troops—Farther Encroachments of Parliament—Opposition of Massachusetts to the new Duties—Dissolution of the Colonial Legislatures—Appointment of Corresponding Committees—Notice of Mr. Carr—Sketch of the Virginia Legislature of 1773—Mr. Henry's Views on the Issue of the Contest with Great Britain—Dissolution of the House of Burgesses—Subsequent Proceedings—Delegates appointed—Mr. Henry appointed a Deputy to a Congress of the Colonies.—The Congress meets at Philadelphia.

At the opening of the next session, the speaker announced the repeal of the stamp-act; and the house of burgesses, in a paroxysm of feeling, voted a statue to the king, and an obelisk to the British patriots by whose exertions the repeal had been effected. But before these monuments of national gratitude could be executed the effervescence subsided; and on the ninth of December, seventeen hundred and sixty-six, the bill which had been prepared for that purpose, was postponed to the first day of the next session; after which, we hear of it no more.

At the session of seventeen hundred and sixty-six, a question of great interest in those days, and one of real importance to the colony, came on to be discussed in the house of burgesses. Mr. Robinson, who had so long held the joint offices of speaker and treasurer, was now dead. The general fact of his delinquency as treasurer was understood, although the sum was not yet ascertained; and that delinquency, whatever it might be, was alleged to have arisen principally from loans made to

* The chronicles of the day exhibit, in a manner very curious and interesting, the progress of these feelings. We have already given a specimen of the drooping spirit of the Pennsylvania Gazette, on the first annunciation of the stamp-act; but after Mr. Henry had touched with his match the train of American courage, its scintillations were seen, sparkling and flashing, on every page of this paper. Thus, in the paper of June twentieth, seventeen hundred and seventy-five: "We learn from the northward, that the stamp-act is to take effect in America on All Saints' day, the first of November next. In the year seventeen hundred and fifty-five, on the first of November, happened that dreadful and memorable earthquake which destroyed the city of Lisbon."

members of the house of burgesses. As the speaker, although elected in the first instance by the house, could not act until approved by the governor, and, when so approved, was in office for seven years, re-eligible indefinitely—and, as in the recent instance of Mr. Robinson, it had been discovered, that an office so held was too apt to generate a devotion to the purposes of the British court—it was considered by the patriots in the house, as a measure of sound policy, to take out of the hands of the speaker so formidable an engine of corruption and power as the treasury of the colony.*

A motion was therefore made to separate the office of treasurer from the speaker's chair, which was supported by Mr. Henry with his usual ability. An arduous struggle ensued. Innovations, however correct in themselves, never fail to startle those who have grown gray in a veneration for the existing order of things. They fancy that they see in every important change an indirect blow at the established government, and at the foundations of their own property. This union of the speaker's chair with the office of treasurer, was one of those errors in policy which time had consecrated, and it required a hand both steady and skilful to remove the veil and expose its deformity. That hand was furnished by Mr. Henry.

The union of boldness and decency which composed his character, of decisive energy in the support of his own opinions, and respectful tenderness toward those of others, fitted him peculiarly for the discharge of this duty. The house admired, on this occasion, the facility with which he could adapt himself to any subject. He had that foundation of strong natural sense, without which genius is a misfortune; an instinctive accuracy of judgment, which always proportioned his efforts to the occasion. He was never guilty of the ridiculous and common error among young members, of attempting to force the subject beyond its nature—of swelling trifles into consequence, and working the ocean into tempest,

"To waft a feather, or to drown a fly."

It is almost superfluous to add, that such a cause, in the hands of such an advocate, did not fail of success. The motion for separating the two offices being carried, a committee was ap-

* A correspondent furnishes the following note on this passage: "There was but one clear and sound bottom on which the separation of the chair and the treasury was decided. The legislature made all the levies of money payable into the hands of their speaker, over whom they had control. The only hold the governor had on him was, a negative on his appointment as speaker at every new election, which amounted, consequently, to a negative on him as treasurer, and disposed him, so far, to be obsequious to the governor."

pointed to examine the accounts of the late treasurer, and their report disclosed an enormous *deficit*, exceeding a hundred thousand pounds.

On the separation of the offices of speaker, and treasurer, Peyton Randolph, the attorney-general, was elected to the chair; and Robert C. Nicholas, an eminent lawyer and a most virtuous man, to the office of treasurer.

After having tried his strength for several years on the legislative floor, against some of the brightest champions of the bar, Mr. Henry came, in the year seventeen hundred and sixty-nine, to the bar itself of the general court. "The profits of his practice, theretofore," says my informant, Judge Winston, "must have been very moderate. For about this time, he informed me that he thought his property was not worth more than fifteen hundred pounds; adding, that if he could only make it double that sum, he should be entirely content."

At this bar, he entered into competition with all the first legal characters in the colony, some of whom had been educated at the Temple. Mr. Pendleton and Mr. Wythe have been already mentioned: but, in addition to these, he had to encounter Mr. John Randolph, Mr. Thompson Mason, Mr. Robert C. Nicholas, Mr. Mercer, Mr. Blair, and Mr. Jefferson; all of them masters of the learning of their profession, and all of them men of pre-eminent abilities.

It cannot be expected from Mr. Henry's legal preparation, that he was able to contend with these gentlemen on a mere question of law. He wanted that learning whose place no splendour of genius can supply to the lawyer; and he wanted those habits of steady and persevering application, without which that learning is not to be acquired. It is said, indeed, that he was wofully deficient as a lawyer; so little acquainted with the fundamental principles of his profession, and so little skilled in that system of artificial reasoning on which the common law is built, as not to be able to see the remote bearings of the reported cases; and hence, it has been said, that it happened with him not unfrequently, whenever he did attempt to argue a question of law, to furnish authorities destructive to his own cause.

Yet he never did and never could vanquish his aversion to the systematic study of the law. On questions turning on the laws of nations, and even on the maritime law, whose basis is natural reason and justice, his vigour of mind made him occasionally very great. One of my correspondents, for example, relates to me an instance of his appearing in the court of admiralty, under the regal government, in behalf of a Spanish captain, whose vessel and cargo had been libelled. A gentleman who was present, and who was very well qualified to judge, was heard to declare, after the trial was over, that he never heard a more eloquent or argumentative speech in his life; that Mr. Henry was on that occasion greatly superior to Mr. Pendleton, Mr. Mason, or any other counsel who spoke to the subject; and that he was astonished how Mr. Henry could have acquired such a knowledge of the maritime law, to which, it was believed, he had never before turned his attention.

But this special preparation on a given subject, and that subject, too, depending on the liberal and equitable principles of the maritime law, is not at all at variance with the report of his inefficiency, on questions to be decided by the common law merely. The power of arguing questions, of the latter description to advantage, requires the mind, in the first place, to be deeply imbued with that peculiar spirit of reasoning which reigns throughout the whole system of the common law; and, in the next, it requires a cool and clear accuracy of thinking, and an elaborate exactness and nicety in the deduction of thought, to which Mr. Henry's early and inveterate habits of indolence, as well as the sublime and excursive fervour of his genius, were altogether hostile.

It was on questions before a jury, that he was in his natural element. There, his intimate knowledge of human nature, and the rapidity as well as justness of his inferences, from the flitting expressions of the countenance, as to what was passing in the hearts of his hearers, availed him fully. The jury might be composed of entire strangers, yet he rarely failed to know them, man by man, before the evidence was closed. There was no studied fixture of features that could long hide the character from his piercing and experienced view. The slightest unguarded turn of countenance, or motion of the eye, let him at once into the soul of the man whom he was observing.

Or, if he doubted whether his conclusions were correct, from the exhibitions of countenance during the narration of the evidence, he had a mode of playing a prelude, as it were, upon the jury, in his exordium, which never failed to "wake into life each silent string," and show him the whole compass as well as pitch of the instrument; and, indeed, (if we may believe all the concurrent accounts of his exhibitions in the general court,) the most exquisite performer that ever "swept the sounding lyre" had not more a sovereign mastery over its powers, than Mr. Henry had over the springs of feeling and thought that belong to a jury. There was a delicacy, a taste, a felicity in his touch, that was perfectly original, and without a rival.

His style of address, on these occasions, is said to have resembled very much that of the scriptures. It was strongly marked with the same simplicity, the same energy, the same pathos. He sounded no alarm; he made no parade, to put the jury on their guard. It was all so natural, so humble, so unassuming, that they were carried imperfectly along, and attuned to his purpose, until some master-touch dissolved them into tears. His language of passion was perfect. There was no word "of learned length or thundering sound," to break the charm. It had almost all the stillness of solitary thinking. It was a sweet revery, a delicious trance.

His voice, too, had a wonderful effect. He had a singular power of infusing it into a jury, and mixing its notes with their nerves, in a manner which it is impossible to describe justly; but which produced a thrilling excitement, in the happiest concordance with his designs. No man knew so well as he did what kind of topics to urge to their understandings; nor what kind of simple imagery to present to their hearts. His eye, which he kept riveted upon them, assisted the process of fascination, and at the same time informed him what theme to press, or at what instant to retreat, if by rare accident he touched an unpropitious string. And then he had such an exuberance of appropriate thoughts, of apt illustrations, of apposite images, and such a melodious and varied roll of the happiest words, that the hearer was never wearied by repetition, and never winced from an apprehension that the intellectual treasures of the speaker would be exhausted.*

The defence of criminal causes was his great professional forte. It seems that the eighth day of the general court was formerly set apart for criminal business. Mr. Henry made

* A striking example of this witchery of his eloquence, even on common subjects, was related by a very respectable gentleman, the late Major Joseph Scott, the marshal of this state. This gentleman had been summoned, at great inconvenience to his private affairs, to attend as a witness a distant court, in which Mr. Henry practised. The cause which had carried him thither having been disposed of, he was setting out in great haste to return, when the sheriff summoned him to serve on a jury. This cause was represented as a complicated and important one; so important as to have enlisted in it all the most eminent members of the bar.

He was therefore alarmed at the prospect of a long detention, and made an unavailing effort with the court to get himself discharged from the jury. He was compelled to take his seat. When his patience had been nearly exhausted by the previous speakers, Mr. Henry rose to conclude the cause, and having much matter to answer, the major stated that he considered himself a prisoner for the evening, if not for the night. But, to his surprise, Mr. Henry appeared to have consumed not more than fifteen minutes in the reply; and he would scarcely believe his own watch, or those of the other jurymen, when they informed him that he had in reality been speaking upward of two hours. So powerful was the charm by which he could bind the senses of his hearers, and make even the most impatient unconscious of the lapse of time.

little or no figure during the civil days of the court; but on the eighth day he was the monarch of the bar. These causes brought him into direct collision with Mr. John Randolph, who had now succeeded Peyton as the attorney-general.

Mr. Randolph, it has been remarked, was, in person and manners among the most elegant gentlemen in the colony, and in his profession one of the most splendid ornaments of the bar. He was a polite scholar, as well as a profound lawyer, and his eloquence also was of a high order. His voice, action, style, were stately, and uncommonly impressive; but gigantic as he was in relation to other men, he was but a pigmy, when opposed in a criminal trial to the arch magician, Henry. In those cases Mr. Henry was perfectly irresistible. He adapted himself, without effort, to the character of the cause: seized with the quickness of intuition, its defensible point, and never permitted the jury to lose sight of it.

Sir Joshua Reynolds has said of Titian, that, by a few strokes of his pencil, he knew how to mark the image and character of whatever object he attempted; and produced by this means a truer representation than any of his predecessors, *who finished every hair*. In like manner, Mr. Henry, by a few master-strokes upon the evidence, could in general stamp upon the cause whatever image or character he pleased; and convert it into tragedy or comedy, at his sovereign will, and with a power which no efforts of his adversary could counteract.

He never wearied the jury by a dry and minute analysis of the evidence; he did not expend his strength *in finishing the hairs;* he produced all his high effect by those rare master-touches, and by the resistless skill with which, in a very few words, he could mould and colour the prominent facts of a cause to his purpose. He had wonderful address, too, in leading off the minds of his hearers from the contemplation of unfavourable points, if at any time they were too stubborn to yield to his power of transformation. He beguiled the hearer so far from them, as to diminish them by distance, and soften, if not entirely cast into shade, their too strong natural colours. At this distance, too, he had a better opportunity of throwing upon them a false light, by an apparently casual ray of refraction from other points in the evidence, whose powers no man better knew how to array and concentrate, in order to disguise or eclipse an obnoxious fact.

It required a mind of uncommon vigilance, and most intractable temper, to resist this charm with which he decoyed away his hearers; it demanded a rapidity of penetration which is rarely, if ever, to be found in the jury-box, to detect the intellectual juggle by which he spread his nets around them; it

6

called for a stubbornness and obduracy of soul which do not exist, to sit unmoved under the pictures of horror, or of pity which started from his canvass.

They might resolve, if they pleased, to decide the cause against him, and to disregard everything which he could urge in the defence of his client. But it was all in vain. Some feint, in an unexpected direction, threw them off their guard, and they were gone; some happy phrase, burning from the soul; some image fresh from Nature's mint, and bearing her own beautiful and genuine impress, struck them with delightful surprise, and melted them into conciliation; and conciliation toward Mr. Henry, was victory inevitable. In short, he understood the human character so perfectly; knew so well all its strength and all its weaknesses, together with every path and by-way which winds around to the citadel of the best fortified heart and mind, that he never failed to take them, either by stratagem or storm. Hence he was, beyond doubt, the ablest defender of criminals in Virginia, and will probably never be equalled again.

It has been observed, that Mr. Henry's knowledge of the common law was extremely defective; but his attendance upon the general court was calculated to cure that defect, in a considerable degree. All legal questions of magnitude or difficulty came before that tribunal, either originally or by appeal; and he had continual opportunities of hearing them discussed in the ablest manner, by the brightest luminaries of the American bar.

His was a mind on which nothing was lost; on which no useful seed could be cast without shooting into all the luxuriance of which its nature was susceptible. Thus improving every hint, and ramifying every principle which was brought into his view, there is reason to believe that a few years must have made him not only a master of the general canons of property, but of the modifications and exceptions of more frequent occurrence, by which those canons are restrained and governed.

In support of this conclusion, I find that in January, seventeen hundred and seventy-three, Robert C. Nicholas, who had enjoyed the first practice at the bar, and who, by virtue of his office of treasurer, was forced to relinquish that practice, committed, by a public advertisement, his unfinished business to Mr. Henry; a step which a man so remarkably scrupulous in the discharge of every moral duty would not have taken, had there been any incompetency on the part of his substitute.

The British ministry, however, did not permit Mr. Henry to waste himself in forensic exertions. The joy of the Americans, on the repeal of the stamp-act, was very short-lived. That measure had not been, on the part of the British parliament, a voluntary sacrifice to truth and right. The ministry and their friends disavowed this ground; and were forward on every occasion, to convince the colonies that they had nothing to expect, either from the clemency or the magnanimity of the British cabinet.

Thus on a question of supplies for the army, in the session of parliament of seventeen hundred and sixty-six and seven, a motion was made in the house of commons, that the revenues arising and *to arise* in America, be applied to subsisting the troops now there, *and those other regiments which it is proposed to send;* in support of which, that brilliant political meteor, Charles Townsend, urged, among other things, "*the propriety of more troops being sent to America, and of their being quartered in the large towns.*"

He said, that he had a plan preparing, which he would lay before the house, *for the raising of supplies in America.* That the legislative authority of Great Britain extended to every colony *in every particular.* That the distinction between *internal* and *external* taxes was *nonsense;* and that he voted for the repeal of the stamp-act, not because it was not a good act, but because, at that time, *there appeared a propriety in repealing it.* He added, that *he repeated the sentence, that the galleries might hear him, and after that, he did not expect to have his statue erected in America:* in all which, Mr. Grenville joined him fully. This temper soon manifested itself in open acts, and turned the late joy of the colonies into mourning.

The first obnoxious measure was a stern demand of satisfaction from the legislatures of the colonies, for the injuries which had been done to the stamp-officers and their adherents. The legislature of Massachusetts, of whom this demand was first made, very respectfully, and with good reason, questioned the propriety and justice of taxing the whole colony for the excesses of a few individuals, which they had neither prompted nor approved; for the sake of peace, however, and in the spirit of accommodation, that satisfaction was given; but they annexed to their vote of satisfaction a grant of pardon to the rioters; and, in England, according to the usual courtesy of that country, nothing was said of the satisfaction, while the pardon was treated as a most insolent and impudent usurpation of the royal authority.

The next step was that suggested by Mr. Townsend, of quartering large bodies of troops upon the chief towns in the colonies, and demanding of the several colonial legislatures a provision for their comfortable support and accommodation. A measure more replete with exasperation could scarcely have been devised. The very presence of those myrmidons was an insult; for it was a direct reflection on the fidelity of the colonists. Their object was perfectly understood: it was to curb the just and honourable spirit of the people; to dragoon them into submission to the parliamentary claim of taxation, and reduce them to the condition of vassals, governed by the right of conquest. The rudeness of the soldiery, too, was well calculated to keep up and increase the irritation, which their presence alone would have been sufficient to excite.

In Boston, they were in the habit of stopping the most respectable citizens in the streets, and compelling them to answer insulting inquiries, or committing them to confinement on their refusal, assigning, as the ground of their conduct, that the town was a garrisoned town. In New York, they provoked a contest with the people, by making war upon a liberty-pole, which was the first object of their earthly devotions, and which the soldiers continually destroyed or attempted to destroy, as soon as it could be replaced. And, as if all this insult and humiliation were not enough, the colonies were to be constrained to tax themselves, to foster and cherish those instruments of their degradation.

The legislature of New York, in a tone at least sufficiently submissive for the occasion, and on the false ground of the inability of the colony, begged to be excused from making the provision. For this high offence, the legislative power of that colony was abolished by act of parliament, until they should submit to make the provision which was required: and they did submit.

A body of British troops, alleged to have been driven by stress of weather into Boston, in the recess of the colonial legislature, had been provided for out of the public moneys, by the governor and his council. The legislature met shortly afterward, and remonstrated against this unconstitutional appropriation, with that Roman firmness and dignity which marked the character of Massachusetts in every stage of the contest. But Governor Bernard, highly indignant at what he affected to consider as presumption, made such a communication upon the subject to the British court, as could have had, and could have been designed to have, no other effect than to widen the breach, and inflame more highly those animosities which already required no new aggravation.

These military preparations were well understood to be the harbingers of some unconstitutional act, the execution of which they were necessary to enforce. Why those preparations were restricted to the northern states, and more particularly to Massachusetts, has never been satisfactorily explained. There was no colony which resisted with more firmness and constancy the pretensions of the British parliament than that of Virginia; yet no military force was thought necessary, during the lives of the governors Fauquier and Bottetourt, to keep down the spirit of rebellion in this colony.

A solution of the difficulty may perhaps be found in the character of the different governors. Virginia had the good fortune, during this period, to be governed by enlightened and amiable men, who saw and did justice to the motives and measure of resistance which was meditated; who were both able and willing to distinguish between reason and force, between remonstrance and rebellion; who perceived with pleasure, the spirit of genuine and unaffected loyalty and affection for the parent-country, which mingled itself with every complaint; and who, in their communications to the British court, were disposed rather "to extenuate," than "to set down aught in malice." Whereas Bernard, the governor of Massachusetts, was the fit instrument and apt representative of the masters whom he served: for he had all their pride and unfeeling insolence, and seems to have enjoyed a kind of fiend-like pleasure, in rendering his province hateful at home, by the most virulent misrepresentations; and in drawing down upon her the accumulated curses and oppressions of the parent-country.*

These preparatory steps having been taken, an act of parliament was passed, imposing certain duties on glass, white and red lead, painters' colours, tea, and paper, imported into the colonies. This act was to take effect on the twentieth of November, seventeen hundred and sixty-seven; and, to insure its operation, another act authorized the king to appoint a board of trade to reside in the colonies, and to instruct them at his pleasure and without limits, as to the mode of executing their duties under this law. A commission accordingly issued, by which the commissioners were armed with a power of search and seizure, at their discretion; with authority to call for aid upon the naval and military establishments within the colony; and *with an exemption from prosecution or responsibility be-*

* Extract of a letter, dated London, June fifth, seventeen hundred and seventy: "The people of England now curse Governor Bernard, as bitterly as those of America. Bernard was drove out of the Smyrna coffee-house, not many days since, by General Oglethorpe, who told him he was a dirty, factious scoundrel, and smelled cursed strong of the hangman; that he had better leave the room, as unworthy to mix with gentlemen of character, but that he would give him the satisfaction of following him to the door, had he any thing to reply. The governor left the house like a guilty coward."—*Pennsylvania Gazette*, August 30th, 1770.

fore any of the king's courts, for whatsoever they might do, by any construction of their commission.

Another measure which gave great offence to the colonies, was the establishment of a board of admiralty, with extensive powers, supported by large salaries independent of the colonies, yet drawn from the revenues compulsorily levied upon them; and the appointment, also, of common law judges, to be paid by the crown out of the revenues of the colony, and to hold their offices during the king's pleasure.

To all these outrages the legislatures of the colonies answered by petitions, memorials, remonstrances, and letters, addressed to the friends of colonial liberty in England; blending, with the strongest professions of loyalty, the expression of their hope, that those obnoxious measures would be reconsidered and reversed, and the colonies protected in their ancient and unalienable rights. In reply, they received from the kindest of their English friends, only exhortations to patience under their sufferings; by the court-party, menaces and anathemas werebrandishedover their heads; and the commissioners of the revenue, together with their auxiliaries, the naval and military officers and soldiery, continued to outrage and insult them, both in their persons and property.

The people of Massachusetts, with the view of frustrating the new revenue-bill, entered into an association, by which they bound themselves not to import from Great Britain, or use any of the articles taxed; and included in the resolution every article of British manufacture which was not of the first and most indispensable necessity. The legislature of that state also resolved on a circular-letter to their sister-colonies, inviting their concurrence and co-operation toward procuring relief, in a constitutional way, from the grievances under which they were all suffering.

This measure having been reported by Governor Bernard, with his usual embellishments, to the Earl of Hilsborough, the British minister for the American department, that minister required the governor to demand of the legislature an immediate rescission of their resolution, on pain of their being forthwith dissolved. They refused to rescind, and were dissolved accordingly. The same minister also addressed a circular-letter to the governors of the other colonies, exhorting them to crush this correspondence and concert among the colonial legislatures in the bud, by exacting from them an assurance that they would not answer the circular of Massachusetts. They refused to give such assurance, and were in their turn dissolved.

These violent measures, however, produced an effect very different from that which was expected to flow from them.

The dissolution of their legislatures swelled the catalogue of their wrongs. and ministered additional fuel to the resentments of the people. The non-importation agreement became general; and, by means of committees established in the several colonies, its execution was guarded with a vigilance which could not be eluded. A breach of it was infamy, inevitable and unpardonable. Its observance was a badge of honour, by which the patriot-colonist was proud to be distinguished.

The privation was, indeed, in many respects severe, but the sufferers were upheld by that kind of holy fortitude which enabled the Christian martyrs, to smile amid the flames and to triumph, even in the agonies of death. Every grade of society, all ages, and both sexes, kindled in this sacred competition of patriotism. The ladies of the colonies, in the dawn, and throughout the whole progress of the revolution, shone with pre-eminent lustre in this war of fortitude and self-denial. They renounced, without a sigh, the use of the luxuries and even of the comforts to which they had been accustomed; and felt a nobler pride in appearing dressed in the simple productions of their own looms, than they had ever experienced from glittering in the brightest ornaments of the East.

The British court looked upon this trial of virtuous fortitude with surly and inexorable rigour. They seemed determined to carry the point, at every hazard. The sufferings of their own merchants and manufacturers were forgotten, in the barbarous pleasure with which they contemplated the sufferings of the colonists. It is not in human nature to continue long to return good for evil, affection for cruelty. The admiration and devotion of the colonies for the parent-country became gradually weaker. This transition of feeling is most interestingly marked in the chronicles of the day. The epithets, "our kind and indulgent mother," with which she was wont to be greeted, were progressively changed into "unnatural parent—cruel stepmother—proud, merciless oppressor—haughty, unfeeling, and unrelenting tyrant."

This state of feeling was aggravated by the collisions which were perpetually occurring between the king's soldiery and the people of the towns in which they were quartered. The streets of New York and of Boston were the theatres of continual riots, ending almost invariably in blood, and not unfrequently in death. The newspapers of the day teem with the detail of scenes of this sort; and from the effect which they produce on the reader at this distance of time, it is not very difficult to conceive what must have been their operation on the people of that day, already goaded to madness by previous injuries.

It is not my purpose to record the series of measures which led to the dismemberment of the British empire. This is the function of the historian. My business is only with Mr. Henry; and, for my purpose, nothing more is necessary than to recall the general character of the contest, for the purpose of showing the part which he bore in it. The revolution may be truly said to have commenced with his resolutions in seventeen hundred and sixty-five.

From that period not an hour of settled peace had existed between the two countries. It is true, that the eruption produced by the stamp-act had subsided with its repeal; and the people had resumed their ancient settlements and occupations; but there was no peace of the heart or of the mind. The rumbling of the volcano was still audible, and the smoke of the crater continually ascended, mingled not unfrequently with those flames and masses of ignited matter which announced a new and more terrible explosion.

These were "the times that tried the souls of men;" and never, in any country or in any age, did there exist a race of men whose souls were better fitted to endure the trial. Patient in suffering, firm in adversity, calm and collected amid the dangers which pressed around them, cool in council, and brave in battle, they were worthy of the cause, and the cause was worthy of them.

The house of burgesses of Virginia, which had led the opposition to the stamp-act, kept their high ground during the whole of the ensuing contest. Mr. Henry, having removed again from Louisa to his native county, in the year seventeen hundred and sixty-seven or sixty-eight, continued a member of the public councils till the close of the revolution; and there could be no want of boldness in any body of which he was a member.

The session of seventeen hundred sixty-eight or sixty-nine, was marked by a set of resolutions so strong as to have excited even the amiable and popular Bottetourt to displeasure. By those resolutions they reasserted, in the most emphatic terms, the exclusive right of the colony to tax themselves in all cases whatever; complained of the recent acts of parliament, as so many violations of the British constitution; and remonstrated, vigorously, against the right of transporting the freeborn subjects of these colonies to England, to take their trial before prejudiced tribunals, for offences alleged to be committed in the colonies.

The tradition with regard to these resolutions is, that they were agreed to in a committee of the whole on one day, but not reported to the house, with the view of preventing their appearance on the journal of the next day, before they could be completely passed through the forms of the house; apprepending, from the fate of the Massachusetts legislature, that a knowledge of these resolutions, on the part of the governor, would produce an immediate dissolution of the house. When the house rose for the evening, however, the fact of their having passed such resolutions was whispered to the governor; and he endeavoured in vain to procure a copy of them from the clerk, (Mr. Wythe.)

On the next day, the house, foreseeing the event, met on the instant of the ringing of the bell, and with closed doors received the report of their resolutions, considered, adopted, and ordered them to be entered upon their journals; which they had scarcely done when they were summoned to attend the governor, and were dissolved. "Mr. Speaker," said he, "and gentlemen of the house of representatives, I have heard of your resolves, and augur ill of their effects; you have made it my duty to dissolve you, and you are accordingly dissolved."

But the dissolution of the house of burgesses did not change the materials of which it had been composed. The same members were re-elected without a single exception, and the same determined spirit of resistance continued to diffuse itself from the legislature over the colony which they represented, and to animate by sympathy the neighbouring colonies. This house had the merit of originating that powerful engine of resistance, corresponding committees between the legislatures of the different colonies.* The measure was brought forward by Mr. Dabney Carr, a new member from the county of Louisa, in a committee of the whole house, on the twelfth of March, seventeen hundred and seventy-three; and the resolutions, as adopted, now stood upon the journals of the day, in the following terms:—

"Whereas, the minds of his majesty's faithful subjects in this colony have been much disturbed by various rumours and reports of proceedings, tending to deprive them of their ancient, legal, and constitutional rights;

"And whereas, the affairs of this colony are frequently connected with those of Great Britain, as well as the neighbouring colonies, which renders a communication of sentiments necessary: in order, therefore, to remove the uneasiness, and to quiet the minds of the people, as well as for the other good purposes above mentioned:—

* The state of Massachusetts is entitled to equal honour: the measures were so nearly coeval in the two states, as to render it impossible that either could have borrowed it from the other. The messengers, who bore the propositions from the two states, are said to have crossed each other on the way. This is Mr. Jefferson's account of it; and Mrs. Warren, in her very interesting history of the revolution, admits, that the measure was original on the part of Virginia. See the note to page 110 of her first volume.

"Be it resolved, That a standing committee of correspondence and inquiry be appointed, to consist of eleven persons, to wit: the Honourable Peyton Randolph, esquire, Robert C. Nicholas, Richard Bland, Richard H. Lee, Benjamin Harrison, Edmund Pendleton, Patrick Henry, Dudley Digges, Dabney Carr, Archibald Cary, and Thomas Jefferson, esquires, any six of whom to be a committee, whose business it shall be to obtain the most early and authentic intelligence of all such acts and resolutions of the British parliament, or proceedings of administration, as may relate to or affect the British colonies in America; and to keep up and maintain a correspondence and communication with our sister-colonies, respecting those important considerations; and the result of such of their proceedings, from time to time, to lay before this house.

"Resolved, That it be an instruction to the said committee, that they do, without delay, inform themselves particularly of the principles and authority on which was constituted a court of inquiry, said to have been lately held in Rhode Island, with powers to transport persons accused of offences committed in America, to places beyond the seas, to be tried.

"The said resolutions being severally read a second time, were, upon the question severally put thereupon, agreed to by the house, *nemine contradicente*.

"Resolved, That the speaker of this house do transmit to the speakers of the different assemblies of the British colonies on the continent, copies of the said resolutions, and desire that they will lay them before their respective assemblies, and request them to appoint some person or persons of their respective bodies, to communicate from time to time with the said committee."

In supporting these resolutions, Mr. Carr made his *debut*, and a noble one it is said to have been. This gentleman by profession a lawyer, had recently commenced his practice at the same bars with Patrick Henry; and although he had not yet reached the meridian of life, he was considered by far the most formidable rival in forensic eloquence that Mr. Henry had ever yet had to encounter. He had the advantage of a person at once dignified and engaging, and the manner and action of an accomplished gentleman.

His education was a finished one; his mind trained to correct thinking; his conceptions quick, and clear, and strong; he reasoned with great cogency, and had an imagination which enlightened beautifully, without interrupting or diverting the course of his argument. His voice was finely toned; his feelings acute; his style free, and rich, and various; his devotion to the cause of liberty verging on enthusiasm; and his spirit firm and undaunted, beyond the possibility of being shaken. With what delight the house of burgesses hailed this new champion, and felicitated themselves on such an accession to their cause, it is easy to imagine. But what are the hopes and expectations of mortals!

> "Ostendent terris hunc tantum fata, neque ultra
> "Esse sinent—"

In two months from the time at which this gentleman stood before the house of burgesses, in all the pride of health, and genius, and eloquence—he was no more: lost to his friends, and to his country, and disappointed of sharing in that noble triumph which awaited the illustrious band of his compatriots.*

Mr. Carr's resolutions were supported successively by Mr. Henry, and Mr. Richard Henry Lee, with their usual ability. The reader will no doubt be gratified by a short sketch of this assembly, as it presented itself to a gentleman who now saw it for the first time, and who looked upon it with an eye of taste and genius; the writer who was then in the ardour of youth, and a stranger in the colony, has since been distinguished by holding and adorning some of the highest offices of the state.

* I cannot withhold from the reader the following note of this transaction and of the character of Mr. Carr, from one who knew him well, and heard this his first and last speech in the house of representatives: "I well remember the pleasure expressed in the countenance and conversation of the members generally, on this *debut* of Mr. Carr, and the hopes they conceived, as well from the talents as the patriotism it manifested. But he died within two months after, and in him we lost a powerful fellow-labourer.

"His character was of a high order: a spotless integrity, sound judgment, handsome imagination, enriched by education and reading, quick and clear in his conceptions, of correct and ready elocution, impressing every hearer with the sincerity of the heart from which it flowed. His firmness was inflexible in whatever he thought right: but when no moral principle was in the way, never had man more of the milk of human kindness, of indulgence, of softness, of pleasantry in conversation and conduct. The number of his friends, and the warmth of their affection, were proofs of his worth and of their estimate of it. To give to those now living an idea of the affliction produced by his death, in the minds of all those who knew him, I liken it to that lately felt by themselves on the death of his eldest son, Peter Carr; so like him in all his endowments and moral qualities, and whose recollection can never recur without a deep-drawn sigh from the bosom of every one who knew him."

Extract from the Virginia Gazette, of May 29, 1773.

"On Sunday, the sixteenth of May, died, at Charlottesville, in the thirtieth year of his age, Dabney Carr, esquire, attorney at law, and member of assembly for the county of Louisa. This excellent person possessed a fine genius, and a benevolent heart, with a taste for all that was polite, elegant, or social; and when occasion offered, displayed a masculine eloquence, and an undaunted love of liberty."

"When I first saw Mr. Henry, which was in March, seventeen hundred and seventy-three, he wore a peach-blossom-coloured coat and a dark wig, which tied behind, and I believe, a bag to it, as was the fashion of the day. When pointed out to me as the orator of the assembly, I looked at him with no great prepossession. On the opposite side of the house sat the graceful Pendleton, and the harmonious Richard Henry Lee, whose aquiline nose, and Roman profile struck me much more forcibly than that of Mr. Henry, his rival in eloquence. The distance from the gallery to the chair, near which these distinguished members sat, did not permit me to have such a view of their features and countenances, as to leave a strong impression, except of Mr. Lee's, whose profile was too remarkable not to have been noticed at an even greater distance.

"I was then between nineteen and twenty, had never heard a speech in public, except from the pulpit—had attached to the idea I had formed of an orator, all the advantages of person which Mr. Pendleton possessed, and even more—all the advantages of voice which delighted me so much in the speeches of Mr. Lee—the fine polish of language, which that gentleman united with that harmonious voice, so as to make me sometimes fancy that I was listening to some being inspired with more than mortal powers of embellishment, and all the advantages of gesture which the celebrated Demosthenes considered as the first, second, and third qualifications of an orator. I discovered neither of these qualifications in the appearance of Mr. Henry, or in the few remarks I heard him deliver during the session.

"It was at this time that Mr. Dabney Carr made a motion for appointing a standing committee of correspondence with the other colonies. I was not present when Mr. Henry spoke on this question; but was told by some of my fellow-collegians, that he far exceeded Mr. Lee, whose speech succeeded the next day. Never before had I heard what I thought oratory; and if his speech was excelled by Mr. Henry's, the latter must have been excellent, indeed. This was the only subject that I recollect, which called forth the talents of the members during that session, and there was too much unanimity to have elicited all the strength of any one of them."

My correspondent had an opportunity of seeing Mr. Henry not long afterward, when speaking on a subject of the highest moment to the liberties of his country, and of witnessing that almost supernatural transformation of appearance, which has been already noticed as being invariably wrought by the excitement of his genius. We shall have his own account of it by-and-by; and shall see that *he* no longer formed an exception to the voice of his country, in assigning the palm of popular eloquence to this most rare and extraordinary favourite of nature.

It is not improbable, as it has been suggested, that the strongly-marked distinction of ranks which prevailed in this country, and the resentment, if not envy, with which the poorer classes looked up to the splendour and ostentation of the landed aristocracy, had a considerable agency in inflaming Mr. Henry's hostility to the British court. He probably regarded the untitled nobles of Virginia as a sort of spurious emanation from the royal stock; connected them in his resentments, and transferred from the effect to the cause, the larger stream of his indignation.

He had a rooted aversion and even abhorrence to everything in the shape of pride, cruelty, and tyranny; and could not tolerate that social inequality from which they proceeded, and by which they were nourished. The principle which he seems to have brought with him into the world, and which certainly formed the guide of all his public actions, was, that the whole human race was one family, equal in their rights, and their birthright liberty.

The elements of his character were most happily mingled for the great struggle which was now coming on. His views were not less steady than they were bold. His vision pierced deeply into futurity; and long before a whisper of independence had been heard in this land, he had looked through the whole of the approaching contest, and saw, with the eye and the rapture of a prophet, his country seated aloft among the nations of the earth.

A striking proof of this prescience, is given in an anecdote communicated to me by Mr. Pope. These are his words:—"I am informed by Colonel John Overton, that before one drop of blood was shed in our contest with Great Britain, he was at Colonel Samuel Overton's, in company with Mr. Henry, Colonel Morris, John Hawkins, and Colonel Samuel Overton, when the last-mentioned gentleman asked Mr. Henry, 'whether he supposed Great Britain would drive her colonies to extremities:—And if she should, what he thought would be the issue of the war.'

"When Mr. Henry, after looking round to see who were present, expressed himself confidentially to the company in the following manner:—'She *will* drive us to extremities—no accommodation *will* take place—hostilities will *soon* commence—and a desperate and bloody touch it will be.'—'But,' said Colonel Samuel Overton, 'do you think, Mr. Henry, that an infant nation as we are, without discipline, arms, ammunition, ships of war, or money to procure them—do you think it

7

possible, thus circumstanced, to oppose successfully the fleets and armies of Great Britain?'

"'I will be candid with you,' replied Mr. Henry. 'I doubt whether we *shall* be able, *alone*, to cope with so powerful a nation. But,' continued he, (rising from his chair, with great animation,) 'where is France? Where is Spain? Where is Holland? the natural enemies of Great Britain.—Where will they be all this while? Do you suppose they will stand by, idle and indifferent spectators to the contest? Will Louis XVI. be asleep all this time? Believe me, *no!*

"'When Louis XVI. shall be satisfied by our serious opposition, and our *Declaration of Independence*, that all prospect of a reconciliation is gone, then, and not till then, will he furnish us with arms, ammunition, and clothing; and not with these only, but he will send his fleets and armies to fight our battles for us; he will form with us a treaty offensive and defensive, against our unnatural mother. Spain and Holland will join the confederation! Our independence will be established! and we shall take our stand among the nations of the earth!'"

Here he ceased; and Colonel John Overton says, he shall never forget the voice and prophetic manner with which these predictions were uttered, and which have been since so literally verified. Colonel Overton says at the word *independence*, the company appeared to be startled; for they had never heard anything of the kind before even suggested.

It was anticipated, that the establishment of corresponding committees would lead eventually to a congress of the colonies, and that measure was brought about by the following circumstances:—

The people of Boston having thrown into the sea a vessel load of tea, which was attempted to be forced upon them, were punished by an act of parliament, which shut up their port, from and after the first day of June, seventeen hundred and seventy-four. The house of burgesses of Virginia being in session when this act arrived, passed an order which stands upon their journal in the following terms:—

"*Tuesday, the 24th of May*, 14 *Geo. III.* 1774.

"This house, being deeply impressed with apprehension of the great dangers to be derived to British America, from the hostile invasion of the city of Boston, in our sister-colony of the Massachusetts bay, whose commerce and harbour are, on the first day of June next, to be stopped by an armed force, deem it highly necessary that the said first day of June next be set apart, by the members of this house, as a day of fasting, humiliation, and prayer, devoutly to implore the Divine interposition for averting the heavy calamity which threatens destruction to our civil rights, and the evils of civil war; to give us one heart and one mind, firmly to oppose, by all just and proper means, every injury to American rights; and that the minds of his majesty and his parliament may be inspired from above with wisdom, moderation, and justice, to remove from the loyal people of America all cause of danger from a continued pursuit of measures pregnant with their ruin.

"*Ordered*, therefore, That the members of this house do attend in their places, at the hour of ten in the forenoon, on the said first day of June next, in order to proceed with the speaker and the mace to the church in this city, for the purpose aforesaid; and that the Reverend Mr. Price be appointed to read prayers, and to preach a sermon suitable to the occasion."

In consequence of this order, Governor Dunmore, on the following day, dissolved the house, with this speech:—"Mr. Speaker, and gentlemen of the house of burgesses: I have in my hand a paper published by order of your house, conceived in such terms as reflect highly upon his majesty and the parliament of Great Britain, which makes it necessary to dissolve you, and you are dissolved accordingly."

The members immediately withdrew to the Raleigh tavern, where they formed themselves into a committee to consider of the most expedient and necessary measures to guard against the encroachments which so glaringly threatened them; and immediately adopted the following spirited association:—

"An association signed by eighty-nine members of the late house of burgesses. We, his majesty's most dutiful and loyal subjects, the late representatives of the good people of this country, having been deprived, by the sudden interposition of the executive part of this government, from giving our countrymen the advice we wished to convey to them, in a legislative capacity, find ourselves under the hard necessity of adopting this, the only method we have left, of pointing out to our countrymen such measures as, in our opinion, are best fitted to secure our dear rights and liberty from destruction, by the heavy hand of power now lifted against North America.

"With much grief we find, that our dutiful applications to Great Britain for the security of our just, ancient, and constitutional rights, have been not only disregarded, but that a determined system is formed and pressed, for reducing the inhabitants of British America to slavery, by subjecting them to the payment of taxes imposed without the consent of the people or their representatives; and that, in pursuit of this system, we find an act of British parliament, lately passed for stopping the harbour and commerce of the town of Boston, in our sister-colony of Massachusetts bay, until the people there submit to the payment of such unconstitutional taxes; and which act most violently and arbitrarily deprives them of their property, in wharves erected by private persons, at their own great and proper expense; which act is, in our opinion, a most dangerous attempt to destroy the constitutional liberty and rights of all North America.

"It is further our opinion, that as tea, on its importation into America, is charged with a duty imposed by parliament, for the purpose of raising a revenue without the consent of the people, it ought not to be used by any person who wishes well to the constitutional rights and liberties of British America. And whereas the India company have ungenerously attempted the ruin of America, by sending many ships loaded with tea into the colonies, thereby intending to fix a precedent in favour of arbitrary taxation, we deem it highly proper and do accordingly recommend it strongly to our countrymen, not to purchase or use any kind of East India commodity whatsoever, except saltpetre and spices, until the grievances of America are redressed.

"We are further clearly of opinion, that an attack made on one of our sister-colonies, to compel submission to arbitrary taxes, is an attack made on all British America, and threatens ruin to the rights of all, unless the united wisdom of the whole be applied. *And for this purpose it is recommended to the committee of correspondence, that they communicate with their several corresponding committees, on the expediency of appointing deputies from the several colonies of British America, to meet in general congress, at such place, annually, as shall be thought most convenient; there to deliberate on those general measures which the united interests of America may from time to time require.*

"A tender regard for the interests of our fellow-subjects, the merchants and manufacturers of Great Britain, prevents us from going further at this time; most earnestly hoping that the unconstitutional principle of taxing the colonies without their consent will not be persisted in, thereby to compel us against our will, to avoid all commercial intercourse with Britain. Wishing them and our people free and happy, we are their affectionate friends, the late representatives of Virginia.

"*The 27th day of May*, 1774."

To give effect to the recommendation of a congress on the part of this colony, delegates were shortly after elected by the several counties to meet in Williamsburgh on the first of August following, to consider further of the state of public affairs, and more particularly, to appoint deputies to the general congress, which was to be convened at Philadelphia, on the fifth of September following. The clear, firm, and animated instructions given by the people of the several counties to their delegates, evince the thorough knowledge of the great parliamentary question which now pervaded the country, and the determined spirit of the colonists to resist the claim of British taxation.

The following are the Instructions from the county of Hanover:—

"*To John Syme and Patrick Henry, Jun., Esquires.*

"Gentlemen, You have our thanks for your patriotic, faithful, and spirited conduct, in the part you acted in the late assembly, as our burgesses, and as we are greatly alarmed at the proceedings of the British parliament respecting the town of Boston, and the province of Massachusetts bay; and as we understand a meeting of delegates from all the counties in this colony is appointed to be in Williamsburgh on the first day of next month, to deliberate on our public affairs, we do hereby appoint you, gentlemen, our delegates; and we do request you, then and there, to meet, consult, and advise, touching such matters as are most likely to effect our deliverance from the evils with which our country is threatened.

"The importance of those things which will offer themselves for your deliberation is exceedingly great; and when it is considered that the effect of the measures you may adopt will reach our latest posterity, you will excuse us for giving you our sentiments, and pointing out some particulars, proper for that plan of conduct we wish you to observe.

"We are freemen; we have a right to be so; and to enjoy all the privileges and immunities of our fellow-subjects in England; and while we retain a just sense of that freedom, and those rights and privileges necessary for its safety and security, we shall never give up the right of taxation. Let it suffice to say, once for all, *we will never be taxed but by our own representatives;* this is the great *badge* of freedom, and British America hath hitherto been distinguished by it; and when we see the British parliament trampling upon that right, and acting with determined resolution to destroy it, we would wish to see the united wisdom and fortitude of America collected for its defence.

"The sphere of life in which we move hath not afforded us lights sufficient to determine with certainty, concerning those things from which the troubles at Boston originated. Whether the people there were warranted by justice, when they destroyed the tea, we know not; but this we know, that the parliament by their proceedings, have made us and all North America parties in the present dispute, and deeply interested in the event of it; insomuch that if our sister-colony of Massachusetts bay is enslaved, *we* cannot long remain free.

"Our minds are filled with anxiety when we view the friendly regard of our parent state turned into enmity; and those powers of government formerly exerted for our aid and protection, formed into dangerous efforts for our destruction. We read our intended doom in the Boston port-bill, in that for altering the mode of trial in criminal cases, and, finally, in the bill for altering the form of government in the Massachusetts bay. These several acts are replete with injustice and oppression, and strongly expressive of the future policy of Britain toward *all* her colonies; if a full and uncontrolled operation is given to this detestable system in its earlier stages, it will probably be fixed upon us for ever.

"Let it, therefore, be your great object to obtain a speedy repeal of those acts; and for this purpose we recommend the adoption of such measures as may produce the hearty union of all our countrymen and sister-colonies. UNITED WE STAND, DIVIDED WE FALL.

"To attain this wished-for union, we declare our readiness to sacrifice any lesser interest arising from a soil, climate, situation, or productions peculiar to us. We judge it conducive to the interests of America, that a general congress of deputies from all the colonies be held, in order to form a plan for guarding the claim of the colonists, and their constitutional rights, from future encroachment, and for the speedy relief of our suffering brethren at Boston.

"For the present, we think it proper to form a general association against the purchase of all articles of goods imported from Great Britain, except negroes' cloths, salt, saltpetre, powder, lead, utensils and implements for handy-craftsmen and manufacturers, which cannot be had in America; books, paper, and the like necessaries; and not to purchase any goods or merchandise that shall be imported from Great Britain, after a certain day that may be agreed on for that purpose by the said general meeting of deputies at Williamsburgh, except the articles aforesaid, or such as shall be allowed to be imported by the said meeting; and that we will encourage the manufactures of America by every means in our power.

"A regard to justice hinders us at this time from withholding our exports; nothing but the direct necessity shall induce us to adopt that proceeding, which we shall strive to avoid as long as possible. The African trade for slaves we consider as most dangerous to the virtue and welfare of this country; we therefore most earnestly wish to see it totally discouraged. A steady loyalty to the kings of England has ever distinguished our country; the present state of things here, as well as the many instances of it to be found in our history, leave no room to doubt it.

"God grant that we may never see the time when that loyalty shall be found incompatible with the rights of freemen. Our most ardent desire is, that we and our latest posterity may continue to live under the genuine, unaltered constitution of England, and be subjects, in the true spirit of that constitution, to his majesty, and his illustrious house; and may the wretches who affirm that we desire the contrary, feel the punishment due to falsehood and villany.

"While prudence and moderation shall guide your councils, we trust, gentlemen, that firmness, resolution, and zeal, will animate you in the glorious struggle. The arm of power, which is now stretched forth against us, is indeed formidable; but we do not despair. Our cause is good; and if it is served with constancy and fidelity, it cannot fail of success. We promise you our best support, and we will heartily join in such measures as a majority of our countrymen shall adopt for securing the public liberty.

"Resolved, That the above address be transmitted to the printers to be published in the gazettes.

"WILLIAM POLLARD, Clerk."

On the first of August, accordingly, the first convention of Virginia delegates assembled in Williamsburgh; and gave a new proof of the invincible energy by which they were actuated, in a series of resolutions, whereby they pledged themselves to make common cause with the people of Boston in every extremity, and broke off all commercial connexion with the mother-country, until the grievances of which they complained should be redressed. By their last resolution they empowered their moderator, Mr. Peyton Randolph, or in case of his death, Robert C. Nicholas, esquire, on any future occasion that might in his opinion require it, to convene the several delegates of the colony, at such time and place as he might judge proper.

They then appointed as deputies to congress on the part of this colony, Messrs. Peyton Randolph, Richard Henry Lee, George Washington, Patrick Henry, Richard Bland, Benjamin Harrison, and Edmund Pendleton, and furnished them with the following firm and spirited letter of instructions:—

"*Instructions for the Deputies appointed to meet in General Congress, on the part of the Colony of Virginia.*

"The unhappy disputes between Great Britain and her American colonies, which began about the third year of the reign of his present majesty, and since continually increasing, have proceeded to lengths so dangerous and alarming, as to excite just apprehensions in the minds of his majesty's faithful subjects of the colony, that they are in danger of being deprived of their natural, ancient, constitutional, and chartered rights, have compelled them to take the same into their most serious consideration; and being deprived of their usual and accustomed mode of making known their grievances, have appointed us their representatives, to consider what is proper to be done in this dangerous crisis of American affairs.

"It being our opinion that the united wisdom of North America should be collected in a general congress of all the colonies, we have appointed the Honourable Peyton Randolph, Richard Henry Lee, George Washington, Patrick Henry, Richard Bland, Benjamin Harrison, and Edmund Pendleton, esquires, deputies to represent this colony in the said congress, to be held at Philadelphia on the first Monday in September next.

"And that they may be the better informed of our sentiments touching the conduct we wish them to observe on this important occasion, we desire that they will express, in the first place, our faith and true allegiance to his majesty, King George III., our lawful and rightful sovereign; and that we are determined, with our lives and fortunes, to support him in the legal exercise of all his just rights and prerogatives. And, however misrepresented, we sincerely approve of a constitutional connexion with Great Britain, and wish most ardently a return of that intercourse of affection and commercial connexion that formerly united both countries; which can only be effected by a removal of those causes of discontent which have of late unhappily divided us.

"It cannot admit of a doubt, but that British subjects in America are entitled to the same rights and privileges as their fellow-subjects possess in Britain; and, therefore, that the power assumed by the British parliament to bind America by their statutes, in all cases whatsoever, is unconstitutional and the source of these unhappy differences.

"The end of government would be defeated, by the British parliament exercising a power over the lives, the property, and the liberty of American subjects, who are not, and from their local circumstances cannot, be there represented. Of this nature we consider the several acts of parliament for raising a revenue in America, for extending the jurisdiction of the courts of admiralty, for seizing American subjects, and transporting them to Britain, to be tried for crimes committed in America, and the several late oppressive acts respecting the town of Boston, and province of Massachusetts bay.

"The original constitution of the American colonies, possessing their assemblies with the sole right of directing their internal polity, it is absolutely destructive of the end of their institution, that their legislatures should be suspended, or prevented, by hasty dissolutions, from exercising their legislative powers.

"Wanting the protection of Britain, we have long acquiesced in their acts of navigation, restrictive of our commerce, which we consider as an ample recompense for such protection; but as those acts derive their efficacy from that foundation alone, we have reason to expect they will be restrained, so as to produce the reasonable purposes of Britain, and not be injurious to us.

"To obtain redress of these grievances, without which the people of America can neither be safe, free, nor happy, they are willing to undergo the great inconvenience that will be derived to them, from stopping all imports whatsoever from Great Britain, after the first day of November next, and also to cease exporting any commodity whatsoever to the same place, after the tenth day of August, seventeen hundred and seventy-five.

"The earnest desire we have to make as quick and full payment as possible of our debts to Great Britain, and to avoid the heavy injury that would arise to this country from an earlier adoption of the non-exportation plan, after the people have already applied so much of their labour to the perfecting of the present crop, by which means they have been prevented from pursuing other methods of clothing and supporting their families, have rendered it necessary to restrain you in this article of non-exportation; but it is our desire that you cordially cooperate with our sister-colonies in general congress, in such other just and proper methods as they, or the majority shall deem necessary for the accomplishment of these valuable ends.

"The proclamation issued by General Gage, in the government of the province of the Massachusetts bay, declaring it treason for the inhabitants of that province to assemble themselves to consider of their grievances, and form associations for their common conduct on the occasion, and requiring the civil magistrates and officers to apprehend all such persons to be tried for their supposed offences, is the most alarming process that ever appeared in a British government; the said General Gage has thereby assumed and taken upon himself powers denied by the constitution to our legal sovereign; he not having condescended to disclose by what authority he exercises such extensive and unheard-of powers, we are at a loss to determine whether he intends to justify himself as the representative of the king, or as the commander-in-chief of his majesty's forces in America.

"If he considers himself as acting in the character of his majesty's representative, we would remind him that the statute 25th, Edward III., has expressed and defined all treasonable offences, and the legislature of Great Britain hath declared that no offence shall be construed to be treason, but such as is pointed out by that statute; and that this was done to take out of the hands of tyrannical kings, and of weak and wicked ministers, that deadly weapon which constructive treason hath furnished them with, and which had drawn the blood of the best and honestest men in the kingdom; and that the king of Great Britain hath no right by his proclamation to subject his people to imprisonment, pains, and penalties.

"That if the said General Gage conceives he is empowered to act in this manner, as the commander-in-chief of his majesty's forces in America, this odious and illegal proclamation must be considered as a plain and full declaration that this despotic viceroy will be bound by no law, nor regard the constitutional rights of his majesty's subjects, whenever they interfere with the plan he has formed for oppressing the good people of Massachusetts bay; and, therefore, that the executing, or attempting to execute, such proclamation, will justify resistance and reprisal."

On the fourth of September, seventeen hundred and seventy-four, that venerable body, the old continental congress of the United States, (toward whom every American heart will bow with pious homage, while the name of liberty shall be dear in our land,) met for the first time at Carpenter's Hall, in the city of Philadelphia. Peyton Randolph, of Virginia, was chosen president, and the house was organized for business with all the solemnities of a regular legislature.*

The most eminent men of the various colonies were now, for the first time, brought together. They were known to each other by fame; but they were personally strangers. The

* Sallust, in his second oration to C. Cesar, *De Republica Ordinanda*, gives a short and animated picture of their Roman ancestors which, with the change of a single word, (*libertate* for *imperio*,) describes so happily our old continental congress, that I am sure I shall gratify the classic reader by its insertion.

"Itaque, majores nostri, cum bellis asperimis premerentur, equis, viris, pecunia amissa, nunquam defessi sunt armati de *libertate* contendere. Non inopia ærarii, non vis hostium, non adversa res, ingentem eorum animum subegit: quem, quæ virtute ceperant, simul cum anima retinerent. Atque ea, magis fortibus consiliis, quam bonis præliis, patrata sunt. Quippe apud illos, una respublica erat; ei consulebant; factio, contra hostes parabatur; corpus atque ingenium, patriæ, non suæ, quisque potentiæ exercitabat."

meeting was awfully solemn. The object which had called them together was of incalculable magnitude. The liberties of no less than three millions of people, with that of all their posterity, were staked on the wisdom and energy of their councils. No wonder, then, at the long and deep silence which is said to have followed upon their organization; at the anxiety with which the members looked around upon each other; and the reluctance which every individual felt to open a business so fearfully momentous.

In the midst of this deep and deathlike silence, and just when it was beginning to become painfully embarrassing, Mr. Henry arose slowly, as if borne down by the weight of the subject. After faltering, according to his habit, through a most impressive exordium, in which he merely echoed back the consciousness of every other heart, in deploring his inability to do justice to the occasion, he launched gradually into a recital of the colonial wrongs. Rising, as he advanced, with the grandeur of his subject, and glowing at length with all the majesty and expectation of the occasion, his speech seemed more than that of mortal man.

Even those who had heard him in all his glory, in the house of burgesses of Virginia, were astonished at the manner in which his talents seemed to swell and expand themselves, to fill the vaster theatre in which he was now placed. There was no rant—no rhapsody—no labour of the understanding—no straining of the voice—no confusion of the utterance. His countenance was erect—his eye, steady—his action, noble—his enunciation, clear and firm—his mind poised on its centre—his views of his subject comprehensive and great—and his imagination coruscating with a magnificence and a variety, which struck even that assembly with amazement and awe. He sat down amid murmurs of astonishment and applause; and as he had been before proclaimed the greatest orator of Virginia, he was now, on every hand, admitted to be the first orator of America.

He was followed by Mr. Richard Henry Lee, who charmed the house with a different kind of eloquence—chaste—classical—beautiful—his polished periods rolling along without effort, filling the ear with the most bewitching harmony, and delighting the mind with the most exquisite imagery. The cultivated graces of Mr. Lee's rhetoric received and at the same time reflected beauty, by their contrast with the wild and grand effusions of Mr. Henry. Just as those noble monuments of art which lie scattered through the celebrated landscape of Naples, at once adorn, and are in their turn adorned by the surrounding majesty of Nature.

Two models of eloquence, each so perfect in its kind, and so finely contrasted, could not but fill the house with the highest admiration; and as Mr. Henry had before been pronounced the Demosthenes, it was conceded on every hand, that Mr. Lee was the Cicero, of America.

CHAPTER IV.

Proceedings of the Congress—Mr. Henry's early Opinion of Washington—Meeting of Delegates in Richmond—Mr. Henry's Resolutions for arming the Militia—Speech on that Occasion—Resolutions Adopted.

It is due, however, to historic truth to record, that the superior powers of these great men were manifested only in debate. On the floor of the house, and during the first days of the session, while general grievances were the topic, they took the undisputed lead in the assembly, and were confessedly, *primi inter pares*. But when called down from the heights of declamation, to that severer test of intellectual excellence, *the details of business*, they found themselves in a body of cool-headed, reflecting, and most able men, by whom they were, in their turn, completely thrown into the shade.

A petition to the king, an address to the people of Great Britain, and a memorial to the people of British America, were agreed to be drawn. Mr. Lee, Mr. Henry, and others, were appointed for the first; Mr. Lee, Mr. Livingston, and Mr. Jay, for the two last. The splendour of their *debut* occasioned Mr. Henry to be designated by his committee, to draw the petition to the king, with which they were charged; and Mr. Lee was charged with the address to the people of England.

The last was first reported. On reading it, great disappointment was expressed in every countenance, and a dead silence ensued for some minutes. At length, it was laid on the table, for perusal and consideration, till the next day: when first one member and then another arose, and paying some faint compliment to the composition, observed that there were still certain considerations not expressed, which should properly find a place in it. The address was, therefore, committed for amendment; and one prepared by Mr. Jay, and offered by Governor Livingston, was reported and adopted, with scarcely an alteration.

These facts are stated by a gentleman to whom they were communicated by Mr. Pendleton and Mr. Harrison, of the Vir ginia delegation, (except that Mr. Harrison erroneously ascribed the draught to Governor Livingston,) and to whom they were afterward confirmed by Governor Livingston himself. Mr. Henry's draught of a petition to the king was equally unsuccessful, and was recommitted for amendment. Mr. John Dickinson (the author of the Farmer's Letters) was added to the committee, and a new draught, prepared by him, was adopted.*

This is one of the incidents in the life of Mr. Henry to which an allusion was made in a former page, when it was observed, that notwithstanding the wonderful gifts which he had derived from nature, he lived himself to deplore his early neglect of literature. But for this neglect, that imperishable trophy won by the pen of Mr. John Dickinson would have been his; and the fame of his genius, instead of resting on tradition, or the short-lived report of his present biographer, would have flourished on the immortal page of the American history.

It is a trite remark, that the talents for speaking and for writing eminently are very rarely found united in the same individual; and the rarity of the occurrence has led to an opinion, that those talents depend on constitutions of mind so widely different, as to render their union almost wholly unattainable. This was not the opinion, however, it is believed, at Athens and at Rome: it cannot, I apprehend, be the opinion either in the united kingdom of Great Britain.

There have been, indeed, in these countries distinguished orators, who have not left behind them any proofs of their eminence in composition; but neither have they left behind them any proofs of their failure in this respect; so that the conclusion of *their* incompetency is rather assumed than established. On the other hand, there have been in all those countries, too many illustrious examples of the union of those talents, to justify the belief of their incongruity by any general law of nature. That there have been many eminent writers who, from physical defects, could never have become orators, is very certain: but is the converse of the proposition equally true? Was there ever an eminent orator who might not, by proper discipline,

* The late Governor Tyler, a warm friend of Mr. Henry, used to relate an anecdote in strict accordance with this statement: it was, that after these two gentlemen had made their first speeches, Mr. Chase, a delegate from Maryland, walked across the house to the seat of his colleague, and said to him, in an under voice: "We might as well go home; we are not able to legislate with these men." But that after the house came to descend to details, the same Mr. Chase was heard to remark: "Well, after all, I find these are but men—and in mere matters of business, *but very common men*."

have become, also, a very eminent writer? What are the essential qualities of the orator? Are they not judgment, invention, imagination, sensibility, taste, and expression, or the command of strong and appropriate language?

If these be the qualities of the orator, it is very easy to understand how they may be improved by the discipline of the closet;* but not so easy to comprehend how they can possibly be injured by it. Is there any danger that this discipline will tame too much the fiery spirit, the enchanting wildness, and magnificent irregularity of the orator's genius? The example of Demosthenes alone is a sufficient answer to this question; and the reader will, at once, recall numerous other examples, corroborative of the same truth, both in ancient and modern times.

The truth seems to be, that this rare union of talents results, not from any incongruity in their nature, but from defective education, taking this word in its larger, Roman sense. If the genius of the orator has been properly trained in his youth to both pursuits, instead of being injured, it will, I apprehend, be found to derive additional grace, beauty, and even sublimity, from the discipline. His flights will be at least as bold—they will be better sustained—and whether he chooses to descend in majestic circles, or to stoop on headlong wing, his performance will not be the worse for having been taught to fly.

For Mr. Henry and for the world, it happened unfortunately, that instead of the advantage of this Roman education, of which we have spoken, the years of his youth had been wasted in idleness. He had become celebrated as an orator before he had learned to compose; and it is not therefore wonderful, that when withdrawn from the kindling presence of the crowd, he was called upon for the first time to take the pen, all the spirit and flame of his genius were extinguished.†

* Nulla enim res tantùm ad dicendum proficit, quantum scriptio.—Cic. Brut. xxiv. 92.

† On this subject, of the rare union of the talents of speaking and writing in the same man, Cicero has a parallel between Galba and Lælius, which is not less just than it is beautiful. After having spoken of Galba as one of those men of great but less cultivated natural powers, who were afraid of lowering the fame of their eloquence by submitting their writings to the world, he proceeds thus:—"Quem (Galbam) fortasse vis non ingenii solum, sed etiam animi, et naturalis quidam dolor dicentem incendebat, effeciebatque, ut et incitata, et gravis, et vehemens esset oratio: dein, cum otiosus stilum prehenderat, motusque omnis animi, tanquam ventus, hominem defecerat, flaccescebat oratio: quod iis, qui limatius dicendi consectantur genus, accidere non solet, propterea quod prudentia nunquam deficit oratorem, qua ille utens, eodem modo possit et dicere et scribere; ardor animi non semper adest, isque cum consedit, omnis illa vis et quasi flamma oratoris extinguitur. Hanc igitur ob

But while, with reference to his own fame and the lasting benefits which he might have conferred on the world, we lament his want of literary discipline, it is not impossible that, for the times in which he lived, and for the more immediate purpose of the American revolution, the popular opinion may be correct.

The people seem to have admired him the more for his want of discipline. "His genius," they say, "was unbroken, and too full of fire, to bear the curb of composition. He delighted to swim the flood, to breast the torrent, and to scale the mountain: and supported as he was, in all public bodies, by masters of the pen, they insist that it was even fortunate for the revolution, that *his* genius was left at large to revel in all the wildness and boldness of nature; that it enabled him to in-

causam, videtur Lælii mens spirare etiam in scriptis, Galbæ autem, vis occidisse." BRUTUS, xxiv. 93.

There seems to have been a strong resemblance between the structure of Galba's eloquence and character, and those of Mr. Henry. In their habits, however, there was this striking difference, that Galba's preparation for speaking was always most elaborate; Mr. Henry's, generally, none at all. On this head, of Galba's anxious preparation, Cicero gives us a very interesting anecdote: Lælius, it seems, was engaged in a great cause, in which he spoke with the peculiar elegance which always distinguished him; but not having succeeded in convincing his judges, the case was adjourned to another day, and a new argument was called for. Lælius again appeared, and surpassed his former exertions, but with the same result, of another adjournment and a call for re-argument. His clients attended him to his house on the rising of the court, expressed their gratitude in the strongest terms, and begged that he would not permit himself to be wearied into a desertion of them. To this Lælius answered, that what he had done for the support of the cause, had, indeed, been diligently and accurately performed; but he was satisfied that *that* cause could be better defended by the more bold and vehement eloquence of Galba.

Galba was accordingly applied to; but was, at first, startled at the idea of succeeding such an orator as Lælius in any cause; more especially, on the short time for preparation that was then allowed him. He yielded, however, to their importunities; and employed the whole of the intermediate day and the morning of that in which the court was to sit, in studying and annotating, with the help of his amanuensis. When the hour of court arrived, his clients called for him, and Galba came out, "with that complexion and those eyes," says Cicero, "which would have led you to suppose that he had been engaged in pleading a cause, and not in studying it." Whence it appears that Galba was not less vehement and inflamed in meditating, than in the act of delivering a speech. His success was proportioned to his preparation. "In the midst of the greatest expectation, surrounded by a vast concourse of hearers, before Lælius himself, he plead the cause with so much force and so much power, that no part of his speech passed without applause, and his clients were discharged, with the approbation of every one." What an impression does this give us of the magnanimity of Lælius, as well as the abilities of Galba! Mr. Henry would not have taken the trouble of Galba's preparation; but he would have gained the cause, if human abilities could have gained it.

fuse, more successfully, his own intrepid spirit into the measures of the revolution; that it rendered his courage more contagious, and enabled him to achieve, by a kind of happy rashness, what perhaps had been lost by a better regulated mind."

But to resume our narrative: congress arose in October, and Mr. Henry returned to his native county. Here, as was natural, he was surrounded by his neighbours, who were eager to hear not only what had been done, but what kind of men had composed that illustrious body.

He answered their inquiries with all his wonted kindness and candour; and having been asked by one of them, "whom he thought the greatest man in congress," he replied: "If you speak of eloquence, Mr. Rutledge, of South Carolina, is by far the greatest orator; but if you speak of solid information and sound judgment, Colonel Washington is, unquestionably, the greatest man on that floor." Such was the penetration which, at that early period of Mr. Washington's life, could pierce through his retiring modesty and habitual reserve, and estimate so correctly the unrivalled worth of his character.

On Monday, the twentieth of March, seventeen hundred and seventy-five, the convention of delegates, from the several counties and corporations of Virginia, met for the second time. This assembly was held in the old church in the town of Richmond. Mr. Henry was a member of that body also. The reader will bear in mind, the tone of the instructions given by the convention of the preceding year to their deputies in congress.

He will remember that, while they recite with great feeling the series of grievances under which the colonies had laboured, and insist with firmness on their constitutional rights, they give, nevertheless, the most explicit and solemn pledge of their faith and true allegiance to his majesty King George III., and avow their determination to support him with their lives and fortunes, in the legal exercise of all his just rights and prerogatives. He will remember, that these instructions contain also, an expression of their sincere approbation of a connexion with Great Britain, and their ardent wishes for a return of that friendly intercourse from which this country had derived so much prosperity and happiness.

These sentiments still influenced many of the leading members of the convention of seventeen hundred and seventy-five. They could not part with the fond hope that those peaceful days would again return which had shed so much light and warmth over the land; and the report of the king's gracious reception of the petition from congress tended to cherish and foster that hope, and to render them averse to any means of violence.

But Mr. Henry saw things with a steadier eye and a deeper insight. His judgment was too solid to be duped by appearances; and his heart too firm and manly to be amused by false and flattering hopes. He had long since read the true character of the British court, and saw that no alternative remained for his country but abject submission or heroic resistance. It was not for a soul like Henry's to hesitate between these courses.

He had offered upon the altar of liberty no divided heart. The gulf of war which yawned before him was indeed fiery and fearful; but he saw that the awful plunge was inevitable. The body of the convention, however, hesitated. They cast around "a longing, lingering look" on those flowery fields on which peace, and ease, and joy, were still sporting; and it required all the energies of a Mentor like Henry to push them from the precipice, and conduct them over the stormy sea of the revolution, to liberty and glory.

The convention being formed and organized for business, proceeded in the first place, to express their unqualified approbation of the measures of congress, and to declare that they considered "this whole continent as under the highest obligations to that respectable body, for the wisdom of their counsels, and their unremitted endeavours to maintain and preserve inviolate the just rights and liberties of his majesty's dutiful and loyal subjects in America."

They next resolve, that "the warmest thanks of the convention, and of all the inhabitants of this colony, were due, and that this just tribute of applause be presented to the worthy delegates, deputed by a former convention to represent this colony in general congress, for their cheerful undertaking and faithful discharge of the very important trust reposed in them."

The morning of the twenty-third of March was opened, by reading a petition and memorial from the assembly of Jamaica, to the king's most excellent majesty: whereupon it was—"Resolved, That the unfeigned thanks and most grateful acknowledgments of the convention be presented to that very respectable assembly, for the exceeding generous and affectionate part they have so nobly taken in the unhappy contest between Great Britain and her colonies; and for their truly patriotic endeavours to fix the just claims of the colonists upon the most permanent constitutional principles:—that the assembly be assured, that it is the most ardent wish of this colony, [and they were persuaded of the whole continent of North America,] to see a speedy return of those halcyon days, when we lived a free and happy people."

These proceedings were not adapted to the taste of Mr.

Henry; on the contrary, they were "gall and wormwood" to him. The house required to be wrought up to a bolder tone He rose, therefore, and moved the following manly resolutions:—

"Resolved, That a well-regulated militia, composed of gentlemen and yeomen, is the natural strength and only security of a free government; that such a militia in this colony would for ever render it unnecessary for the mother-country to keep among us, for the purpose of our defence, any standing army of mercenary soldiers, always subversive of the quiet, and dangerous to the liberties of the people, and would obviate the pretext of taxing us for their support.

"That the establishment of such militia is, *at this time*, peculiarly necessary, by the state of our laws, for the protection and defence of the country, some of which are already expired, and others will shortly be so: and that the known remissness of government in calling us together in legislative capacity, renders it too insecure, in this time of danger and distress, to rely that opportunity will be given of renewing them, in general assembly, *or making any provision to secure our inestimable rights and liberties, from those further violations with which they are threatened.*

"Resolved, therefore, *That this colony be immediately put into a state of defence, and that*
be a committee to prepare a plan for imbodying, arming and disciplining such a number of men, as may be sufficient for that purpose."

The alarm which such a proposition must have given to those who had contemplated no resistance of a character more serious than petition, non-importation, and passive fortitude, and who still hung with suppliant tenderness on the skirts of Britain, will be readily conceived by the reflecting reader. The shock was painful. It was almost general. The resolutions were opposed as not only rash in policy, but as harsh and well nigh impious in point of feeling. Some of the warmest patriots of the convention opposed them. Richard Bland, Benjamin Harrison, and Edmund Pendleton, who had so lately drunk of the fountain of patriotism in the continental congress, and Robert C. Nicholas, one of the best as well as ablest men and patriots in the state, resisted them with all their influence and abilities.

They urged the late gracious reception of the congressional petition by the throne. They insisted that national comity, and much more filial respect, demanded the exercise of a more dignified patience. That the sympathies of the parent-country were now on our side. That the friends of American liberty in parliament were still with us, and had, as yet, had no cause to blush for our indiscretion. That the manufacturing interests of Great Britain, already smarting under the effects of our non-importation, co-operated powerfully toward our relief. That the sovereign himself had relented, and showed that he looked upon our sufferings with an eye of pity.

"Was this a moment," they asked, "to disgust our friends, to extinguish all the conspiring sympathies which were working in our favour, to turn their friendship into hatred, their pity into revenge? And what was there, they asked, in the situation of the colony, to tempt us to this? Were we a great military people? Were we ready for war? Where were our stores—where were our arms—where our soldiers—where our generals—where our money, the sinews of war? They were nowhere to be found.

"In truth, we were poor—we were naked—we were defenceless. And yet we talk of assuming the front of war! of assuming it, too, against a nation, one of the most formidable in the world? A nation ready and armed at all points! Her navies riding triumphant in every sea; her armies never marching but to certain victory! What was to be the issue of the struggle we were called upon to court? What *could* be the issue, in the comparative circumstances of the two countries, but to yield up *this country* an easy prey to Great Britain, and to convert the illegitimate right which the British parliament now claimed, into a firm and indubitable right, *by conquest!*

"The measure might be brave; but it was the bravery of madmen. It had no pretension to the character of prudence; and as little to the grace of genuine courage. It would be time enough to resort to measures of *despair*, when every well-founded *hope* had entirely vanished."

To this strong view of the subject, supported as it was by the stubborn fact of the well-known helpless condition of the colony, the opponents of these resolutions superadded every topic of persuasion which belongs to the cause.

"The strength and lustre which we have derived from our connexion with Great Britain—the domestic comforts which we had drawn from the same source, and whose value we were now able to estimate by their loss—that ray of reconciliation which was dawning upon us from the east, and which promised so fair and happy a day:—with this they contrasted the clouds and storms which the measure now proposed was so well calculated to raise—and in which we should not have even the poor consolation of being pitied by the world, since we should have so needlessly and rashly drawn them upon ourselves."

These arguments and topics of persuasion were so well justified by the appearance of things, and were moreover so entirely in unison with that love of ease and quiet which is natural to man, and that disposition to hope for happier times, even under the most forbidding circumstances, that an ordinary man, in Mr. Henry's situation, would have been glad to compound with the displeasure of the house, by being permitted to withdraw his resolutions in silence.

Not so Mr. Henry. His was a spirit fitted to raise the whirlwind, as well as to ride in and direct it. His was that comprehensive view, that unerring prescience, that perfect command over the actions of men, which qualified him not merely to guide, but almost to create the destinies of nations.

He rose at this time with a majesty unusual to him in an exordium, and with all that self-possession by which he was so invariably distinguished. "No man," he said, "thought more highly than he did of the patriotism, as well as abilities, of the very worthy gentlemen who had just addressed the house. But different men often saw the same subject in different lights; and, therefore, he hoped it would not be thought disrespectful to those gentlemen, if, entertaining as he did, opinions of a character very opposite to theirs, he should speak forth *his* sentiments freely, and without reserve.

"This," he said, "was no time for ceremony. The question before this house was one of awful moment to the country. For his own part, he considered it as nothing less than a question of freedom or slavery. And in proportion to the magnitude of the subject, ought to be the freedom of the debate. It was only in this way that they could hope to arrive at truth, and fulfil the great responsibility which they held to God and their country. Should he keep back his opinions at such a time, through fear of giving offence, he should consider himself as guilty of treason toward his country, and of an act of disloyalty toward the Majesty of heaven, which he revered above all earthly kings.

"Mr. President," said he, "it is natural to man to indulge in the illusions of hope. We are apt to shut our eyes against a painful truth—and listen to the song of that siren, till she transforms us into beasts. Is this," he asked, "the part of wise men, engaged in a great and arduous struggle for liberty? Were we disposed to be of the number of those, who having eyes, see not, and having ears, hear not, the things which so nearly concern their temporal salvation? For his part, whatever anguish of spirit it might cost, *he* was willing to know the whole truth; to know the worst, and to provide for it.

"He had," he said, "but one lamp by which his feet were guided; and that was the lamp of experience. He knew of no way of judging of the future but by the past. And judging by the past, he wished to know what there had been in the conduct of the British ministry for the last ten years, to justify those hopes with which gentlemen had been pleased to solace themselves and the house? Is it that insidious smile with which our petition has been lately received? Trust it not, sir; it will prove a snare to your feet. Suffer not yourselves to be betrayed with a kiss.

"Ask yourselves how this gracious reception of our petition comports with those warlike preparations which cover our waters and darken our land. Are fleets and armies necessary to a work of love and reconciliation? Have we shewn ourselves so unwilling to be reconciled, that force must be called in to win back our love? Let us not deceive ourselves, sir. These are the implements of war and subjugation—the last arguments to which kings resort.

"I ask gentlemen, sir, what means this martial array, if its purpose be not to force us to submission? Can gentlemen assign any other possible motive for it? Has Great Britain any enemy in this quarter of the world, to call for all this accumulation of navies and armies? No, sir, she has none. They are meant for us: they can be meant for no other. They are sent over to bind and rivet upon us those chains which the British ministry have been so long forging. And what have we to oppose them? Shall we try argument? Sir, we have been trying that for the last ten years. Have we anything new to offer upon the subject? Nothing. We have held the subject up in every light of which it is capable; but it has been all in vain. Shall we resort to entreaty and humble supplication? What terms shall we find, which have not been already exhausted?

"Let us not, I beseech you, sir, deceive ourselves longer. Sir, we have done everything that could be done, to avert the storm which is now coming on. We have petitioned—we have remonstrated—we have supplicated—we have prostrated ourselves before the throne, and have implored its interposition to arrest the tyrannical hands of the ministry and parliament. Our petitions have been slighted; our remonstrances have produced additional violence and insult; our supplications have been disregarded; and we have been spurned, with contempt, from the foot of the throne.

"In vain, after these things, may we indulge the fond hope of peace and reconciliation. *There is no longer any room for hope.* If we wish to be free—if we mean to preserve inviolate those inestimable privileges for which we have been so long contending—if we mean not basely to abandon the noble struggle in which we have been so long engaged, and which we have pledged ourselves never to abandon, until the glorious object of our contest shall be obtained!—we must fight!—I repeat it, sir, we must fight!!! An appeal to arms and to the God of hosts, is all that is left us!*

"They tell us, sir," continued Mr. Henry, "that we are weak—unable to cope with so formidable an adversary. But when shall we be stronger. Will it be the next week or the next year? Will it be when we are totally disarmed, and when a British guard shall be stationed in every house? Shall we gather strength by irresolution and inaction? Shall we acquire the means of effectual resistance by lying supinely on our backs, and hugging the delusive phantom of hope, until our enemy shall have bound us hand and foot? Sir, we are not weak, if we make a proper use of those means which the God of nature hath placed in our power.

"Three millions of people armed in the holy cause of liberty, and in such a country as that which we possess, are invincible by any force which our enemy can send against us. Besides, sir, we shall not fight our battles alone. There is a just God who presides over the destinies of nations, and who will raise up friends to fight our battles for us. The battle, sir, is not to the strong alone; it is to the vigilant, the active, the brave. Besides, sir, we have no election. If we were base enough to desire it, it is now too late to retire from the contest. There is no retreat but in submission and slavery! Our chains are forged. Their clanking may be heard on the plains of Boston! The war is inevitable—and let it come!! I repeat it, sir, let it come!!!

"It is vain, sir, to extenuate the matter. Gentlemen may cry, peace, peace—but there is no peace. The war is actually begun! The next gale that sweeps from the north will bring to our ears the clash of resounding arms! Our brethren are already in the field! Why stand we here idle? What is it that gentlemen wish? What would they have? Is life so dear, or peace so sweet, as to be purchased at the price of chains and slavery? Forbid it, Almighty God!—I know not

* "Imagine to yourself," says my correspondent, (Judge Tucker,) "this sentence delivered with all the calm dignity of Cato, of Utica—imagine to yourself the Roman senate, assembled in the capitol, when it was entered by the profane Gauls, who, at first, were awed by their presence, as if they had entered an assembly of the gods!—imagine that you heard that Cato addressing such a senate—imagine that you saw the handwriting on the wall of Belshazzar's palace—imagine you heard a voice as from heaven uttering the words: '*We must fight*,' as the doom of fate, and you may have some idea of the speaker, the assembly to whom he addressed himself, and the auditory, of which I was one."

what course others may take; but as for me," cried he, with both his arms extended aloft, his brows knit, every feature marked with the resolute purpose of his soul, and his voice swelled to its boldest note of exclamation—"give me liberty, or give me death!"

He took his seat. No murmur of applause was heard. The effect was too deep. After the trance of a moment, several members started from their seats. The cry, "to arms!" seemed to quiver on every lip, and gleam from every eye. Richard H. Lee arose and supported Mr. Henry, with his usual spirit and elegance. But his melody was lost amid the agitations of that ocean, which the master-spirit of the storm had lifted up on high. That supernatural voice still sounded in their ears, and shivered along their arteries. They heard, in every pause, the cry of liberty or death. They became impatient of speech, their souls were on fire for action.*

The resolutions were adopted; and Patrick Henry, Richard H. Lee, Robert C. Nicholas, Benjamin Harrison, Lemuel Riddick, George Washington, Adam Stevens, Andrew Lewis, William Christian, Edmund Pendleton, Thomas Jefferson, and Isaac Zane, esquires, were appointed a committee to prepare the plan called for by the last resolution.†

* Mr. Randolph, in his manuscript history, has given a most eloquent and impressive account of this debate. Since these sheets were prepared for the press, and at the moment of their departure from the hands of the author, he has received from Chief Justice Marshall, a note in relation to the same debate, which he thinks too interesting to suppress. It is the substance of a statement made to the chief justice (then an ardent youth, feeling a most enthusiastic admiration of eloquence, and panting for war) by his father, who was a member of this convention. Mr. Marshall, (the father,) after speaking of Mr. Henry's speech, "as one of the most bold, vehement, and animated pieces of eloquence that had ever been delivered," proceeded to state, that "he was followed by Mr. Richard H. Lee, who took a most interesting view of our real situation. He stated the force which Britain could probably bring to bear upon us, and reviewed our resources and means of resistance. He stated the advantages and disadvantages of both parties, and drew from this statement auspicious inferences. But he concluded with saying, admitting the probable calculations to be against us, we are assured in holy writ that "the race is not to the swift, nor the battle to the strong; and if the language of genius may be added to inspiration, I will say with our immortal bard:—

"'*Thrice* is he armed, who hath his quarrel just!
And he but naked, though locked up in steel,
Whose conscience with injustice is oppressed!'"

† Colonel Robert Carter Nicholas (although opposed like all the older patriots, from the considerations which have been stated in the text, to resistance at this particular point of time) was, nevertheless, one of the firmest supporters of the principles of the revolution. As soon, therefore, as the measure of resistance was carried, in order to give to it the greatest effect, he rose and

the charges of transportation, and other necessary expenses." At the same session of the convention, I find that the alert and inquiring spirit of Mr. Henry laid hold of another instance of royal misrule.

Governor Dunmore, it seems, by a recent proclamation, had declared that his majesty had given orders for all vacant lands within this colony to be put up in lots at public sale; and that the highest bidder for such lots should be the purchaser thereof, and should hold the same, subject to a reservation of one half-penny *per* acre, by way of annual quitrent, and of all mines of gold, silver, and precious stones. These terms were deemed an innovation on the established usage of granting lands in this colony; and this sagacious politician saw in the proceeding, not only an usurpation of power, but a great subduction of the natural wealth of the colony, and the creation, moreover, of a separate band of tenants and retainers, devoted to the vilest measures of the crown. With a view, therefore, to defeat this measure, he moved the following resolution, which was adopted:—

"Resolved, That a committee be appointed to inquire whether his majesty may of right advance the terms of granting lands in this colony, and make report thereof to the next general assembly or convention; and that, in the meantime, it be recommended to all persons whatever, to forbear purchasing or accepting lands on the conditions before mentioned." Of this committee he was of course the chairman; and the other members were Richard Bland, Thomas Jefferson, Robert C. Nicholas, and Edmund Pendleton, esquires.

The convention having adopted a plan for the encouragement of arts and manufactures in this colony, and reappointed their former deputies to the continental congress, with the substitution of Mr. Jefferson for Mr. Peyton Randolph, in case of the non-attendance of the latter;* and having also provided for a re-election of delegates to the next convention, came to an adjournment. It is curious to read in the file of papers from which the foregoing proceedings are extracted, and immediately following them, this proclamation of his Excellency Lord Dunmore:—

"Whereas, certain persons, styling themselves delegates of several of his majesty's colonies in America, have presumed, without his majesty's authority or consent, to assemble together at Philadelphia, in the months of September and October last, and have thought fit, among other unwarrantable proceedings,

* He was speaker of the house of burgesses, a call of which was expected, and did accordingly take place.

to resolve that it wil. be necessary that another congress should be held at the same place on the tenth of May next, unless redress of certain pretended grievances be obtained before that time: and to recommend that all the colonies of North America should choose deputies to attend such congress: *I am commanded by the king*, and I do accordingly issue this my proclamation, to require all magistrates and other officers to use their utmost endeavours to prevent any such appointment of deputies, and to exhort all persons whatever within this government, to desist from such an unjustifiable proceeding, so highly displeasing to his majesty."

This proclamation was published while the convention was in session, and was obviously designed to have an effect on their proceedings. It passed by them, however, "as the idle wind which they regarded not." The age of proclamations was gone, and the glory of regal governors pretty nearly extinguished for ever.

It ought not to be omitted, however, that this very convention passed resolutions complimentary to Lord Dunmore, and the troops which he had commanded in an expedition of the preceding year against the Indians: a compliment which, as we shall see, was afterward found to be unmerited. As the resolution in regard to Lord Dunmore does honour to the candour of the convention, and shows also how little personality there was in the contest, I take leave to subjoin it:—

"Resolved, *unanimously*, That the most cordial thanks of the people of this colony are a tribute justly due to our worthy governor, Lord Dunmore, for his truly noble, wise, and spirited conduct, on the late expedition against our Indian enemy—a conduct which at once evinces his excellency's attention to the true interests of this colony, and a zeal in the executive department which no dangers can divert, or difficulties hinder, from achieving the most important services to the people who have the happiness to live under his administration."

Lord Dunmore was not a man of popular manners; he had nothing of the mildness, the purity, the benevolence and suavity of his predecessor. On the contrary, he is represented as having been rude and offensive; coarse in his figure, his countenance and his manners. Yet he received from the house of burgesses the most marked respect.

Thus, in seventeen hundred and seventy-four, while the liberties of the colonies were bleeding at every pore, and while the house was smarting severely, under the recent news of the occlusion of the port of Boston, they paid to Lady Dunmore, who had just arrived at Williamsburgh, the most cordial and elegant attentions, congratulated his Lordship on this increase to his domestic felicity; and even, after their abrupt dissolution, complimented the inhabitants of the palace with a splendid ball and entertainment, in honour of the arrival of the Countess Dunmore and her family.

CHAPTER V.

The Export of Powder from Great Britain prohibited—Seizure of the Military Stores in Massachusetts and other Colonies—Magazine at Williamsburgh plundered by Order of Governor Dunmore—Address of the Common Council—Lord Dunmore's Reply—Excitement occasioned by the Proceedings—Mr. Henry's View as to the Result of these Events—He is invested with the Command of the Hanover Volunteers and marches for Williamsburgh—The Affair of the Powder Compromised—Lord Dunmore's Proclamation against Mr. Henry.

THE storm of the revolution now began to thicken. The cloud of war had actually burst on the New England states, while as yet the middle and southern colonies were in comparative repose. The calm, however, was deceitful, and of short duration; and, as far as Virginia was concerned, had been occasioned rather by the absence of Governor Dunmore on an Indian expedition, than any disposition on his part to favour the colony. His return to Williamsburgh was the signal for violence.

It seems to have been a matter of concert among the colonial governors, if indeed the policy was not dictated by the British court, to disarm the people of all the colonies at one and the same time, and thus incapacitate them for united resistance.

To give effect to this measure, the export of powder from Great Britain was prohibited; and an attempt was generally made about the same period to seize the powder and arms in the several provincial magazines. Gage, the successor of Hutchinson in the government of Massachusetts, set the example, by a seizure of the ammunition and military stores at Cambridge, and the powder in the magazines at Charlestown, and other places. His example was followed by similar attempts in other colonies to the north.

And on Thursday, the twentieth of April, seventeen hundred and seventy-five, Captain Henry Collins, of the armed schooner Magdalen, then lying at Burwell's ferry, on James river, came up at the head of a body of marines, and, acting under the orders of Lord Dunmore, entered the city of Williamsburgh in the dead of the night, and carried off from the public magazine about twenty barrels of powder, which he placed on board his schooner before the break of day.

Clandestine as the movement had been, the alarm was given to the inhabitants early on the next morning. Their exasperation may be easily conceived. The town was in tumult. A considerable body of them flew to arms, with the determination to compel Captain Collins to restore the powder. With much difficulty, however, they were restrained by the graver inhabitants of the town, and by the members of the common council, who assured them that proper measures should be immediately used to produce a restoration of the powder, without the effusion of human blood. The council, therefore, met in their corporate character, and addressed the following letter to Governor Dunmore:—

"To his Excellency the Right Honourable John, Earl of Dunmore, his majesty's lieutenant, governor-general, and commander-in-chief of the colony and dominion of Virginia:—
The humble address of the mayor, recorder, aldermen, and common council of the city of Williamsburgh:—

"My Lord—We, his majesty's dutiful and loyal subjects, the mayor, recorder, aldermen and common council of the city of Williamsburgh, in common hall assembled, humbly beg leave to represent to your excellency, that the inhabitants of this city were this morning exceedingly alarmed by a report that a large quantity of gunpowder was, in the preceding night, while they were sleeping in their beds, removed from the public magazine in this city, and conveyed under an escort of marines, on board one of his majesty's armed vessels lying at a ferry on James river.

"We beg leave to represent to your excellency, that, as the magazine was erected at the public expense of this colony, and appropriated to the safe-keeping of such munition as should be there lodged, from time to time, for the protection and security of the country, by arming thereout such of the militia as might be necessary in cases of invasions and insurrections, they humbly conceive it to be the only proper repository to be resorted to in times of imminent danger.

"We further beg leave to inform your excellency, that from various reports at present prevailing in different parts of the country, we have too much reason to believe that some wicked and designing persons have instilled the most diabolical notions into the minds of our slaves; and that, therefore, the utmost attention to our internal security is become the more necessary.

"The circumstances of this city, my lord, we consider as peculiar and critical. The inhabitants, from the situation of the magazine in the midst of their city, have for a long tract of time, been exposed to all those dangers which have happened in many countries from explosions and other accidents. They have, from time to time, thought it incumbent on them to guard the magazine. For their security they have, for some time past, judged it necessary to keep strong patrols on foot; in their present circumstances, then, to have the chief and necessary means of their defence removed, cannot but be extremely alarming.

"Considering ourselves as guardians of the city, we therefore humbly desire to be informed by your excellency, upon what motives, and for what particular purpose, the powder has been carried off in such a manner; and we earnestly entreat your excellency to order it to be immediately returned to the magazine."

To which his excellency returned this verbal answer:—that "hearing of an insurrection in a neighbouring county, he had removed the powder from the magazine, where he did not think it secure, to a place of perfect security; and that, *upon his word and honour*, whenever it was wanted on any insurrection, it should be delivered in half an hour; that he had removed it in the night-time, to prevent any alarm, and that Captain Collins had his express commands for the part he had acted; he was surprised to hear the people were under arms on this occasion, and that he should not think it prudent to put powder into their hands in such a situation."

This conditional promise of the return of the powder, supported by the influence of Mr. Peyton Randolph, Mr. Robert C. Nicholas, and other characters of weight, had the effect, it seems, of quieting the inhabitants for that day. On the succeeding night, however, a new alarm took place, on a report that a number of armed men had again landed from the Magdalen, about four miles below the city, with a view, it was presumed, of making another visit of nocturnal plunder. The inhabitants again flew to arms; but, on the interposition of the same eminent citizens, the ferment was allayed, and nothing more was done than to strengthen the usual patrol for the defence of the city.

On the next day, Saturday the twenty-second of April, when everything was perfectly quiet, Lord Dunmore, with rather more heat than discretion, sent a message into the city, by one of the magistrates, and which his lordship had delivered with the most solemn asseverations, that if any insult were offered to Captain Foy, (a British captain residing at the palace, as his secretary, and considered to be the instigator of the governor to his violences,) or to Captain Collins, *he would declare freedom to the slaves, and lay the town in ashes;* and he added, that he could easily depopulate the whole country. At this time, both Captains Foy and Collins were and had been continually walking the streets, at their pleasure, without the slightest indication of disrespect. The effect of a threat, so diabolically ferocious, directed toward the people who had ever shown him and his family such enthusiastic marks of respect and attention, and following so directly the plunder of the magazine, will be readily conceived. Yet it broke not out into any open act. His lordship remained unmolested even by a disrespectful look. The augmented patrol was kept up; but no defensive preparation was made by the inhabitants of the city.

The transactions which were passing in the metropolis circulated through the country with a rapidity proportioned to their interests, and with this farther aggravation, which was also true in point of fact, that in addition to the clandestine removal of the powder, the governor had caused the muskets in the magazine to be stripped of their locks.

In the midst of the irritation excited by this intelligence, came the news of the bloody battles of Lexington and Concord, resulting from an attempt of the governor-general Gage, to seize the military stores deposited at the latter place. The system of colonial subjugation was now apparent: the effect was instantaneous. The whole country flew to arms. The independent companies, formed in happier times for the purpose of military discipline, and under the immediate auspices of Lord Dunmore himself, raised the standard of liberty in every county.

By the twenty-seventh of April, there was assembled at Fredericksburgh upward of seven hundred men well-armed and disciplined, "friends of constitutional liberty and America." Their march, however, was arrested by a letter from Mr. Peyton Randolph, in reply to an express, and received on the twenty-ninth, by which they were informed that the gentlemen of the city and neighbourhood of Williamsburgh, had had full assurance from his excellency, that the affair of the powder should be accommodated, and advising that the gentlemen of Fredericksburgh should proceed no farther.

On the receipt of this letter, a council was held of one hundred and two members, delegates of the provincial convention, and officers and special deputies of fourteen companies of light-horse, then rendezvoused on the ground; who, after the most spirited expression of their sentiments on the conduct of the governor, and after giving a mutual pledge to be in readiness at a moment's warning, to reassemble, and by force of arms

to remember that the same God whose power divided the Red sea for the deliverance of Israel, still reigned in all his glory, unchanged and unchangeable—was still the enemy of the oppressor, and the friend of the oppressed—that he would cover them from their enemies by a pillar of cloud by day, and guide their feet through the night by a pillar of fire—that for his own part, he was anxious that his native county should distinguish itself in this grand career of liberty and glory, and snatch the noble prize which was now offered to their grasp—that no time was to be lost—that their enemies in this colony were now few and weak—that it would be easy for them, by a rapid and vigorous movement, to compel the restoration of the powder which had been carried off, or to make a reprisal on the king's revenues in the hands of the receiver-general, which would fairly balance the account—that the Hanover volunteers would thus have an opportunity of striking the first blow in this colony, in the great cause of American liberty, and would cover themselves with never-fading laurels.

These were heads of his harangue. I presume not to give the colouring. That was Mr. Henry's own, and beyond the power of any man's imitation. The effect, however, was equal to his wishes. The meeting was in a flame, and a decision immediately taken, that the powder should be retrieved, or counterbalanced by a reprisal.

Captain Samuel Meredith, who had heretofore commanded the Independent Company, resigned his commission in Mr. Henry's favour, and the latter gentleman was immediately invested with the chief command of the Hanover volunteers. Mr. Meredith accepted the commission of lieutenant; and the present Colonel Parke Goodall was appointed the ensign of the company. Having received orders from the committee, correspondent with his own suggestions, Captain Henry forthwith took up his line of March for Williamsburgh.

Ensign Goodall was detached, with a party of sixteen men, to cross the river into King William county, the residence of Richard Corbin, the king's receiver-general; to demand from him three hundred and thirty pounds, the estimated value of the powder; and, in the event of his refusal to make him a prisoner. He was ordered, in this case, to treat his person with all possible respect and tenderness, and to bring him to Doncastle's ordinary, about sixteen miles above Williamsburgh, where the ensign was required, at all events, to rejoin the main body.

The detachment, in pursuance of their orders, reached the residence of the receiver-general some hours after bedtime, and a guard was stationed around the house until morning. About daybreak, however, the ladies of the family made their appearance, and gave the commanding officer of the detachment the firm and correct assurance, that Colonel Corbin was not at home; but that the house, nevertheless, was open to search, if it was the pleasure of the officer to make it. The manner of the assurance, however, was too satisfactory to render this necessary, and the detachment hastened to form the junction with the main body which had been ordered.

In the meantime, the march of his gallant corps, in arms, headed by a man of Mr. Henry's distinction, produced the most striking effects in every quarter. Corresponding companies started up on all sides, and hastened to throw themselves under the banners of Henry. It is believed that five thousand men at least, were in arms, and were crossing the country to crowd around his standard, and support it with their lives. The march was conducted in the most perfect order, and with the most scrupulous respect to the country through which they passed. The ranks of the royalists were filled with dismay. Lady Dunmore, with her family, retired to the Fowey man-of-war, then lying off the town of Little York. Even the patriots in Williamsburgh were daunted by the boldness, and, as they deemed it, the rashness of the enterprise.

Messenger after messenger was despatched to meet Mr. Henry on the way, and beg him to desist from his purpose, and discharge his men. It was in vain. He was inflexibly resolved to effect the purpose of his expedition or to perish in the attempt. The messengers were therefore detained, that they might not report his strength; and the march was continued with all possible celerity. The governor issued a proclamation, in which he denounced the movement, and called upon the people of the country to resist it. He could as easily have called "spirits from the vasty deep." He seems not to have relied much, himself, on the efficacy of his proclamation. The palace was therefore filled with arms, and a detachment of marines ordered up from the Fowey. Before daybreak, on the morning of the fourth of May, Captain Montague, the commander of that ship, landed a party of men, with the following letter, addressed to the Honourable Thomas Nelson, the president of his majesty's council:—

"*Fowey, May 4th,* 1775.

"SIR,—I have this morning received certain information that his excellency Lord Dunmore, governor of Virgina, is threatened with an attack at daybreak, this morning, at his palace in Williamsburgh, and have thought proper to send a detachment from his majesty's ship under my command, to support his excellency: therefore strongly pray you to make use of every endeavour to prevent the party from being molested and attacked, as in that case I must be under a necessity to fire upon this town. From

"GEORGE MONTAGUE."

Lord Dunmore, however, thought better of this subject, and caused Mr. Henry to be met at Doncastle's, about sunrise on the same morning, with the receiver-general's bill of exchange, for the sum required. It was accepted as a satisfaction for the powder, and the following receipt was passed by Mr. Henry:—

"*Doncastle's Ordinary, New Kent, May 4th,* 1775.

"Received from the Honourable Richard Corbin, Esq., his majesty's receiver-general, three hundred and thirty pounds, as a compensation for the gunpowder lately taken out of the public magazine by the governor's order; which money I promise to convey to the Virginia delegates at the general congress, to be, under their direction, laid out in gunpowder for the colony's use, and to be stored as they shall direct, until the next colony convention, or general assembly; unless it shall be necessary, in the meantime, to use the same in the defence of this colony. It is agreed, that in case the next convention shall determine that any part of the said money ought to be returned to his majesty's said receiver-general, that the same shall be done accordingly. "PATRICK HENRY, jun.

"Test—SAMUEL MEREDITH,
PARKE GOODALL."

The march of the marines from the Fowey had, however, produced the most violent commotion both in York* and Wil-

* "The town of York being somewhat alarmed by a letter from Captain Montague, commander of his majesty's ship the Fowey, addressed to the Hon. Thomas Nelson, esquire, president of his majesty's council in Virginia; and a copy of said letter being procured, a motion was made, that the copy should be laid before the committee, and considered. The copy was read, and is as follows:—

"'*Fowey, May* 4, 1775.

"'SIR—I have this morning received certain information that his excellency the Lord Dunmore, governor of Virginia, is threatened with an attack at day-break this morning, at his palace in Williamsburgh, and have thought proper to send a detachment from his majesty's ship under my command to support his excellency; therefore, strongly pray you to make use of every endeavour to prevent the party from being molested and attacked, as in that case I must be under the necessity to fire upon this town. From GEORGE MONTAGUE.

"'*To the Hon. Thomas Nelson.*'

"The committee, together with Capt. Montague's letter taking into consideration the time of its being sent, which was too late to permit the president to use his influence, had the inhabitants been disposed to *molest and attack* the detachment; and further considering that Col. Nelson, who, had his threat been carried into execution, must have been a principal sufferer, was at that

liamsburgh, Mr. Henry himself seemed to apprehend that the public treasury would be the next object of depredation and that a pretext would be sought for it in the reprisal which had just been made. He therefore addressed, from Doncastle's, the following letter to Robert Carter Nicholas, esquire, the treasurer of the colony:—

"*May* 4, 1775.

"SIR—The affair of the powder is now settled, so as to produce satisfaction to me, and I earnestly wish to the colony in general. The people here have it in charge from Hanover committee, to tender their service to you, as a public officer, for the purpose of escorting the public treasury to any place in this colony, where the money would be judged more safe than in the city of Williamsburgh. The reprisal now made by the Hanover volunteers, though accomplished in a manner less liable to the imputation of violent extremity, may possibly be the cause of future injury to the treasury. If, therefore, you apprehend the least danger, a sufficient guard is at your service. I beg the return of the bearer may be instant, because the men wish to know their destination. With great regard, I am, sir, your most humble servant, "PATRICK HENRY, jun."

To this letter an answer was received from Mr. Nicholas, importing that he had no apprehension of the necessity, or *propriety* of the proffered service: and Mr. Henry understanding, also, that the private citizens of Williamsburgh were in a great measure quieted from their late fears for their persons and property, judged it proper to proceed no farther. Their expedition having been crowned with success, the volunteers returned in triumph to their respective homes.

The committee of Hanover again met; gave them their warmest thanks for the vigour and propriety with which they

very moment exerting his utmost endeavours in behalf of government, and the safety of his excellency's person, unanimously come to the following resolutions:—

"Resolved, That Capt. Montague, in threatening to fire upon a defenceless town, in case of an attack upon the detachment, in which said town might not be concerned, has testified a spirit of cruelty unprecedented in the annals of civilized times; that, in his late notice to the president, he has added insult to cruelty; and that considering the circumstances already mentioned, of one of the most considerable inhabitants of said town, he has discovered the most hellish principles that can actuate a human mind.

"Resolved, That it be recommended to the inhabitants of this town, and to the country in general, that they do not entertain or show any other mark of civility to Capt. Montague, besides what common decency and absolute necessity require.

"Resolved, That the clerk do transmit the above proceedings to the public printers, to be inserted in the Virginia gazettes.

(A true copy,) "WILLIAM RUSSELL, Cl'k Com."

had conducted the enterprise; and returned their acknowledgments, in suitable terms, to the many volunteers of the different counties, who joined and were marching, and ready to coöperate with the volunteer company of Hanover.

Two days after the return of the volunteers, and when all was again quiet, the governor thundered the following anathema from the palace:—

"By his excellency, the Right Honourable John, Earl of Dunmore, his majesty's lieutenant and governor-general of the colony and dominion of Virginia, and vice-admiral of the same:—

"A PROCLAMATION.

"Virginia, to wit:—Whereas, I have been informed, from undoubted authority, that *a certain Patrick Henry*, of the county of Hanover, and a number of deluded followers, have taken up arms, chosen their officers, and styling themselves an Independent Company, have marched out of their county, encamped, and put themselves in a posture of war; and have written and despatched letters to divers parts of the country, exciting the people to join in these outrageous and rebellious practices, to the great terror of his majesty's faithful subjects, and in open defiance of law and government; and have committed other acts of violence, particularly in extorting from his majesty's receiver-general the sum of three hundred and thirty pounds, under pretence of replacing the powder I thought proper to order from the magazine: whence it undeniably appears, that there is no longer the least security for the life or property of any man; wherefore I have thought proper with the advice of his majesty's council, and in his majesty's name, to issue this my proclamation, strictly charging all persons upon their allegiance, not to aid, abet, or give countenance to the said Patrick Henry, or any other persons concerned in such unwarrantable combinations; but, on the contrary, to oppose them and their designs by every means; which designs must otherwise inevitably involve the whole country in the most direful calamity, as they will call for the vengeance of offended majesty, and the insulted laws, to be exerted here to vindicate the constitutional authority of government.

"Given under my hand and seal of the colony, at Williamsburgh, this sixth day of May, seventeen hundred and seventy-five, and in the fifteenth year of his majesty's reign.

"DUNMORE.

"God save the king."

But Lord Dunmore's threats and denunciations had no other effect than to render more conspicuous and more honourable the man who was the object of them. Mr. Henry, who had been on the point of setting out for congress at the time when he had been called off by the intelligence from Williamsburgh, now resumed his journey, and was escorted in triumph by a large party of gentlemen, as far as Hooe's ferry, on the Potomac. Messengers were sent after him from all directions, bearing the thanks and the applauses of his assembled countrymen, for his recent enterprise; and in such throngs did these addresses come, that the necessity of halting to read and answer them converted a journey of one day into a triumph of many. Thus the same man, whose genius had in the year seventeen hundred and sixty-five given the first political impulse to the revolution, had now the additional honour of heading the first military movement in Virginia, in support of the same cause.

CHAPTER VI.

Second Session of the Delegates to Congress—Attachment of the People of Virginia to Lady Dunmore—Barbarous Proceeding of Lord Dunmore—Takes his Residence on board the Fowey—His Correspondence with the Committee—Mr. Henry is appointed Colonel of one of the Regiments raised by the Colonial Convention—Tender of the British sloop Otter is burnt by the People—Correspondence with Capt. Squire in relation to that Event—Lord Dunmore heads a Body of Recruits—Col. Woodford is sent to oppose his Progress—Circumstances leading to Mr. Henry's resignation—He is elected a Delegate to the Convention—Declaration of Rights—Mr. Henry elected Governor of Virginia—Addresses connected with that Event.

I CANNOT learn that Mr. Henry distinguished himself peculiarly at this session of congress. The spirit of resistance was sufficiently excited; and nothing remained but to organize that resistance, and to plan and execute the details which were to give it effect. In business of this nature, Mr. Henry as we have seen, was not efficient. It has been already stated that he was unsuccessful in composition, of which much was done, and eminently done, at this session; and the lax habits of his early life had implanted in him an insuperable aversion to the drudgery of details. He could not endure confinement of any sort, nor the labour of close and solitary thinking.

His habits were all social, and his mind delighted in unlimited range. His conclusions were never reached by an elaborate deduction of thought; he gained them as it were *per saltem*; yet with a certainty not less infallible than that of the driest and severest logician. It is not wonderful, therefore, that he felt himself lost amid the operations in which congress was now engaged, and that he enjoyed the relief which was afforded him, by a military appointment from his native state. It will be proper, however, to explain particularly the proceedings which led to this incident in the life of Mr. Henry.

Shortly after the affair of the gunpowder, Lord North's conciliatory proposition, popularly called the Olive Branch, arrived in America. Hereupon the governor of Virginia called a meeting of the house of burgesses; and as if the quarrel were now completely over, Lady Dunmore and her family returned from the Fowey to the palace.

If an estimate may be formed from the newspapers of the day, into which the people seem to have poured their feelings without reserve, that lady was eminently a favourite in this colony. Her residence here had been short; yet the exalted virtues which marked her character, and those domestic graces and attractions which shone with the more lustre by contrast with his lordship, had already endeared her to the people; and would have consecrated her person, and those of her children, amid the wildest tumult to which this colony could possibly be excited. The people had been extremely wounded by her late departure for the Fowey: they considered it as a measure of his lordship, and as an unjust reflection both upon the judgment and generosity of the people of this country.

They had told him intelligibly enough, that they had formed a much more correct estimate of her worth than he himself appeared to have done; and that so far from her being insecure in the bosom of a people who thus admired, respected, and loved her, his lordship would have acted much more wisely to have kept her near his person, and covered himself under the sacred shield which sanctified her in the eyes of Virginians. In proportion to their regret and mortification at her departure, was the ardour of delight with which they hailed her return. A paragraph in Purdie's paper assured her, that "her arrival at the palace was to the great joy of the citizens of Williamsburgh, and of the people of the whole country, who had the most unfeigned regard and affection for her ladyship, and wished her long to live among them."

On Thursday, the first of June, the general assembly according to the proclamation of Lord Dunmore, met at the capitol in the city of Williamsburgh. He addressed them with great earnestness on the alarming state of the colony; and exhibited the conciliatory proposition of the British ministry, as an advance on the part of the mother-country, which it was the duty of the colonists to meet with gratitude and devotion. The council answered him in a manner perfectly satisfactory; but before he could receive the answer of the house of burgesses, an incident occurred, which drove his lordship precipitately from his palace, and terminated for ever all friendly relations between himself and the people of Virginia.

It seems, that during the late ferment, produced by the removal of the powder, and while Mr. Henry was on his march toward Williamsburgh, some of the inhabitants of the town, to the great offence of the graver citizens, had possessed themselves of a few of the guns which still remained in the magazine. This step gave great displeasure as well as alarm to the governor; and although the mayor and council, as well as all the more respectable inhabitants of the town, condemned it in terms as strong as his own, and sincerely united in the means which were used to recover the arms, yet his lordship continued to brood over it in secret, until, with the aid of the minions of the palace, he hatched a scheme of low and cruel revenge, sufficient of itself to cover him with immortal infamy.

It was on Monday night, the fifth of June, that this scheme discovered itself. "Last Monday night," says Purdie, "an unfortunate accident happened to two persons of this city, who, with a number of others, had assembled at the magazine, to furnish themselves with arms. Upon their entering the door, one of the guns, which had a spring to it, and was charged eight fingers deep with swan-shot, went off, and lodged two balls in one of their shoulders, another entered at his wrist, and is not yet extracted: the other person had one of his fingers shot off, and the next to it so much shattered as to render it useless, by which sad misfortune he is deprived of the means of procuring a livelihood by his business. Spring-guns, it seems, were placed at other parts of the magazine, *of which the public were totally ignorant;* and certainly had any person lost his life, the perpetrator or perpetrators of this diabolical invention might have been justly branded with the opprobrious title of murderers. O tempora! O mores!"

The indignation naturally excited by this piece of deliberate and barbarous treachery, which was at once traced to Lord Dunmore, was farther aggravated by a discovery that several barrels of powder had been buried in the magazine, with the purpose, it was reasonably conjectured, of being used as a mine, and thus producing still more fatal destruction, when the occasion should offer. Early on the next morning, Lord Dunmore with his family, including Captain Foy, fled from the palace to return to it no more, and took shelter on board the Fowey, from the vengeance which he knew he so justly deserved. No commotion, however, had ensued to justify his retreat.

The people, indeed, were highly indignant, but they were

silent and quiet. The suggestions of his lordship's conscience had alone produced his flight. He left behind him a message to the speaker and house of burgesses, in which he ascribed this movement to apprehensions for his personal safety; stated that he should fix his residence on board the Fowey; that no interruption should be given to the sitting of the assembly; that he should make the access to him easy and safe; and thought it would be more agreeable to the house to send to him, from time to time, one or more of their members, as occasion might require, than to put the whole body to the trouble of moving to be near him.

On receiving this message, the house immediately resolved itself into a committee of the whole, and prepared an answer, in which they expressed their deep concern at the step which he had taken—assuring him that his apprehensions of personal danger were entirely unfounded; regretting that he had not expressed them to the house previous to his departure, since, from their zeal and attachment to the preservation of order and good government, they should have judged it their indispensable duty to have endeavoured to remove any cause of disquietude. They express the anxiety with which they contemplate the very disagreeable situation of his most amiable lady and her family, and assure him, that they should think themselves happy in being able to restore their perfect tranquillity, by removing all their fears.

They regret his departure and the manner of it, as tending to keep up the great uneasiness which had of late so unhappily prevailed in this country; and declared that they will cheerfully concur in any measure that may be proposed, proper for the security of himself and his family; they remind him how impracticable it will be to carry on the business of the session with any tolerable degree of propriety, or with that despatch which the advanced season of the year required, while his lordship was so far removed from them, and so inconveniently situated; and conclude with entreating him, that he would be pleased to return with his lady and family to the palace, which they say, they are persuaded will give the greatest satisfaction, and be the most likely means of quieting the minds of the people.

This communication was carried down to him by a deputation of two members of the council, and four of the house of burgesses; and in reply to language so respectful, and assurances so friendly and conciliatory, his lordship returned an answer in which he charged them with having slighted his offers of respect and civility, with giving countenance to the violent and disorderly proceeding of the people, and with a usurpation of the executive power in ordering and appointing guards to mount in the city of Williamsburgh, with the view, *as was pretended,* to protect the magazine, but which might well be doubted, as there then remained nothing therein which required being guarded; he exhorts them to return within the pale of their constitutional power; to redress the many grievances which existed; to open the courts of justice; to disarm the independent companies, and what was not less essential by their own example, and every means in their power, to abolish the spirit of persecution which pursued, with menaces and acts of oppression, all his majesty's loyal and orderly subjects.

For the accomplishment of which ends, he invited them to adjourn to the town of York, opposite to which the Fowey lay, where he promised to meet and remain with them till their business should be finished. But with respect to their entreaty that he would return to the palace, he represents to them that unless they closed in with the conciliatory proposition now offered to them by the British parliament, his return to Williamsburgh would be as fruitless to the people, as possibly it might be dangerous to himself. So that he places the event of his returning, on their acceptance of Lord North's offer of conciliation.

The house of burgesses now took up that proposition; and having examined it in every light, with the utmost attention, they conclude with a firm and dignified rejection of it, and an appeal "to the even-handed justice of that Being who doth no wrong; earnestly beseeching him to illuminate the councils, and prosper the endeavours, of those to whom America had confided her hopes, that, through their wise direction, we may again see reunited the blessings of liberty and prosperity, and the most permanent harmony with Great Britain."*

A correspondence on another topic was now opened between the council and burgesses, and the governor, Dunmore.

The former addressed him with a request, that he would order a large parcel of arms which he had left in the palace to be removed to the public magazine, a place of greater safety. This he peremptorily refused; and ordered that those arms, *belonging to the king*, should not be touched without his express permission. In their reply, they say, that the arms may in some sort be considered as belonging to the king, as the supreme head of the government, and that they were properly under his lordship's direction; yet they humbly conceived, that they were originally provided and had been preserved for the use of the country in cases of emergency.

* This vigorous and eloquent production is from the same pen which drew the Declaration of American Independence.

The palace, they say, had indeed been hitherto much respected, but not so much out of regard to the building, as the residence of his majesty's representative. Had his lordship thought fit to remain there, they would have had no apprehensions of danger; but considering these arms at present as exposed to his lordship's servants, *and every rude invader*, the security derived from his lordship's presence could not now be relied on. They, therefore, again entreat him to order the removal of the arms to the magazine. They then proceed to state, that they cannot decline representing to him that the important business of the assembly had been much impeded by his excellency's removal from the palace—that this step had deprived them of that free and necessary access to his lordship, to which they were entitled by the constitution of the country—that there were several bills of the last importance to the country, now ready to be presented to his excellency for his assent.

They complain of the inconvenience to which they had been put in sending their members twelve miles to wait on his excellency, on board of one of his majesty's ships of war, to present their addresses—they state that they think it would be highly improper, and too great a departure from the constitutional and accustomed mode of transacting business, to meet his excellency at any other place than the capitol, to present such bills as were ready for his signature—and, therefore, beseech him to return for this purpose.

To all this he gave a very short answer; that, as to the arms, he had already declared his intention, and conceived they were meddling with a subject which did not belong to them; he desired to know whom they designed by the term *rude invader;* that the disorders in Williamsburgh and other parts of the country, had driven him from the palace; and that, if any inconvenience had arisen to the assembly on that account, he was not chargeable with it; that they had not been deprived of any necessary or free access to him; that the constitution undoubtedly vested him with the power of calling the assembly to any place in the colony, which exigency might requre; that not having been made acquainted with the whole proceedings of the assembly, he knew of no bills of importance, which, if he were inclined to risk his person again among the people, the assembly had to present to him, nor whether they were such as he could assent to.

In the course of their correspondence he required the house to attend him on board the Fowey, for the purpose of obtaining his signature to the bills; and some of the members to prevent an actual dissolution of the government, and to give effect to the many necessary bills which they had passed, proposed to yield to this extraordinary requisition. The project, however, was exploded by a member's rising in his place, and relating the fable of the sick lion and the fox.

The governor having thus virtually abdicated his office, the government was in effect dissolved. The house hereupon resolved, "That his Lordship's message, requiring the house to attend him on board one of his majesty's ships-of-war, is a high breach of the rights and privileges of this house."—"That the unreasonable delays thrown into the proceedings of this house by the governor, and his evasive answers to the sincere and decent addresses of the representatives of the people, give us great reason to fear, that a dangerous attack may be meditated against the unhappy people of this colony."—"It is, therefore, our opinion, they say, that they prepare for the preservation of their property, and their inestimable rights and liberties with the greatest care and attention."

"That we do and will bear faith and true allegiance to our most gracious sovereign, George III., our only lawful and rightful king: that we will, at all times, to the utmost of our power, and at the risk of our lives and properties, maintain and defend his government in this colony, as founded on the established laws and principles of the constitution: that it is our most earnest desire to preserve and strengthen those bonds of amity, with all our fellow-subjects in Great Britain, which are so very essential to the prosperity and happiness of both countries." Having adopted these resolutions without a dissenting voice, they adjourned themselves to the twelfth of October following; and the delegates were summoned to meet in convention at the town of Richmond, on the seventeenth of July.*

Immediately on the adjournment of the house of burgesses, a very full meeting of the citizens of Williamsburgh convened, on the call of Peyton Randolph, at the court-house in that city, "to consider of the expediency of stationing a number of men there for the public safety; as well to assist the citizens in their nightly watches, as to guard against any surprise from our enemies; whereupon it was unanimously agreed (until the general convention should meet) to invite down from a number of counties, to the amount of two hundred and fifty men. Meanwhile, until they arrived, the neighbouring counties, they say, were kind enough to lend them their assistance.

* On this occasion, Richard H. Lee, standing with two of the burgesses in the porch of the capitol, inscribed with his pencil on a pillar of the capitol, these prophetic lines, from Shakspeare:—

"When shall we three meet again?
In thunder, lightning, and in rain;
When the hurly-burly's done,
When the battle's lost and won."

On the twenty-ninth of June, the Fowey ship, and Magdalen schooner, sailed from York; on board the latter went Lady Dunmore, and the rest of the governor's family, bound for England; and the colony was for a short time relieved by the report that the Fowey carried Lord Dunmore and Captain Foy on a visit to General Gage, at Boston. This report, however, was unfounded. The Fowey merely escorted the Magdalen to the Capes, and then returned again to her moorings, before York. The Otter sloop-of-war, commanded by Captain Squire, thereupon fell down to the mouth of York river, with the intention of cruising along the coast, and seizing all provision vessels; and soon became distinguished at least for the malignity of her attempts. The Fowey was relieved by the ship Mercury, of twenty-four guns, John Macartney, commander, and departed for Boston, and carrying with her the now obnoxious Captain Foy. The governor's domestics left the palace, and removed to his farm at Montibello, about six miles below Williamsburgh; and the governor himself fixed his station at the town of Portsmouth. In this posture of things, on Monday, the twenty-fourth of July, seventeen hundred and seventy-five, the colonial convention met at the city of Richmond.

The proceedings of this convention were marked by a character of great decision and vigour. One of their first measures was an ordinance for raising and imbodying a sufficient force for the defence and protection of the colony. By this ordinance it was provided, that two regiments of regulars, to consist of one thousand and twenty privates, rank and file, should be forthwith raised and taken into the pay of the colony; and a competent regular force was also provided for the protection of the western frontier. The whole colony was divided into sixteen military districts; with a provision, that a regiment of six hundred and eighty men, rank and file, should be raised on the eastern shore district, and a battalion of five hundred in each of the others; to be forthwith armed, trained, furnished with all military accoutrements, and ready to march at a minute's warning.

A committee, called the committee of safety, was also organized, with functions and powers analogous to those of the executive department, and apparently designed to supply the vacancy occasioned by the governor's abdication of that branch of the government.

The convention now proceeded to the appointment of officers to command the regular forces. The lofty stand which Mr. Henry had taken in the American cause, his increasing popularity, and the prompt and energetic movement which he had made in the affair of the gunpowder, brought him strongly before the view of the house; and he was elected the colonel of the first regiment, *and the commander of all the forces raised, and to be raised, for the defence of the colony.* Mr. William Woodford, who is said to have distinguished himself in the French and Indian war, was appointed to the command of the second regiment.

The place of rendezvous for the troops was the city of Williamsburgh. Mr. Henry was at his post on the twentieth of September, examining the grounds adjacent to the city, for the purpose of selecting an encampment; and the place chosen was at the back of William and Mary college. The troops were recruited and poured in with wonderful rapidity. The papers of the day teem with the annunciation of company after company, both regulars and minute-men, with the highest encomiums on the appearance and spirit of the troops; and had the purpose been offensive war, Colonel Henry was soon in a situation to have annihilated any force that Lord Dunmore could at that time have arrayed against him.

But there was, in truth, something extremely singular and embarrassing in the situation of the parties in regard to each other. It was not war, nor was it peace. The very ordinance by which these troops were raised, was filled with professions of allegiance and fidelity to George III.—professions, whose sincerity there is the less reason to doubt, because they are confined to the exercise of his constitutional powers, and stand connected with an expression of their firm determination to resist any attempt on the liberties of the country. The only intelligible purpose, therefore, for which these troops were raised, was a preparation for defence; and for defence against an attempt to enforce the parliamentary taxes upon this colony. With respect to Lord Dunmore, he was indeed considered as having abandoned the duties of his office: yet still he was regarded as the governor of Virginia; and there seems to have been no disposition to offer violence to his person.

Dunmore, on his part, considered the colony as in a state of open and general rebellion; not merely designing to resist an attempt to enforce upon them an obnoxious tax, but to subvert the regal government wholly and entirely; and had his power been equal to his wishes, there is no reason to doubt that he would have disarmed the colony, and hung up without ceremony, the leaders of this traitorous revolt, as he affected to consider it. His impotence, however, and the aversion of the colonists to act otherwise than defensively, produced a suspense full of the most painful anxiety.

In the meantime, Captain Squire, commander of his majesty's sloop, the Otter, had been labouring throughout the summer with some success, to change the defensive attitude of the colony. He was engaged in cruising continually in James and York rivers, plundering the defenceless shores, and carrying off the slaves, wherever seduction or force could place them in his power. These piratical excursions had wrought up the citizens who were not in arms to a very high pitch of resentment; and an accident soon gave them an opportunity of partial reprisal, which they did not fail to seize.

On the second of September, the captain, sailing in a tender, on a marauding expedition from James to York river, was encountered by a violent tempest, and his tender was driven on shore upon Back river, near Hampton. It was night, and the storm still raging:—the captain and his men, distrusting (unjustly, as it would seem from the papers) the hospitality of the inhabitants, made their escape through the woods; the vessel was on the next day discovered and burnt by the people of the neighbourhood. In consequence of this act, the captain addressed the following letter to the committee of the town of Hampton:—

"*Otter sloop, Norfolk river, Sept.* 10, 1775.

"GENTLEMEN—Whereas, a sloop-tender, manned and armed in his majesty's service, was, on Saturday the second instant, in a violent gale of wind, cast on shore in Back river, Elizabeth county, having on board the undermentioned king's stores, which the inhabitants of Hampton thought proper tc seize: I am therefore to desire, that the king's sloop, with all the stores belonging to her, be immediately returned; or the people of Hampton, who committed the outrage, must be answerable for the consequences.

"I am, gentlemen, your humble servant,

"MATTHEW SQUIRE."

This letter, with a catalogue of the stores having been communicated to the committee of Williamsburgh, and by them having been laid before the commanding officer of the volunteers of that place, Major James Innes, at the head of a hundred men, who courted the enterprise, flew to Hampton to repel the threatened invasion. Squire, however, satisfied himself for the present, by falling down to Hampton road, where he seized the passage-boats, with the negroes in them, by way of reprisal, as he alleged, for the stores, &c., taken out of his tender when driven ashore in the late storm; "which boats and negroes," adds Purdie's paper of the day, "it is likely he intends taking into the *king's service*, to send out a pirating for hogs, fowls, &c. A very pretty occupation for the captain of one of his majesty's ships-of-war."

The next paper announces the movements of Squire by a

paragraph, which I extract *verbatim*, as showing in an amusing light, the spirit of the times, and as Camden says, "the plain and jolly mirth of our ancestors," even in the midst of misfortunes:—"We hear that the renowned Captain Squire, of his majesty's sloop Otter, is gone up the bay for Baltimore in Maryland; on his *old trade*, it is to be presumed, of negro-catching, pillaging the farms and plantations of their stock and poultry, and other *illustrious actions*, highly becoming a *Squire* in the king's navy. Some say, his errand was to watch for a quantity of gunpowder intended for this colony; but that *valuable* is now safely landed where he dare not come to *smell* it." The same paper contains the following answer from the committee of Hampton to Squire's letter:—

"To Matthew Squire, Esq., commander of his majesty's sloop Otter, lying in Hampton roads.

"*Hampton, September* 16, 1775.

"Sir—Yours of the tenth instant, directed to the committee of the town of Hampton, reciting, that a sloop-tender on his majesty's service was, on the second instant, cast on shore near this place, having on board some of the king's stores, which you say were seized by the inhabitants, and demanding an immediate return of the same, or that the people of Hampton must answer the consequences of such outrage, was this day laid before them, who knowing the above recital to be injurious and untrue think proper here to mention the facts relative to this matter. The sloop we apprehend, was not in his majesty's service, as we are well assured that you were on a pillaging or pleasuring party; and although it gives us pain to use indelicate expressions, yet the treatment received from you calls for a state of facts, in the simple language of truth, however harsh it may sound.

"To your own heart we appeal for the candour with which we have stated them—to that heart which drove you into the woods in the most tempestuous weather, in one of the darkest nights, to avoid the much-injured and innocent inhabitants of this county, who had never threatened or ill-used you—and who would at that time have received you, we are assured, with humanity and civility, had you made yourself and situation known to them.

"Neither the vessel nor stores were seized by the inhabitants of Hampton; the gunner, one Mr. Gray—and the pilot, one Mr. Ruth—who were employed by you on this party, are men, we hope, who will still assert the truth. From them, divers of our members were informed that the vessel and stores together with a good seine, (which you, without cause, so hastily deserted,) were given up as irrecoverably lost, by the officers, and some of the proprietors, to one Finn, near whose house you were driven on shore, as a reward for his entertaining you, &c., with respect and decency.

"The threats of a person whose conduct hath evinced that he was not only capable, but desirous of doing us, in our then defenceless state, the greatest injustice, we confess, were somewhat alarming; but with the greatest pleasure we can inform you, our apprehensions are now removed.

"Although we know that we cannot legally be called to account for that which you are pleased to style an outrage, and notwithstanding we have hitherto, by you been treated with iniquity, we will, as far as in our power lies, do you right upon just and equitable terms.

"First. We, on behalf of the community, require from you the restitution of a certain Joseph Harris, the property of a gentleman of our town, and all other our slaves whom you may have on board; which said Harris, as well as other slaves, hath been long harboured, and often employed, with your knowledge, (as appeared to us by the confession of Ruth and others, and is well known to all your men,) in pillaging us under cover of night, of our sheep and other live stock.

"Secondly. We require that you will send on shore all boats, with their hands, and every other thing you have detained on this occasion.

"And lastly. That you shall not, by your own arbitrary authority, undertake to insult, molest, interrupt, or detain, the persons or property of any one passing to and from this town, as you have frequently done for some time past.

"Upon complying with those requisitions, we will endeavour to procure every article left on our shore, and shall be ready to deliver them to your pilot and gunner, of whose good behaviour we have had some proofs.

"We are, &c.,

"*The Committee of Elizabeth City county, and town of Hampton.*"

In the meantime, Squire's threat against Hampton was not an empty one, as is proven by the following account of the attempt to execute it: the article is extracted from a supplement to Purdie's paper of October twenty-seventh, seventeen hundred and seventy-five:—

"After Lord Dunmore, with his troops and the navy, had been for several weeks seizing the persons and property of his majesty's peaceable subjects in this colony—on Wednesday night last, a party from an armed tender landed near Hampton, and took away a valuable negro slave and a sail from the owner. Next morning there appeared off the mouth of Hampton river, a large armed schooner, a sloop, and three tenders, with soldiers on board, and a message was received at Hampton from Captain Squire, on board the schooner, that he would that day land and burn the town; on which a company of regulars, and a company of minute-men,* who had been placed there in consequence of former threats denounced against that place, made the best disposition to prevent their landing, aided by a body of militia who were suddenly called together on the occasion.

"The enemy accordingly attempted to land, but were retarded by some boats sunk across the channel for that purpose. Upon this they fired several small cannon at the provincials without any effect, who in return discharged their small arms so effectually, as to make the enemy move off, with the loss of several men, as it is believed. But they had, in the meantime, burnt down a house belonging to Mr. Cooper, on the river. On intelligence of this reaching Williamsburgh, about nine o'clock at night, a company of riflemen was despatched to the aid of Hampton, *and the colonel of the second regiment* sent to take the command of the whole; who with the company, arrived about eight o'clock next morning.

"The enemy had in the night cut through the boats sunk, and made a passage for their vessels, which were drawn close up to the town, and began to fire upon it soon after the arrival of the party from Williamsburgh; but as soon as our men were so disposed as to give them a few shot, they went off so hastily that our people took a small tender, with five white men, a woman, and two slaves, six swivels, seven muskets, some small arms, a sword, pistols, and other things, and several papers belonging to Lieutenant Wright, who made his escape by jumping overboard and swimming away with Mr. King's man, who are on shore, and a pursuit it is hoped may overtake them.

"There were two of the men in the vessel mortally wounded; one is since dead, and the other near his end. Besides which, we are informed, nine were seen to be thrown overboard from one of the vessels. We have not a man even wounded. The vessels went over to Norfolk, and we are informed the whole force from thence is intended to visit Hampton this day. If they should, we hope our brave troops are prepared for them; as we can with pleasure assure the public,

*"Captain George Nicholas commanded the regulars, and Captain Lyne the minute-men; Captain Nicholas, therefore, as being in the regular service, had the command of the whole in the first skirmish. This gentleman was the eldest son of Colonel Robert C. Nicholas; and on the return of peace became highly distinguished both as a politician and a lawyer.

that every part of them behaved with spirit and bravery, and are wishing for another skirmish."

The next paper contains the following card to Captain Squire, which is inserted merely as another specimen of the character of the times :—

"*Williamsburgh, November 3d.*

"The riflemen and soldiers of Hampton desire their compliments to Captain Squire and his squadron, and wish to know how they approve the reception they met last Friday. Should he incline to renew his visit, they will be glad to see him; otherwise, in point of complaisance, they will be under the necessity of returning the visit. If he cannot find the *ear* that was cut off, they hope he will wear a *wig* to hide the mark; for perhaps it may not be necessary that all should know *chance* had effected that which the *laws* ought to have done."

In the meantime, Lord Dunmore, with a motley band of tories, negroes, and recruits from St. Augustine's, was "cutting such fantastic capers" in the country round about Norfolk, as made it necessary to crush him or drive him from the state. With this view, the committee of safety (who, by their constitution, were authorized to direct all military movements) detached Colonel Woodford, at the head of about eight hundred men to cross James river at Sandy Point, and go in pursuit of his lordship. Colonel Henry himself had been anxious for this service, and is said to have solicited it in vain. But the committee of safety* seem to have distrusted too much his want of military experience, to confide to him so important an enterprise.

The disgust which Mr. Henry had conceived at the palpable reflection on his military capacity was increased by Colonel Woodford's refusal to acknowledge his superiority in command. This gentleman, after his departure from Williamsburgh, on the expedition against Dunmore, considered himself as no longer under Mr. Henry's authority; and consequently addressed all

* The committee of safety was composed of the following gentlemen :—Edmund Pendleton, George Mason, Hon. John Page, Richard Bland, Thomas Ludwell Lee, Paul Carrington, Dudley Digges, William Cabell, Carter Braxton, James Mercer, and John Tabb, esquires. The clause of the ordinance of convention which authorized this committee to direct all military movements, is the following :—

"And whereas it may be necessary for the public security, that the forces to be raised by virtue of this ordinance should, as occasion may require, be marched to different parts of the colony, and that the officers should be subject to a proper control, *Be it ordained by the authority aforesaid*, That the officers and soldiers under such command shall in all things, not otherwise particularly provided for by this ordinance, and the articles established for their regulation, be under the control, and subject to the order of the general committee of safety."

his communications to the convention when in session, and when not so, to the committee of safety. On the sixth December, seventeen hundred and seventy-five, Mr. Henry sent an express to Colonel Woodford, with the following letter:—

"*On Virginia service.*

"To William Woodford, Esq., colonel of the second regiment of the Virginia forces.

"*Headquarters, Dec.* 6, 1775.

"SIR—Not hearing of any despatch from you for a long time, I can no longer forbear sending to know your situation, and what has occurred. Every one as well as myself, is vastly anxious to hear how all stands with you. In case you think anything could be done to aid and forward the enterprise you have in hand, please to write it. But I wish to know your situation, particularly with that of the enemy, that the whole may be laid before the convention now here. The number and designs of the enemy, as you have collected it, might open some prospects to us, that might enable us to form some diversion in your favour. The bearer has orders to lose no time, and return with all possible haste. I am, sir, your most humble servant, "P. HENRY, jun.

"P. S. Captain Alexander's company is not yet come.

"Col. WOODFORD."

To this letter, on the next day, he received the following answer from Colonel Woodford:—

"*Great Bridge, 7th Dec.*, 1775.

"SIR—I have received yours per express; in answer to which must inform you, that, understanding you were out of town, I have not written you before last Monday, by the return of the honourable the convention's express, when I referred you to my letter to them for every particular respecting mine and the enemy's situation. I wrote them again yesterday and this morning, which no doubt they will communicate to you, as commanding officer of the troops at Williamsburgh. When joined, I shall always esteem myself immediately under your command, and will obey accordingly; but when sent to command a separate and distinct body of troops, under the immediate instructions of the committee of safety—whenever that body or the honourable convention is sitting, I look upon it as my indispensable duty to address my intelligence to them, as the supreme power in this colony.

"If I judge wrong, I hope that honourable body will set me right. I would wish to keep up the greatest harmony between us, for the good of the cause we are engaged in; but cannot bear to be supposed to have neglected my duty, when I have done everything I conceived to be so. The enemy are strongly fortified on the other side the bridge, and a great number of negroes and tories with them; my prisoners disagree as to the numbers. We are situate here in mud and mire, exposed to every hardship that can be conceived, but the want of provisions, of which our stock is but small, the men suffering for shoes; and if ever soldiers deserved a second blanket in any service, they do in this; our stock of ammunition much reduced, no bullet-moulds that were good for anything sent to run up our lead, till those sent the other day by Mr. Page. If these necessaries and better arms had been furnished in time for this detachment, they might have prevented much trouble and great expense to this colony.

"Most of those arms I received the other day from Williamsburgh are rather to be considered as lumber, than fit to be put in men's hands, in the face of an enemy: with much repair, some of them will do; with those, and what I have taken from the enemy, hope to be better armed in a few days. I have written to the convention, that it was my opinion, the greatest part of the first regiment ought immediately to march to the scene of action with some cannon, and a supply of ammunition, and every other necessary for war that the colony can muster, that a stop may be put to the enemy's progress.

"As to the Carolina troops and cannon, they are by no means what I was made to expect: sixty of them are here, and one hundred will be here to-morrow; more, it is said, will follow in a few days, under Colonel Howe; badly armed, cannon not mounted, no furniture to them. How long these people will choose to stay, it is impossible for me to say; ninety-nine in one hundred of these lower people rank tories. From all these informations, if you can make a diversion in my favour, it will be of service to the colony, and very acceptable to myself and soldiers; whom, if possible, I will endeavour to keep easy under their hard duty, but begin to doubt whether it will be the case long."

In two days after the receipt of this letter, came the news of the victory of the Great Bridge, by which Colonel Woodford at once threw into the shade the military pretensions of all the other state officers; a circumstance not very well calculated to gild the pill of contumacy, which he had just presented to the commander-in-chief. The committee of safety had now a delicate part to act between these two officers; they were extremely anxious to avoid the decision of the question which had arisen between them, seeing very distinctly that their decision could not but disappoint very painfully that gentleman who was their favourite officer.

They seem to have been apprehensive that Colonel Woodford would be led, by that decision, to resign in disgust; and were justly alarmed at the idea of losing the services of so valuable an officer, especially after the distinction which he had recently gained at the Great Bridge. Mr. Henry, however, insisted that the committee or convention should determine the question, as being the only way to settle the construction of his commission. It was accordingly taken up, and decided by the following order of the committee:—

"*In Committee—December*, MDCCLXXV

"Resolved, unanimously, That Colonel Woodford, although acting upon a separate and detached command, ought to correspond with Colonel Henry, and make returns to him at proper times of the state and condition of the forces under his command; and also that he is subject to his orders, when the convention, or the committee of safety, is not sitting, but that while either of those bodies are sitting, he is to receive his orders from one of them."

The address which was thought necessary in communicating this resolution to Colonel Woodford, is a proof of the very high estimate in which he was held by the committee; and the same evidence furnishes very decisive proof that Colonel Henry had not owed his military appointment to the suffrage of those members of the committee who maintained the correspondence. Thus, on the thirteenth of December, seventeen hundred and seventy-five, a member of the convention addressed a letter to Colonel Woodford, which seems to have been a preparative for the resolution of the committee, and is certainly suited, with great dexterity, to that object; the writer, after some introductory observations, says:—"Whether you are obliged to make your returns to Colonel H—y, and to send your despatches through him to the convention and committee of safety, and also from those bodies through him to you, must depend upon the ordinance and the commission he bears.

"You will observe his commission is strongly worded, beyond what I believe was the intention of the person who drew it*—but the ordinance, I think, clearly gives the convention,

* The committee appointed to draw up and report the forms of commissions, for the officers of the troops to be raised by order of the convention of the summer of 1775, were, Mr. Banister, Mr. Lawson, Mr. Walkins, and Mr. Holt; and on the 26th of August, 1775, Mr. Banister from this committee reported the following:—

"*Form of a commission for the colonel of the first regiment, and commander of the regular forces.*

"The committee of safety for the colony of Virginia to Patrick Henry, Esq.

"Whereas by a resolution of the delegates of this colony, in convention assembled, it was determined that you, the said Patrick Henry, Esq., should be

and committee of safety acting under their authority, the absolute direction of the troops. The dispute between you must be occasioned, I suppose, (for I have not seen your letter to the colonel,) by disregard of him as a commander, after the adjournment of the committee of safety, and before the meeting of the convention; at which time, I am apt to think, though I am not military man enough to determine, your correspondence should have been with him as commanding officer.

"I have talked with Colonel Henry about this matter; he thinks he has been ill treated, and insists the officers under his command shall submit to his orders. I recommended it to him to treat the business with caution and temper; as a difference at this critical moment between our troops would be attended with the most fatal consequences; and took the liberty to assure him you would, I was certain, submit to whatever was thought just and reasonable. He has laid the letter before the committee of safety, whose sentiments upon the subject I expect you must have received before this. I hope it will not come before the convention, but from what Colonel Henry said, he intimated it must, as it could be no otherwise determined.

"My sentiments upon that delicate point, I partly communicated upon the expected junction of the Carolina troops with

colonel of the first regiment of regulars, and commander-in-chief of all the forces to be raised for the protection and defence of this colony; and by an ordinance of the same convention it is provided, that the committee of safety should issue all military commissions: Now, in pursuance of the said power to us granted, and in conformity to the appointment of the convention, we, the said committee of safety, do constitute and commission you, the said Patrick Henry, Esq., colonel of the first regiment of regulars, and *commander-in-chief of all such other forces as may, by order of the convention, or committee of safety, be directed to act in conjunction with them;* and with the said forces, or any of them, you are hereby empowered to resist and repel all hostile invasions, and quell and suppress any insurrections which may be made or attempted against the peace and safety of this his majesty's colony and dominion.

"And we do require you to exert your utmost efforts for the promotion of discipline and order among the officers and soldiers under your command, agreeable to such ordinances, rules, and articles, which are now or hereafter may be, instituted for the government and regulation of the army; and that you pay due obedience to all orders and instructions, which, from time to time, you may receive from the convention or committee of safety; to hold, exercise, and enjoy the said office of colonel and commander-in-chief of the forces, and to perform and execute the power and authority aforesaid, and all other things which are truly and of right incidental to your said office, during the pleasure of the convention, and no longer. *And we do hereby require and command all officers and soldiers, and every person whatsoever, in any way concerned, to be obedient and assisting to you in all things, touching the due execution of this commission, according to the purport or intent thereof.*

"Given under our hands at this day of Anno Dom. 177 ."

ours which I presume you have received. By your letter yesterday to the president, I find you agree with me. I very cordially congratulate you on the success at the Bridge and the reduction of the fort, which will give our troops the benefit of better and more wholesome ground. Your letter came to the convention just time enough to read it before we broke up, as it was nearly dark; it was however proposed and agreed, that the president should transmit you the approbation of your conduct in treating with kindness and humanity the unfortunate prisoners; and that your readiness to avoid dispute about rank with Colonel Howe, they consider as a further mark of your attachment to the service of your country.

"I have had it in contemplation paying you a visit, but have not been able to leave the convention, as many of our members are absent and seem to be in continual rotation, some going, others returning. We shall raise many more battalions, and, as soon as practicable, arm some vessels. A commander or general, I suppose, will be sent us by the congress, as it is expected our troops will be upon continental pay. I pray God to protect you, and prosper all your endeavours."

But the letter from the chairman of the committee, which enclosed the resolution is a masterpiece of address, so far as relates to the feelings of Colonel Woodford; though certainly not well judged to promote the permanent harmony of those officers, by inspiring sentiments of respect and subordination for the superior. The letter bears date on the twenty-fourth of December, seventeen hundred and seventy-five; it is written in a strain of the most frank and conciliatory friendship—full of deserved eulogy on Colonel Woodford's conduct—and very far from complimentary to the colonel of the first regiment.

In relation to this gentleman, (after having mentioned the resolution of raising other regiments,) he says: "The field-officers to each regiment will be named here, and recommended to congress; in case our army is taken into continental pay, they will send commissions. A general officer will be chosen there, I doubt not, and sent us; *with that matter, I hope we shall not intermeddle, lest it should be thought propriety requires our calling or rather recommending our present first officer to that station.*

"Believe me, sir, the unlucky step of calling that gentleman from our councils, where he was useful, into the field, in an important station, the duties of which he must, in the nature of things, be an entire stranger to, has given me many an anxious and uneasy moment. In consequence of this mistaken step, which cannot now be retracted or remedied, for he has done nothing worthy of degradation, and must keep his rank, we must be deprived of the service of some able officers, whose honour and former ranks will not suffer them to act under him in this juncture, when we so much need their services; however, I am told, that Mercer, Buckner, Dangerfield, and Weeden, will serve, and are all thought of. I am also told, that Mr. Thurston and Mr. Millikin are candidates for regiments: the latter, I believe, will raise, and have a German one. In the course of these reflections, my great concern is on your account.

"The pleasure I have enjoyed in finding your army conducted with wisdom and success, and your conduct meet with the general approbation of the convention and country, makes me more uneasy at a thought that the country should be deprived of your services, or you made uneasy in it, by any untoward circumstances. I had seen your letter to our friend Mr. Jones, (now a member of the committee of safety,) and besides that, Colonel Henry has laid before the committee your letter to him, and desired our opinion whether he was to command you or not.

"We never determined this till Friday evening; a copy of the resolution I enclose you. If this will not be agreeable, and prevent future disputes, I hope some happy medium will be suggested to effect the purpose, and make you easy; for the colony cannot part with you, while troops are necessary to be continued."

Mr. Henry had too much sagacity not to perceive the light in which he was viewed by the committee of safety, and too much sensibility not to be wounded by the discovery. His situation was indeed, at this time, most painfully embarrassing. The rank which he had held was full of the promise of honour and distinction; he was *the first officer of the Virginia forces;* the celebrity which he had already attained among his countrymen, not only by his political resistance to the measures of the British parliament, but by the bold and daring military enterprise which he had headed the preceding year, in the affair of the gunpowder, led his countrymen to expect, that the appointment which he now held would not be a barren one, but that he would mark it with the characters of his extraordinary genius, and become as distinguished in the field as he had been in the senate.

He knew that these expectations *were* entertained, and had every disposition to realize them; but his wishes and his hopes were perpetually overruled by the committee of safety, who commanded over him, and who gratuitously distrusting his capacity for war, would give him no opportunity of making trial of it. Yet Mr. Henry, untried, has been most unjustly slighted as a soldier, and spoken of as a mere military cipher! If I have not been misinformed, some of those who composed this very committee did, in aftertimes, frequently allude to this period of his life, to prove the practical inutility of his character, and have applied to him the saying, which Wilkes applied to Lord Chatham, that "all his power and efficacy was seated in his tongue."*

What figure he might have made in war, had the opportunity been allowed him, can now be only matter of speculation. His personal bravery, so far as I have heard, has never been called in question; or if it has, it has been without evidence: and neither his ardour in the public cause, nor his strong natural sense, can with any colour of justice be disputed. If we superadd to these qualities that presence of mind, that promptitude, boldness, and novelty of view—that dexterous address, and fertility of expedient, for which he was remarkable—I can see no reason to doubt, that he would have justified the highest expectations of his admirers, had he been permitted to command the expedition which he courted.

As to his want of experience, the alleged ground for keeping him so ignominiously confined to headquarters, he possessed pretty nearly as much experience as Colonel Washington had when he covered the retreat of Braddock's routed forces; as much, too, as those young generals of ours who have recently covered themselves with so much glory on our northern frontier: nor would it seem to comport with that respect which the committee owed to the convention, from whom both Colonel Henry and themselves had received their respective appointments, to arrogate the power of reversing the decree of the convention, and practically degrading the officer of their first choice. It is certain that the committee were severely spoken of at the day, and that the people, as well as the soldiery, did not hesitate openly to impute their conduct toward Mr. Henry to personal envy.

Other humiliations yet awaited him. Shortly after the affair of the Great Bridge, Colonel Howe, of North Carolina, at the head of five or six hundred men of that state, joined Colonel Woodford; and taking the command of the whole, with the consent of the latter gentleman, who yielded to the seniority of his commission, marched with their united forces into Norfolk, which had been evacuated by the British. From this post Colonel Howe continually addressed his communications to the committee of safety, or to the convention; and Colonel Henry,

*—*homines inertissimi, quorum omnis vis, virtusque in lingua sita est.*
Sallust Oratio sec. De Rep. Ord.

after having seen his lawful rights and honours transferred in the first instance, to an inferior officer of his own, had now the mortification of seeing himself completely superseded, and almost annihilated, by an officer from another state of only equal rank.

But even this was not all: six additional regiments had been raised by the convention, and congress had been solicited to take the Virginia troops on continental establishment. They resolved to take the six *new* regiments, passing by the two first; a discrimination which conveys so palpable a reflection on the two first regiments, that it is difficult to account for it, except by the secret influence of that unfriendly star, which had hitherto controlled and obscured Mr. Henry's military destinies. The measure was so exactly adjusted to the wish expressed by Colonel Woodford's correspondent, that congress would not devolve the chief command of the Virginia forces on Colonel Henry, that it is difficult to avoid the suspicion that the suggestion came from the same quarter.

The convention, however, now interfered in behalf of their favourite; and remonstrated against this degradation of the officers of their first choice; earnestly recommending it to congress, if they adhered to their resolution of taking into continental pay no more than six regiments, to suffer the two first to stand first in the arrangement. This course was accordingly adopted; *but, at the same time, commissions of brigadier-general were forwarded by congress to Colonel Howe, and Colonel Andrew Lewis.*

The reader, if he knows anything of the scrupulous and even fastidious delicacy with which military officers watch the most distant reflection upon their competency, will not be surprised that Mr. Henry refused the continental commission of colonel,* which was now offered to him and immediately re-

* The following is an exact copy of the commission sent from the general congress to the committee of safety, appointing Colonel Henry to the command of the first regiment, or battalion, in this colony, taken upon the continental establishment, agreeable to the requisition of the last convention :—

"In Congress.

"The delegates of the United Colonies of New Hampshire, Massachusetts bay, Rhode Island, Connecticut, New York, New Jersey, Pennsylvania, the counties of New Castle, Kent, and Sussex, on Delaware, Maryland, Virginia, North Carolina, South Carolina, and Georgia, to Patrick Henry, Esq. :—

"We, reposing especial trust and confidence in your patriotism, valour, conduct, and fidelity, do, by these presents constitute and appoint you to be colonel of the first battalion of Virginia forces, in the army of the United Colonies, raised for the defence of American liberty, and for repelling every hostile invasion thereof. You are, therefore, carefully and diligently to discharge

signed that which he held from the state. His resignation produced a commotion in the camp, which wore at first an alarming aspect; and would probably have had an extremely unpropitious effect on the military efforts of the state, had it not been instantaneously quelled by his own patriotic exertions. The following is the notice of this transaction from Purdie's paper of March first, seventeen hundred and seventy-six:—

"Yesterday morning, the troops in this city being informed that Patrick Henry, esquire, commander-in-chief of the Virginia forces, was about to leave them, the whole went into deep mourning, and being under arms, waited on him at his lodgings, when they addressed him in the following manner:—

"'*To Patrick Henry, jun., Esquire.*

"'Deeply impressed with a grateful sense of the obligations we lie under to you, for the polite, humane, and tender treatment manifested to us through the whole of your conduct, while we had the honour of being under your command, permit us to offer you our sincere thanks, as the only tribute we have in our power to pay to your real merits. Notwithstanding your withdrawing yourself from the service fills us with the most poignant sorrow, as it at once deprives us of our father and general; *yet, as gentlemen, we are compelled to applaud your spirited resentment to the most glaring indignity.* May your merit shine as conspicuous to the world in general, as it hath done to us, and may Heaven shower its choicest blessings upon you!'

"To which he returned the following answer:—

"'GENTLEMEN—I am exceedingly obliged to you for your approbation of my conduct. Your address does me the highest honour. This kind testimony of your regard to me would have been an ample reward for services much greater than

the duty of colonel, by doing and performing all manner of things thereunto belonging.

"And we do strictly charge and require all officers and soldiers under your command to be obedient to your orders as colonel. And you are to observe and follow such orders and directions, from time to time, as you shall receive from this or a future congress of the United Colonies, or committee of congress, for that purpose appointed, or commander-in-chief for the time being of the army of the United Colonies, or any other superior officer, according to the rules and discipline of war, in pursuance of the trust reposed in you. This commission to continue in force until revoked by this or a future congress.

"By order of the Congress,

"JOHN HANCOCK, President.

"Attest,

"CHARLES THOMSON, Secretary.

"*Philadelphia, Feb. 13th,* 1776."

those *I have had the power to perform.* I return you, and each of you, gentlemen, my best acknowledgments for the spirit, alacrity, and zeal you have constantly shown in your several stations. I am unhappy to part with you. I leave the service, but I leave my heart with you. May God bless you, and give you success and safety, and make you the glorious instrument of saving our country.'

"After the officers had received Colonel Henry's kind answer to their address, they insisted upon his dining with them at the Raleigh tavern, before his departure: and after dinner a number of them proposed escorting him out of town, but were prevented in their resolution by some uneasiness getting among the soldiery, who assembled in a tumultuous manner, and demanded their discharge, declaring their unwillingness to serve under any other commander; upon which Colonel Henry found it necessary to stay a night longer in town; which he spent in visiting the several barracks, and used every argument in his power with the soldiery, to lay aside their imprudent resolution, and to continue in the service which he had quitted from motives in which *his honour alone was concerned;* and that, although he was prevented from serving his country in a military capacity, yet his utmost abilities should be exerted for the real interest of the united colonies, in support of the glorious cause in which they have engaged.

"This, accompanied with the extraordinary exertions of Colonel Christian and other officers present, happily produced the desired effect, the soldiers reluctantly acquiescing: and we have now the pleasure to assure the public, that those brave fellows are now pretty well reconciled, and will spend the last drop of their blood in their country's defence."

This is the man who has been sometimes branded as a turbulent, seditious, factious demagogue! Had he been of this character, what an occasion was here to have provoked it to action! This love for the man and the officer, and this resentment of the indignities to which he had been subjected, were not confined to the camp at Williamsburgh; they pervaded the whole army, and were felt and expressed by the following address, signed by upward of ninety officers at Kemp's landing and Suffolk, (*in Colonel Woodford's camp,*) as well as at Williamsburgh; and printed by their desire in Purdie's paper of the twenty-second of March, seventeen hundred and seventy-five:—

"SIR—Deeply concerned for the good of our country, we sincerely lament the unhappy necessity of your resignation, and with all the warmth of affection assure you, that, whatever may have given rise to the *indignity* lately offered to you, we *join with the general voice of the people*, and think it our duty to make this public declaration of our high respect for your distinguished merit. To your vigilance and judgment as a senator this united continent bears ample testimony; while she prosecutes her steady opposition to those destructive ministerial measures *which your eloquence first pointed out and taught to resent, and your resolution led forward to resist.*

"To your extensive popularity the service also is greatly indebted, for the expedition with which the troops were raised; and, while they were continued under your command, the firmness, candour, and politeness, which formed the complexion of your conduct toward them, obtained the signal approbation of the wise and virtuous, and will leave upon our minds the most grateful impression. Although retired from the immediate concerns of war, we solicit the continuance of your kindly attention. We know your attachment to the best of causes; we have the fullest confidence in your abilities, and in the rectitude of your views; and *however willing the envious may be to undermine an established reputation*, we trust the day will come, when justice shall prevail, and thereby secure you an honourable and happy return to the glorious employment of conducting our councils, and hazarding your life in the defence of your country.

"With the most grateful sentiments of regard and esteem, we are, sir, very respectfully, your most obliged and obedient humble servants."

If any doubt can be entertained as to the body to which this imputation of *envy* pointed, it will be removed by the following defence of the committee of safety, extracted from the supplement to Purdie's paper of the fifteenth of March, seventeen hundred and seventy-six:—

"Mr. Purdie—I am informed a report is prevailing through the colony, that the committee of safety were the cause of Colonel Henry's resigning the command of his battalion; which it is supposed hath received confirmation from the address of the officers to that gentleman, in which they speak of *a glaring indignity* having been offered him, if it was not wholly derived from that source. That the good people of the country may be truly informed in this matter, the following state of facts is submitted, without comment, to the impartial judgment of the public:—

"As soon as the last convention had voted the raising seven new battalions of troops, besides augmenting the old ones, the committee of safety informed our delegates to congress of that vote, desiring they would use their best endeavours to have the whole supported at continental expense; in answer to which, a letter was received from the delegates, dated the thirtieth of December, of which the following is an extract: 'The resolutions of congress for taking our six additional [they would not agree to take our other two] battalions, into continental pay, and for permitting an exportation for supplying our countrymen with salt, are enclosed.'

"It was supposed from hence, an intention prevailed in congress to pass by the two old battalions, and take six of the new ones into continental pay; which, as it was said those officers would take precedency of provincial ones of equal rank, was generally thought wrong, since it would degrade the officers of the two first battalions; and, to avoid this, the convention came to a resolution, the tenth of January, of which the following is part: 'Should the congress adhere to their resolution of taking into continental pay no more than six battalions, let it be earnestly recommended to them to suffer our two present battalions (to be completed as before mentioned) to stand first in the arrangement; since, otherwise, the officers first appointed by this convention, most of whom have already gone through a laborious and painful service, will be degraded in their ranks, and there is too much reason to apprehend that great confusion will ensue.'

"The worthy gentlemen (*not a member of the committee of safety*) who proposed this resolution, informed the convention, he had consulted some of the officers of the first regiment, who wished to have their rank preserved, though it was foreseen the pay would be reduced.

"The committee of safety, in a letter to the delegates, dated the twenty-fifth of January, enclosing this resolution, thus write: 'You have a list of the field officers as they stand recommended, and we doubt not receiving the commissions in the like order, with blanks for the proper number of captains and subalterns. If, however, the resolution of congress should be unalterably fixed to allow us but six battalions, you will please to attend to that part of the resolve which recommends their being the first six, as a point of great consequence to our harmony, in which may be involved the good of the common cause.'

"The committee of safety afterward received the commissions wholly filled up for the field officers of six battalions, in the rank they stood recommended by the convention, beginning with Colonel Henry, and ending with Colonel Buckner of the sixth battalion, with directions to deliver them. Colonel Henry was accordingly offered his commission, which he declined accepting, and retired without assigning any reasons.

"As to the general officers, the convention left them entirely to the choice of the congress, without recommendation; nor did the committee of safety at all intermeddle in that choice. "A FRIEND TO TRUTH."

Immediately following this defence of the committee, in the same paper, are the two following articles:—

"MR. PURDIE—The address of the officers to Colonel Henry, and the colonel's reply, have led some of our enemies to hope that there would be great discontent in the army, by which our military operations would be retarded, and that there would be a considerable murmuring against the congress; but they are much mistaken. It is true the soldiers and officers were very unhappy at parting with so amiable a commander as Colonel Henry; and might be a little imprudent in some expressions on the occasion; but there is not a man of them who is not so warmly attached to the glorious cause he is engaged in, as to serve with alacrity under any commander, rather than it should suffer.

"And Colonel Henry himself is a gentleman of so much honour, and so true a patriot, that he will never countenance a murmur against the congress; nay so far from it, that it is highly probable he will soon be found in that august assembly, urging with his powerful eloquence, the necessity of prosecuting the war with redoubled vigour. I am a sincere friend to the congress and to Colonel Henry."

"Mr Purdie,

"'*Envy* will merit as its shade pursue:
But, like the shadow, proves the substance true.'—POPE.

"I was not surprised to see, in your last week's gazette, the resignation of Patrick Henry, esquire, late commander-in-chief of all the Virginia forces, and colonel of the first regiment. From that gentleman's amiable disposition, his invariable perseverance in the cause of liberty, *we apprehend that envy strove to bury in obscurity his martial talents. Fettered and confined, with only an empty title, the mere echo of authority, his superior abilities lay inactive, nor could be exerted for his honour, or his country's good.*

"Virginia may truly boast, that in him she finds the able statesman, the soldier's father, the best of citizens, and liberty's dear friend. Clad with innocence, as in a coat-of-mail, he is proof against *every serpentile whisper*. The officers and soldiers, who know him, are riveted to his bosom; when he speaks, all is silence; when he orders, they cheerfully obey; and in the field, under so sensible, so prudent an officer, though hosts oppose them, with shouts they meet their armed foe, the sure presages of victory and success.

"Let us, my countrymen, with grateful hearts, remember that he carried off the standard of liberty, and defeated Grenville in his favourite *stamp-act*.

"'While many dreaded, till with pleasing eye,
Saw tyranny before brave Henry fly.'

"I am, Mr. Purdie, your friend, and a well-wisher to Virginia. "AN HONEST FARMER."

It is very clear from the last piece, as well as from the address of the ninety officers, which has been already given, and which was published by their desire in a paper *subsequent to that which contains the defence of the committee*, that *that* defence had been by no means satisfactory; and that either the committee as a body, or what is more probable, some individual or individuals of it, were still believed to have had a secret hand in planning and directing the series of indignities which had driven Mr. Henry from a military life.

It would seem that the truly respectable and venerable chairman of that committee came in at the time for his full proportion of this censure, and that he smarted severely under it: this I infer, from a letter of his to Colonel Woodford some time afterward, in answer to one by which that gentleman had consulted him as to the propriety of *his* resigning his commission. After having dissuaded him from this step by other topics, he proceeds thus:—"I am apprehensive that your resignation will be handled to your disadvantage, *from a certain quarter, where all reputations are sacrificed for the sake of one;* what does it signify, that *he* resigned without any such cause, or assigning any reason at all? *it is not without example, that others should be censured for what he is applauded for.*"

This acrimony, so unusual from a man of Mr Pendleton's benevolence and courtesy, could have been wrung from him only by the bitterest provocations; and renders it highly probable, that the numerous and enthusiastic admirers of Mr. Henry had implicated this gentleman deeply in the indignities which had recently been offered to their favourite.

The necessity of placing this incident of Mr. Henry's life in its true light, upon the evidence in my possession, has imposed upon me a very painful duty in regard to Mr. Pendleton. With the justice or injustice of the construction placed upon his conduct in relation to Mr. Henry, I have nothing to do. Even if just, the infirmity of human nature may be easily excused in feeling some uneasiness at the eclipsing brightness with which Mr. Henry had rushed, like a comet, to the head of affairs in Virginia.

It demands, however, no uncommon measure of charity to believe, that what was imputed to envy at the time, proceeded, so far as Mr. Pendleton was concerned, from a single eye to the public good, and a sincere belief on his part, (an opinion in which he was by no means singular,) that Mr. Henry's inexperience in military affairs made it unsafe to commit to his management the infancy of our war.

The people required to be animated by success in the onset; and it was therefore very natural in the committee of safety, on whom the responsibility for the management of the war devolved, to select, for the first enterprises, the most experienced commander. Mr. Pendleton was too virtuous a man, and too faithful a patriot, to have yielded consciously to any other motive of action than the public good. His country has fixed its seal upon his exalted character, and the writer of these sketches is much more disposed to brighten than to efface the impression.

The motives of Mr. Henry's resignation of his commission which have been stated, are very easily and clearly deducible from the papers of the day, and were expressly avowed by him to his confidential friends and brother-in-law, Colonel Meredith.* To other friends, however, he stated that he was the more reconciled to the necessity which had compelled him to resign, because he believed that he could perhaps serve the cause of his country more effectually in the public councils than in the field.†

Immediately upon his resignation he was elected a delegate to the convention from the county of Hanover. The session of that body, which was now coming on, was pregnant with importance. Dunmore had abdicated the chair of government, and the royal authority in the colony was seen and felt no longer, but in acts of hostility.

The king had declared from his throne, that the colonists must be reduced by force to submit to the British claim of taxation; and the colonists, on their part, had avowed that they never would submit to this prostration of their rights; but, on

* These are Colonel Meredith's words:—"P. H. in a communication to Colonel M. stated his motives for resigning his commission as colonel. He conceived himself neglected, by younger officers having been put above him, and preferred to him; particularly in the affair of the Great Bridge, where he wished to have commanded; but Colonel Woodford received that appointment. He disliked his being kept in and about Williamsburgh, and not appointed to some important post or expedition. He was thus induced to think he was neglected by those who had the power of appointment. He therefore resigned."

† Judge Tyler, and Captain George Dabney.

the contrary, that they would hand down to their children the birthright of liberty which they had enjoyed, or perish in the attempt. On this quarrel arms had been taken up on both sides, and the appeal had been made to the God of battles. The war had assumed a regular and settled form; blood had been profusely shed in various parts of the continent, and reconciliation had become hopeless.

The people being thus abandoned by their king, put out of his protection, declared in a state of open rebellion, and treated as enemies, the social compact which had united the monarch with his subjects was at an end; the colonial constitution, which could be set and kept in motion only by the presence and agency of the king or his representative, was of course dissolved; and all the rights and powers of government reverted, of necessity, to their source, the people. These causes produced the convention.

It was the organ by which the people chose to exercise the fundamental rights thus thrown back upon them, by the dissolution of the regal government. It was the substitute for the whole government which had been withdrawn—legislative, executive, and judiciary. It represented the whole political power of the people; and had been expressly elected *to take care of the republic.* The means of accomplishing this object were left to themselves, without limitation or restriction on the part of the people.

Hitherto, while any hope of a restoration of the original government on just terms could be entertained, the convention had been satisfied with temporary expedients; the first convention, however, had exercised the power of the people in their highest capacity, by adopting a species of constitution, and organizing a government under it; thus they erected an executive, under the name of a committee of safety, which the people recognised as flowing directly from themselves.

Before the meeting of the convention of seventeen hundred and seventy-six, however, it was seen and well understood on every hand, that the contest could not be maintained by the people, without the aid of regular government: and that the political malady of which they complained, could be extirpated in no other way than by applying the knife to the root. The newspapers of the preceding year contain frequent suggestions of this kind; the impression had now become universal; and the papers present specimens of explicit instructions from the people to their delegates to this effect.*

*The following are instructions from the freeholders of James' city to their delegates:—

Thus instructed in the sentiments of their constituents, and representing the people in their highest sovereign capacity, the convention met on the sixth of May, seventeen hundred and seventy-six, in the old capitol in the city of Williamsburgh. Mr. Pendleton having been elected president, after having thanked the house for the honour done him, addressed them with great solemnity, in the following terms :—"We are now met in general convention according to the ordinance for our election, at a time truly critical, when subjects of the most important, and interesting nature require our serious attention.

"The administration of justice, and almost all the powers of government, have now been suspended for near two years. It will become us to reflect whether we can longer sustain the great struggle we are making in this situation." Having then directed their attention to certain specific subjects which required attention, he concluded his short, but impressive address, by exhorting the members to calmness, unanimity, and diligence.

"*To Robert C. Nicholas, and William Norvell, Esquires :—*

"Gentlemen—In vain do we congratulate ourselves on the impotency of the minister to divide us, if our union amounts to nothing more than a union in one common lethargy. War hath been brought into our houses, heightened by terrors and cruelties which the justest cause wants even palliatives for; but faint advances toward peace, insidiously urged, have caught the ear of the credulous, and groundless hopes of accommodation deluded the timid, so that the free military system remains untouched in most essential points. As if our inexperience, poverty in warlike stores, and the infancy of our navy, were of trifling moment, we have ventured to neglect resources in such difficulties, which Heaven hath placed within our attainment.

"Alliances may be formed at an easy price, capable of supplying these disadvantages, but an independent state disdains to humble herself to an equality in treaty with another, who cannot call her politics her own; or to be explicit, she cannot enter into a negotiation with those who denominate themselves rebels, by resistance, and confession of a dependancy.

"Reasons, drawn from *justice, policy, and necessity*, are everywhere at hand *for a radical separation from Great Britain*. From *justice; for the blood of those who have fallen in our cause cries aloud*, 'It is time to part.' From *necessity*, because she hath, of herself, repudiated us by a rapid succession of *insult, injury, robbery, murder*, and *a formal declaration of war*. These are but few, and some of the weakest arguments which the great volume of our oppression opens to every spirited American.

"It cannot be a violation of our faith now to reject the terms of 1763. They are a qualified slavery at best, and were acceptable to us, not as the extent of our right, but the probable cause of peace; but since the day in which they were most humbly offered as the end of animosities, an interval hath passed, marked with *tyranny intolerable*.

"We, therefore, whose names are hereunto subscribed, do request and instruct you, our delegates, (provided no just and honourable terms are offered by the king,) to exert your utmost ability, in the next convention, *toward dissolving the connexion between America and Great Britain*, TOTALLY, FINALLY AND IRREVOCABLY."

On the fifteenth of May, Mr. Cary reported from the committee of the whole house on the state of the colony, the following preamble and resolutions, which were unanimously adopted:—

"Forasmuch as all the endeavours of the United Colonies, by the most decent representations and petitions to the king and parliament of Great Britain, to restore peace and security to America under the British government, and a reunion with that people upon just and liberal terms, instead of a redress of grievances, have produced, from an imperious and vindictive administration, increased insult, oppression, and a vigorous attempt to effect our total destruction. By a late act, all these colonies are declared to be in rebellion, and out of the protection of the British crown; our properties subjected to confiscation; our people, when captivated, compelled to join in the murder and plunder of their relations and countrymen; and all former rapine and oppression of Americans declared legal and just. Fleets and armies are raised, and the aid of foreign troops engaged to assist these destructive purposes.

"The king's representative in this colony hath not only withheld all the powers of government from operating for our safety, but, having retired on board an armed ship, is carrying on a piratical and savage war against us; tempting our slaves, by every artifice, to resort to him, and training and employing them against their masters. In this state of extreme danger, we have no alternative left, but an abject submission to the will of those overbearing tyrants, or a total separation from the crown and government of Great Britain: uniting and exerting the strength of all America for defence, and forming alliances with foreign powers for commerce and aid in war.

"Wherefore, appealing to the Searcher of hearts for the sincerity of former declarations, expressing our desire to preserve the connexion with that nation, and that we are driven from that inclination by their wicked councils, and the eternal laws of self-preservation,

"Resolved, *unanimously*, That the delegates appointed to represent this colony in general congress, be instructed to propose to that respectable body, to DECLARE THE UNITED COLONIES FREE AND INDEPENDENT STATES, absolved from all allegiance to, or dependance upon, the crown or parliament of Great Britain; and that they give the assent of this colony to such declaration, and to whatever measures may be thought proper and necessary by the congress for forming foreign alliances, and A CONFEDERATION OF THE COLONIES, at such time, and in the manner, as to them shall seem best. Provided, that the power of forming government for, and the regulation of, the internal concerns of each colony, be left to the respective colonial legislatures.

"Resolved, *unanimously*, That a committee be appointed to prepare A DECLARATION OF RIGHTS, and such a plan of government as will be most likely to maintain peace and order in this colony, and secure substantial and equal liberty to the people."

This measure was followed by the most lively demonstrations of joy. The spirit of the times, is interestingly manifested by the following paragraph from Purdie's paper of the seventeenth of May, which immediately succeeds the annunciation of the resolutions:—

"In consequence of the above resolutions, universally regarded as the only door which will lead to safety and prosperity, some gentlemen made a handsome collection for the purpose of treating the soldiery, who next day were paraded in Waller's grove, before Brigadier-General Lewis, attended by the gentlemen of the committee of safety, the members of the general convention, the inhabitants of this city, &c., &c. The resolutions being read aloud to the army, the following toasts were given, each of them accompanied by a discharge of the artillery and small arms, and the acclamations of all present:—

"1. The American Independent States.

"2. The grand Congress of the United States, and their respective legislatures.

"3. General Washington, and victory to the American arms.

"The Union Flag of the American States waved upon the capitol during the whole of this ceremony; which being ended, the soldiers partook of the refreshments prepared for them by the affection of their countrymen, and the evening concluded with illuminations, and other demonstrations of joy; every one seeming pleased that the domination of Great Britain was now at an end, so wickedly and tyrannically exercised for these twelve or thirteen years past, notwithstanding our repeated prayers and remonstrances for redress."

The committee appointed to prepare the declaration and plan of government, called for by the last resolution, were the following:—Mr. Archibald Cary, Mr. Meriwether Smith, Mr. Mercer, Mr. Henry Lee, Mr. Treasurer, Mr. Henry, Mr. Dandridge, Mr. Gilmer, Mr. Bland, Mr. Digges, Mr. Carrington, Mr. Thomas Ludwell Lee, Mr. Cabell, Mr. Jones, Mr. Blair, Mr. Fleming, Mr. Tazewell, Mr. Richard Cary, Mr. Bullitt, Mr. Watts, Mr. Bannister, Mr. Page, Mr. Starke, Mr. David Mason, Mr. Adams, Mr. Reed, and Mr. Thomas Lewis; to whom were afterward successively added, Mr. Madison, Mr.

Ruthford, Mr. Watkins, Mr. George Mason, Mr. Harvie, Mr. Curle, and Mr. Holt.

On Wednesday, the twelfth of June following, that declaration of rights which stands prefixed to our statutes, was reported and adopted without a dissenting voice; as was also, on Saturday, the twenty-ninth of the same month, the present plan of our government.

The striking similitude between the recital of wrongs prefixed to the constitution of Virginia, and that which was afterward prefixed to the Declaration of Independence of the United States, is of itself sufficient to establish the fact that they are from the same pen. But the constitution of Virginia preceded the Declaration of Independence, by nearly a month; and was wholly composed and adopted while Mr. Jefferson is known to have been out of the state, attending the session of congress at Philadelphia. From these facts alone, a doubt might naturally arise whether he was, as he has always been reputed, the author of that celebrated instrument, the Declaration of American Independence, or at least the recital of grievances which ushers it in; or whether this part of it, at least, had not been borrowed from the preamble to the constitution of Virginia.

To remove this doubt, it is proper to state, that there now exists among the archives of this state an original rough draught of a constitution for Virginia, in the hand-writing of Mr. Jefferson, containing this identical preamble, and which was forwarded by him from Philadelphia, to his friend Mr. Wythe, to be submitted to the committee of the house of delegates. The body of the constitution is taken principally from a plan proposed by Mr. George Mason; and had been adopted by the committee before the arrival of Mr. Jefferson's plan; his preamble, however, was prefixed to the instrument; and some of the modifications proposed by him introduced into the body of it.

The salary of the governor to be appointed under the new constitution was immediately fixed by a resolution of the house at one thousand pounds per annum; and the house proceeded to elect forthwith the first republican governor for the commonwealth of Virginia. This was the touchstone of public favour. The office was of the first importance; and the whole state was open to the choice of the house. The question was decided on the first ballot. The vote stood thus:—

For Patrick Henry, jun. Esq. - - -	60
Thomas Nelson, Esq. - - - -	45
John Page, Esq. - - - - - -	1

Whereupon it was "Resolved, That the said Patrick Henry,

jun. Esq., be governor of this commonwealth, to continue in that office until the end of the succeeding session of assembly after the last of March next; and that Mr. Mason, Mr. Henry Lee, Mr. Digges, Mr. Blair, and Mr. Dandridge, be a committee to wait upon him, and notify such appointment."

On Monday, the first of July, Mr. George Mason, of this committee, reported, that they had performed the duty assigned them, and that the governor had been pleased to return the following answer to the convention:—

"*To the Honourable the President and House of Convention:*—

"Gentlemen—The vote of this day, appointing me governor of the commonwealth, has been notified to me in the most polite and obliging manner, by George Mason, Henry Lee, Dudley Digges, John Blair, and Bartholomew Dandridge, esquires.

"A sense of the high and unmerited honour conferred upon me by the convention, fills my heart with gratitude, which I trust my whole life will manifest. I take this earliest opportunity to express my thanks, which I wish to convey to you, gentlemen, in the strongest terms of acknowledgment.

"When I reflect that the tyranny of the British king and parliament hath kindled a formidable war, now raging throughout this wide-extended continent, and in the operations of which this commonwealth must bear so great a part; and that, from the events of this war, the lasting happiness or misery of a great proportion of the human species will finally result; that, in order to preserve this commonwealth from anarchy, and its attendant ruin, and to give vigour to our councils, and effect to all our measures, government hath been necessarily assumed, and new-modelled; that it is exposed to numberless hazards, and perils, in its infantine state; that it can never attain to maturity, or ripen into firmness, unless it is guarded by an affectionate assiduity, and managed by great abilities; I lament my want of talents; I feel my mind filled with anxiety and uneasiness, to find myself so unequal to the duties of that important station, to which I am called by the favour of my fellow-citizens at this truly critical conjuncture. The errors of my conduct shall be atoned for, so far as I am able, by unwearied endeavours to secure the freedom and happiness of our common country.

"I shall enter upon the duties of my office, whenever you, gentlemen, shall be pleased to direct; relying upon the known wisdom and virtue of your honourable house to supply my defects, and to give permanency and success to that system of government which you have formed, and which is so wisely

CHAPTER VII.

Mr. Henry's Administration as Governor of Virginia—Disasters of the Revolution—Their Effects—A prospect of making a Dictator is originated in Virginia—Mr. Henry vindicated—His Re-election in 1777—The plot to supplant General Washington—Anonymous Disclosures to Mr. Henry—Letters to Washington on that subject—Washington's Reply—Mr. Henry again re-elected in 1778—Narration of the Case of Josiah Philips—Mr. Henry declines a fourth Election—Death of his Wife—He remarries—General Gates enters Richmond in disgrace—Mr. Henry's Resolution in favour of that Officer—General Gates's Reply—Dispiriting State of Affairs—Meeting of the Assembly at Richmond—Mr. Harrison elected Speaker—Tarlton makes a Descent upon the Town—Arrival of the French—Termination of the Revolution—Mr. Henry's Course as Member of the Assembly—He advocates the Return of the Refugees—Sentiments on Freedom of Commerce—Bill for Intermarriages with the Indians—Incorporation of religious Societies—Bill for establishing a Provision for Teachers of Religion—Visit of Lafayette and Washington to Richmond—Reminiscences of Mr. Henry by a Cotemporary—Comparison between Him and Mr. Lee—Judge Stuart's delineation of Mr. Henry's Eloquence—He is again elected Governor of Virginia in 1784—Resigns in 1786—Resumes the Practice of the Law—The Federal Constitution adopted at Philadelphia.

Shortly after Mr. Henry's election as governor, Lord Dunmore was driven from Gwinn's Island, and from the state, to return to it no more; and Virginia was left in repose from every external enemy. No opportunity, therefore, was afforded to the governor to distinguish himself in the exercise of that important constitutional power which created him the commander-in-chief of the forces of the state. Duties, however, of more importance than lustre, remained for the executive of the state—in keeping up the ardour of the commonwealth in the public cause—in furnishing and forwarding their quota of military supplies to the grand continental army—in awakening the spirit of the state to the importance of discipline, and preparing the militia for the effectual discharge of their *routine* of duty—in watching and crushing the intrigues of the tories who still infested the state, and went about clandestinely, preaching disaffection to the patriot cause, and submission to Great Britain—in counteracting the schemes of speculating monopolists and extortioners, who sought to avail themselves of the necessities of the times, and to grow rich by preying on the misfortunes of the people—in short, in eradicating and removing those numerous moral diseases, which spring up with so much fecundity, and flourish so luxuriantly, amid the calamities of a revolution—and in keeping the body politic pure and healthy in all its parts.

The numerous and well directed proclamations with which the papers of the day abounded, attest the vigilance and energy with which these duties were performed. To enter upon a detail of them, would be to write the history of Virginia during this period, instead of the life of Mr. Henry; a work wholly unnecessary, since it has been already executed with minuteness and fidelity by an elegant writer, * whose work will probably see the light before these sketches. I shall confine myself to a few prominent incidents of Mr. Henry's administration, on account of some of which a degree of censure has been unjustly, I think, attached to his character.

The fall of the year 1776 was one of the darkest and most dispiriting periods of the revolution. The disaster at Long Island had occurred, by which a considerable portion of the American army had been cut off—a garrison of between three and four thousand men had been taken at Fort Washington—and the American general, with the small remainder, disheartened, and in want of every kind of comfort, was retreating through the Jerseys before an overwhelming power, which spread terror, desolation, and death, on every hand. This was the period of which Paine, in his Crisis, used that memorable expression:—"These are the times which try the souls of men!" For a short time the courage of the country fell. Washington alone remained erect, and surveyed with godlike composure the storm that raged around him. Even the heroism of the Virginia legislature gave way; and, in a season of despair, the mad project of a dictator was seriously meditated.

That Mr. Henry was thought of for this office, has been alleged, and is highly probable; but that the project was suggested by him, or even received his countenance, I have met with no one who will venture to affirm. There is a tradition that Colonel Archibald Cary, the speaker of the senate, was principally instrumental in crushing this project; that meeting Colonel Syme, the step-brother of Colonel Henry, in the lobby of the house, he accosted him very fiercely in terms like these:—"I am told that your brother wishes to be dictator: tell him from me, that the day of his appointment shall be the day of his death—for he shall feel my dagger in his heart before the sunset of that day;" and the tradition adds, that Colonel Syme, in great agitation, declared, "that if such a project existed, his brother had no hand in it, for that nothing could be more foreign to him, than to countenance any office which could endanger, in the most distant manner, the liberties of his country."

The intrepidity and violence of Colonel Cary's character renders the tradition probable; but it furnishes no proof of Mr. Henry's implication in the scheme. It is most certain, that both himself and his friends have firmly and uniformly

* Mr. L. H. Girardin, the continuator of Burk's History of Virginia.

persisted in asserting his innocence; and there seems to be neither candour or justice in imputing to him, without evidence, a scheme which might just as well have originated in the assembly itself. It was not more than a month afterward, that *congress* actually did, with relation to General Washington, very nearly what the Virginia legislature are said to have contemplated in regard to Mr. Henry; they invested him with powers very little short of dictatorial: yet no one ever suspected General Washington of having prompted the measure Why then shall Mr. Henry be suspected?

Neither General Washington himself, nor any other patriot, had maintained the principles of the revolution with more consistency and uniformity than Patrick Henry; and it will certainly never satisfy a fair inquirer, to attempt to balance a suspicion, without the shadow of proof, against the whole course of a long and patriotic life. The charge, moreover, seems preposterous. What advantage could a rational man promise himself from the dictatorship of a single state, embarked with twelve other sovereign and independent states, in one common cause; a cause, too, now so well understood by the whole body of the American people, and in which all their souls were so intensely engaged? The man who was at the head of the armies of the union, might have played the part of Cesar or Cromwell, had he possessed their wicked spirit; but what could the dictator of a *single state do*, and that, too, a *state of firm and enlightened patriots?*

It is impossible to believe that the legislature themselves could have entertained a doubt of Mr. Henry's innocence; since at the next annual election for governor, which took place on the thirtieth of May, seventeen hundred and seventy-seven, he was re-elected *unanimously;* the house being composed of nearly the same members, and the same Colonel Cary being speaker of the senate. This honourable proof of confidence, by those who best knew the whole case—who watched, with a scrutiny so severely jealous, the conduct of our prominent men—and among whom were some who derived no pleasure from the public honours of Mr. Henry—will be decisive of this question, with every man who is dispassionately searching for the truth, and is willing to find it.

This very honourable mark of the confidence of the legislature, in re-electing him unanimously to the office of governor, affected Mr. Henry most sensibly; and to the committee who announced it to him, he gave the following answer:—

"GENTLEMEN: The *signal* honour conferred on me by the general assembly in their choice of me to be the governor of this commonwealth, demands my best acknowledgments, which

I beg the favour of you to convey to them in the most acceptable manner.

"I shall execute the duties of that high station, to which I am again called by the favour of my fellow-citizens, according to the best of my abilities, and I shall rely upon the candour and wisdom of the assembly, to excuse and supply my defects. The good of the commonwealth shall be the only object of my pursuit, and I shall measure my happiness according to the success which shall attend my endeavours to establish the public liberty. I beg to be presented to the assembly; and that they and you will be assured, that I am, with every sentiment of the highest regard, their and your most obedient and very humble servant,

"P. Henry."

It was in the course of this year's administration of the government by Mr. Henry, that that memorable plot which disgraces our history, was formed to supplant General Washington. This is said to have proceeded from the glory which General Gates had gained by the capture of Burgoyne and his army at Saratoga, and was believed to have been suggested by General Gates himself. The plot is said to have been an extensive one, and to have embraced some of the members of congress, and many officers of the army. The high estimate which Mr. Henry had formed of the abilities of General Washington, while that illustrious man was comparatively unknown to his countrymen, has been already stated. This estimate, instead of having been lowered, had been confirmed and raised by subsequent events.

Mr. Henry was too cool and judicious an observer of events, to have imputed to the commander-in-chief the disasters of the autumn of seventeen hundred and seventy-six. His masterly retreat through the Jerseys, the brilliant strokes of generalship exhibited at Trenton and Princeton, and above all, that singular constancy of soul with which he braved adversity, had excited his grateful admiration, and established Washington in his heart as one of the first of human beings. He not only admired him as a general, but revered him as a patriot, and loved him as a friend. Feeling for General Washington sentiments like these, the reader may judge of the indignation and horror with which he read the following anonymous letter, addressed to him by one of the conspirators against that father of his country:—

"Yorktown, *January 12th*, 1778.

"Dear sir: The common danger of our country first brought you and me together. I recollect with pleasure the influence of your conversation and eloquence upon the opinions of this country, in the beginning of the present controversy. You first taught us to shake off our idolatrous attachment to royalty and to oppose its encroachments upon our liberties, with our very lives. By these means you saved us from ruin. The independence of America is the offspring of that liberal spirit of thinking and acting which followed the destruction of the sceptres of kings, and the mighty power of Great Britain.

"But, sir, we have only passed the Red sea. A dreary wilderness is still before us, and unless a Moses or a Joshua *are* raised up in our behalf, we must perish before we reach the promised land. We have nothing to fear from our enemies on the way. General Howe, it is true, has taken Philadelphia; but he has only changed his prison. His dominions are bounded on all sides, by his out-sentries. America can only be undone by herself. She looks up to her councils and arms for protection; but alas! what are they? Her representation in congress dwindled to only twenty-one members—her Adams—her Wilson—her Henry, are no more among them. Her councils weak—and partial remedies applied constantly for universal diseases.

"Her army—what is it? a major-general belonging to it, called it a few days ago, in my hearing, a *mob*. Discipline unknown or *wholly* neglected. The quartermaster and commissary's departments filled with idleness, ignorance, and peculation—our hospitals crowded with six thousand sick, but half provided with necessaries or accommodations, and more dying in them in one month, than perished in the field during the whole of the last campaign. The money depreciating, without any effectual measures being taken to raise it—the country distracted with the Don Quixote attempts to regulate the prices of provisions—an *artificial* famine created by it, and a *real* one dreaded from it—the spirit of the people failing through a more intimate acquaintance with the causes of our misfortunes—many submitting daily to General Howe—and more wishing to do it, only to avoid the calamities which threaten our country.

"But is our case desperate? by no means. We have wisdom, virtue, and strength *enough* to save us, if they could be called into action. *The northern army* has shown us what Americans are capable of doing, with a *general* at their head. The spirit of the southern army is no way inferior to the spirit of the northern. A Gates, a Lee, or a Conway, would in a few weeks render them an irresistible body of men. The last of the above officers has accepted of the new office of inspector-general of our army, in order to reform abuses; but the remedy is only a palliative one.

"In one of his letters to a friend, he says, 'a great and good

God hath decreed America to be free—or the * * * * * * and weak counsellors, would have ruined her long ago.' You may rest *assured* of *each* of the facts related in this letter. The author of it is one of your Philadelphia friends. A hint of his name, if found out by the handwriting, must not be mentioned to your most intimate friend. Even the letter *must* be thrown in the fire. But some of its contents ought to be made public, in order to awaken, enlighten, and alarm our country. I rely upon your prudence, and am, dear sir, with my usual attachment to *you*, and to our beloved independence, yours sincerely.

"*His Excellency P. Henry.*"

Mr. Henry did not hesitate a moment as to the course which it was proper for him to take with this perfidious letter: he enclosed it forthwith to General Washington, in the following frank and high-minded communication:—

"WILLIAMSBURGH, *February* 20, 1770.

"DEAR SIR: You will no doubt, be surprised at seeing the enclosed letter, in which the encomiums bestowed on me are as undeserved, as the censures aimed at you are unjust. I am sorry there should be one man who counts himself my friend, who is not yours.

"Perhaps I give you needless trouble in handing you this paper. The writer of it may be too insignificant to deserve any notice. If I knew this to be the case, I should not have intruded on your time, which is so precious. But there may possibly be some scheme or party forming to your prejudice. The enclosed leads to such a suspicion. Believe me, sir, I have too high a sense of the obligations America has to you, to abet or countenance so unworthy a proceeding. The most exalted merit hath ever been found to attract envy. But I please myself with the hope, that the same fortitude and greatness of mind which have hitherto braved all the difficulties and dangers inseparable from your station, will rise superior to every attempt of the envious partisan.

"I really cannot tell who is the writer of this letter, which not a little perplexes me. The handwriting is altogether strange to me.

"To give you trouble of this gives me pain. It would suit my inclination better to give you some assistance in the great business of the war. But I will not conceal any thing from you by which you may be affected; for I really think, your personal welfare and the happiness of America are intimately connected. I beg you will be assured of that high regard and esteem, with which I ever am, dear sir, your affectionate friend and very humble servant, "P. HENRY

"*His Excellency General Washington.*"

Not having received any answer to this letter, and being filled with solicitude by the wicked conspiracy, he again wrote to General Washington, as follows:—

"WILLIAMSBURGH, *March* 5, 1778.

"DEAR SIR: By an express which Colonel Finnie sent to camp, I enclosed you an anonymous letter, which I hope got safe to hand. I am anxious to hear something that will serve to explain the strange affair, which I am now informed is taken up respecting you. Mr. Curtis has just paid us a visit, and by him I learn sundry particulars concerning General Mifflin, that much surprised me. It is very hard to trace the schemes and windings of the enemies to America. I really thought that man its friend: however, I am too far from him to judge of his present temper.

"While you face the armed enemies of our liberty in the field, and by the favour of God have been kept unhurt, I trust your country will never harbour in her bosom the miscreant who would ruin her best supporter. I wish not to flatter; but when arts, unworthy honest men, are used to defame and traduce you, I think it not amiss, but a duty, to assure you of that estimation in which the public hold you.

"Not that I think any testimony I can bear is necessary for your support, or private satisfaction; for a bare recollection of what is past must give you sufficient pleasure in every circumstance of life. But I cannot help assuring you, on this occasion, of the high sense of gratitude which all ranks of men, in this your native country, bear to you. It will give me sincere pleasure to manifest my regards, and render my best services to you or yours. I do not like to make a parade of these things, and I know you are not fond of it: however, I hope the occasion will plead my excuse.

"The assembly have, at length, empowered the executive here, to provide the Virginia troops serving with you with clothes, &c. I am making provision accordingly, and hope to do something toward it. Every possible assistance from government is afforded the commissary of provisions, whose department has not been attended to. It was taken up by me too late to do much. Indeed, the load of business devolved on me is too great to be managed well. A French ship, mounting thirty guns, that has been long chased by the English cruisers, has got into Carolina, as I hear last night.

"Wishing you all possible felicity, I am, my dear sir,

"Your ever affectionate friend,

"And very humble servant,

"P. HENRY.

"*His Excellency General Washington.*"

In reply, Mr. Henry received, shortly afterward the two following very cordial letters from the general:—

"Valley Forge, *March* 27, 1778.

"Dear Sir: About eight days past, I was honoured with your favour of the 20th ultimo. Your friendship, sir, in transmitting me the anonymous letter you had received, lays me under the most grateful obligations; and, if anything could give a still a further claim to my acknowledgments, it is the very polite and delicate terms in which you have been pleased to make the communication.

"I have ever been happy in supposing that I held a place in your esteem, and the proof of it you have afforded on this occasion makes me peculiarly so. The favourable light in which you hold me is truly flattering; but I should feel much regret if I thought the happiness of America so intimately connected with my personal welfare, as you so obligingly seem to consider it. All I can say is, that she has ever had, and I trust she ever will have, my honest exertions to promote her interests. I cannot hope that my services have been the best, but my heart tells me they have been the best that I could render.

"That I may have erred in using the means in my power for accomplishing the objects of the arduous, exalted station with which I am honoured, I cannot doubt: nor do I wish my conduct to be exempted from the reprehension it may deserve. Error is the portion of humanity, and to censure it, whether committed by this or that public character, is the prerogative of freemen.

* * * * * * *

"This is not the only secret and insidious attempt that has been made to wound my reputation. There have been others equally base, cruel, and ungenerous; because conducted with as little frankness, and proceeding from views, perhaps, as personally interested.

"I am, dear sir, &c.

"George Washington.

"*To his excellency Patrick Henry, Esq., Governor of Virginia.*"

"Camp, *March* 28, 1778.

"Dear Sir: Just as I was about to close my letter of yesterday, your favour of the fifth instant came to hand. I can only thank you again in the languague of the most undissembled gratitude for your friendship, and assure you, the indulgent disposition which Virginia in particular, and the states in general, entertain toward me, gives me the most sensible pleasure. The approbation of my country is what I wish; and as far as my abilities and opportunity will permit, I hope I shall endeavour to deserve it. It is the highest reward to a feeling mind; and happy are they who so conduct themselves as to merit it. The anonymous letter with which you were pleased to favour me, was written by * * * *, so far as I can judge from the similitude of hands. * * * * * *

"My caution to avoid everything that could injure the service, prevented me from communicating, except to a very few of my friends, the intrigues of a faction which I knew was formed against me, since it might serve to publish our internal dissensions; but their own restless zeal to advance their views has too clearly betrayed them and made concealment on my part fruitless. I cannot precisely mark the extent of their views; but it appeared, in general, that General Gates was to be exalted on the ruin of my reputation and influence.

"This I am authorized to say from undeniable facts in my own possession—from publications, the evident scope of which could not be mistaken—and from private detractions industriously circulated. * * * * *, it is commonly supposed, bore the second part in the cabal; and General Conway, I know, was a very active and malignant partisan; but I have good reason to believe, that their machinations have recoiled most sensibly upon themselves.

"I am, dear sir, &c., "GEO. WASHINGTON.

"*His excellency Patrick Henry, Esq.*
Governour of Virginia."

The plot did recoil on its contriver, and left General Washington more firmly established than ever in the confidence of his countrymen.

At the spring session of seventeen hundred and seventy-eight, Mr. Henry was again unanimously re-elected to the office of governor. Mr. Jefferson, Mr. Dandridge, and Mr. Page, the committee appointed to announce to him that event, received and reported the following answer:—

"GENTLEMEN: The general assembly in again electing me governor of this commonwealth, have done me very signal honour. I trust that their confidence thus continued in me, will not be misplaced.

"I beg you will be pleased, gentlemen, to present me to the general assembly, in terms of grateful acknowledgment for this fresh instance of their favour toward me; and to assure them, that my best endeavours shall be used to promote the public good, in that station to which they have once more been pleased to call me."

At this same session an act was passed, on account of which both Mr. Henry and the legislature have been, it is thought, improperly censured. I mean the act to attaint Josiah Philips. This man, in the summer of seventeen hundred and seventy-seven, at the head of a banditti, commenced a course of crimes in the counties of Norfolk and Princess Anne, which spread terror and consternation on every hand. Availing himself of the disaffection which prevailed in that quarter, and taking refuge from occasional pursuit in the fastnesses of the Dismal Swamp, he had carried on a species of war against the innocent and defenceless, at the bare mention of which humanity shudders.

Scarcely a night passed without witnessing the shrieks of women and children, flying by the light of their own burning houses, from the assaults of these merciless wretches; and every day was marked by the desolation of some farm, by robberies on the highway, or the assassination of some individual whose patriotism had incurred the displeasure of this fierce and bloody leader of banditti. Every attempt to take them had hitherto proved abortive; when in May, seventeen hundred and seventy-eight, the governor received the following letter from Colonel John Wilson:—

"NORFOLK COUNTY, *May* 20, 1778.

"HONOURABLE SIR: I received your letter the fourteenth instant of the twelfth April, respecting the holding the militia in readiness, and my attention to the arms and accoutrements, which I shall endeavour to comply with as far as in my power: that much, however, may not be expected from this county, I beg to observe, that the militia, of late, fail much in appearing at musters, submitting to the trifling fine of five shillings, which, they argue, they can afford to pay, by earning more at home; but I have reason to fear, through disaffection. With such a set of men, it is impossible to render any service to country or county.

"A few days since, hearing of the ravages committed by Philips and his notorious gang, I ordered fifty men to be raised out of four companies, consisting of upward of two hundred: of those only ten appeared, and it being at a private muster, I compelled twenty others into duty, putting them under the command of Captain Josiah Wilson, who immediately marched after the insurgents; and that very night, one fourth of his men deserted. Captain Wilson still pursued, but to no purpose: they were either taken to their secret places in the swamp, or concealed by their friends, that no intelligence could be obtained. He then returned, his men declaring they could stay no longer, on account of their crops.

"I consider, therefore, that rather than that they should wholly desert, it might be better to discharge them, and wait the coming of the Nansemond militia, when I trusted something might be done: but of those men I can hear no tidings; and unless they or some other better men do come, it will be out of my power to effect anything with the militia of this county; for such is their cowardly disposition, joined to their disaffection, that scarce a man, without being forced, can be raised to go after the outlyers.

"We have lost Captain Wilson since his return: having some private business at a neighbour's, within a mile of his own house, he was fired on by four men concealed in the house, and wounded in such a manner that he died in a few hours; and this will surely be the fate of a few others, if their request of the removal of the relations and friends of those villains be not granted, which I am again pressed to solicit for, and in which case neither assistance, pay, nor plunder, is expected; conceiving that to distress their supporters is the only means by which we can root those wretches from us, and thereby establish peace and security to ourselves and families.

"I am, with great respect, honourable sir,

"Your most obedient humble servant,

"John Wilson."

"*May* 24.—A company of about fifty men are now come from Nansemond; but I am informed by the captain, that they will not be kept above two days, five having deserted already.

"John Wilson."

The governor immediately enclosed this letter to the house of delegates, with the following communication:—

"*The Honourable Benjamin Harrison, Esq., Speaker of the House of Delegates.*

"Williamsburgh, *May* 27, 1778.

"Sir: I was always unwilling to trouble the general assembly with anything that seemed of too little consequence for deliberation. In that view I have for some time considered the insurrection in Princess Anne and Norfolk. I have from time to time given orders to the commanding officers of those counties, to draw from the militia a force sufficient to quell it. These officers have often complained of the difficulty of the business, arising partly from the local circumstances attending it, but chiefly from the backwardness and even disaffection of the people. In order to remove the latter obstacle, I gave orders for one hundred men to be drawn out into this service, from Nansemond county; but I am sorry to say, the almost total want of discipline in that and too many other militias in the state, seems to forbid the hope of their doing much to effect.

"Col. Wilson, whose letter I enclose, has several times given me to understand, that, in his opinion, the removal of such families as are in league with insurgents, was a step absolutely necessary, and has desired me to give orders accordingly. But thinking that the executive power is not competent to such a purpose, I must beg leave to submit the whole matter to the assembly, who are the only judges how far the methods of proceeding directed by law are to be dispensed with on this occasion.

"A company of regulars, drawn from the several stations, will be ordered to co-operate with the militia, though indeed their scanty numbers will not permit it to be done without hazard. But I cannot help thinking this ought to be encountered; for an apparent disposition to disturb the peace of this state has been manifested by these people during the whole course of the present war. It seems, therefore, that no effort to crush these desperadoes should be spared.

"My duty would no longer suffer me to withhold these several matters from the view of the general assembly, to whom I beg leave to refer them through you.

"With great regard,
"I have the honour to be, sir,
"Your most obedient humble servant,
"P. HENRY."

This letter was communicated to the house on the day of its date, and was immediately referred to a committee of the whole house, on the state of the commonwealth. That committee was immediately formed; but not having time to go through the subject, had leave to sit again. On the next day the house again resolved itself into a committee of the whole, and after some time spent therein, the speaker resumed the chair, and Mr. Carter reported on the subject of Philips, as follows:—

"Information being received, that a certain Philips, with divers others, his associates and confederates, have levied war against this commonwealth within the counties of Norfolk and Princess Anne, committing murders, burning houses, wasting farms, and doing other acts of enormity, in defiance of the officers of justice—

"Resolved, That it is the opinion of this committee, that if the said Philips, his associates, and confederates, do not render themselves to some officer, civil or military, within this commonwealth, on or before day of June, in this present year, such of them as fail so to do, ought to be attainted of high treason; and that in the meantime, and before such render, it shall be lawful for any person, with or without orders, to pursue and slay, or otherwise to take and deliver to justice, the said Philips, his associates and confederates."

Mr. Jefferson, Mr. Smith, and Mr. Tyler, were the committee appointed to prepare and bring in a bill, pursuant to this resolution, which was reported on the same day, and read the first time. *On the two succeeding days* it was read a *second* and *third* time; and thus *regularly passed through the forms of the lower house.* It was communicated to the senate by Mr Jefferson, on the thirtieth day of the month, and returned, passed by them, without amendment, on the first day of June, which was the last day of the session. The act, as it stands upon the statute book of the session, is as follows:—

"*An act to attaint Josiah Philips and others, unless they render themselves to justice within a certain time.*

"Whereas a certain *Josiah Philips*, labourer, of the parish of *Lynhaven* and county of *Princess Anne*, together with divers others, inhabitants of the counties of *Princess Anne*, and *Norfolk*, and citizens of this commonwealth, contrary to their fidelity, associating and confederating together, have levied war against this commonwealth, within the same, committing murders, burning houses, wasting farms, and doing other acts of hostility in the said counties of *Princess Anne* and *Norfolk*, and still continue to exercise the same enormities on the good people of this commonwealth; and, whereas, the delays which would attend the proceeding to outlaw the said offenders, according to the usual forms and procedures of the courts of law, would leave the said good people, for a long time exposed to murder and devastation:—

"*Be it, therefore, enacted by the general assembly*, That if the said *Josiah Philips*, his associates and confederates, shall not, on or before the last day of *June*, in the present year, render themselves to the governor, or to some member of the privy council, judge of the general court, justice of the peace, or commissioned officer of the regular troops, navy or militia of this commonwealth, in order to their trials for the treasons, murders, and other felonies by them committed, that, then, such of them, the said *Josiah Philips*, his associates and confederates, as shall not so render him or themselves, shall stand and be convicted and attainted of high treason, and shall suffer the pains of death, and incur all forfeitures, penalties, and disabilities, prescribed by the law against those convicted and attainted of high treason; and that execution of this sentence of attainder shall be done, by order of the general court, to be entered so soon as may be conveniently, after notice that any of the said offenders are in custody of the keeper of the public jail.

"And if any person committed to the custody of the keeper of the public jail, as an associate or confederate of the said *Josiah Philips*, shall allege that he has not been of his associates or confederates, at any time after the first day of *July*, in the year of our Lord one thousand seven hundred and seventy-seven, at which time the said murders and devastations were begun, a petit jury shall be summoned and charged, according to the forms of the law, to try, in the presence of the said court, the fact so alleged; and if it be found against the defendant, execution of this act shall be done as before directed.

"And that the good people of this commonwealth may not, in the meantime, be subject to the unrestrained hostilities of the said insurgents: *Be it further enacted*, That from and after the passing of this act, it shall be lawful for any person, with or without orders, to pursue and slay the said *Josiah Philips*, and any others who have been of his associates or confederates, at any time after the said first day of *July* aforesaid, and shall not have previously rendered him or themselves to any of the officers, civil or military, before described, or otherwise to take and deliver them to justice, to be dealt with according to law. *Provided*, that the person so slain be in arms at the time, or endeavouring to escape being taken."

Philips was apprehended in the course of the autumn, and indicted by Mr. Edmund Randolph, attorney-general, *for highway-robbery*, simply. *On this charge he was tried* at the October term of the general court, *convicted*, and *executed:* so that the act of attainder was never brought to bear upon him at all. This is the whole case of Josiah Philips. The reader will judge whether Mr. Henry deserves censure for having communicated to the legislature the letter of Col. Wilson; or whether that body acted with too much severity toward a wretch, who had not only set the laws of his country at defiance, but was waging a cruel and dastardly war upon men without arms, upon women and children; and acting, not the part of a brave and open enemy, but that of an enemy of the human family.

Just at the close of Mr. Henry's administration, Virginia suffered an invasion of a few days, under the British officers Collin and Matthew. They seized Fort Nelson, near Norfolk, destroyed the naval stores at Gosport, burnt Suffolk, and disappeared before the militia could be rallied to chastise their insolence. This occurred in the month of May, seventeen hundred and seventy-nine; and the facility and impunity with which the enterprise was accomplished, very probably suggested the more serious invasion of the state, which afterward took place under the traitor Arnold.

It would seem, that a wish was entertained to re-elect Mr. Henry to the office of governor a fourth time, although the constitution declared him ineligible after the third year. The impression seems to have been that his appointment for the first year, not having been made by delegates who had themselves been elected under the constitution, ought not to be counted as one of the constitutional years of service. Mr. Henry, however, had too scrupulous a respect for that instrument to accept the office, even in a doubtful case; and, therefore, addressed the following letter to the speaker:—

"*May* 28, 1779.

"SIR: The term for which I had the honour to be elected governor by the late assembly being just about to expire, and the constitution, *as I think*, making me ineligible to that office, I take the liberty to communicate to the assembly through you, sir, my intention to retire in four or five days.

"I have thought it necessary to give this notification of my design, in order that the assembly may have the earliest opportunity of deliberating upon the choice of a successor to me in office. With great regard,

"I have the honour to be, sir,

"Your most obedient servant,

"P. HENRY."

Thus closed Mr. Henry's administration: and although he had not an opportunity of distinguishing it by any splendid achievements, it is honour enough that he had given universal satisfaction, and that he retired with a popularity confirmed and increased.

It has been thought best not to break the chain of the narrative, as to his public character, by noticing the changes which had before this time occurred in his domestic relations. It may be proper to pause here for the purpose of supplying this omission.

His wife, the partner of his youth, and the solace of his early adversities, had died in the year seventeen hundred and seventy-five, after having made him the father of six children. The anguish of this blow was mitigated by the circumstance of her having been, for several years, in a state of ill health and of suffering, from which there was no hope of recovery; and to her, therefore, death indeed "came like a friend to relieve her from pain."

Neither had the father lived to witness the promotion of his son to the highest honours of the republic. He had lived however, long enough to enjoy the first bloom of his fame, and to see him the most celebrated and rising character in the state. He had died about the year seventeen hundred and seventy, and left behind him a name highly respectable for every private and social virtue.

His uncle, for whom he seems to have had a strong affection, had died during his government, and in token of his affection and respect, had appointed him the executor of his will.

His tender and indulgent mother still survived, and felt all that pure and exquisite delight, which the well-deserved honours of her son were calculated to inspire.

After the death of his wife, Mr. Henry sold the farm called Scotch Town, on which he had resided in Hanover, and purchased eight or ten thousand acres of valuable land in the county of *Henry;* a county which had been erected during his government, and which had taken its name from him, as did afterward its neighbouring county of *Patrick*. In the year seventeen hundred and seventy-seven, he intermarried with Dorothea, the daughter of Mr. Nathaniel W. Dandridge, with whom, after the resignation or expiration of his office, he removed to his newly-acquired estate, called Leatherwood, and there resumed the practice of the law. In the year seventeen hundred and eighty, we find him again in the assembly, and one of the most active members in the house.

During the winter session of this year, General Gates entered the city of Richmond from his southern campaign, where he had most wofully fulfilled General Lee's prediction.* His total defeat at Camden, and a series of subsequent ill fortune, had left South Carolina completely in the hands of the victorious British; and to increase his humiliation, congress had not only superseded him in that command, by the substitution of General Greene, but had passed a resolution requiring the commander-in-chief to order a court of inquiry on his conduct. Under these accumulated disgraces, the unfortunate general entered the city of Richmond; when Mr. Henry moved a resolution which displays, in a most engaging light, the delicate and generous sensibility of his character; it was as follows:—

"Resolved, That a committee of four be appointed to wait on Major-general Gates, and to assure him of the high regard and esteem of this house; that the remembrance of his former glorious services cannot be obliterated by any reverse of fortune; but that this house, ever mindful of his great merit, will omit no opportunity of testifying to the world, the gratitude which, as a member of the American union, this country owes to him in his military character."

The author may be permitted to say of a state, which is *his* only by adoption, that in an assembly of Virginians, this generous resolution could not fail to pass *unanimously*. The committee appointed to communicate it to the general, were, Mr. Henry, Mr. Richard H. Lee, Mr. Zane, and General Nelson. We may be assured, that a committee, chosen with so

* When Gen. Charles Lee heard of Gen. Gates's appointment to the command of the southern army, he foretold that "his *northern laurels* would be turned into *southern willows*."

much judgment,* discharged their duty in a manner the most grateful to the wounded feelings of the general; and on the next day, Mr. Henry reported the following answer, which was spread upon the journal:—

"RICHMOND, *December* 28, 1780.

"SIR: I shall ever remember with the utmost gratitude, the high honour this day done me by the honourable the house of delegates of Virginia. When engaged in the noble cause of freedom and the United States, I devoted myself entirely to the service of obtaining the great end of their union. That I have been once unfortunate is my great mortification; but, let the event of my future services be what they may, they will, as they always have been, be directed by the most faithful integrity, and animated by the truest zeal for the honour and interest of the United States. "HORATIO GATES."

The spring and summer of the next year presented a period of even deeper darkness than the autumn of seventeen hundred and seventy-six. Virginia, had not, hitherto, been the theatre of hostile operations of a very serious character; her sufferings had been rather those of sympathy with her northern and southern sisters; but in this year the calamities of war were brought home to her own bosom. Arnold's invasion took place in January: having carried his ravages as high up as Richmond and Westham, he retired to Portsmouth, where he rested till April, when General Philips succeeded to the command, and paid another visit of desolation to Manchester.

In the next month came Lord Cornwallis, with his victorious army from the south, driving everything before him, and striking terror into whatsoever quarter he approached. Having formed a junction between his forces and those under the command of General Philips, there was no longer a military force in the state which had the power to resist him. The inferior body of republican troops, under the Marquis la Fayette, moved before him, without the ability to strike a blow; and Cornwallis roamed at pleasure, and without any apprehension, through the interior of the state.

The seventh of May was the day appointed by law for the meeting of the assembly at Richmond. A few members met and took the oaths prescribed by law; but the number not being sufficient to proceed to business, the house was adjourned from day to day until the tenth; when, upon information of the ap-

* Mr. Henry, the mover, had recently closed his administration with honour, as the first republican governor of Virginia, and was the most considerable man in the commonwealth; Mr. Lee was a member of the congress, whose vote we have just mentioned; Mr. Zane represented the county in which Gen. Gates lived; and Gen. Nelson was the most popular military character in the state.

proach of the enemy, they adjourned to the twenty-fourth, to meet at Charlottesville. It was not until the twenty-eighth, that a house was formed to proceed to business at this place; when Mr. Benjamin Harrison was elected speaker, and after making the usual acknowledgments for that honour, proceeded to address the following remarks to the house; which I quote, not because they are a very favourable specimen of Mr. Harrison's oratory, but to show the panic which prevailed even among the first men of the country:—

"The critical and dangerous situation of our country leads me to hope, that my recommending it to you to *despatch* the weighty matters that will be under your consideration, *with all convenient speed*, will not be taken amiss; the people expect that effectual and decisive measures will be taken to rid them of an implacable enemy, that are now roaming at large in the very bowels of our country, and I have no doubt of your answering their expectations; the mode of doing this may indeed be difficult: but it not being my province to point it out, I shall leave it to your wisdom, in full confidence that everything that is necessary for quieting the minds and dispelling the fears of our constituents, will be done."

Eight days after this address, Mr. John Jouett, a citizen of the place, entered the town on horseback, at full speed, and announced the near and rapid approach of Tarlton, at the head of three hundred cavalry and mounted infantry. The house had just met, and was about to commence business, when the alarming cry of "Tarlton and the British," was spread through the village; and they had scarcely taken time to adjourn informally to Staunton, when Tarlton rushed like a thunderbolt into the village, in the confident expectation of seizing the whole assembly; but the birds had flown. He made seven of them only prisoners. The rest reassembled in Staunton, on the seventh of June. On the tenth of June, a false report of his approach produced another panic; and the house having merely taken time to resolve that they would meet at the Warm Springs, if it should be found dangerous to meet in Staunton on the next day; and on their failure so to do, that the speaker might call a meeting, when and where he pleased, again broke up and dispersed.

It was at this period of almost hopeless darkness, when the energies of the state seemed to have been pretty nearly paralyzed, that the project of a dictator was again revived; and it is again highly probable, that Mr. Henry was the character who was in view for that office. Inquiries have been made of the surviving members of that assembly to ascertain whether the project could be traced to him, or whether he had any kind of participation in the proposal; but those inquiries have resulted in a conviction of his entire innocence. The project came from other quarters, and seems to have been the last refuge of that general despair which for a short time pervaded the whole commonwealth.

But this period of deep darkness was the harbinger of breaking day. The morning dawned with the arrival of those aids from France, which Mr. Henry had so long ago predicted; and the sun of American independence arose to set no more. He lived to witness the glorious issue of that revolution which his genius had set in motion; and (to repeat his own prophetic language, before the commencement of the struggle) "to see America take her stand among the nations of the earth." The contest closed with the capture of Cornwallis, at Little York, on the nineteenth of October, seventeen hundred and eighty-one; and thus, the ball of the revolution rested in the same state in which it had received the first impulse.

This enlightened and patriotic statesman, however, was not yet inclined to indulge himself in that repose to which he was so well entitled. The constitution of the state had as yet been tried only in war, when the sense of common danger, and their ardour in the common cause, might of themselves have been sufficient to keep the people together, and to supply, in a good degree, the place of government. It was necessary to see how the instrument would work in peace; what assurance it gave of public order and well-regulated liberty; or whether any, and what defects in the plan required amendment.

There were other considerations, too, which called loudly for attention. The war had left the country in a most deplorable situation; poor and in debt; its warriors unrequited; its finances wholly deranged; its jurisprudence unsettled; and all its faculties weak, disordered, and exhausted. This was no time for the patriot to quit his post. It demanded all his vigilance to guard the infant republic against the machinations of its enemies, both abroad and at home; it required all his care and all his skill to heal the numerous disorders which had flowed from the war; to nurse the new-born nation into health and strength; to develop its resources, moral and physical; and thus to give security and permanence to its liberties.

With the view of contributing his aid to those great objects, Mr. Henry still continued to represent the county of his residence, in the legislature of the state, and controlled the proceedings of that body, with a weight of personal authority, and a power of eloquence, which it was extremely difficult, and indeed almost impossible to resist. A striking evidence of this power was given, immediately on the close of the revolution, in his advocating the return of the British refugees. The measure was most vehemently opposed. There was no class of human beings against whom such violent and deep-rooted prejudices existed. The name of "British tory," was of itself enough, at that period, to throw almost any company in Virginia into flames, and was pretty generally a signal for a coat of tar and feathers; a signal which was not very often disobeyed. Mr. Henry's proposition in favour of a class of people so odious could not fail to excite the strongest surprise; and was, at first, received with a repugnance apparently insuperable.

The late Judge Tyler, then the speaker of the house, opposed it in the committee of the whole, with great warmth; and in the course of the discussion, turning from the chairman to Mr. Henry, he asked him, "how *he*, above all other men, could think of inviting into his family, an enemy, from whose insults and injuries he had suffered so severely?" To this Mr. Henry answered, that "the personal feelings of a politician ought not to be permitted to enter those walls. The question," he said, "was a national one, and in deciding it, if they acted wisely, nothing would be regarded but the interest of the nation.

"On the altar of his country's good he was willing to sacrifice all personal resentments, all private wrongs—and he flattered himself, that he was not the only man in the house who was capable of making such a sacrifice. We have, sir," said he, "an extensive country, *without population*—what can be a more obvious policy than that this country ought to be peopled? —*people*, sir, form the strength, and constitute the wealth of a nation. I want to see our vast forests filled up by some process a little more speedy than the ordinary course of nature. I wish to see these states rapidly ascending to that rank which their natural advantages authorize them to hold among the nations of the earth. Cast your eyes, sir, over this extensive country—observe the salubrity of your climate; the variety and fertility of your soil—and see that soil intersected in every quarter by bold, navigable streams, flowing to the east and to the west, as if the finger of Heaven were marking out the course of your settlements, inviting you to enterprise, and pointing the way to wealth.

"Sir, you are destined, at some time or other, to become a great agricultural and commercial people; the only question is, whether you choose to reach this point by slow gradations, and at some distant period; lingering on through a long and sickly minority; subjected, meanwhile, to the machinations, insults, and oppressions of enemies, foreign and domestic, without sufficient strength to resist and chastise them; or whether you choose rather to rush at once, as it were, to the full enjoyment of those high destinies, and be able to cope, single-handed, with the proudest oppressor of the old world.

If you prefer the latter course, as I trust you do, encourage emigration; encourage the husbandmen, the mechanics, the merchants of the old world, to come and settle in this land of promise; make it the home of the skilful, the industrious, the fortunate and happy, as well as the asylum of the distressed; fill up the measure of your population as speedily as you can, by the means which Heaven hath placed in your power; and I venture to prophesy there are those now living, who will see this favoured land among the most powerful on earth; able, sir, to take care of herself, without resorting to that policy which is always so dangerous, though sometimes unavoidable, of calling in foreign aid.

"Yes, sir; they will see her great in arts and in arms—her golden harvests waving over fields of immeasurable extent; her commerce penetrating the most distant seas, and her cannon silencing the vain boasts of those who now proudly affect to rule the waves. But, sir, you must have *men;* you cannot get along without them; those heavy forests of valuable timber, under which your lands are groaning, must be cleared away; those vast riches which cover the face of your soil, as well as those which lie hid in its bosom, are to be developed and gathered only by the skill and enterprise of men; your timber, sir, must be worked up into ships, to transport the productions of the soil from which it has been cleared; then you must have commercial men and commercial capital, to take off your productions, and find the best markets for them abroad; your great want, sir, is the want of men; and these you must have, and will have speedily, if you are wise.

"Do you ask how you are to get them? Open your doors, sir, and they will come in; the population of the old world is full to overflowing; that population is ground, too, by the oppressions of the governments under which they live. Sir, they are already standing on tiptoe upon their native shores, and looking to your coasts with a wistful and longing eye; they see here a land blessed with natural and political advantages, which are not equalled by those of any other country upon earth; a land on which a gracious Providence hath emptied the horn of abundance; a land over which peace hath now stretched forth her white wings, and where content and plenty lie down at every door!

"Sir, they see something still more attractive than all this; they see a land in which liberty, hath taken up her abode; that liberty, whom they had considered as a fabled goddess, existing only in the fancies of poets; they see her here, a real divinity; her altars rising on every hand throughout these happy states; her glories chanted by three millions of tongues; and the whole region smiling under her blessed influence. Sir, let but this our celestial goddess, liberty, stretch forth her fair hand toward the people of the old world; tell them to come, and bid them welcome; and you will see them pouring in from the north, from the south, from the east, and from the west; your wildernesses will be cleared and settled; your deserts will smile; your ranks will be filled; and you will soon be in a condition to defy the powers of any adversary.

"But gentlemen object to any accession from Great Britain; and particularly to the return of the British refugees. Sir, I feel no objection to the return of these deluded people; they have, to be sure mistaken their own interests most wofully, and most wofully have they suffered the punishment due to their offences. But the relations which we bear to them and to their native country are now changed; their king hath acknowledged our independence;—the quarrel is over; peace hath returned and found us a free people. Let us have the magnanimity, sir, to lay aside our antipathies and prejudices, and consider the subject in a political light.

"Those are an enterprising, moneyed people; they will be serviceable in taking off the surplus produce of our lands, and supplying us with necessaries, during the infant state of our manufactures. Even if they be inimical to us in point of feeling and principle, I can see no objection, in a political view, in making them tributary to our advantage. And as I have no prejudices to prevent my making this use of them, so, sir, I have no fear of any mischief that they can do us. Afraid of *them!*—what, sir,"—said he, rising to one of his loftiest attitudes, and assuming a look of the most indignant and sovereign contempt,—"shall *we*, who have laid the proud British *lion* at our feet, now be afraid of his *whelps?*"

The force of this figure, and the energy with which it was brought out, are said to have produced an effect that made the house start simultaneously. It continued to be admired, long after the occasion which gave it birth had passed away, and was frequently quoted by Mr. Wythe to his students, while professor of law at William and Mary college, as a happy specimen of those valuable figures, which unite the beauty of decoration with the effect of argument.

The gentleman (Judge Tyler) to whom I am indebted for the preceding incident, has favoured me also with the following one, which I shall give in his own words:—

"Mr. Henry espoused the measure which took off the restraints on British commerce, before any treaty was entered into; in which I opposed him on this ground, that that measure would expel from this country the trade of every other nation, on account of our habits, language, and the manner of conducting business on credit between us and them: also on this ground, in addition to the above, that if we changed the then current of commerce, we should drive away all competition, and never perhaps should regain it, (which has literally happened.) In reply to these observations, he was beyond all expression eloquent and sublime.

"After painting the distresses of the people, struggling through a perilous war, cut off from commerce so long that they were naked, and unclothed, he concluded with a figure, or rather a series of figures, which I shall never forget, because, beautiful as they were in themselves, their effect was heightened beyond all description, by the manner in which he acted what he spoke:—'Why,' said he, 'should we fetter commerce? If a man is in chains, he droops and bows to the earth, for his spirits are broken,' looking sorrowfully at his feet; 'but let him twist the fetters from his legs, and he will stand erect,—straightening himself, and assuming a look of proud defiance. Fetter not commerce, sir—let her be as free as air—she will range the whole creation, and return on the wings of the four winds of heaven, to bless the land with plenty.'"

In the fall session of seventeen hundred and eighty-four, Mr. Henry proposed and advocated several measures which deserve particular mention:—one of them, on account of the originality and boldness of mind from which it proceeded; and others, because they have sometimes been made the subjects of censure against him. The first respects the Indians. Those unfortunate beings, the natural enemies of the white people, whom they regarded as lawless intruders into a country set apart for themselves by the Great Spirit, had continued, from their first landing, to harass the white settlements, and hang, like a pestilence on their frontier, as it advanced itself toward the west.

The story of their accumulated wrongs, handed down by tradition from father to son, and emblazoned with all the colours of Indian oratory, had kept their war-fires smoking from age to age, and the hatchet and scalping-knife perpetually bright. They had long since abandoned the hope of being able, by their single strength, to exterminate the usurpers of their soil; but either from the spirit of habitual and deadly revenge, or from the policy of checking, as far as they could, the perpetually extending encroachments of the white men, they had waged an unremitting war upon their borders, marked with horrors which eclipse the wildest fictions of the legendary tale. These people, too, besides the mischiefs to which they were prompted by their own feelings and habits, were an ever-ready and a most terrific scourge, in the hands of any enemy with whom this country might be at variance.

The stories of these border skirmishes, which yet live in the traditions of the west, are highly worthy of collection. They exhibit scenes of craft, boldness, and ferocity, on the part of the savages, and of heroic and desperate defence by the semi-barbarous men, women, and children, who were the objects of these attacks, which mark the characters of both sides in a most interesting manner. Those tales of the long, obstinate, and bloody defence of log-cabins; of the almost incredible achievements of women and little boys; of the sometimes total and sometimes partial havoc of families; of the captivity, tortures, and death of some; and the miraculous escape, wanderings, and preservation of others—would form a book of more interest than any other that could be put into the hands of a Virginia reader; and would furnish the subject of many a novel, drama, and painting. The adventure of Captain Smith and Pocahontas, if you put aside the dignity of their characters, is cold and tame, when compared with some which are related among the western inhabitants of this state.

Dunmore, although thanked at the time for his services, was afterward believed, by the house of burgesses, to have made use of them in the years seventeen hundred and seventy-four and five, in order to draw off the attention of the colonists from the usurpation of the British court: and, in the recent war of the revolution, that merciless enemy had been again let loose upon our frontier, with all the terrors of savage warfare. The return of peace with Britain had given us but a short respite from their hostilities. I perceive, by the journal of the house of delegates, that on the fifth of November, seventeen hundred and eighty-four, it was, on the motion of Mr. Henry,

"Resolved, That the governor, with the advice of council, be requested to adopt such measures as may be found necessary to avert the danger of hostilities with the Indians, and to incline them to treat with the commissioners of congress; and for that purpose to draw on the treasury for any sum of money not exceeding one thousand pounds, which shall stand charged to the account of money issued for the contingent charges of government."

A treaty with the Indians, however, was well known to be a miserable expedient; the benefits of which would scarcely last as long as the ceremonies that produced it. The reflecting politician could not help seeing, that, in order to remove the annoyance effectually, the remedy must go to the root of the disease—that that inveterate and fatal enmity which rankled in the hearts of the Indians must be eradicated—that a common interest and congenial feelings between them and their white neighbours must be created—and humanity and civilization gradually superinduced upon the Indian character. The difficulty lay in devising a mode to effect these objects. The white people who inhabited the frontier, from the constant state of warfare in which they lived with the Indians, had imbibed much of their character; and learned to delight so highly in scenes of crafty, bloody, and desperate conflict, that they as often gave as they received the provocation to hostilities.

Hunting, which was their occupation, became dull and tiresome, unless diversified occasionally by the more animated and piquant amusement of an Indian skirmish; just as "the blood more stirs to rouse a lion than to start a hare." The policy, therefore, which was to produce the deep and beneficial change that was meditated, must have respect to both sides, and be calculated to implant kind affections in bosoms which at present were filled only with reciprocal and deadly hatred. The remedy suggested by Mr. Henry was to encourage marriages between these conterminous enemies; and having succeeded, in the committee of the whole house, in procuring the report of a resolution to this effect, he prepared a bill which he is said to have advocated with irresistible earnestness and eloquence. The inducements held out by this bill, to promote these marriages, were, pecuniary bounties to be given on the certificate of marriage, and to be repeated at the birth of each child; exemption from taxes; and the free use of a seminary of learning, to be erected for the purpose, and supported at the expense of the state.

This bill, which is thought worthy of preservation, as a political curiosity, is as follows:—

"*A bill for the encouragement of marriages with the Indians.*

"Whereas, intermarriages between the citizens of this commonwealth and the Indians living in its neighbourhood, may have great effect in conciliating the friendship and confidence of the latter, whereby not only their civilization may in some degree be finally brought about, but in the meantime, their hostile inroads be prevented: for encouraging such intermarriages,

Be it enacted by the General Assembly, That if any free white male inhabitant of this commonwealth shall, according to the laws thereof, enter into the bonds of matrimony with an Indian female, being of lawful age, and under no precontract to any Indian male, and shall thereby induce her to become an inhabitant of this commonwealth, and to live with him in the character of a wife, such male inhabitant, on producing a certificate of such marriage, under the hand and seal of the person cohabitating the same, shall be entitled to receive a premium of ——— pounds, out of any unappropriated money which the treasurer may have in his hands, or of such money as may hereafter be appropriated to such use; shall, over and above such premium, be entitled to the sum of —— pounds, for every child proceeding from such marriage, on a certificate of the birth thereof, and their apparent cohabitancy, under the hand and seal of any one justice of the peace of the county in which he resides, and shall, moreover, be exempted from all taxes on his person and property for and during the time of such cohabitancy.

"*And be it further enacted,* That if any free female inhabitant of this commonwealth shall, in like manner, intermarry with any male Indian of lawful age, they shall, on a certificate thereof, as aforesaid, be entitled to —— pounds, to be paid as aforesaid, and laid out under the direction of the court of the county within which such marriage shall be celebrated, in the purchase of live stock, for his and her use, and such male Indian shall be annually, on the first day of October, entitled to —— pounds, to be paid as aforesaid, and laid out under the direction of the said court, in the purchase of clothes for his use; and each male child proceeding from such intermarriage, shall, at the age of ——— be removed to such public seminary of learning, as the executive may direct, and be there educated until the age of twenty-one, at the public expense, to be defrayed out of such funds as may hereafter be appropriated to the same. And the governor, with the advice of council, is hereby authorized and desired to cause the benefit of this provision to be extended to all such male children; and if any such male Indian shall become an inhabitant of this commonwealth, he shall be moreover exempted from all taxes on his person or the property he may acquire.

"*And be it further enacted,* That the offspring of the intermarriages aforesaid, shall be entitled, in all respects, to the same rights and privileges, under the laws of this commonwealth, as if they had proceeded from intermarriages among free white inhabitants thereof.

"*And be it further enacted,* That the executive do take the most effectual and speedy measures for promulgating this act to such tribe or tribes of Indians as they may think necessary."

On the third reading of the bill, the first blank was filled with *ten*—the second with *five*—the third with *ten*—the fourth with *three*—and the fifth with *ten years*.

While Mr. Henry continued a member of the house, the progress of this bill was unimpeded. It passed through a first and second reading, and was engrossed for its final passage, when his election as governor took effect, and displaced him from the floor: on the third day after which event the bill was read a third time and rejected.

It were a useless waste of time to speculate on the probable effects of this measure, had it succeeded. It is considered, however, as indicative of great humanity of character, and as marked with great boldness, if not soundness of policy. Mr. Henry is said to have been extremely sanguine as to its efficacy, and to have supported it by some of the highest displays of his eloquence.

The other two measures to which I have adverted, as having been patronised by Mr. Henry, at this session, were, the incorporation of the Protestant Episcopal church, and what is called "a general assessment." These measures have been frequently stated, in conversation, as proofs of a leaning on the part of Mr. Henry, toward an established church, and that, too, the aristocratic church of England. To test the justness of this charge, the journals of the house of delegates have been examined, and this is the result of the evidence which they furnish: on the seventeenth of November, seventeen hundred and eighty-four, Mr. Matthews reported from the committee of the whole house, on the state of the commonwealth, the following resolution:—

"*Resolved*, That it is the opinion of this committee, that acts ought to pass for the incorporation of *all societies of the Christian religion, which may apply for the same.*"

The ays and noes having been called for, on the passage of this resolution, were, ays, sixty-two, noes, twenty-three; Mr. Henry being with the majority.

The principle being thus established in relation to *all* religious societies, which should desire a legal existence for the benefit of acquiring and holding property to the use of their respective churches, leave was given, on the same day, to bring in a bill to incorporate the clergy of the Protestant Episcopal church, which had brought itself within that principle by having applied for an act of incorporation; and Mr. Henry was one, but not the chairman,* of the committee appointed to bring in that bill.

How a measure which holds out to *all* religious societies, *equally*, the same benefit, can be charged with partiality, because accepted by one only, it is not very easy to discern. It would seem, to an ordinary mind, that on the same principle, the Christian religion itself might be charged with partiality, since its offers, though made to all, are accepted but by a few: and it is very certain, that if Mr. Henry is to be suspected of

* The chairman was Mr. Carter H. Harrison; the rest of the committee were, Mr. Henry, Mr. Thomas Smith, Mr. William Anderson, and Mr. Tazewell

a bias toward an established church, on account of this vote, the charge will reach some of the foremost and best-established republicans in the state, whose names stand recorded with Mr. Henry's on this occasion, and who hold to this day the undiminished confidence of their countrymen.

The other measure, the general assessment, proceeded from a number of petitions from different counties of the commonwealth, which prayed that as all persons enjoyed the benefits of religion, all might be required to contribute to the expense of supporting *some form of worship or other.* The committee to whom these petitions were referred, reported a bill whose preamble sets forth the grounds of the proceeding, and furnishes a conclusive refutation of the charge of partiality to any particular form of religion. The bill is entitled, "A bill, establishing a provision for teachers of the Christian religion;" and its preamble is in the following words:—

"Whereas the general diffusion of Christian knowledge hath a natural tendency to correct the morals of men, restrain their vices, and preserve the peace of society; which cannot be effected without a competent provision for learned teachers, who may be thereby enabled to devote their time and attention to the duty of instructing such citizens as, from their circumstances and want of education, cannot otherwise attain such knowledge; and it is judged such provision may be made by the legislature, *without counteracting the liberal principle heretofore adopted and intended to be preserved, by abolishing all distinctions of pre-eminence among the different societies or communities of Christians.*"

The provisions of the bill are in the strictest conformity with the principles announced in the close of the preamble; the persons subject to taxes are required, at the time of giving in a list of their titheables, to declare to what particular religious society they chose to appropriate the sums assessed upon them, respectively; and, in the event of their failing or declining to specify any appropriation, the sums thus circumstanced are directed to be paid to the treasurer, and applied by the general assembly to the encouragement of *seminaries of learning*, in the counties where such sums shall arise.

If there be any evidence of a leaning toward any particular religious sect in this bill, or any indication of a desire for an established church, the author of these sketches has not been able to discover them. Mr. Henry was a sincere believer in the Christian religion, and had a strong desire for the successful propagation of the gospel, but there was no tincture of bigotry or intolerance in his sentiments; nor have I been able to learn that he had a punctilious preference for any particular form of worship. His faith regarded the vital spirit of the gospel, and busied itself not at all with external ceremonies or controverted tenets.

Both these bills, "for incorporating the Protestant Episcopal church," and "establishing a provision for teachers of the Christian religion," were reported after Mr. Henry had ceased to be a member of the house; but the resolutions on which they were founded were adopted while he continued a member, and had his warmest support. The first bill passed into a law; the last was rejected by a small majority on the third reading.

The same session afforded Mr. Henry a double opportunity of gratifying, in the most exquisite manner, that naturally bland and courteous spirit, which so eminently distinguished his character. General Washington and the Marquis la Fayette, both of them objects of the warmest love and gratitude to this country, visited Richmond in November. They arrived on different days. The general entered the city on the fifteenth, and the journal of the next morning exhibits the following order:—

"The house being informed of the arrival of General Washington in this city, *Resolved, nemine contradicente*, that as a mark of their reverence for his character, and affection for his person, a committee of five members be appointed to wait upon him, with the respectful regard of this house, to express to him the satisfaction they feel in the opportunity afforded by his presence of offering this tribute to his merits; and to assure him that as they not only retain the most lasting impressions of the transcendant services rendered in his late public character, but have, since his return to private life, experienced proofs that no change of situation can turn his thoughts from the welfare of his country, so his happiness can never cease to be an object of their most devout wishes and fervent supplications.

"And a committee was appointed of Mr. Henry, Mr. Jones, (of King George,) Mr. Madison, Mr. Carter H. Harrison, and Mr. Carrington."

To this spontaneous and unanimous burst of feeling, General Washington returned an answer marked with his characteristic modesty, and full of the most touching sensibility. It is worthy of insertion, as showing, in a soft and winning light, a character with which we are apt to associate only the images of a dignity and reserve, approaching to sternness. "Gentlemen," said he, "my sensibility is deeply affected by this distinguished mark of the affectionate regard of your honourable house. I lament, on this occasion, the want of those powers which would enable me to do justice to my feelings; and shall rely upon your indulgent report to supply the defect: at the same time, I pray you to present for me, the strongest assurances of unalterable affection and gratitude, for this last pleasing and flattering attention of my country."

The marquis, who had been to France since the close of hostilities, made his entree on the morning of the seventeenth of November; and the house, immediately on its meeting, came to the following resolution:—

"The house being informed of the arrival, this morning, of the Marquis de la Fayette in this city, Resolved, *nemine contradicente,* that a committee of five be appointed, to present to him the affectionate respects of this house, to signify to him their sensibility to the pleasing proof given by this visit to the United States, and to this state in particular, that the benevolent and honourable sentiments which originally prompted him to embark in the hazardous fortunes of America, still render the prosperity of its affairs an object of his attention and regard; and to assure him, that they cannot review the scenes of blood and danger through which we have arrived at the blessings of peace, without being touched, in the most lively manner, with the recollection, not only of the invaluable services for which the United States at large are so much indebted to him, but of that conspicuous display of cool intrepidity and wise conduct, during his command in the campaign of seventeen hundred and eighty-one, which, by having so essentially served this state in particular, have given him so just a title to its particular acknowledgments. That, impressed as they thus are with the distinguished lustre of his character, they cannot form a wish more suitable, than that the lesson it affords may inspire all those whose noble minds may emulate his glory, to pursue it by means equally auspicious to the interests of humanity.

"And a committee was appointed of Mr. Henry, Mr. Madison, Mr. Jones, (of King George,) Mr. Matthews, and Mr. Brent."

To this address, the marquis made the following polite and feeling answer:—

"Gentlemen: With the most respectful thanks to your honourable body, permit me to acknowledge, not only the flattering favour they are now pleased to confer, but also the constant partiality, and unbounded confidence of this state, which in trying times, I have so happily experienced. Through the continent, gentlemen, it is most pleasing for me to join with my friends in mutual congratulations; and I need not add what my sentiments must be in Virginia, where step by step have I so keenly felt for her distress, so eagerly enjoyed her recovery.

"Our armed force was obliged to retreat, but your patriotic hearts stood unshaken; and while, either at that period, or in our better hours, my obligations to you are numberless; I am happy in this opportunity to observe, that the excellent services of your militia were continued with unparalleled steadiness. Impressed with the necessity of federal union, I was the more pleased in the command of an army so peculiarly federal; as Virginia herself freely bled in defence of her sister states.

"In my wishes to this commonwealth, gentlemen, I will persevere with the same zeal, that once and for ever has devoted me to her. May her fertile soil rapidly increase her wealth—may all the waters which so luxuriantly flow within her limits, be happy channels of the most extensive trade—and may she in her wisdom, and the enjoyment of prosperity, continue to give the world unquestionable proofs of her philanthropy and her regard for the liberties of all mankind.

"LA FAYETTE."

Time had now brought forward several new political characters, who had risen high in the public estimation: but Mr. Henry and Mr. Lee still kept their ground far in the van. A gentleman of great distinction, who began his public career in seventeen hundred and eighty-three, found both these eminent men in the house of delegates, and heard them for the first time in debate: he served through the two sessions of that and those of the following year, and has communicated to me so vivid and interesting a comparison of their merits, as they struck his young and ardent mind, that I cannot consent to withhold it from the reader.

"I met with Patrick Henry in the Assembly in May, seventeen hundred and eighty-three. I also then met with Richard H. Lee. I lodged with Mr. Lee one or two sessions, and was perfectly acquainted with him, while I was yet a stranger to Mr. Henry. These two gentlemen were the great leaders in the house of delegates, and were almost constantly opposed: there were many other great men who belonged to that body; but, as orators, they cannot be named with Henry or Lee. Mr. Lee was a polished gentlemen: he had lost the use of one of his hands, but his manner was perfectly graceful.

"His language was always chaste, and although somewhat too monotonous, his speeches were always pleasing; yet he did not ravish your senses, nor carry away your judgment by storm. His was the mediate class of eloquence described by Rollin in his *belles lettres;* he was like a beautiful river, meandering through a flowery mead, but which never overflowed its banks. It was Henry who was the mountain torrent that swept away everything before it: it was he alone who thundered and lightened: he alone attained that sublime species of eloquence also mentioned by Rollin.

"It has been one of the greatest pleasures of my life to hear these two great masters, almost constantly opposed to each other, for several sessions. I had no relish for any other speaker. Henry was almost always victorious. He was as much superior to Lee in temper as in eloquence; for while, with a modesty approaching almost to humility, he would apologise to the house for being so often 'obliged to differ from the honourable gentleman, which he assured them, was from no want of respect for him.' Lee was frequently much chafed by the opposition; and I once heard him say aloud, and petulantly, after sustaining a great defeat, that, 'if the votes were weighed instead of being counted, he should not have lost it.'*

"Mr. Henry was inferior to Mr. Lee in the gracefulness of his action, and perhaps also in the chasteness of his language: yet his language was seldom incorrect, and his address always striking. He had a fine blue eye, and an earnest manner, which made it impossible not to attend to him. His speaking was unequal, and always rose with the subject and the exigency. In this respect he differed entirely from Mr. Lee, who was always equal, and therefore less interesting. At some times, Mr. Henry would seem to hobble, (especially at the beginning of his speeches,) and at others, his tones would be almost disagreeable: yet it was by means of his tones, and the happy modulation of his voice, that his speaking had perhaps its greatest effect.

* This hit of Mr. Lee was thought a very happy one at the time. I have heard it mentioned by several others who were members of the house, particularly by Judge Tyler. This gentleman represented it as having occurred after a division and count of the house, and just as the members were about to return to their seats. A member who was in the majority, and who was not very remarkable either for intellect or urbanity, said, with a coarse laugh, to Mr. Lee, "Well, you see you have lost it." Upon which the latter, looking at him with rather a contemptuous and sneering countenance, answered, "Yes, *I have* lost it, but if votes were *weighed* instead of being *counted*, I should *not* have *lost* it."

Was this thought original in Mr. Lee, or had he unconsciously borrowed it from the younger Pliny? "Sed hoc pluribus [levius] visum est. *Numerantur enim sententiæ, non ponderantur:* nec aliud in publico consilio potest fieri, in quo nihil est tam inæquale, quam æqualitas ipsa; nan cum sit impar prudentia, par omnium jus est."—PLIN. Epist. Lib. II. Epist. XII.

"Yet these reflections, it seems, made no impression upon the majority. *Votes go by number, not weight;* nor can it be otherwise in assemblies of this kind, where nothing is more unequal than that equality which prevails in them; for though every member has the same weight of suffrage, every member has not the same strength of judgment."—MELMOTH's Translation of Pliny. London, 1748.

"He had a happy articulation—a clear, bold, strong voice—and every syllable was distinctly uttered. He was always very unassuming, and very respectful toward his adversaries; the consequence was, that no feeling of disgust or animosity was arrayed against him. He was great at a reply, and greater in proportion to the pressure which was bearing upon him; and it seemed to me, from the frequent opportunities of observation afforded me during the period of which I have spoken, that the resources of his mind and of his eloquence were equal to any drafts which could possibly be made upon them."

This inequality in the speeches of Mr. Henry, was imputed by some of his observers to art. He always spoke, they say, for victory, and wishing to carry every one with him, adapted the different parts of his discourse to their different capacities. A critic of a higher order would sometimes think him trifling, when in truth he was making a most powerful impression on the weaker members of the house. By these means it is said, he contrived to worm his way through the whole body, and to insinuate his influence into every mind. When he hobbled, it was like the bird that thus artfully seeks to decoy away the foot of the intruder from the precious deposite of her brood; and at the moment when it would be thought that his strength was almost exhausted, he would spring magnificently from the earth, and tower above the clouds.

He knew all the local interests and prejudices of every quarter of the state, and of every county in it; and whether these prejudices were rational or irrational, it is said that he would appeal to them without hesitation, and, whenever he found it necessary, enlist them in his cause. His address on these occasions has been highly admired even by those who have censured the course as deficient in dignity and candour. It was executed with so much delicacy and adroitness, and covered under a countenance of such apostolic solemnity, that the persons on whom he was operating were unconscious of the design.

Winding his way thus artfully through the house, from county to county, from prejudice to prejudice, with the power of moving them, when he pleased, from tears to laughter, from laughter to tears, of astonishing their imaginations, and overwhelming their judgments and hearts, it is easy to conceive how irresistible he must have been. When with these prodigious faculties the reader connects his engaging deportment out of the house—the uncommon kindness and gentleness of his nature—the simplicity, frankness, and amenity of his manners—the innocent playfulness and instruction of his conversation—the integrity of his life—and the high sense of the services which he had rendered to the cause of liberty and his country—he will readily perceive, that the opinions and wishes of such a man would be, of themselves, almost decisive of any question.

The artifice of resorting to erroneous local prejudices, in a legislative debate, is certainly not to be commended. Truth stands in need of no such aids. It must be admitted that there is more purity as well as dignity, in supporting a sound measure by sound arguments only: and we must be prepared to become Jesuits, before we can justify a resort to wrong means to promote even a right end. In excuse of Mr. Henry, we have nothing to urge except immemorial and almost universal usage; and it is moreover highly probable, that many of the instances, in which he was accused of resorting improperly to local prejudices, were cases in which the questions were, from their nature, to be decided in a great measures by local interests. Of this description is the following one, now furnished, at my request, in writing, by Judge Archibald Stuart, from whom I had the pleasure to hear it in conversation several years ago:—

"At your request, I attempt a narrative of the extraordinary effects of Mr. Henry's eloquence in the Virginia legislature, about the year seventeen hundred and eighty-four, when I was present as a member of that body.

"The finances of the country had been much deranged during the war, and public credit was at a low ebb; a party in the legislature thought it then high time to place the character and credit of the state on a more respectable footing, by laying taxes commensurate with all the public demands. With this view, a bill had been brought into the house, and referred to a committee of the whole; in support of which the then speaker, (Mr. Tyler,) Henry Tazewell, Mann Page, William Ronald, and many other members of great respectability, (including, to the best of my recollection, Richard H. Lee, and, perhaps, Mr. Madison,) took an active part. Mr. Henry, on the other hand, was of opinion that this was a premature attempt; that policy required that the people should have some repose after the fatigues and privations to which they had been subjected, during a long and arduous struggle for independence.

"The advocates of the bill, in committee of the whole house, used their utmost efforts, and were successful in conforming it to their views, by such a majority (say thirty) as seemed to ensure its passage. When the committee rose, the bill was instantly reported to the house; when Mr. Henry, who had been excited and roused by his recent defeat, came forward again in all the majesty of his power. For some time after he commenced speaking, the countenances of his opponents indicated no apprehension of danger to their cause.

"The feelings of Mr. Tyler, which were sometimes warm, could not on that occasion be concealed, even in the chair. His countenance was forbidding, even repulsive, and his face turned from the speaker. Mr. Tazewell was reading a pamphlet: and Mr. Page was more than usually grave. After some time, however, it was discovered that Mr. Tyler's countenance gradually began to relax; he would occasionally look at Mr. Henry: sometimes smile; his attention by degrees became more fixed; at length it became completely so:—he next appeared to be in good humour; he leaned toward Mr. Henry—appeared charmed and delighted, and finally lost in wonder and amazement. The progress of these feelings was legible in his countenance.

"Mr. Henry drew a most affecting picture of the state of poverty and suffering in which the people of the upper counties had been left by the war. His delineation of their wants and wretchedness was so minute, so full of feeling, and withal so true, that he could scarcely fail to enlist on his side every sympathetic mind. He contrasted the severe toil by which *they* had to gain their daily subsistence, with the facilities enjoyed by the people of the lower counties. The latter, he said, residing on the salt rivers and creeks, could draw their supplies at pleasure, from the waters that flowed by their doors; and then he presented such a ludicrous image of the members who had advocated the bill, (the most of whom were from the lower counties,) peeping and peering along the shores of the creeks, to pick up their mess of crabs, or addling off to the oyster-rocks, to rake for *their daily bread*,* as filled the house with a roar of merriment. Mr. Tazewell laid down his pamphlet, and shook his sides with laughter; even the gravity of Mr. Page was affected: a corresponding change of countenance prevailed through the ranks of the advocates of the bill, and you might discover that they had surrendered their cause. In this they were not disappointed; for on a division, Mr. Henry had a majority of upward of thirty against the bill."

If this be a fair specimen of the cases (as probably it is) in which Mr. Henry was accused of appealing improperly to local prejudices, the censure seems undeserved. It is obvious that the consideration urged by him, on this occasion, belonged properly to the subject, and that the appeal to local circumstances was fairly made. Candour will justify us in looking,

* At that day, (and perhaps still,) the poorer people on the salt creeks, lived almost exclusively on fish; passing whole days, and sometimes weeks, without seeing a grain of bread.

with great distrust, to the censures cast on this extraordinary man, by rivals whom he had obscured.

On the seventeenth of November, seventeen hundred and eighty-four, Mr. Henry was again elected governor of Virginia, to commence his service from the thirtieth day of the same month. The communication made by him to the first legislature which met after his election, is inserted in the Appendix; it is given at large, as a specimen of Mr. Henry's style in more extended compositions than have yet been submitted to the reader, and for the further purpose of showing, that the objects with which a governor of Virginia, acting within the pale of the constitution, is conversant in time of peace, are not such as to shed much lustre on his character, or to solicit very powerfully the attention of his biographer. (See Appendix, Note B.)

In examining the public archives of this date, there is a circumstance whose frequent and indeed constant recurrence, presses itself most painfully on the attention: I mean the resignation of state officers, on the plea of a necessity to resort to some more effectual means of subsistence. It is not generally known, that the councils of Virginia were, during the period of which we are now speaking, enlightened and adorned by some of the brightest of her sons; much less is it known that they were driven from those councils, by that wretched policy which has always regulated the salaries of officers in Virginia. The letters of resignation, during the years seventeen hundred and eighty-four, five, and six, which now stand on the public files, afford the best comment on this policy.

Virginia lost during those years, the services of such men as have rarely existed in this or any other country; and such as she can never hope to see again in her councils, until the system of penury shall yield to that of liberality. At the close of the war, indeed, there was some apology for this penury; the country was wretchedly poor and in debt. But this cause has long since ceased, and with it also should cease the affect.

Virginia is now rich, and may fill her offices with the flower of her sons; but can it be expected that men who wish to live free from debt, and to leave their families independent at their deaths will relinquish the pursuits by which they are able to affect these objects, and enter upon a service full of care, responsibility, and anxiety; a service whose certain fruits (if it be their only dependance) must be a life of pecuniary embarrassment; and (what is still worse) their wives and children, after their deaths, must be cast on the charity of a cold and unfeeling world. Ought such a sacrifice to be expected? and yet must it not be the inevitable consequence of an exclusive dependance on the salary of any office in Virginia, which requires talents of the highest order?

How affecting is that spectacle which we have seen of a public officer, who, having worn out the prime and vigour of life in the service of his country, instead of being enabled to retire, in old age, to the repose and peace which he so justly deserved, is compelled to toil on for subsistence, though trembling, perhaps, under the weight of eighty winters, oppressed by debt, harassed by his creditors, with the certainty before him of dying poor and involved; and leaving his posterity, if he have any, on the parish! How forcibly does it remind us of that pathetic exclamation of Wolsey:—

"O Cromwell, Cromwell,
Had I but served my God, with half the zeal
I served my king, he would not, in mine age
Have left me naked to my enemies!"

Is it in reference to the warm and generous state of Virginia, that these reflections can be made, and made too with truth and justice!

These remarks are not foreign to our story: in the fall of seventeen hundred and eighty-six, while yet a year remained of his constitutional term, Mr. Henry was under the necessity of retiring from the office of governor. There never was a man whose style of living was more perfectly unostentatious, temperate and simple; yet the salary had been inadequate to the support of his family; and, at the end of two years, he found himself involved in debts, which for the moment, he saw no hope of paying, but by the sacrifice of a part of his estate. Let it be remembered, that this occurred in the year seventeen hundred and eighty-six; and let it be further remembered, that the salary was then very nearly what it still remains!

In consequence of Mr. Henry's declining a re-election, the legislature proceeded to appoint his successor; and then, on the succeeding twenty-fifth of November, the house of delegates came to the following resolution:—

"Resolved, *unanimously*, That a committee be appointed to wait on his excellency the governor, and present him the thanks of this house, for his wise, prudent, and upright administration, during his last appointment of chief magistrate of this commonwealth, assuring him that they retain a perfect sense of his abilities, in the discharge of the duties of that high and important office, and wish him all domestic happiness, on his return to private life."

To this resolution, Mr. Corbin, one of the committee, reported the following answer from Mr. Henry:—

"GENTLEMEN: The house of delegates have done me distinguished honour, by the resolution they have been pleased to communicate to me through you. I am happy to find my endeavours to discharge the duties of my station, have met with their favourable acceptance.

"The approbation of my country is the highest reward to which my mind is capable of aspiring, and I shall return to private life, highly gratified in the recollection of this instance of regard shown me by the house; having only to regret that my abilities to serve my country have come so short of my wishes.

"At the same time that I make my best acknowledgments to the house for their goodness, I beg leave to express my particular obligations to you, gentlemen, for the polite manner in which this communication is made to me."

On the fourth of December, in the same year, Mr. Henry was appointed by the legislature, one of seven deputies from this commonwealth to meet a convention proposed to be held in Philadelphia, on the following May, for the purpose of revising the federal constitution. On this list of deputies, his name stands next to that of him, who stood of right before all others in America; the order of appointment as exhibited by the journals being as follows: George Washington, Patrick Henry, Edmund Randolph, John Blair, James Madison, George Mason, and George Wythe.

The same cause, however, which had constrained Mr. Henry's retirement from the executive chair of state, disabled him now from obeying this honourable call of his country. On his resigning the government, he retired to Prince Edward county, and endeavoured to cast about for the means of extricating himself from his debts. At the age of fifty years, worn down by more than twenty years of arduous service in the cause of his country, eighteen of which had been occupied by the toils and tempests of the revolution, it was natural for him to wish for rest, and to seek some secure and placid port in which he might repose himself from the fatigues of the storm. This, however, was denied him; and after having devoted the bloom of youth and the maturity of manhood to the good of his country, he had now in his old age to provide for his family.

"*He had never*," says a correspondent, (Judge Winston,) "*been in easy circumstances;* and soon after his removal to Prince Edward county, conversing with his usual frankness with one of his neighbours, he expressed his anxiety under the debts which he was not able to pay; the reply was to this effect: 'Go back to the bar; your tongue will soon pay your debts. If you will promise to go, I will give you a retaining fee on the spot.'

"This blunt advice determined him to return to the practice of the law; which he did in the beginning of seventeen hundred and eighty-eight; and during six years he attended regularly the district courts of Prince Edward and New London."

Direful must have been the necessity which drove a man of Mr. Henry's disposition and habits, at his time of life, and tempest-beaten as he was, to resume the practice of such a profession as the law. He would not, however, undertake the technical duties of the profession; his engagements were confined to the argument of the cause; and his clients had of course, to employ other counsel, to conduct the pleadings, and ripen their cases for hearing. Hence his practice was restricted to difficult and important cases; but his great reputation kept him constantly engaged; he was frequently called to distant courts; the light of his eloquence shone in every quarter of the state, and thousands of tongues were everywhere employed in repeating the fine effusions of his genius.

The federal constitution, the fruit of the convention at Philadelphia, had now come forth, and produced an agitation which had not been felt since the return of peace. The friends and the enemies to its adoption were equally zealous and active in their exertions to promote their respective wishes; the presses throughout the continent teemed with essays on the subject; and the rostrum, the pulpit, the field, and the forest, rung with declamations and discussions of the most animated character. Every assemblage of people, for whatsoever purpose met, either for court or church, muster or barbecue, presented an *arena* for the political combatants; and in some quarters of the union, such was the public anxiety of the occasion, that gentlemen in the habit of public speaking, converted themselves into a sort of itinerant preachers, going from county to county, and from state to state, collecting the people by distant appointments, and challenging all adversaries to meet and dispute with them the propriety of the adoption of the federal constitution.

All who sought to distinguish themselves by public speaking, all candidates for popular favour, and especially the junior members of the bar, flocked to these meetings from the remotest distances, and entered the lists with all the ardour, and gallantry of the knights of former times at their tilts and tournaments. Never was there a theme more fruitful of discussion, and never was there one more amply or ably discussed.

Of the convention which was to decide the fate of this instrument in Virginia, Mr. Henry was chosen a member for the county of Prince Edward. Although the constitution had come forth with the sanction of the revered name of Washington, and carried with it all the weight of popularity which that name could not fail to attach to any proposition, it had not the good fortune to be approved by Mr. Henry. He was (to use his own expression) "most awfully alarmed" at the idea of its adoption; for he considered it as threatening the liberties of his country; and he determined, therefore, to buckle on once more the armour which he had hung up in the temple of peace, and try the fortune of this, the last of his political fields.

CHAPTER VIII.

Convention at Richmond on the Adoption of the Federal Constitution—Uncommon Array of Men of Talent in the Convention—Mr. Henry's Reply to Gen. Lee—To Mr. Pendleton—Synopsis of the chief Objections to the Constitution—Mr. Henry's Reply to Mr. Madison and Mr. Corbin—Singular Incident connected with Mr. Henry's closing Address—Session of the Assembly in October—Mr. Henry nominates Richard H. Lee and Mr. Grayson as Senators in Opposition to Mr. Madison—His Resolutions in the Assembly on the Subject of the Constitution—Anecdote of his Retaliation upon a young Member—Draft of Letters to Governor Clinton and to several States.

The convention met in Richmond, on the second of June, seventeen hundred and eighty-eight, and exhibited such an array of variegated talents, as had never been collected before within the limits of the state, and such a one as it may well be feared we shall never see again. A few of the most eminent of these statesmen are still alive; of whom, therefore, delicacy forbids us to speak as they deserve. Their powers, however, and the peculiar characters of their intellectual excellence, are so well known that their names will be sufficient to speak their respective eulogies.

We may mention, therefore, Mr. Madison, the late president of the United States; Mr. Marshall, the chief-justice; and Mr. Monroe, now the president. What will the reader think of a body, in which men like these were only among their equals! Yet such is the fact; for there were those sages of other days, Pendleton and Wythe; there was seen displayed the Spartan vigour and compactness of George Nichols; and there shone the radiant genius and sensibility of Grayson; the Roman energy and the Attic wit of George Mason was there; and there, also, the classic taste and harmony of Edmund Randolph; "the splendid conflagration" of the high-minded Innis; and the matchless eloquence of the immortal Henry!

The debates and proceedings of this Convention, by Mr. David Robertson, of Petersburgh, have passed through two editions; yet it is believed that their circulation has been principally confined to Virginia; and even in this state, from the rapid progress of our population, that book is supposed to be in, comparatively, few hands. Hence it has been thought proper to give a short sketch of Mr. Henry's course in this body. It ought to be premised, however, that the published debates have been said, by those who attended the convention, to present but an imperfect view of the discussion of that body. In relation to Mr. Henry, they are confessedly imperfect; the reporter having sometimes dropped him in those passages in which the reader would be most anxious to follow him.

From the skill and ability of the reporter, there can be no doubt that the substance of the debates, as well as their general course, are accurately preserved. The work is, therefore, a valuable repository of the arguments by which the constitution was opposed on one hand, and supported on the other; but it must have been utterly impossible for a man who possesses the sensibility and high relish for eloquence which distinguish the reporter, not to have been so far transported by the excursions of Mr. Henry's genius, as sometimes, unconsciously, to have laid down his pen.

It was not until the fourth, that the preliminary arrangements for the discussion were settled. Mr. Pendleton had been unanimously elected the president of the convention; but it having been determined that the subject should be debated in committee of the whole, the house on that day resolved itself into committee, and the venerable Mr. Wythe was called to the chair. In conformity with the order which had been taken, to discuss the constitution, clause by clause, the clerk now read the preamble, and the two first sections; and the debate was opened by Mr. George Nicholas.

He confined himself strictly to the sections under consideration, and maintained their policy with great cogency of argument. Mr. Henry rose next, and soon demonstrated that his excursions were not to be restrained by the rigour of rules. Instead of proceeding to answer Mr. Nicholas, he commenced by sounding an alarm calculated to produce a most powerful impression. The effect, however, will be entirely lost upon the reader, unless he shall associate with the speech which I am about to lay before him, that awful solemnity and look of fearful portent, by which Mr. Henry could imply even more than he expressed; and that slow, distinct, emphatic enunciation, by which he never failed to move the souls of his hearers.

"Mr. Chairman: The public mind, as well as my own, is

extremely uneasy at the proposed change of government. Give me leave to form one of the number of those who wish to be thoroughly acquainted with the reasons of this perilous and uneasy situation—and why we are brought hither to decide on this great national question. I consider myself as the servant of the people of this commonwealth—as a sentinel over their rights, liberty, and happiness. I represent their feelings when I say, that they are exceedingly uneasy, being brought from that state of full security which they enjoyed, to the present *delusive appearance of things.*

"A year ago, the minds of our citizens were at perfect repose. Before the meeting of the late federal convention at Philadelphia, a general peace and a universal tranquillity prevailed in this country—but since that period, they are exceedingly uneasy and disquieted. When I wished for an appointment to this convention, my mind was extremely agitated for the situation of public affairs. I conceive the republic to be in extreme danger.

"If our situation be thus uneasy, whence has arisen this fearful jeopardy? It arises from this fatal system—it arises from a proposal to change our government—a proposal that goes to the utter annihilation of the most solemn engagements of the states—a proposal of establishing nine states into confederacy, to the eventual exclusion of four states. It goes to the annihilation of those solemn treaties we have formed with foreign nations. The present circumstances of France—the good offices rendered us by that kingdom, require our most faithful and most punctual adherence to our treaty with her.

"We are in alliance with the Spaniards, the Dutch, the Prussians: those treaties bound us as thirteen states, confederated together. Yet here is a proposal to sever that confederacy. Is it possible that we shall abandon all our treaties and national engagements? And for what? I expected to have heard the reasons of an event, so unexpected to my mind and many others. Was our civil polity or public justice endangered or sapped? Was the real existence of the country threatened—or was this preceded by a mournful progression of events?

"This proposal of altering our federal government is of a most alarming nature. Make the best of this new government—say it is composed by anything but inspiration—you ought to be extremely cautious, watchful, jealous of your liberty; for instead of securing our rights, you may lose them for ever. If a wrong step be now made, the republic may be lost for ever. If this new government will not come up to the expectation of the people, and they should be disappointed, their liberty will be lost, and tyranny must and will arise.

"I repeat it again, and I beg gentlemen to consider, that a wrong step made now, will plunge us into misery, and our republic will be lost. It will be necessary for this convention to have a faithful historical detail of the facts that preceded the session of the federal convention, and the reason that actuated its members in proposing an entire alteration of government, and to demonstrate the dangers that awaited us: if they were of such awful magnitude, as to warrant a proposal so extremely perilous as this, I must assert, that this convention has an absolute right to a thorough discovery of every circumstance relative to this great event.

"And here I would make this inquiry of those worthy characters who composed a part of the late federal convention. I am sure they were fully impressed with the necessity of forming a great consolidated government, instead of a confederation. That this *is* a consolidated government is demonstrably clear; and the danger of such a government is to my mind very striking. I have the highest veneration for those gentlemen: but, sir, give me leave to demand, what right had they to say, *we, the people?*

"My political curiosity, exclusive of my anxious solicitude for the public welfare, leads me to ask, who authorized them to speak the language of, *we, the people,* instead of, *we, the states? States* are the characteristics, and the soul of *a confederation.* If the *states* be not the agents of this compact, it must be one *great, consolidated, national government of the people of all the states.* I have the highest respect for those gentlemen who formed the convention; and were some of them not here, I would express some testimonial of esteem for them.

"America had, on a former occasion, put the utmost confidence in them; a confidence which was well-placed; and I am sure, sir, I would give up anything to them; I would cheerfully confide in them as my representatives. But, sir, on this great occasion, I would demand the cause of their conduct. Even from that illustrious man, who saved us by his valour, I would have a reason for his conduct—that liberty which he has given us by his valour, tells me to ask this reason—and sure I am, were he here, he would give us that reason: but there are other gentlemen here who can give us this information. *The people* gave them no power to use their name. That they exceeded their power is perfectly clear.

"It is not mere curiosity that actuates me—I wish to hear the real, actual, existing danger, which should lead us to take those steps so dangerous in my conception. Disorders have arisen in other parts of America; but here, sir, no dangers, no insurrection, or tumult, has happened—everything has been calm and tranquil. But, notwithstanding this, *we are wandering on the great ocean of human affairs. I see no landmark to guide us. We are running we know not whither.*

"Difference in opinion has gone to a degree of inflammatory resentment, in different parts of the country, which has been occasioned by this perilous innovation. The federal convention ought to have *amended the old system*—for *this* purpose they were *solely* delegated: the object of their mission extended to no other consideration. You must therefore forgive the solicitation of one unworthy member, to know what danger could have arisen under the present confederation, and what are the causes of this proposal to change our government?"

This inquiry was answered by an eloquent speech from Mr. Randolph; and the debate passed into other hands; until on the next day, General Lee, in reference to Mr. Henry's opening speech, addressed the chair, as follows:—

"Mr. Chairman: I feel every power of my mind moved by the language of the honourable gentleman, yesterday. The *eclat* and brilliancy which have distinguished that gentleman, the honours with which he has been dignified, and the brilliant talents which he has so often displayed, have attracted my respect and attention. On so important an occasion, and before so respectable a body, I expected a new display of his powers of oratory: but, instead of proceeding to investigate the merits of the new plan of government, the *worthy character* informed us of *horrors* which he felt, of *apprehensions* in his mind, which made him *tremblingly fearful of the fate of the commonwealth.*

"Mr. Chairman: Was it proper to appeal to the *fear* of this house? The question before us belongs to the *judgment* of this house; I trust he is come to *judge* and not to *alarm.* I trust that he, and every other gentleman in this house, comes with a firm resolution, coolly and calmly to examine, and fairly and impartially to determine."

In the further progress of his speech, General Lee again said, rather tauntingly, of Mr. Henry—"The gentleman sat down as he began, leaving us to ruminate *on the horrors* with which he opened."

Mr. Henry, rising immediately after these sarcastic remarks, gave a striking specimen of that dignified self-command, and that strict and uniform *decorum*, by which he was so pre-eminently distinguished in debate. Far from retorting the sarcasms of his adversary, he seemed to have heard nothing but the compliments with which they stood connected, and rising slowly from his seat, with a countenance expressive of unaffected humility, he began with the following modest and disqualifying exordium:—

"Mr. Chairman: I am much obliged to the very worthy gentleman for his encomium. I wish I *was* possessed of talents, or possessed of *anything*, that might enable me to elucidate this great subject. I own, sir, I am not free from suspicion. I am apt to entertain doubts. I rose, on yesterday, not to enter upon the discussion, but merely to ask a question which had arisen in my own mind. When I asked that question, I thought the meaning of my interrogation was obvious. The fate of America may depend on this question.

"Have they said, *we, the states?* Have they made a proposal of a compact between *states?* If they *had*, this would be a confederation; it is, otherwise, most clearly, *a consolidated government*. The whole question turns, sir, on that *poor little thing*, the expression, *we, the people*, instead of, *the states* of America."

He then proceeded to set forth, in terrible array, his various objections to the constitution; not confining himself to the clauses under debate, but ranging through the whole instrument, and passing from objection to objection, as they followed each other in his mind. This departure from the rule of the house, although at first view censurable, was insisted upon by himself and his colleagues, as being indispensable to a just examination of the particular clause under consideration; because the policy or impolicy of any provision did not always depend upon itself alone, but on other provisions with which it stood connected, and, indeed, upon the whole system of powers and checks that were associated with it in the same instrument, and thus formed only parts of one entire whole.

The truth of this position, in relation to some of the provisions, could not be justly denied; and a departure once made from the rigour of the rule, the debate became at large, on every part of the constitution; the disputants at every stage looking forward and backward throughout the whole instrument, without any control other than their own discretion. Thus freed from restraints, under which his genius was at all times impatient, uncoupled and let loose to range the whole field at pleasure, Mr. Henry seemed to have recovered, and to luxuriate in all the powers of his youth. He had, indeed, occasion for them all; for while he was supported by only three effective auxiliaries, opposed to him stood a phalanx, most formidable both for talents and weight of character; and several of whom it might be said, with truth, that *each* was "*in himself a host;*" for at the head of the opposing ranks stood Mr. Pendleton, Mr. Wythe, Mr. Madison, Mr. Marshall, Mr. Nicholas, Mr. Randolph, Mr. Innis, Mr. Henry Lee, and Mr. Corbin. Fearful odds! and such as called upon him for the most strenuous exertion of all his faculties.

Nor did he sink below the occasion. For twenty days, during which this great discussion continued without intermission, his efforts were sustained, not only with undiminished strength, but with powers which seemed to gather new force from every exertion. All the faculties useful for debate were found united in him, with a degree of perfection, in which they are rarely seen to exist, even separately, in different individuals: irony, ridicule, the purest wit, the most comic humour, exclamations that made the soul start, the most affecting pathos, and the most sublime apostrophes, lent their aid to enforce his reasoning, and to put to flight the arguments of his adversaries.

The objection that the constitution substituted a consolidated in lieu of a confederated government, and that this new consolidated government threatened the total annihilation of the state sovereignties, was pressed by him with most masterly power: he said there was no necessity for a change of government so entire and fundamental—and no inducement to it, unless it was to be found in this *splendid government*, which we were told was to make us *a great and mighty people*.

"We have no detail," said he, "of those great considerations, which, in my opinion, ought to have *abounded*, before we should recur to a government of this kind. Here is a revolution as *radical* as that which separated us from Great Britain. It is as radical, if in this transition our rights and privileges are endangered, and the sovereignty of the states be relinquished: and cannot we plainly see, that this is actually the case? The rights of conscience, trial by jury, liberty of the press, all your immunities and franchises, all pretensions to human rights and privileges, are rendered insecure, if not lost, by this change so loudly talked of by some, and so inconsiderately by others. Is this tame relinquishment of rights worthy of freemen? Is it worthy of that manly fortitude that ought to characterize republicans?

"It is said eight states have adopted this plan: I declare, that if *twelve states and a half* had adopted it, I would with manly firmness, and in spite of an erring world, reject it. You are not to inquire how your trade may be increased, nor how you are to become *a great and powerful people*, but how *your liberties* can be secured; for *liberty* ought to be the *direct end* of your government. Is it necessary for your *liberty*, that you should abandon those great rights by the adoption of this system? Is the relinquishment of the trial by jury, and the liberty of the press, necessary for your liberty? Will the abandonment of your most sacred rights tend to the security of your liberty? Liberty, the greatest of all earthly blessings—*give us that precious jewel, and you may take everything else!*

"But I am fearful I have lived long enough to become an old-fashioned fellow. Perhaps an invincible attachment to the dearest rights of man, may, *in these refined, enlightened days*, be deemed *old-fashioned:* if so, I am contented to be so: I say, the time has been, when every pulse of my heart beat for American liberty, and which, I believe, had a counterpart in the breast of every true American; but suspicions have gone forth—suspicions of my integrity—publicly reported that my professions are not real—twenty-three years ago was I supposed a traitor to my country: I was then said to be a bane of sedition because I supported the rights of my country: I may be thought suspicious, when I say our privileges and rights are in danger: but, sir, a number of the people of this country are weak enough to think these things are too true.

"I am happy to find, that the gentleman on the other side declares they are groundless: but, sir, suspicion is a virtue, as long as its object is the preservation of the public good, and as long as it stays within proper bounds: should it fall on me, I am contented; conscious rectitude is a powerful consolation: I trust there are many who think my professions for the public good to be real. Let your suspicion look to both sides: there are many on the other side, who possibly may have been persuaded of the necessity of these measures, which I conceive to be dangerous to your liberty.

"Guard with jealous attention the public liberty. Suspect every one who approaches that jewel. Unfortunately, nothing will preserve it but downright force: whenever you give up that force, you are inevitably ruined. I am answered by gentlemen, that though I might speak of terrors, yet the fact was, that we were surrounded by none of the dangers I apprehended. I conceive this new government to be one of those dangers: it has produced those horrors which distress many of our best citizens. We are come hither to preserve the poor commonwealth of Virginia, if it can be possibly done: something must be done to preserve your liberty and mine.

"The confederation, this same despised government, merits, in my opinion, the highest encomium: it carried us through a long and dangerous war: it rendered us victorious in that bloody conflict with a powerful nation: it has secured us a territory greater than any European monarch possesses: and shall a government which has been thus strong and vigorous, be accused of imbecility, and abandoned for want of energy? Consider what you are about to do, before you part with this government. Take longer time in reckoning things; revolutions like this have happened in almost every country of Europe: similar examples are to be found in ancient Greece and ancient Rome: instances of the people losing their liberty by their own carelessness and the ambition of a few.

"We are cautioned, by the honourable gentleman who presides, against faction and turbulence: I acknowledge that licentiousness is dangerous, and that it ought to be provided against: I acknowledge, also, the new form of government may effectually prevent it: yet there is another thing it will as effectually do—it will oppress and ruin the people. There are sufficient guards placed against faction and licentiousness: for when power is given to this government to suppress these, or for any other purpose, the language it assumes is clear, express, and unequivocal: but when this constitution speaks of privileges, there is an *ambiguity*, sir, a *fatal ambiguity, an ambiguity* which is very astonishing!"

The adoption of the instrument had been maintained upon the ground that it would increase our military strength, and enable us to resist the lawless ambition of foreign princes: it had been urged, too, that if the convention should rise without adopting the instrument, disunion and anarchy would be the certain consequences. In answer to these topics he said:—

"Happy will you be, if you miss the fate of those nations, who, omitting to resist their oppressors, or negligently suffering their liberty to be wrested from them, have groaned under intolerable despotism! Most of the human race are now in this deplorable condition. And those nations who have gone in search of *grandeur*, *power*, and *splendour*, have also fallen a sacrifice, and been the victims of their own folly. While they acquired those visionary blessings, they lost their freedom.

"My great objection to this government is, that it does not leave us the means of defending our rights, or of waging war against tyrants. It is urged by some gentlemen, that this new plan will bring us an acquisition of strength, an army, and the militia of the states. This is an idea extremely ridiculous: gentlemen cannot be in earnest. *This acquisition will trample on your fallen liberty!* Let my beloved Americans guard against that fatal lethargy that has pervaded the universe. Have we the means of resisting disciplined armies, when our only defence, the militia, is put into the hands of congress?

"The honourable gentleman said, that great danger would ensue, if the convention rose without adopting this system. I ask, where is that danger? I see none. Other gentlemen have told us within these walls, that the union is gone—or, that the union will be gone. Is not this trifling with the judgment of their fellow-citizens? Till they tell us the ground of their fears, I will consider them as imaginary. I rose to make inquiry where those dangers were; they could make no answer: I believe I never shall have that answer.

"Is there a disposition in the people of this country to revolt against the dominion of laws? Has there been a single tumult in Virginia? Have not the people of Virginia, when labouring under the severest pressure of accumulated distresses, manifested the most cordial acquiescence in the execution of the laws? What could be more lawful than their unanimous acquiescence under general distresses? Is there any revolution in Virginia? *Whither is the spirit of America gone? Whither is the genius of America fled? It was but yesterday when our enemies marched in triumph through our country. Yet the people of this country could not be appalled by their pompous armaments: they stopped their career, and victoriously captured them!* Where is the peril now compared to that?

"Some minds are agitated by foreign alarms. Happily for us, there is no real danger from Europe: that country is engaged in more arduous business: from that quarter there is no cause of fear: you may sleep in safety for ever for them.. Where is the danger? If sir, there was any, I would recur to the American spirit to defend us—that spirit which has enabled us to surmount the greatest difficulties: to that illustrious spirit I address my most fervent prayer, to prevent our adopting a system destructive to liberty.

"Let not gentlemen be told that it is not safe to reject this government. Wherefore is it not safe? We are told there are dangers; but those dangers are ideal; they cannot be demonstrated. To encourage us to adopt it, they tell us that there is a plain, easy way of getting amendments. When I come to contemplate this part, I suppose that I am mad, or, that my countrymen are so. The way to amendment is, in my conception, shut. Let us consider this *plain, easy way.*"

He then proceeds to demonstrate, that as the constitution required the concurrence of three fourths of the states to any amendment, it followed that six tenths of the people, in four of the smallest states, (not containing collectively one-tenth part of the population of the United States,) would have it in their power to defeat the most salutary amendments; and then asks, "Is this, sir, an easy mode of securing the public liberty? It is, sir, a most fearful situation, when the most contemptible minority can prevent the alteration of the most oppressive government: for it may, in many respects, prove to be such. Is this the spirit of republicanism? What, sir, is the genius of democracy? Let me read that clause of the bill of rights of Virginia, which relates to this:—

"'Third Article. That government is, or ought to be, instituted for the common benefit, protection, and security of the people, nation, or community; of all the various modes and forms of government, that is best which is capable of producing the greatest degree of happiness and safety, and is most effectually secured against the danger of mal-administration; and that whenever any government shall be found inadequate, or contrary to these purposes, *a majority of the community* hath an indubitable, unalienable, and indefeasible right to reform, alter, or abolish it, in such manner as shall be judged most conducive to the public weal.'

"This, sir, is the language of democracy, *that a majority of the community* have a right to alter their government when found to be oppressive; but how different is the genius of your new constitution from this? How different from the sentiments of freemen, that a contemptible minority can prevent the good of the majority? If, then, gentlemen, standing on this ground, are come to that point, that they are willing to bind themselves and their posterity to be oppressed, *I am amazed, and inexpressibly astonished!*

"If this be the opinion of the majority, I must submit; but to me, sir, it appears perilous and destructive; I cannot help thinking so; perhaps it may be the result of my age; these may be feelings natural to a man of my years, when the American spirit has left him, and his mental powers, like the members of the body, are decayed. If, sir, amendments are left to the twentieth, or to the tenth part of the people of America, your liberty is gone for ever.

"We have heard that there is a great deal of bribery practised in the house of commons in England; and that many of the members raised themselves to preferments by selling the rights of the people. But, sir, the tenth part of that body cannot continue oppressions on the rest of the people. English liberty is, in this case, on a firmer foundation than American liberty. It will be easily contrived to procure the opposition of one tenth of the people to any alteration, however judicious."

Mr. Pendleton had repelled the idea of danger from the adoption of the constitution, on the ground of the facility with which the people could recall their delegated powers, and change their servants. "We will assemble in convention," said Mr. Pendleton, "wholly recall our delegated powers, or reform them so as to prevent such abuse, and punish our servants." In reply to this, Mr. Henry said:—"The honourable gentleman who presides told us, that, to prevent abuses in our government, we will assemble in convention, recall our delegated powers, and punish our servants for abusing the trust reposed in them. *Oh, sir, we should have fine times, indeed, if to punish tyrants, it were only necessary to assemble the people! Your arms* wherewith you *could* defend yourselves, are gone! and you have no longer an aristocratical, no longer a democratical spirit. Did you ever read of any revolution in any nation, brought about by the punishment of those *in power*, inflicted by those who had *no power at all?* You read of a riot act in a country which is called one of the freest in the world, where a few neighbours cannot assemble, without the risk of being shot by a hired soldiery, the engines of despotism.

"*We may see such an act in America. A standing army we shall have also, to execute the execrable commands of tyranny;* and how are you to punish them? *Will you order them to be punished? Who shall obey these orders? Will your mace-bearer be a match for a disciplined regiment?* In what situation are we to be? The clause before you gives a power of direct taxation, unbounded and unlimited; exclusive power of legislation, in all cases whatsoever, for ten miles square; *and over all places purchased for the erection of forts, magazines, arsenals, dock-yards, &c. What resistance could be made? The attempt would be madness.* You will find all the strength of this country in the hands of your enemies; those garrisons will naturally be the strongest places in the country. Your militia is given up to congress, also, in another part of this plan; they will therefore act as they think proper; all power will be in their own possession; you cannot force them to receive their punishment."

He continued to ridicule, very successfully, the alluring idea of the expected splendour of the new government, and the imaginany checks and balances which were said to exist in this constitution: "If we admit," said he, "this consolidated government, it will be because we like *a great splendid one. Some way or other we must be a great and mighty empire; we must have an army, and a navy, and a number of things!* When the American spirit was in its youth, the language of America was different: *liberty*, sir, was *then* the *primary object.*" And again: "This constitution is said to have beautiful features; when I come to examine these features, sir, they appear to me horribly frightful! Among other deformities, it has an *awful squinting; it squints toward monarchy!* And does not this raise indignation in the heart of every true American?

"Your president may easily become king; your senate is so imperfectly constructed, that your dearest rights may be sacrificed by what may be a small minority; and a very small minority may continue, *for ever, unchangeable*, this government, although horridly defective; where are your checks in this government? Your strong hold will be in the hands of your enemies; it is on a supposition that your American governors shall be honest, that all the good qualities of this government are founded; but its defective and imperfect construction puts it in their power to perpetrate the worst of mischiefs, should they be bad men; and, sir, would not all the world, from the eastern to the western hemisphere, blame our distracted folly in resting our rights *upon the contingency of our rulers being good or bad?*

"Show me that age and country, where the rights and liberties of the people were placed on the sole chance of their rulers being good men, without a consequent loss of liberty? I say, that the loss of that dearest privilege has ever followed, with absolute certainty, every such mad attempt. If your American chief be a man of ambition and abilities, how easy is it for him to render himself absolute! The army is in his hands; and if he be a man of address, it will be attached to him; and it will be the subject of long meditation with him to seize the first auspicious moment to accomplish his design; and, sir, will the American spirit, solely, relieve you when this happens?

"I would rather *infinitely*, and I am sure most of this convention are of the same opinion, have a king, lords, and commons, than a government so replete with such insupportable evils. If we make a king, we may prescribe the rules by which he shall rule his people, and interpose such checks as shall prevent him from infringing them: but the president in the field, at the head of his army, can prescribe the terms on which he shall reign master, so far that it will puzzle any American ever to get his neck from under the galling yoke. I cannot, with patience, think of this idea. If ever he violates the laws, one of two things will happen: he will come at the head of his army to carry everything before him; or he will give bail, or do what Mr. Chief Justice will order him. If he be guilty, will not the recollection of his crimes teach him to make one bold push for the American throne? Will not the immense difference between being master of everything, and being ignominiously tried and punished, powerfully excite him to make this bold push?

"But, sir, where is the existing force to punish him? Can he not, at the head of his army, beat down every opposition? Away with your president; we shall have a king: the army will salute him monarch; your militia will leave you, and assist in making him king, and fight against you: and what have you to oppose this force? What will then become of you and your rights? Will not absolute despotism ensue?" [Here Mr. Henry strongly and pathetically expatiated on the probability of the president's enslaving America, and the horrid consequences that must result.]

After the frank admission of the reporter, exhibited by the words contained in these brackets, that he had not attempted to follow Mr. Henry in this pathetic excursion, the reader will perceive, that it would be doing injustice to the memory of that eminent man, to multiply extracts from this book, as specimens of his eloquence. The stenographer who should be able to take down Mr. Henry's speeches, word for word, must have other qualities besides the perfect mastery of his art; he must have the perfect mastery of himself, and be able, for the moment, to play the mere *automaton;* for without such self-command, no man, who had a human heart in his bosom, could listen to his startling exclamations, or horror-breathing tones, without keeping his eyes immovably riveted upon the speaker. His dominion over his hearers was so absolute, that it was idle to think of resisting him; you would as soon think of resisting the lightning of heaven.

The very tone of voice in which he would address the chairman, when he felt the inspiration of his genius rising—"Mr. Chairman!"—and the awful pause which followed this call—fixed upon him at once every eye in the assembly: and then *his own rapt countenance!*—those eyes which seemed to beam with light from another world, and under whose fiery glance the crest of the proudest adversary fell! his majestic attitudes, and that bold, strong, and varied action, which *spoke* forth, with so much power, the energies of his own great spirit, rendered his person a spectacle so sublime, and so awfully interesting, that to look in any other direction when the spell was upon him was not to be expected from any man who had eyes to see and ears to hear. Little cause have we, therefore, to wonder or to complain, that a gentleman of Mr. Robertson's lively admiration of genius, and of his quick and kindling sensibility, was sometimes bedimmed by his own tears, and at others torn from his task by those master-flights, which rushed like a mighty whirlwind from the earth, and carried up everything in their vortex.

The chief objections taken to the constitution are reducible to the following heads:—

I. That it was a consolidated, instead of a confederated government: that in making it so, the delegates at Philadelphia had transcended the limits of their commission: changed fundamentally the relations which the states had chosen to bear to each other: annihilated their respective sovereignties: destroyed the barriers which divided them: and converted the whole into one solid empire. To this leading objection, almost all the rest had reference, and were urged principally with the view to illustrate and enforce it.

2. The vast and alarming array of specific powers given to the general government, and the wide door opened for an unlimited extension of those powers, by the clause which authorized congress *to pass all laws necessary to carry the given powers into effect.* It was urged that this clause rendered the previous specification of powers an idle illusion; since, by the force of construction arising from that clause, congress might easily do anything and everything it chose, under the pretence of giving effect to some specified power.

3. The unlimited power of taxation of all kinds: the states were no longer to be required, in their federative characters, to contribute their respective proportions toward the expenses and engagements of the general government: but congress were authorized to go directly to the pockets of the people, and to sweep from them *en masse*, from north to south, whatever portion of the earnings of the industrious poor the rapacity of the general government, or their schemes of ambitious grandeur, might suggest.

It was contended, that such a power could not be exercised, without just complaint, over a country so extensive, and so diversified in its productions and the pursuits of its people: that it was impossible to select any subject of general taxation which would not operate unequally on the different sections of the union, produce discontent and heart-burnings among the people, and most probably terminate in open resistance to the laws: that the representatives in congress were too few to carry with them a knowledge of the wants and capacities of the people in the different parts of a large state, and that the representation could not be made full enough to attain that object, without becoming oppressively expensive to the country: that hence taxation ought to be left to the states themselves, whose representation was full, who best knew the habits and circumstances of their constituents, and on what subjects a tax could be most conveniently laid. Mr. Henry said that he was willing to grant this power conditionally; that is, upon the failure of the states to comply with requisitions from congress: but that the absolute and unconditional grant of it, in the first instance, filled his mind with the most awful anticipations.

It was resolved, he saw clearly, that we must be a great and splendid people; and that in order to be so, immense revenues must be raised from the people: the people were to be bowed down under the load of their taxes, direct and indirect; and a swarm of federal tax-gatherers were to cover this land, to blight every blade of grass, and every leaf of vegetation, and consume its productions for the enrichment of themselves and their masters: it was not contended, he supposed, but that the state legislature, also, might impose taxes for their own internal purposes: thus the people were to be doubly oppressed, and between the state sheriffs and the federal sheriffs to be ground to dust: on this subject he drew such a vivid and affecting picture of these officers, entering in succession the cabin of the broken-hearted peasant, and the last one rifling the poor remains which the first had left as is said to have drawn tears from every eye.

4. The power of raising armies and building navies, and still more emphatically, the control given to the general government over the militia of the states, was most strenuously opposed. The power thus given was a part of the means of that aggrandizement which was obviously meditated, and there could be no doubt that it would be exercised: so that this republic, whose best policy was peace, was to be saddled with the expense of maintaining standing armies and navies, useless for any other purpose than to insult her citizens, to afford a pretext for increased taxes, and an augmented public debt, and finally to subvert the liberties of her people: her militia, too, her last remaining defence, was gone.

"Congress," said Mr. Henry, "by the power of taxation—by that of raising an army and navy—and by their control over the militia—have the sword in the one hand, and the purse in the other. Shall we be safe without either? Congress have an unlimited power over both; they are entirely given up by us. Let him (Mr. Madison) candidly tell me where and when did freedom exist, when the sword and purse were given up from the people? Unless a miracle in human affairs shall interpose, no nation ever did or ever can retain its liberty, after the loss of the sword and the purse."

The unlimited control over the militia was vehemently opposed, on the ground, that the marching militia from distant states to quell insurrection, and repel invasions, and keeping the free yeomanry of the country under the lash of martial law, would, in the first instance, produce an effect extremely inimical to the peace and harmony of the union; and in the next, harass the agricultural body of the people so much, as to reconcile them, as a less evil, to that curse of nations, and bane of freedom, a standing army:—and secondly, this power was opposed, on the ground that congress, under the boundless charter of constructive power which it possessed, might transfer to the president the power of calling forth the militia, and thus enable him to disarm all opposition to his schemes.

5. The several clauses providing for the federal judiciary were objected to, on the ground of the clashing jurisdictions of the

state and federal courts; and secondly, because infinite power was given to congress to multiply inferior federal courts at pleasure; a power which they would not fail to exercise, in order to swell the patronage of the president, *to their own emolument;* and thus enable him to reward their devotion to his views, by bestowing on them and their dependants those offices which they had themselves created.

6. It was contended that the trial by jury was gone in civil cases, by that clause which gives to the supreme court appellate power over the law and the fact in every case; and which thereby enabled that tribunal to annihilate both the verdict and judgment of the inferior courts: and that in criminal cases also, the trial by jury was worse than gone, because it was admitted, that the common law, which alone gave the challenge for favour, would not be in force as to the federal courts; and hence a jury might, in every instance, be packed to suit the purpose of the prosecution.

7. The authority of the president to take the command of the armies of the United States, in person, was warmly resisted, on the ground, that if he were a military character, and a man of address, he might easily convert them into an engine for the worst of purposes.

8. The cession of the whole treaty-making power to the president and senate, was considered as one of the most formidable features in the instrument, inasmuch as it put it in the power of the president and any ten senators, who might represent the five smallest states, to enter into the most ruinous foreign engagements, and even to cede away by treaty any portion of the territory of the larger states: it was insisted, that the lower house, who were the immediate representatives of the people, instead of being excluded as they were by the constitution from all participation in the treaty-making power, ought at least to be consulted, if not to have the principal agency in so interesting a national act.

9. The immense patronage of the president was objected to: because it placed in his hands the means of corrupting the congress, the navy, and army, and of distributing, moreover, throughout the society, a band of retainers in the shape of judges, revenue officers, and tax-gatherers, which would render him irresistible in any scheme of ambition that he might meditate against the liberties of his country.

10. The irresponsibility of the whole *gang* of federal officers (as they were called) was objected to: there was indeed, in some instances, a power of impeachment pretended to be given, but it was mere *sham* and mockery; since, instead of being tried by a tribunal, zealous and interested to bring them to jus-

tice, they were to try each other for offences, in which, probably, they were all mutually implicated.

11. It was insisted, that if we must adopt a constitution ceding away such vast powers, express and implied, and so fraught with danger to the liberties of the people, it ought at least to be guarded by a bill of rights; that in all free governments, and in the estimation of all men attached to liberty, there were certain rights unalienable—imprescriptible—and of so sacred a character, that they could not be guarded with too much caution: among these were the liberty of speech and of the press—what security had we, that even *these* sacred privileges would not be invaded? Congress might think it necessary, in order to carry into effect the given powers, to silence the clamours and censures of the people; and, if they meditated views of lawless ambition, they certainly will so think: what then would become of the liberty of speech and of the press?

Several objections of a minor character were urged, such as:—

1. That the ambiguity with which the direction for publishing the proceedings of congress was expressed, ("from time to time,") put it in their power to keep the people in utter ignorance of their proceedings; and thus to seize the public liberties "by ambuscade."

2. That the ninth section of the first article, professing to set out restrictions upon the power of congress, gave them, by irresistible implication, the sovereign power over all subjects not excepted, and thus enlarged their constructive powers, *ad infinitum.*

3. That congress had the power of involving the southern states in all the horrors which would result from a total emancipation of their slaves; and that the northern states, uninterested in the consequences of such an act, had a controlling majority, which possessed the power, and would not probably want the inclination to effect it.

4. That the pay of the members was by the constitution to be fixed by themselves, without limitation or restraint. "They may, therefore," said Mr. Henry, "indulge themselves in the fullest extent. They will make their compensation as high as they please. I suppose, if they be good men, their own delicacy will lead them to be satisfied with *moderate salaries.* But there is no security for this, should they be otherwise inclined."

These objections, and many others which it were tedious to enumerate, were pressed upon the house day after day, with all the powers of reasoning and of eloquence; and where argument and declamation were found unavailing, the force of ridicule was freely resorted to. Thus, in relation to the objection of consolidation, Mr. Madison had said:—

"There are a number of opinions as to the nature of the government; but the principal question is, whether it be a federal or consolidated government. In order to judge properly of the question before us, we must consider it minutely in its principal parts. I conceive, myself, that it is of a mixed nature:—it is, in a manner, unprecedented: we cannot find one express example in the experience of the world—it stands by itself. In some respects, it is a government of a federal nature; in others, it is of a consolidated nature."

He then proceeds to point out and discriminate its federal from its national features. Mr. Corbin, on the same side, expressed himself satisfied with Mr. Madison's definition of the instrument; but begged leave to call it by another name, viz., "*a representative federal government*, as contradistinguished from a confederacy."

Mr. Henry, in replying to these gentlemen, says:—"This government is so new, *it wants a name! I wish its other novelties were as harmless as this.* We are told, however, that, *collectively taken*, it is *without an example!*—that it is *national* in this part, and *federal* in that part, &c. We may be amused, if we please, by a treatise of *political anatomy. In the brain* it is *national:* the *stamina* are *federal—some limbs* are *federal, others national.* The senators are voted for by the state legislatures—*so far it is federal.* Individuals choose the members of the first branch—*here it is national.*

"It is *federal* in conferring general powers; but *national* in retaining them. It is not to be supported by the states—the pockets of individuals are to be searched for its maintenance. *What signifies it to me, that you have the most curious anatomical description of it in its creation?* To all the common purposes of legislation, it is *a great consolidation of government.* You are not to have the right to legislate in any but trivial cases; you are not to touch private contracts: you are not to have the right of having armies in your own defence: you cannot be trusted with dealing out justice between man and man.

"*What shall the states have to do? Take care of the poor—repair and make highways—erect bridges—and so on, and so on! Abolish the state legislatures at once.* What purposes should they be continued for? Our legislature will indeed be a ludicrous spectacle—one hundred and eighty men, marching in solemn farcical procession, exhibiting a mournful proof of the lost liberty of their country, without the power of restoring it. But, sir, we have the consolation, that it is a mixed government! that is, it may work sorely in your neck; but you will have some comfort by saying, that it was a federal government in its origin!"

Notwithstanding this ridicule, however, thrown on some of their arguments, Mr. Henry did not fail, on every proper occasion, to do justice to the great abilities and merits of his adversaries. To the eloquence of Col. Innis he paid a memorable tribute; and in one short sentence sketched a picture of it so vivid, and so faithful, that it would be injustice to both gentlemen not to give it a place:—"That honourable gentleman is endowed with great eloquence—eloquence splendid, magnificent, and sufficient to shake the human mind!"

No circumlocution could have described with half the spirit and truth, that rare union of pomp and power which distinguished Col. Innis; whose car of triumph was always a chariot of war; *pugnæ vel pompæ, pariter aptus.* One of the most singular instances on record of the fallacy of the human memory, occurred in the course of these debates: this was in relation to the case of Josiah Phillips, which has been already mentioned. Mr. Randolph, in answer to Mr. Henry's panegyrics on the constitution of the state of Virginia, brought forward that case in the following terms:—

"There is one example of this violation (of the state constitution) in Virginia, of a most striking and shocking nature; an example so horrid, that if I conceived my country would passively permit a repetition of it, dear as it is to me, I would seek means of expatriating myself from it. A man, who was then a citizen, was deprived of his life thus:—from a mere reliance on general reports, *a gentleman in the house of delegates informed the house*, that a certain man (Josiah Philips) had committed several crimes, and was running at large perpetrating other crimes; he, therefore, moved for leave to attaint him; he obtained that leave instantly; no sooner did he obtain it, than he drew from his pocket a bill ready written for that effect; it was read three times in one day, and carried to the senate; I will not say that it passed the same day through the senate; but he was attainted very speedily and precipitately, without any proof better than vague reports!

"Without being confronted with his accusers and witnesses: without the privilege of calling for evidence in his behalf, he was sentenced to death, and was afterward actually executed. Was this arbitrary deprivation of life, the dearest gift of God to man, consistent with the genius of a republican government? Is this compatible with the spirit of freedom? This, sir, has made the deepest impression in my heart, and I cannot contemplate it without horror." Now the reader, by adverting to the statement which has been already given of Philips's case, and which is founded on record, will find that there is not one word of this eloquent invective that is consistent with the facts.

What makes the case still more strange is, that Mr. Randolph, at the happening of the occurrence to which he alludes, held the double office of clerk of the house of delegates, and attorney-general of the commonwealth; in the first character, he had, only ten years before, been officially informed, that the bill of attainder had not been founded on report, but on a communication of the governor, enclosing the letter of the commanding officer of the militia in the quarter which was the theatre of Philips's ravages; that that letter had been in due form committed to the whole house on the state of the commonwealth, whose resolutions led to the bill in question; and that the bill, instead of being read three times in one day, had been regularly, and according to the forms of the house, read on three several days.

While in his character of attorney-general, he had himself endicted and prosecuted Philips for highway robbery—confronted him with the witnesses, whose names are given at the foot of the endictment, still extant among our records, and endorsed in Mr. Randolph's own hand-writing; *convicted him on that charge*, on *which charge*, and on *which alone*, Philips, was *regularly sentenced* and *executed*. Yet, not only Mr. Randolph, but all the other members who had occasion to advert to the circumstance, and even Mr. Henry, on whom it is supposed to have been designed to bear, proceed in their several criminations and defences, upon the admission that Philips had fallen a victim to the bill of attainder. Had the incident been of a common character, there would have been nothing strange in its having been forgotten; but it is one of so singular and interesting a nature, that this total oblivion of it by the principal actors themselves becomes a matter of curious history. (See Appendix. Note C.)

The convention had been attended, from its commencement, by a vast concourse of citizens of all ages and conditions. The interest so universally felt in the question itself, and not less the transcendent talents which were engaged in its discussion, presented such attractions as could not be resisted. Industry deserted its pursuits, and even dissipation gave up its objects, for the superior enjoyments which were presented by the hall of the convention. Not only the people of the town and neighbourhood, but gentlemen from every quarter of the state, were seen thronging to the metropolis, and speeding their eager way to the building in which the convention held its meetings.

Day after day, from morning till night, the galleries of the house were continually filled with an anxious crowd, who forgot the inconvenience of their situation in the excess of their enjoyment; and far from giving any interruption to the course of the debate, increased its interest and solemnity by their silence and attention. No bustle, no motion, no sound was heard among them, save only a slight movement when some new speaker arose, whom they were all eager to see as well as to hear; or when some masterstroke of eloquence shot thrilling along their nerves, and extorted an involuntary and inarticulate murmur. Day after day was this banquet of the mind and of the heart, spread before them, with a delicacy and variety which could never cloy.

There every taste might find its peculiar gratifications—the man of wit—the man of feeling—the critic—the philosopher—the historian—the metaphysician—the lover of logic—the admirer of rhetoric—every man who had an eye for the beauty of action, or an ear for the harmony of sound, or a soul for the charms of poetic fancy—in short, every one who could see, or hear, or feel, or understand, might find in the wanton profusion and prodigality of that attic feast, some delicacy adapted to his peculiar taste. Every mode of attack and of defence, of which the human mind is capable, in decorous debate—every species of weapon and armour, offensive and defensive, that could be used with advantage, from the Roman javelin to the Parthian arrow, from the cloud of Eneas to the shield of Achilles—all that could be accomplished by human strength, and almost more than human activity, was seen exhibited on that celebrated floor.

Nor did the debate become oppressive by its unvarying formality. The stateliness and sternness of extended argument were frequently relieved by quick and animated dialogue. Sometimes the conversation would become familiar and friendly. The combatants themselves would seem pleased with this relief; forget that they were enemies, and by a sort of informal truce put off their armour, and sit down amicably together to repose, as it were, in the shade of the same tree. By this agreeable intermixture of colloquial sprightliness and brilliancy with profound, and learned, and vigorous argument—of social courtesy, and heroic gallantry, the audience, far from being fatigued with the discussion, looked with regret to the hour of adjournment.

In this great competition of talents, Mr. Henry's powers of debate still shone pre-eminent. They were now exhibiting themselves in a new aspect. Hitherto his efforts, however splendid, had been comparatively short and occasional. In the house of burgesses in seventeen hundred and sixty-five, in the congress of seventeen hundred and seventy-four, and the state convention of seventeen hundred and seventy-five, he had exhibited the impetuous charge of the gallant Francis the First: but now, in combination with this fiery force, he was displaying all the firm and dauntless constancy of Charles the Fifth. No shock of his adversaries could move him from his ground. His resources never failed. His eloquence was poured from inexhaustible fountains, and assumed every variety of hue and form and motion, which could delight or persuade, instruct or astonish.

Sometimes it was the limpid rivulet sparkling down the mountain's side, and winding its silver course between margins of moss—then gradually swelling to a bolder stream, it roared in the headlong cataract, and spread its rainbows to the sun—now, it flowed on in tranquil majesty, like a river of the west, reflecting from it polished surface, forest, and cliff, and sky—anon, it was the angry ocean, chafed by the tempest, hanging its billows, with deafening clamours, among the cracking shrouds, or hurling them in sublime defiance at the storm that frowned above.

Toward the close of the session, an incident occurred of a character so extraordinary as to deserve particular notice. The question of adoption or rejection was now approaching. The decision was still uncertain, and every mind and every heart was filled with anxiety. Mr. Henry partook most deeply of this feeling; and while engaged, as it were, in his last efforts, availed himself of the strong sensations which he knew to pervade the house, and made an appeal to it which, in point of sublimity, has never been surpassed in any age or country of the world.

After describing, in accents which spoke to the soul, and to which every other bosom deeply responded, the awful immensity of the question to the present and future generations, and the throbbing apprehensions with which he looked to the issue, he passed from the house and from the earth, and looking as he said, "beyond that horizon which binds mortal eyes," he pointed—with a countenance and action that made the blood run back upon the aching heart—to those celestial beings who were hovering over the scene, and waiting with anxiety for a decision which involved the happiness or misery of more than half the human race.

To those beings—with the same thrilling look and action—he had just addressed an invocation that made every nerve shudder with supernatural horror—when, lo! a storm at that instant arose, which shook the whole building, and the spirits whom he had called seemed to have come at his bidding. Nor did his eloquence, or the storm immediately cease—but availing himself of the incident, with a master's art, he seemed to mix in the fight of his ethereal auxiliaries, and "rising on the wings of the tempest, to seize upon the artillery of Heaven, and direct its fiercest thunders against the heads of his adversaries." The scene became insupportable; and the house rose without the formality of adjournment, the members rushing from their seat with precipitation and confusion.*

But all his efforts were in vain. Either the justice of the opposing cause, or the powers of his adversaries, or the prejudged opinions and instructions of the members, rendered his reasoning and his eloquence equally unavailing. Out of a house, composed of one hundred and sixty-eight members, the question of ratification was carried by a majority of ten. Mr. Henry seemed to have a presage of this result. After the storm which has been mentioned, Colonel Innis, who, in his character of attorney-general, had been hitherto attending a court of *oyer and terminer*, came into the house, and the debate was renewed. Mr. Henry, in answering him, closed the last speech which he delivered on the floor, with the following remarks:—

"I beg pardon of this house for having taken up more time than came to my share; and I thank them for the patience and polite attention with which I have been heard. If I shall be in the minority, I shall have those painful sensations which arise from a conviction of being overpowered in a good cause. Yet, I will be a peaceable citizen! My head, my hand, and my heart shall be free to retrieve the loss of liberty, and remove the defects of that system, in a *constitutional way*. I wish not to go to violence, but will wait with hopes that the spirit which predominated in the revolution is not yet gone: nor the cause of those who are attached to the revolution yet lost—I shall therefore patiently wait, in expectation of seeing that government changed, so as to be compatible with the safety, liberty, and happiness of the people."

The objections, however, which had been urged, and the arguments by which they had been supported, although they had not succeeded in preventing the ratification of the constitution, had produced a very serious effect on the house. Before their final dissolution, they agreed to a bill of rights, and a series of amendments (twenty in number,) embracing and providing for the objections of Mr. Henry and his associates. A copy of these amendments, engrossed on parchment, and

* The words above quoted are those of Judge Archibald Stewart; a gentleman who was present, a member of the convention, and one of those who voted against the side of the question supported by Mr. Henry. The incident, as given in the text, is wholly founded on the statements of those who were witnesses of the scene; and by comparing it with the corresponding passage in the printed debates, the reader may decide how far these are to be relied on as specimens of Mr. Henry's eloquence.

signed by the president of the convention, was ordered to be transmitted to congress, together with the instrument of ratification. Similar copies were ordered to be transmitted to the executive and legislatures of the several states; and fifty copies of the ratification and proposed amendments were ordered to be struck for the use of each county in this commonwealth.

Mr. Henry lost no ground with the people, at the time, for the part which he had taken on this occasion; and when afterward the constitution began to develop its tendencies by practical operation, so many of his predictions were believed by a majority of the people of Virginia to be fulfilled, and so many more in a rapid progress of fulfilment, that his character for political penetration rose higher than ever. That he had lost no ground at the time, two signal proofs were given in the session of assembly immediately following that of the convention. The latter body rose on the twenty-seventh of June, and the assembly met on the twentieth of October following. This interval had been too short to permit the subsidence of that high excitement, which the canvass of the constitution had provoked; and the assembly was consequently discriminated by feelings of party as strong and determined, as those which had characterized the convention itself.

The constitution having been adopted by a sufficient number of states to carry it into effect, it became necessary at this session to provide for its organization, and, among other measures, to choose two senators to represent this state, in the congress of the United States. For this office, Mr. Madison was presented by those who were at that time distinguished by the appellation of *federalists;* by which nothing more was then meant, than that they were advocates for the adoption of the new federal constitution.

The anti-federalists, on the contrary, who were alarmed by the vast powers which they considered as granted by the constitution, regarded it as a salutary check on the constructive extension of those powers, and as the best means of securing those amendments which they deemed essential to the liberties of the people, that the first congress should be composed of men of their own sentiments. In opposition to Mr. Madison, therefore, Mr. Henry took the unusual liberty of nominating two candidates, Mr. Richard H. Lee and Mr. Grayson; and, notwithstanding the great accession of character which Mr. Madison had acquired by the ability with which he had espoused the ratification of the constitution, those gentlemen were elected by a considerable majority.

At the same session of the assembly, Mr. Henry, whose mind seems to have been filled with the most oppressive solicitude by the unconditional adoption of the constitution, and who brooded with correspondent anxiety over the most effect ive means of procuring amendments, moved, in the committee of the whole house, the following preamble and resolutions:—

"Whereas the convention of delegates of the people of this commonwealth did ratify a constitution or form of government for the United States, referred to them for their consideration, and did also declare that sundry amendments to exceptionable parts of the same ought to be adopted; and whereas the subject-matter of the amendments agreed to by the said convention involves all the great, essential, and unalienable rights, liberties, and privileges of freemen; many of which, if not cancelled, are rendered insecure under the said constitution, until the same shall be altered and amended:—

"*Resolved*, That it is the opinion of this committee, that for quieting the minds of the good citizens of this commonwealth—and securing their dearest rights and liberties—and preventing those disorders which must arise under a government not founded in the confidence of the people—application be made to the congress of the United States, as soon as they shall assemble under the said constitution, *to call a convention* for proposing amendments to the same, according to the mode therein directed.

"*Resolved*, That it is the opinion of this committee, that a committee ought to be appointed to draw up and report to the house, a proper instrument of writing, expressing the sense of the general assembly, and pointing out the reasons which induce them to urge their application thus early, for calling the aforesaid convention of the states.

"*Resolved*, That it is the opinion of this committee, that the said committee ought to be instructed to prepare the draft of a letter, in answer to one received from his excellency George Clinton, Esq., president of the convention of New York—and a circular letter, on the aforesaid subject, to the other states in the union, expressive of the wish of the general assembly of this commonwealth, that they may join in an application to the new congress, to appoint a convention of the states, so soon as the congress shall assemble under the new constitution."

These were carried in committee, and immediately reported to the house; when a motion was made to amend them, by striking out from the word "whereas," and substituting in lieu of the original, the following preamble and resolutions:—

"*Whereas*, the delegates appointed to represent the good people of this commonwealth, in the late convention held in the month of June last, did, by their act of the twenty-fifth of the same month, assent to and ratify the constitution, recommended on the seventeenth day of September, seventeen hundred and eighty-seven, by the federal convention for the government of the United States, declaring themselves, with a solemn appeal to the Searcher of hearts for the purity of their intentions, under the conviction, "that whatsoever imperfections might exist in the constitution, ought rather to be examined in the mode prescribed therein, than to bring the Union into danger by a delay, with a hope of obtaining amendments previous to the ratification.

"And whereas, in pursuance of the said declaration, the same convention did, by their subsequent act of the twenty-seventh of June, aforesaid, agree to such amendments to the said constitution of the government for the United States, as were by them deemed necessary to be recommended to the consideration of the congress which shall first assemble under the said constitution, to be acted upon according to the mode prescribed in the fifth article thereof; at the same time enjoining it upon their representatives in congress, to exert all their influence, and use all reasonable and legal methods, to obtain a ratification of the foregoing alterations and provisions, in the manner provided by the fifth article of the said constitution, and in all congressional laws to be passed in the meantime, to conform to the spirit of those amendments as far as the said constitution would admit.

"*Resolved*, Therefore, that it is the opinion of this committee, that an application ought to be made, in the name and on the behalf of the legislature of this commonwealth, to the congress of the United States, so soon as they shall assemble under the said constitution, to pass an act recommending to the legislatures of the several states, the ratification of a bill of rights, and of certain articles of amendment, proposed by the convention of this state, for the adoption of the United States; and that, until the said act shall be ratified in pursuance of the fifth article of the said constitution of the government for the United States, congress do conform their ordinances to the true spirit of the said bill of rights and articles of amendment.

"*Resolved*, That it is the opinion of this committee, that the executive ought to be instructed to transmit a copy of the foregoing resolution to the congress of the United States, so soon as they shall assemble, and to the legislatures and executive authorities of each state in the union."

On this proposal of amendment a very animated debate ensued, which resulted in its rejection, and the adoption of the original report, by a majority of more than two for one.

These two measures—the election of the senators named by Mr. Henry, in opposition to so formidable a competitor as Mr. Madison—and the carrying so strong a measure as the call of a new continental convention, for the purpose of revising and altering the constitution—certainly furnish the most decisive proof, that his influence remained unimpaired by the part which he had taken in the convention of the state.

It was in the course of the debate which has been just mentioned, that Mr. Henry was driven from his usual *decorum* into a retaliation, that became a theme of great public merriment at the time, and has continued ever since one of the most popular anecdotes that relate to him.

He had insisted, it seems, with great force, that the speedy adoption of the amendments was the only measure that could secure the great and unalienable rights of the freemen of this country—that the people were known to be exceedingly anxious for this measure—that it was the only step which could reconcile them to the new constitution—and assure that public contentment, security, and confidence, which were the sole objects of government, and without which no government could stand—that whatever might be the individual sentiments of gentlemen, yet the wishes of the people, the foundation of all authority, being known, they were bound to conform to those wishes—that, for his own part, he considered *his* opinion as nothing, when opposed to those of his constituents; and that he was ready and willing *at all times* and *on all occasions*, "*to bow, with the utmost deference, to the majesty of the people.*"

A young gentleman, on the federal side of the house, who had been a member of the late convention, and had in that body, received, on one occasion, a slight touch of Mr. Henry's lash, resolved now, in an ill-fated moment, to make a set charge upon the veteran, and brave him to the combat. He possessed fancy, a graceful address, and an easy, sprightly elocution; and had been sent by his father, (an opulent man, and an officer of high rank and trust under the regal government,) to finish his education in the colleges of England, and acquire the polish of the court of St. James; *where he had passed the whole period of the American revolution.*

Returning with advantages which were rare in this country, and with the confidence natural to his years, presuming a little too far upon those advantages, he seized upon the words, "bow to the majesty of the people," which Mr. Henry had used, and rung the changes upon them with considerable felicity.

He denied the solicitude of the people for the amendments, so strenuously urged on the other side; he insisted that the people thought their "*great* and *unalienable* rights" sufficiently secured by the constitution which they had adopted: that the preamble of the constitution itself, which was now to be considered as the language of the people, declared its objects to be, among others, the security of those very rights; the people then declare the constitution the guarantee of their rights, while the gentleman, in opposition to this public declaration of their sentiments, insists upon *his amendments* as furnishing that guarantee; yet the gentleman tells us, that "he bows to the majesty of the people:" these words he accompanied with a most graceful bow.

"The gentleman," he proceeded, "had set himself in opposition to the will of the people, throughout the whole course of this transaction: the people approved of the constitution: the suffrage of their constituents in the last convention had proved it—the people wished, most anxiously wished, the adoption of the constitution, as the only means of saving the credit and the honour of the country, and producing the stability of the union: the gentleman, on the contrary, had placed himself at the head of those who opposed its adoption—*yet, the gentleman is ever ready and willing, at all times and on all occasions, to bow to the majesty of the people*," (with another profound and graceful bow.)

Thus he proceeded, through a number of animated sentences, winding up each one with the same words, sarcastically repeated, and the accompaniment of the same graceful obeisance. Among other things, he said, "it was of little importance whether a country was ruled by a despot, with a tiara on his head, or by a demagogue in a red cloak, a caul-bare wig," &c., (describing Mr. Henry's dress so minutely, as to draw every eye upon him,) "although he *should profess on all occasions to bow to the majesty of the people*."

A gentleman who was present, and who, struck with the singularity of the attack, had the curiosity to number the vibrations on those words, and the accompanying action, states, that he counted *thirteen* of the most graceful bows he had ever beheld. The friends of Mr. Henry considered such an attack on a man of his years and high character as very little short of sacrilege; on the other side of the house, there was, indeed, a smothered sort of dubious laugh, in which there seemed to be at least as much apprehension as enjoyment. Mr. Henry had heard the whole of it without any apparent mark of attention.

The young gentleman having finished his philipic, very much at least to his own satisfaction, took his seat, with the gayest expression of triumph in his countenance—"*Heu! Nescia mens hominum, fati, sortisque futuræ!*" Mr. Henry raised himself up, heavily, and with affected awkwardness—

"Mr. Speaker," said he, "I am a plain man, and have been educated altogether in Virginia. My whole life has been spent among planters, and other plain men of similar education, who have never had the advantage of that polish which a court alone can give, and which the gentleman over the way has so happily acquired; indeed, sir, the gentleman's employments and mine (in common with the great mass of his countrymen) have been as widely different as our fortunes; for while that gentleman was availing himself of the opportunity which a splendid fortune afforded him, of acquiring a foreign education, mixing among the great, attending levees and courts, *basking in the beams of royal favour at St. James'*, and exchanging courtesies with crowned heads, I was engaged in the arduous toils of the revolution; and was probably as far from thinking of acquiring those polite accomplishments which the gentleman has so successfully cultivated, as that gentleman *then* was from sharing in the toils and dangers in which *his unpolished countrymen* were engaged.

"I will not, therefore, presume to vie with the gentleman in those courtly accomplishments, of which he has just given the house so agreeable a specimen; yet such a bow as I can make, shall be ever at the service of the people."—Herewith, although there was no man who could make a more graceful bow than Mr. Henry, he made one so ludicrously awkward and clownish, as took the house by surprise, and put them into a roar of laughter.—"The gentleman, I hope, will commiserate the disadvantages of education under which I have laboured, and will be pleased to remember, that I have never been a favourite with that monarch, whose gracious smile he has had the happiness to enjoy."

He pursued this contrast of situations and engagements, for fifteen or twenty minutes, without a smile, and without the smallest token of resentment, either in countenance, expression, or manner. "You would almost have sworn," says a correspondent, "that he thought himself making his apology for his own awkwardness, before a full drawing-room at St. James.' I believe there was not a person that heard him, the sufferer himself excepted, who did not feel every risible nerve affected. His adversary meantime hung down his head, and sinking lower and lower, until he was almost concealed behind the interposing forms, submitted to the discipline as quietly as a Russian malefactor, who had been beaten with the knout, till all sense of feeling was lost."

The documents reported, and adopted by the house of delegates, in consequence of the foregoing resolutions, are the following—which are given because they are said to be from the pen of Mr. Henry:—

"*Resolved*, That it is the opinion of this committee, that an application ought to be made, in the name and on behalf of the legislature of this commonwealth, to the congress of the United States, in the following words, to wit:—

"The good people of this commonwealth,

"In convention assembled, having ratified the constitution submitted to their consideration, this legislature has, in conformity to that act, and the resolutions of the United States in congress assembled, to them transmitted, thought proper to make the arrangements that were necessary for carrying it into effect. Having thus shown themselves obedient to the voice of their constituents, all America will find that so far as it depends on them, that plan of government will be carried into immediate operation. But the sense of the people of Virginia would be but in part complied with, and but little regarded, if we went no further.

"In the very moment of adoption, and coeval with the ratification of the new plan of government, the general voice of the convention of this state pointed to objects no less interesting to the people we represent, and equally entitled to your attention. At the same time that, from motives of affection for our sister states, the convention yielded their assent to the ratification, they gave the most unequivocal proofs that they dreaded its operation under the present form.

"In acceding to a government under this impression, painful must have been the prospect, had they not derived consolation from a full expectation of its imperfections being speedily amended. In this resource, therefore, they placed their confidence—a confidence that will continue to support them, while they have reason to believe they have not calculated upon it in vain.

"In making known to you the objections of the people of this commonwealth to the new plan of government, we deem it unnecessary to enter into a particular detail of its defects, which they consider as involving all the great and unalienable rights of freemen: For their sense on this subject, we refer you to the proceedings of their late convention, and the sense of this general assembly, as expressed in their resolutions of the —— day of ——.

"We think proper, however, to declare that, in our opinion, as those objections were not founded on speculative theory, but deduced from principles which have been established by the melancholy example of other nations, in different ages—so they never will be removed, until the cause itself shall cease to exist. The sooner, therefore, the public apprehensions are quieted, and the government is possessed of the confidence of the people, the more salutary will be its operations, and the longer its duration.

"The cause of amendments we consider as a common cause; and since concessions have been made from political motives, which *we* conceive may endanger the republic, we trust that a commendable zeal will be shown for obtaining those provisions, which experience has taught us are necessary to secure from danger the unalienable rights of human nature.

"The anxiety with which our countrymen press for the accomplishment of this important end, will ill admit of delay. The slow forms of congressional discussion and recommendation, if indeed they should ever agree to any change, would we fear be less certain of success. Happily for their wishes, the constitution hath presented an alternative, by submitting the decision to a convention of the states. To this, therefore, we resort, as the source from whence they are to derive relief from their present apprehensions.

"We do, therefore, in behalf of our constituents, in the most earnest and solemn manner, make this application to congress, that a convention be immediately called, of deputies from the several states, with full power to take into their consideration the defects of this constitution that have been suggested by the state conventions, and report such amendments thereto as they shall find best suited to promote our common interests, and secure to ourselves, and our latest posterity, the great and unalienable rights of mankind."

Draft of a letter to Governor Clinton on the same subject:—

"SIR: The letter from the convention of the state of New-York hath been laid before us since our present session. The subject which it contemplated was taken up, and we have the pleasure to inform you of the entire concurrence in sentiment, between that honourable body and the representatives in senate and assembly of the freemen of this commonwealth.

"The propriety of immediately calling a convention of the states, to take into consideration the defects of the constitution was admitted; and in consequence thereof, an application agreed to, to be presented to the congress, so soon as it shall be convened for the accomplishment of that important end. We herewith transmit to your excellency, a copy of this application, which we request may be laid before your assembly at their next meeting. We take occasion to express our most earnest wishes that it may obtain the approbation of New-York, and of all other sister states."

Draft of a letter to the several states on the same subject:—

"The freemen of this commonwealth, in convention assembled, having, at the same time that they ratified the federal constitution, expressed a desire that many parts, which they considered as exceptionable parts, should be amended—the general assembly, as well from a sense of duty as a conviction of its defects, have thought proper to take the earliest measures in their power, for the accomplishment of this important object. They have accordingly agreed upon an application to be presented to the congress, so soon as it shall be assembled, requesting that honourable body to call a convention of deputies from the several states, to take the same into their consideration, and report such amendments as they shall find best calculated to answer the purpose.

"As we conceive that all the good people of the United States are equally interested in obtaining those amendments that have been proposed, we trust that there will be a harmony in their sentiments and measures, upon this very interesting subject. We herewith transmit to you a copy of this application, and take the liberty to subjoin our earnest wishes that it may have your concurrence."

In the two remaining years during which Mr. Henry continued a member of the assembly, I find nothing worthy of particular remark. In the spring of seventeen hundred and ninety-one, he declined a re-election, with the purpose of bidding a final adieu to public life: and although the tender of the most honourable appointments, the solicitations of his numerous friends and admirers, and ultimately his own wishes conspired to draw him from his retreat, he never again made his appearance in a public character.

CHAPTER IX.

Mr. Henry continues the Practice of the Law—Case of "the British Debts" —Uncommon Interest elicited to hear Mr. Henry on this Case—His Speech —Mode of answering opposing Counsel—Sketch of Him in his professional Character—His Defence of the Son of Dr. Holland on his Trial for Murder —Anecdote of the Case of John Hook—He bids a final Adieu to his Profession in 1794.

Mr. Henry still continued, however, rather through necessity than choice, the practice of the law: and in the fall of this year, seventeen hundred and ninety-one, a cause came on to be argued before the circuit court of the United States, in which he made what has been considered his most distinguished display of professional talents. This was the celebrated case of the British debts; a case in which, from its great and extensive interest, the whole power of the bar of Virginia was embarked, and which was discussed with so much learning, argument, and eloquence, as to have placed that bar, in the estimation of the federal judges, (if the reports of the day may be accredited,) above all others in the United States.

The cause was argued first in seventeen hundred and ninety-one, before Judges Johnson and Blair, of the supreme court, and Griffin, judge of the district; and afterward in seventeen hundred and ninety-three, before Judges Jay and Iredell, and the same district judge. Mr. Henry was one of the counsel for the defendant, and argued the cause on both occasions. The deep interest of the question, in a national point of view, and the manner in which it involved more particularly the honour of the state of Virginia, and the fortunes of her citizens, had excited Mr. Henry to a degree of preparation which he had never before made; and he came forth, on this occasion, a perfect master of every principle of law, national and municipal, which touched the subject of investigation in the most distant point.

Of the first argument, a manuscript report is still extant, taken in shorthand by Mr. Robertson, the same gentleman who reported the debates of the convention of Virginia in seventeen hundred and eighty-eight. The second argument was not reported; because, as Mr. Robertson states, he was informed by the counsel, that it would be nothing more than a repetition of the first; and he adds, that he was afterward told it was much inferior. What must we conclude, then, as to the powers displayed by Mr. Henry in the first argument, when, in the course of the second and inferior one, he extorted from Judge Iredell, as he sat on the bench, the exclamation:—"Gracious God!—He *is* an *orator indeed!*"

The report of the first argument, as deciphered by Mr. Robertson, from his stenographic notes, has been obligingly submitted to the author of these sketches, and he has extracted from it an imperfect analysis of Mr. Henry's speech. The report may unquestionably be relied on, so far as it professes to state the principles of law, and the *substance* of the arguments urged by the very eminent counsel engaged in the cause; and in this point of view, it is to be lamented that so valuable a work should still exist only in the form of a manuscript. But, as a sample of Mr. Henry's peculiar and inimitable eloquence, it is subject to all the objections which have been already urged to the printed debates of the Virginia convention.

This manuscript report bears upon its face the most conclusive proof of its inaccuracy in those passages in which it attempts to exhibit either the captivating flights of Mr. Henry's fancy, or those unexpected and overwhelming assaults which he made upon the hearts of his judges; for in *all* such passages, (it is believed, without an exception,) the pen has been drawn through the sentence as originally written, in such a manner, however, as to leave the words still legible; while the same thought, or something like it, has been interlined in other words; and even the interlineations themselves are oftener than otherwise erased, altered, and farther interlined, for the purpose of seeking to amend the expression: so that, in casting one's eyes over the manuscript report of Mr. Henry's speech, in order to single out the most brilliant passages, those which are the most blotted and blurred by erasures and interlineations may be selected at once, without the hazard of mistake. Hence, it is obvious, that the reporter had not in his stenographic notes, the *very expression* of the speaker; but some hint merely of the thought, which he was afterward unable to fill up to his own satisfaction. If farther evidence on this subject were required, it is found in this circumstance: that, on reading Mr. Robertson's imitations of the splendid parts of Mr. Henry's speech to several of those who heard it delivered, there has not been one who has not turned off from the recital with the strongest expressions of disappointment, and in several instances corrected by memory the language of the reporter.

This explanation is equally due to the memory of Mr. Henry, to the reader, and the author; for the author is fully aware, that if the truth of the general character which he has attempted to give of Mr. Henry's eloquence shall be tested by those imperfect specimens to which, for want of more accurate ones, he has been compelled to resort, discredit will be thrown upon the whole work, and it will be regarded rather as romance than history. But the ingenuous and candid reader will look beyond those poor and wretched imitations, and my own equally poor and wretched descriptions, to that proof of Mr. Henry's eloquence which is furnished by its practical effects. Can there be any doubt of the supreme eloquence of that man who awakened and hushed at his pleasure, "the stormy wave of the multitude?" who, by his powers of speech, roused the whole American people from north to south? put the revolution into motion, and bore it upon his shoulder, as Atlas is said to do the heavens? to whose charms of persuasion, not the rabble merely, but all ranks of society, have borne the most unanimous evidence? who moved not merely the populace, the rocks, and stones of the field, but, "by the summit took the mountain-oak, and made him stoop to the plain?"

Instead, then, of comparing our descriptions of Mr. Henry's eloquence with the specimens which his reporters have made of it, let the reader compare that description with the effects which it actually wrought, and the universal testimony which is borne to it, by the rapturous admiration of every one who ever had the happiness to hear him; and the author so far from being afraid of the charge of exaggeration, will be apprehensive only of that of presumption, in attempting a description of powers so perfectly undescribable.

But to return to his argument in the case of the British debts. In order to render intelligible the analysis which we propose to give to the reader, it will be necessary to prefix to it a statement of the case, of the pleadings, and the points made in argument, by the opening counsel.

William Jones, a British subject, as surviving partner of the mercantile house of Farrell and Jones, brought an action of debt in the federal circuit court at Richmond, against Doctor Thomas Walker, of the county of Albemarle, in Virginia, on a bond which bore date before the revolutionary war; to wit, on the eleventh of May, seventeen hundred and seventy-two. To this action the defendant pleaded five several pleas:—

1. The first was, the plea of payment generally, on which the plaintiff took issue; but it was not tried, the cause having gone off on the demurrers growing out of the subsequent pleadings.

2. In his second plea, the defendant relies on the act of sequestration, passed by the legislature of Virginia during the revolutionary war, to wit, on the twentieth of October, seventeen hundred and seventy-seven; by which it was enacted, that "it should be lawful for any citizen of this commonwealth, owing money to a subject of Great Britain, to pay the same, or any part thereof, from time to time, as he should think fit, into the loan office of the state; taking thereout a certificate for the same in the name of the creditor, with an endorsement under the hand of the commissioner of the loan office, expressing the name of the payee, delivering such certificate to the governor and council, *whose receipt should discharge him from so much of the debt:*"—and the defendant exhibits the governor's receipt for two thousand one hundred and fifty-one pounds and eighteen shillings, which he offers in bar to so much of the plaintiff's demand.

3. In his third plea, he sets out the act of forfeiture, passed by the assembly on the third of May, seventeen hundred and seventy-nine, whereby it was, among other things, enacted, "that all the property, real and personal, within the common-

wealth, belonging at that time to any British subject, should be deemed to be vested in the commonwealth;" as also the act of the sixth of May, seventeen hundred and eighty-two, whereby it was enacted, "that no demand whatsoever, originally due to a subject of Great Britain, should be recoverable in any court of this commonwealth, although the same might be transferred to a citizen of this state, or to any other person capable of maintaining such action, unless the assignment had been or might be made for a valuable consideration *bona fide* paid before the first of May, seventeen hundred and seventy-seven:" and the plea insists that the debt, in the declaration mentioned, was personal property of a British subject, forfeited to the commonwealth under the first-mentioned act, and a demand, whose recovery in the courts of the commonwealth was barred by the last.

4. The fourth plea takes the ground, that the king of Britain and his subjects were still alien enemies, and that the state of war still continued, on the ground of the several direct violations of the definitive treaty of peace, which follow:—

First, in continuing to carry off the negroes in his possession, the property of American citizens, and refusing to deliver them, or permit the owners to take them, according to the express stipulations of that treaty:—

Secondly, in the forcible retention of the forts Niagara and Detroit, and the adjacent territory:—

Thirdly, in supplying the Indians, who were at war with the United States, with arms and ammunition, furnished within the territories of the United States, to wit, at the forts Detroit and Niagara, and at other forts and stations forcibly held by the troops and armies of the king, within the United States; and in purchasing from the Indians, within the territories aforesaid, the plunder taken by them in war from the United States, and the persons of American citizens made prisoners; which several infractions, the plea contends, had abolished the treaty of peace, and placed Great Britain and the United States in a state of war; and that hence, the plaintiff, being an alien enemy, had no right to sue in the courts of the United States.

5. The fifth plea sets forth, that at the time of contracting the debt in the declaration mentioned, the plaintiff and the defendant were fellow-subjects of the same king and government; that on the fourth of July, seventeen hundred and seventy-six, the government of the British monarch in this country was dissolved, and the coallegiance of the parties severed; whereby the plea contends, that the debt in the declaration mentioned was annulled.

To the second plea the plaintiff replied, insisting on the treaty of peace of seventeen hundred and eighty-three, whereby it was stipulated, that creditors on either side should meet with no lawful impediment to the recovery of the full value, in sterling money, of all *bona fide* debts theretofore contracted; and also on the constitution of the United States of seventeen hundred and eighty-seven, by which it had been expressly declared, that treaties which were *then* made, or which should *thereafter* be made, under the authority of the United States, should be *the supreme law of the land*, anything in the constitution, *or the laws of any state, to the contrary notwithstanding*.

The defendant rejoined, that the treaty had been annulled by the infractions of it on the part of Great Britain, and so could not aid the cause of the plaintiff; and farther, that the debt in the declaration mentioned was not *bona fide* due, and owing to the plaintiff at the date of the treaty, insomuch as the same (or at least two thousand one hundred and fifty-one pounds and eighteen shillings of it) had been discharged by the payment set forth in the second plea; and hence, that it was not a subsisting debt, within the terms and provisions of the treaty.

To this rejoinder, as also to the third, fourth, and fifth pleas of the defendant, the plaintiff demurred; and the cause came on to be argued, on these demurrers, at Richmond, on the twenty-fourth of November, seventeen hundred and ninety-one.

The Virginian reader will readily estimate the splendour and power of the discussion in this case, when he learns the names of the counsel engaged in it; on the part of the plaintiff, then, were Mr. Ronald, Mr. Baker, Mr. Wickham, and Mr. Starke; and on that of the defendant, Mr. Henry, Mr. Marshall, (afterward chief justice of the United States,) Mr. Alexander Campbell, and Mr. Innis, the attorney-general of Virginia: I mention their names in the order in which they spoke on their respective sides.

The cause was opened with great fairness and ability, by Mr. Ronald and Mr. Baker, in succession; they were answered by all the counsel of the defendant; and Mr. Wickham, Mr. Starke, and Mr. Baker, were heard in the reply. The opening counsel made the following points:—

First, that debts were not a subject of confiscation in war.

Secondly, that if they were, Virginia, at the time of passing the acts relied on by the defendant, was not a sovereign and independent state, Great Britain not having at that time assented to her independence; and hence, that she had not the power of legislating away the debts of fellow-subjects not represented in her legislative councils—which councils, were themselves a usurpation in the eye of the law.

Thirdly, that if debts were subject to confiscation, and Virginia were competent to pass laws to that effect, she had not done so; and Mr. Baker particularly entered into a minute and ingenious scrutiny of the language of the several acts of assembly, to prove that, so far from having been forfeited, the debts were recognised as existing British debts down to the year seventeen hundred and eighty-two.

Fourthly, that if all these points were against the plaintiff. the right of recovering those debts was restored by the treaty of seventeen hundred and eighty-three, and the constitution of the United States, which recognised that treaty as the supreme law of the land; and,

Fifthly, that the alleged infractions of the treaty on the part of Great Britain did not produce the effect of abolishing the treaty; that this was a national concern, with which the individual plaintiff and defendant had nothing to do; that the question of infraction was one to be decided by the supreme power of the nation only, and one of which the court could not, with any propriety, take cognizance.

Mr. Baker closed his opening speech on Thursday evening, the twenty-fourth of November, and it was publicly understood that Mr. Henry was to commence his reply on the next day. The legislature was then in session; but when eleven o'clock, the hour for the meeting of the court, arrived, the speaker found himself without a house to do business. All his authority and that of his sergeant-at-arms were unavailing to keep the members in their seats; every consideration of public duty yielded to the anxiety which they felt, in common with the rest of their fellow-citizens, to hear this great man on this truly great and extensively-interesting question.

Accordingly, when the court was ready to proceed to business, the court-room of the capitol, large as it is, was insufficient to contain the vast concourse that was pressing to enter it. The portico, and the area in which the statue of Washington stands, were filled with a disappointed crowd, who, nevertheless, maintained their stand without. In the court-room itself, the judges through condescension to the public anxiety, relaxed the rigour of respect which they were in the habit of exacting, and permitted the vacant seats of the bench, and even the windows behind it, to be occupied by the impatient multitude. The noise and tumult, occasioned by seeking a more favourable station, were at length hushed, and the profound silence which reigned within the room gave notice to those without, that the orator had risen, or was on the point of rising.

Every eye in front of the bar was riveted upon him with the most eager attention; and so still and deep was the silence, that every one might hear the throbbing of his own heart. Mr. Henry, however, appeared wholly unconscious that all this preparation was on his account, and rose with as much simplicity and composure, as if the occasion had been one of ordinary occurrence. Nothing can be more plain, modest, and unaffected, than his exordium:—"I stand here, may it please your honours, to support, according to my power, that side of the question which respects the American debtor.

"I beg leave to beseech the patience of this honourable court; because the subject is very great and important, and because I have not only the greatness of the subject to consider, but those numerous observations which have come from the opposing counsel to answer. Thus, therefore, the matter proper for my discussion is unavoidably accumulated. Sir, there is a circumstance in this case, that is more to be deplored than that which I have just mentioned, and that is this: those animosities which the injustice of the British nation hath produced, and which I had well hoped would never again be the subject of discussion, are necessarily brought forth.

"The conduct of that nation, which bore so hard upon us in the late contest, becomes once more the subject of investigation. I know, sir, how well it becomes a liberal man and a Christian to forget and to forgive. As individuals professing a holy religion, it is our bounden duty to forgive injuries done us as individuals. But when to the character of Christian you add the character of patriot, you are in a different situation. Our mild and holy system of religion inculcates an admirable maxim of forbearance. If your enemy smite one cheek, turn the other to him. But you must stop there. You cannot apply this to your country. As members of a social community, this maxim does not apply to you. When you consider injuries done to your country, your political duty tells you of vengeance. Forgive as a private man, but never forgive public injuries. Observations of this nature are exceedingly unpleasant, but it is my duty to use them."

With the same primeval simplicity, he enters upon the argument; not making a formal division of the whole subject, but merely announcing the single proposition which he was about to maintain for the time; thus, immediately after the exordium which has been quoted he proceeds thus:—

"The first point which I shall endeavour to establish will be, that debts in common wars become subject to forfeiture; and if forfeited in common wars, much more must they be so in a revolution war, as the late contest was. In considering this subject, it will be necessary to define what a debt is. I mean by it an engagement, or promise, by one man to pay another, for a valuable consideration, an adequate price. By a contract thus made, for a valuable consideration, there arises what, in the law phrase, is called a *lien* on the body and goods of the promissor or debtor. This interest, which the creditor becomes entitled to, in the goods and body of his debtor, is such as may be taken from the creditor, if he be found the subject of a hostile country.

"This position is supported by the following authorities." He then cites and reads copious extracts from Grotius and Vattel, which seem to support his position decisively—and then proceeds thus:—"This authority decides in the most clear and satisfactory manner, that, as a nation, we had powers as extensive and unlimited as any nation on earth. This great writer, after stating the equality and independence of nations, and who are, and who are not enemies, does away the distinction between corporeal and incorporeal rights, and declares that war gives the same right *over the debts*, as over the other goods of an enemy.

"He illustrates his doctrine by the instance of Alexander's remitting to the Thessalians, a debt due by them to the Theban commonwealth: this is a case in point—for supposing the subjects of Alexander had been indebted to the Thebans, might he not have remitted the debts due by them to that people, as well as the debts due them by his allies, the Thessalians? Let me not be told that he was entitled to the goods of the Thebans, because he had conquered them. If he could remit a debt due by those whose claim of friendship was so inferior, those who were only attached to him by the feeble ties of contingent and temporary alliance—if his Macedonians, his immediate and natural subjects, were indebted to the Thebans, could he not have remitted *their* debts?

"This author states, in clear, unequivocal terms, by fair inference and unavoidable deduction, that when two nations are at war, either nation has a right, according to the laws of nature and nations, to remit to its own citizens debts which they may owe to the enemy. If this point wanted further elucidation, it is pointedly proved by the authority which I first quoted from Grotius, that it is an inseparable concomitant of sovereign power, that debts and contracts similar to those which existed in America, at the time the war with Great Britain broke out, may, in virtue of the eminent domain, or right, be cancelled and destroyed.

"'*A king has a greater right in the goods of his subjects, for the public advantage, than the proprietors themselves. And when the exigency of the state requires a supply, every man is more obliged to contribute toward it, than to satisfy his creditors.* The sovereign may discharge a debtor from *the obligation of paying, either for a certain time, or for ever*' What language can be more expressive than this? Can the mind of man conceive anything more comprehensive?

"Rights are of two sorts, private and inferior, or *eminent* and *superior*, such as the community hold over the persons and estates of its members for the common benefit. The latter is paramount to the former. A king or chief of a nation has a greater right than the owner himself over any property in the nation. The individual who owns private property cannot dispose of it, contrary to the will of his sovereign, to injure the public. This author is known to be no advocate for tyranny, yet he mentions that a king has a superior power over the property in his nation, and that by virtue thereof, he may discharge his subjects for ever from debts which they owe to an enemy.

"The instance which our author derives from the Roman history, affords a striking instance of the length to which the necessities and exigencies of a nation will warrant it to go. It was a juncture critical to the Roman affairs. But their situation was not more critical or dangerous than ours at the time these debts were confiscated. It was after the total defeat and dreadful slaughter at Cannæ, when the state was in the most imminent danger. Our situation in the late war was equally perilous. Every consideration must give way to the public safety.

"That admirable Roman maxim, *salus populi suprema lex*, governed that people in every emergency. It is a maxim that ought to govern every community. It was not peculiar to the Roman people. The impression came from the same source from which we derive our existence. Self-preservation, that great dictate implanted in us by nature, must regulate our conduct; we must have a power to act according to our necessities, and it remains for human judgment to decide what are the proper occasions for the exercise of this power. Call to your recollection our situation during the late arduous contest. Was it not necessary in our day of trial, to go to the last iota of human right? The Romans fought for their altars and household gods. By these terms they meant everything dear and valuable to men. Was not our stake as important as theirs?

"But many other nations engage in the most bloody wars for the most trivial and frivolous causes. If other nations who carried on wars for a mere point of honour, or a punctilio of gallantry, were warranted in the exercise of this power, were not we, who fought for everything most inestimable and valuable to mankind, justified in using it? Our finances were in a more distressing situation than theirs at this awful period of our existence. Our war was in opposition to the most grievous oppression—we resisted, and our resistance was approved and blessed by Heaven.

"The most illustrious men who have considered human affairs, when they have revolved human rights, and considered how far a nation is warranted to act in cases of emergency, declare that the only ingredient essential to the rectitude and validity of its measures is, that they be for the public good. I need hardly observe that the confiscation of these debts was for the public good. Those who decided it were constitutionally enabled to determine it. Grotius shows that you have not only power over the goods of your enemies, but according to the exigency of affairs, you may seize the property of your citizens."

After reading the apposite passage from Grotius, he says:—"I read these authorities to prove, that the property of an enemy is liable to forfeiture, and that debts are as much the subject of hostile contest as tangible property. And Vattel, page 484, as before mentioned, pointedly enumerates *rights* and *debts* among such property of the enemy as is liable to confiscation. To this last author I must frequently resort in the course of my argument. I put great confidence in him, from the weight of his authority—for he is universally respected by all the wise and enlightened of mankind, being no less celebrated for his great judgment and knowledge, than for his universal philanthropy. One of his first principles of the law of nations is, a perfect equality of rights among nations; that each nation ought to be left in the peaceable enjoyment of that liberty it has derived from nature.

"I refer your honours to his preliminary discourse from 6th to the 12th page; and as it will greatly elucidate the subject, and tend to prove the position I have attempted to support, I will read sections 17, 18, 19, and 20, of this discourse." Having read these sections, he touches transiently, but powerfully, the objection to the want of national independence to pass the laws of forfeiture, till that independence was assented to by the king of Great Britain. "When the war commenced," said he, "these things, called British debts, lost their quality of external obligation, and became matters of internal obligation, because the creditors had no right of constraint over the debtors. They were before the war, matters of perfect external obligation, accompanied by a right of constraint; but the war having taken away this right of constraint over the debtors, they were changed into an internal obligation, binding the conscience only. For it will not surely be denied, that the creditor lost the right of constraint over his debtor.

"From the authority of this respectable author, therefore—from the clearest principles of the laws of nature and nations, these debts became subject to forfeiture or remission. Those authors state, in language as emphatic and nervous as the human mind can conceive, or the human tongue can utter, that independent nations have the power of confiscating the property of their enemies; and so had this gallant nation. America, being a sovereign and complete nation, in all its forms and departments, possessed all the rights of the most powerful and ancient nations. Respecting the power of legislation, it was a nation complete, and without human control. Respecting public justice, it was a nation blessed by Heaven, with the experience of past times; not like those nations, whose crude systems of jurisprudence originated in the ages of barbarity and ignorance of human rights.

"America was a sovereign nation, when her sons stepped forth to resist the unjust hand of oppression, and declared themselves independent. The consent of Great Britain was not necessary (as the gentlemen on the other side urge) to create us a nation. Yes, sir, we were a nation, long before the monarch of that little island in the Atlantic ocean gave his *puny* assent to it."—These words he accompanied by a most significant gesture—rising on tiptoe—pointing as to a vast distance, and half-closing his eyelids, as if endeavouring with extreme difficulty, to draw a sight on some object almost too small for vision —and blowing out the words *puny* assent, with lips curled with unutterable contempt.—

"America was, long before that time, a great and gallant nation. In the estimation of *other nations* we *were* so: the beneficent hand of Heaven enabled her to triumph, and secured to her the most sacred rights mortals can enjoy. When these illustrious authors, these friends to human nature, these kind instructers of human errors and frailties,* contemplate the obligations and corresponding rights of nations, and define the internal right, which is without constraint and not binding, do they not understand such rights as these, which the British creditors now claim? Here this man tells us what conscience says ought to be done, and what is compulsory. These British debts must come within the grasp of human power, like all other human things. They ceased to have that external quality, and fell into that mass of power which belonged to our legislature by the law of nations."

He comes now to a very serious obstacle, which it required both address and vigour to remove. Vattel, whom he had cited to support his position of the forfeitable character of debts, and who, so far as Mr. Henry had read him, does support him explicitly, annexes a qualification to the principle, which had been pressed with great power by the gentlemen who opened the cause. The curiosity of the reader will be gratified by seeing the manner in which he surmounted the

* In the second argument, he eulogized the writers on the laws of nations, as "benevolent spirits, who held up the torch of science to a benighted world."

objection. "But we are told, that admitting this to be true in the fullest latitude, yet the customary law of Europe is against the exercise of this power of confiscation of debts; in support of which position, they rely on what is added by Vattel, p. 484.

Let us examine what he says:—'The sovereign has naturally the same right over what his subjects may be indebted to enemies: therefore, he may confiscate debts of this nature, if the term of payment happen in the time of war, or at least he may prohibit his subjects from paying while the war lasts. *But at present, in regard to the advantage and safety of commerce, all the sovereigns of Europe have departed from this rigour. And as this custom has generally been received, he who should act contrary to it, would injure the public faith; for strangers trusted his subjects only, from a firm persuasion,* that the general custom would be observed.'

"Excellent man! and excellent sentiments! The principle cannot be denied to be good: but when you apply it to the case before the court, does it warrant their conclusions? The author says, that although a nation has a right to confiscate debts due by its people to an enemy, yet, *at present the custom of Europe is contrary.* It is not enough for this author to tell us that this *custom* is contrary to the *right.* He admits the *right.* Let us see whether this custom has existence here. Vattel, having spoken of the necessary law of nations, which is immutable, and the obligations whereof are indispensable, proceeds to distinguish the several other kinds of natural law in the same preliminary discourse, pp. 11 and 12, thus:—

"'Certain maxims and customs consecrated by long use, and observed by nations between each other, as a kind of law, form this *customary law of nations*, or the custom of nations. This law is founded on a tacit consent, or, if you will, on a tacit convention *of the nations that observe it with respect to each other.* Whence, it appears, that *it is only binding to those nations that have adopted it,* and that is not universal, any more than *conventional laws.* It must be here also observed of this *customary law,* that the particulars relating to it do not belong to a systematic treatise on the law of nations, but that we ought to confine ourselves to the giving a general theory of it, that is, to the rules which here ought to be observed, as well with respect to its effects, as in relation to the matter itself: and in this last respect, these rules will serve to distinguish the lawful and innocent customs, from those that are unjust and illegal!

"'When a custom is generally established, either between all the polite nations in the world, or only between those of a certain continent, as of Europe for example; or those who have a more frequent correspondence; if that custom is in its own nature indifferent, and much more, if it be a wise and useful one, it ought to be obligatory on *all those nations who are considered as having given their consent to it.* And *they* are bound to observe it *with respect to each other*, while they have not expressly declared that they will not adhere to it. But if that custom contains anything unjust or illegal, it is of no force; and every nation is under an obligation to abandon it, nothing being able to oblige or permit a nation to violate a natural law.

"'These three kinds of the law of nations, *voluntary, conventional* and *customary*, together, compose the *positive law of nations.* For they all proceed from the volition of nations; the *voluntary law*, from their presumed consent: the *conventional law*, from an express consent; and the *customary law, from a tacit consent:* and as there can be no other manner of deducing any law from the will of nations, there are only these three kinds of the *positive law of nations.*'

"This excellent author, after having stated the voluntary law of nations to be the result of the equality of nations, and the conventional law to be particular compacts or treaties, *binding only on the contracting parties*, declares, *that the customary law of nations is only binding to those nations that have adopted it;* that it is a *particular* and not a *universal* law; that it applies *only* to distinct nations. The case of Alexander and the Thebans is founded on the *general* law of nations, applicable to nations at war. It is enough for me, then, to show that America, being at war, was entitled to the privilege of national law. But, says Vattel, the present state of European refinement controls the general law (of which he had been before speaking).

"We know that the customary law of nations can only bind *those who are parties to the custom.* In the year 1776, when America announced her will to be free, or in the year 1777, when the law concerning British debts passed, was there a customary law *of America* to this effect? Or were the customary laws of *Europe* binding on *America?* Were *we* a *party to any such customary law?* Was there anything in our constitution or laws which tied up our hands? No, sir. To make this customary law obligatory, the assent of *all the parties to be bound by it is necessary. There must be an interchange of it.*

"It is not for *one* nation or community to say to *another*, you are bound by this law, because *our kingdom* approves of it. It must not only be *reciprocal* in its *advantages* and *principles*, but it must have been *reciprocal in its exercise.* Virginia could not, therefore, be bound by it. Let us see whether it could be a hard case on the British creditors, that this customary law of nations did not apply in their favour. Were these debts contracted *from a persuasion of its observance? Did the creditors trust to this customary law of nations?* No, sir. They trusted to what they thought as firm, the *statute* and *common law of England.*

"Victorious and successful as their nation had lately been, when they, in their pride and inconsiderate self-confidence, stretched out the hand of oppression, their subjects placed no reliance on the *customs of particular nations.* They put confidence in those barriers of right, which were derived from their own nation. Their reliance was, that the tribunals established in this country, under the same royal authority, as in England, would do them justice. If we were not willing, they possessed the power of compelling us to do them justice. The debts, having, therefore, not been contracted *from any reliance on the customary law of nations,* were they contracted *from a regard 'to the rights of commerce?'*

"From a view of promoting the commerce of *those little things called colonies?* This regard could not have been the ground they were contracted on, for their *conduct* evinced that *they wished to take the right of commerce from us.* What other ingredient remains to show the operation of this custom in their favour? The book speaks of strangers trusting subjects of a different nation, from a reliance on the observance of the customary law.

"The fact here was, that fellow-subjects trusted us, on the footing just stated; trusted to the existing compulsory process of law, not relying on a passive inert custom. A fearful, plodding, sagacious trader, would not rely on so flimsy, so uncertain a dependance. Something similar to what he thought positive satisfaction, he relied on. Were we not subject to the same king? The cases are then at variance. He states the custom to exist for the advantage of commerce, and that a departure from it would injure the public faith. Public faith is in this case out of the question.

"The public faith was not pledged—it could not therefore be injured. I have already read to your honours from the 11th page of the preliminary discourse of Vattel, '*that the customary law of nations is only binding on those who have adopted it, and that it is not universal, any more than conventional laws.'* It is evident we could not be bound by any convention or treaty to which we ourselves were not a party: and from this authority it is equally obvious that we could not be bound by any customary law to which we were not parties.

"I think, therefore, with great submission to the court, that the right for which I contended, that is, that in common wars between independent nations, either of the contending parties has a right to confiscate or remit debts due by its people to the enemy, is not shaken by the customary law of nations, as far as it regards us, because the custom could not affect us. But gentlemen say we were not completely independent till the year 1783! To take them on their own ground, their arguments will fail them. There is a customary law which will operate pretty strongly on our side of the question. What were the inducements of the debtors? On what did the American debtor rely?

"Sir, he relied for protection on that system of common and statute law on which the creditors depended. Was he deceived in that reliance? That he was most miserably deceived, I believe will not admit of a doubt. The customary law of nations will only apply to distinct nations, mutually consenting thereto. When tyranny attempted to rivet her chains upon us, and we boldly broke them asunder, we were remitted to that amplitude of freedom which the beneficent hand of Nature gave us. We were not bound by fetters which are of benefit to one party, while they are destructive to the other. Would it be proper that we should be bound, and they unrestrained?"

As a still farther answer to the objection, and as giving the only rule of restraint in operating on the property of a belligerant, he cites the following principle from Vattel, and applies it to the actual state of America: "Vattel, book the 3d, ch. 8, sect. 137, says, that 'the lawful end gives a true right only to those means *which are necessary for obtaining such end.* Whatever exceeds this, is censured by the laws of nature as faulty, and will be condemned at the tribunal of conscience. Hence it is, that the right to such or such acts of hostility varies according to their circumstances. What is just and perfectly innocent in a war, in one particular situation, is not always so in another. *Right goes hand in hand with necessity,* and the exigency of the case; but never exceeds it.'

"This, sir, is the first dictate of nature, and the practice of of nations; and if your misfortunes and distresses should be sad and dreadful, you are let loose from those common restraints which may be proper on common occasions, in order to preserve the great rights of human nature.

"This is laid down by that great writer in clear and unequivocal terms. If then, sir, it be certain from a recurrence to facts, that it was necessary for America to seize on British property, this book warrants the legislature of this state in passing those confiscating and prohibitory laws. I need only refer to your recollection, for our pressing situation during the late contest; and happy am I, that this all-important question comes on, before the heads of those, who were actors in the great scene, are laid in the dust. An uninformed posterity would be unacquainted with the awful necessity which impelled us on.

"If the means were within reach, we were warranted by the laws of nature and nations to use them. The fact was, that we were attacked by one of the most formidable nations under heaven; a nation that carried terror and dread with its thunder to both hemispheres."—[This illustration of the power of Great Britain was, if we may trust respectable tradition, much more expanded than we find it in the report; and such was the force of his imagination, and the irresistible energy of his delivery and action, that the audience now felt themselves instinctively recoiling from the tremendous power of that very nation, which but a short time before had been exhibited as a mere dot in the Atlantic, a point so microscopic as to be scarcely visible to the naked eye: he proceeds to close the first member of his first point thus:]

"Our united property enabled us to look in the face that mighty people. Dared we to have gone in opposition to them bound hand and foot? Would we have dared to resist them fettered? for we should have been fettered, if we had been deprived of so considerable a part of our little stock of national resources. In that most critical and dangerous emergency, our all was but a little thing. Had we a treasury?—an exchequer? Had we commerce? Had we any revenue? Had we anything from which a nation could draw wealth? No, sir. Our credit became the scorn of our foes. However, the efforts of certain patriotic characters (there were not a few of them, thank Heaven) gave us credit among our own people.

"But we had not a farthing to spare. We were obliged to go on a most grievous anticipation, the weight of which we feel at this day. Recur to our actual situation, and the means which we had of defending ourselves. The actual situation of America is described here, where this author says, '*that right goes hand in hand with necessity.*' The necessity of being great and dreadful, you are warranted to lay hold of every atom of money within your reach, especially if it be the money of your enemies. It is prudent and necessary to strengthen yourselves and weaken your enemies.

"Vattel, book 3d, ch. 8, sect. 138, says, 'The business of a just war being to suppress violence and injustice, it gives a right to compel, by force, him who is deaf to the voice of justice. It gives a right of doing against the enemy, whatever is necessary for weakening him—for disabling him from making any farther resistance in support of his injustice—and the most effectual, the most proper methods may be chosen, provided they have nothing odious, be not unlawful in themselves, or exploded by the law of nature.' Here let me pause for a moment, and ask, whether it be odious in itself, or exploded by the law of nature, to seize those debts?

"No—because the money was taken from the very offenders. We fought for the great, unalienable, hereditary rights of human nature. An unwarrantable attack was made upon us. An attack, not only not congenial with motherly or parental tenderness, but incompatible with the principles of humanity or civilization. Our defence then was a necessary one. What says Vattel, book 3d, chapter 8, section 136?—'The end of a just war is to *revenge or prevent injury;* that is, to procure by force the justice which cannot otherwise be obtained; to compel an unjust person to repair an injury already done, or to give securities against any wrong threatened by him.

"'On a declaration of war, therefore, this nation has a right of doing against the enemy whatever is necessary to this justifiable end of bringing him to reason, and obtaining justice and security from him.' We have taken nothing in this necessary defence, but from the very offenders—those who unjustly attacked us: for we had a right of considering every individual of the British nation as an enemy. This I prove by the same great writer, p. 519, section 139, of the same book:—'An enemy attacking me unjustly gives an undoubted right of repelling his violences; and he who opposes me in arms, when I demand only my right, becomes himself the real aggressor, by his unjust resistance. He is the first author of violence, and obliges me to make use of force, for securing myself against the wrongs intended me either in my person or possessions; for if the effects of this force proceed so far as to take away his life, he owes the misfortune to himself; for, if by sparing him, I should submit to the injury, the good would soon become the prey of the wicked.

"'Hence the right of *killing* enemies in a just war is derived; when their resistance cannot be suppressed—when they are not to be reduced by milder methods, *there is a right of taking away their life.* Under the *name of enemies,* as we have already shown, are comprehended not only the first author of the war, but likewise *all who join him, and fight for his cause.*' Thus I think the first part of my position confirmed and unshaken; that in common wars, a nation not restrained by the customary law of nations, has a right to confiscate debts."

In the second member of that point, he is released from the

servility of quotation; and, to borrow a phrase of his own, "remitted to the amplitude" of his natural genius: the reader will therefore be amused by a more copious extract:—"From this I will go on to the other branch of my position: that if, in common wars, debts be liable to forfeiture, *a fortiori*, must they be so in a revolution war. Let me contrast the late war with wars in common. According to those people called kings, wars in common are systematic and produced for trifles; for not conforming to imaginary honours; because you have not lowered your flag before him at sea; or for a supposed affront to the person of an ambassador.

"Nations are set by the ears, and the most horrid devastations are brought on mankind, for the most frivolous causes. If then, when small matters are in contest, debts be forfeitable, what must have accrued to *us*, as engaged in the late revolution war—a war commenced in attainder, perfidy, and confiscation? If we take with us this great principle of Vattel, that *right goes in hand with necessity*, and consider the peculiar situation of the American people, we will find reason more than sufficient to give us a right of confiscating those debts.

"The most striking peculiarity attended the American war. In the first of it, we were stripped of every municipal right. Rights and obligations are correspondent, co-extensive, and inseparable—they must exist together, or not at all. We were, therefore, when stripped of all our municipal rights, clear of every municipal obligation, burden, and onerous engagement. If then the obligation be gone, what is become of the correspondent right? They are mutually gone."

These little words, "they are mutually gone," which would have made no figure in the pronunciation of an ordinary speaker, are said to have formed a beautiful picture, as delivered by Mr. Henry: his eyes seemed to have pursued these associated objects to the extremest verge of mortal sight, while the fall of his voice, and correspondent fall of his extended hand, with the palm downward, depicted the idea of evanescence with indescribable force: the audience might imagine, that they saw the objects at the very instant when they vanished in the distance, and became commingled with the air: and all this, too, without any affected pause to give it effect; without any apparent effort on his part; but with all the quickness of thought and all the ease of nature.

"The case of sovereign and independent nations at war is far different; because, there private right is respected, and domestic *asylum* held sacred. Was it the case in our war? No, sir. Daggers were planted in your chambers, and mischief, death, and destruction, might meet you at your fireside.

"There is an essential variance between the late war and common wars. In common wars, children are not obliged to fight against their fathers, nor brothers against brothers, nor kindred against kindred. Our men were compelled, contrary to the most sacred ties of humanity, to shed the blood of their dearest connexions. In common wars, contending parties respect municipal rights, and leave even to those they invade, the means of paying debts, and complying with obligations; they touch not private property. For example, when a British army lands in France, they plunder nothing: they pay for what they have, and respect the tribunals of justice, unless they have a mind to be called a savage nation.

"Were we thus treated? Were we permitted to exercise industry and to collect debts, by which we might be enabled to pay British creditors? Had we a power to pursue commerce? No, sir. What became of our agriculture? Our inhabitants were mercilessly and brutally plundered, and our enemies professed to maintain their army by those means only. Our slaves carried away, our crops burnt, a cruel war carried on against our agriculture—disability to pay debts produced by pillage and devastation, contrary to every principle of national law. From that series of plenty in which we had been accustomed to live and to revel, we were plunged into every species of human calamity.

"Our lives attacked—charge of rebels fixed upon us—confiscation and attainder denounced against the whole continent; and he that was called king of England sat judge upon our case—he pronounced his judgment, not like those to whom poetic fancy has given existence—not like him who sits in the infernal regions, and dooms to the Stygian lake those spirits who deserve it, because *he* spares the innocent, and sends *some* to the fields of Elysium—not like *him* who sat in ancient imperial Rome, and wished the people had but one neck, that he might at one blow strike off their heads, and spare himself the trouble of carnage and massacre, because *one city* would have satisfied his vengeance—not like any of his fellow-men, for nothing would satiate his sanguinary ferocity, but the indiscriminate destruction of a whole continent—involving the innocent with the guilty.

"Yes, *he* sat in judgment with his coadjutors, and pronounced proscription, attainder, and forfeiture, against men, women, and even children at the breast. Is not this description pointedly true in all its parts? And *who* were his coadjutors and executioners in this strange court of judicature? Like the fiends of poetic imagination—*Hessians, Indians* and *Negroes*, were his coadjutors and executioners. Is there anything in this sad detail of offences which is unfounded? anything not enforced by the act of parliament against America? We were thereby driven out of their protection, and branded by the epithet *rebels*. The term *rebel* may not now appear in all its train of horrid consequences.

"We know that when a person is called *rebel* by that government, his goods and life are forfeited, and his very blood pronounced to be corrupted, and the severity of the punishment entailed on his posterity. To whom may we apply for the verity of this? The jurisprudence and history of that nation prove, that, when they speak of rebels, nothing but blood will satisfy them. Is there nothing hideous in this part of the portrait? It is unparalleled in the annals of mankind. Though I have respect for individuals of that nation, my duty constrains me to speaks thus.

"When we contemplate this mode of warfare, and the sentiments of the writers on natural law on this subject, we are justified in saying, that in this revolution war, we had a right to consider British debts as subject to confiscation—and to seize the property of those who originated that war. As to the injuries done to agriculture, they appear in a diminutive view, when compared to the injuries and indignities offered to persons, and mansions of abode. Sir, from your seat you might have seen instances of the most grievous hostility: not only private property wantonly pillaged, but men, women, and children, dragged publicly from their habitations, and indiscriminately devoted to destruction. The rights of humanity were sacrificed. We were then deprived not only of the benefits of municipal, but natural law.

"If there shall grow out of these considerations a palpable disability to pay those debts, I ask if the claim be just? For that disability was produced by those excesses—by those very men who come on us now for payment. Here give me leave to say, that they sold us a bad title in whatever they sold us—in real as well as in personal property. Describe the nature of a debt: it is an engagement or promise to pay—but it must be for a valuable consideration. If this be clear, was not the title, to whatever property they sold us, bad in every sense of the word, when the war followed? What can add value to property? Force.

"Notwithstanding the equity and fairness of the debt when incurred, if the security of the property received was afterward destroyed, the title has proved defective. Suppose millions were contracted for and received, those millions give you no advantage without force to protect them. This necessary protection is withdrawn by the very men who were bound to afford it, and who now demand payment. Neither lands, slaves, nor other property, are worth a shilling, without protecting force. This title was destroyed, when the act of parliament, putting us out of their protection, passed against America. I say, sir, the title was destroyed by the very offenders who come here now and demand payment. Justice and equity cancel the obligation as to the price that was to be given for it, because the tenure is destroyed, and the effects purchased have no value.

"Such a claim is unsupported by the plainest notions of right and wrong. For this long catalogue of offences committed against the citizens of America, every individual of the British nation is accountable. How are you to be compensated for those depredations on persons and property? Are you to go to the kingdom of England, to find the very individual who did you the outrage, and demand satisfaction of him? To tell you of such a remedy as this, is adding insult to injury. Every individual is chargeable with national offences."

To maintain this last position, he cites an authority expressly in point, from Vattel, and proceeds thus:—"These observations of Vattel amount to this: that a king or conductor of a nation is considered as a moral person, by means of whom the nation acquires or loses its rights, and subjects itself to penalties. The individuals, and the nation which they compose are one. I will therefore take it for granted, that whatever violences and excesses were committed on this continent are chargeable to the plaintiff in this very action. Recollect our distressed situation. We had no exchequer, no finances, no army, no navy, no common means of defence.

"Our necessity—dire necessity compelled us to throw aside those rules which respect private property, and to make impresses on our own citizens to support the war. Right and necessity being co-extensive, we were compelled to exert a right the most eminent over the whole community. The *salus populi* demanded what we did. If we had a right to disregard the legal fences thrown round the property of our citizens, had we not a greater right to take British property?

"Another peculiarity contributes to aid our defence. The want of an exchequer obliged us to emit paper money, and compel our citizens to receive it for gold. In the ears of some men this sounds harshly. But they are young men, who do not know and feel the irresistible necessity that urged us. Would your armies have been raised, clothed, maintained, or kept together without paper money? Without it, the war would have stood still, resistance to tyranny would have stopped, and despotism, with all its horrid train of appurtenances, must have depressed your country. We compelled the people to receive it in payment of all debts—we induced and invited them (if we did not compel them) to put it into the treasury, as a complete discharge from their debts.

"Sir, I trust I shall not live to see the day, when the public counsels of America, will give ground to say that this was a state trick, contrived to delude and defraud the citizens. What must it be ostensibly, when, by the compact of your nation, they had publicly bound and pledged themselves, that it was and should be money, if afterward, in the course of human events, when temptations present themselves, they shall declare that it is not money?

"Sir, the honest planter is unskilled in political tricks and deceptions. His interest ought never to be sacrificed. The law is his guide. The law compelled him to receive it, and his countrymen would have branded him with the name of enemy if he had refused it. The laws of the country are as sacred as the imaginary sanctity of British debts. Sir, national engagements ought to be held sacred; the public violation of this solemn engagement will destroy all confidence in the government. If you depart from the national compact one iota, you give a dangerous precedent, which may imperceptibly and gradually introduce the most destructive encroachment on human rights."

He then proceeds to notice more directly the objection, that we were not a people competent for legislation till the assent of the British king was given to our independence:—"I will beg leave here to dissent from the position of the gentleman on the other side, which denied that we were a people, till our enemies were pleased to say we were so. That we were a people, and had a right to do everything which a great and a royal—nay, an imperial people could do, is clear and indisputable. Though under the humble appearance of republicanism, our government and national existence, when examined, are as solid as a rock—not resting on the mere fraud and oppression of rulers, nor the credulity nor barbarous ignorance of the people; but founded on the consent and conviction of enlightened human nature. That we had every right that completely independent nations can have, will be satisfactorily proved to your honours, by again referring to Vattel."

He then cites and reads a passage from Vattel, the effect of which is, that during a civil war, the parties, acknowledging no common judge on earth, are to be considered as two distinct people; and to govern themselves in the conduct of the war by the general laws of nations. After which he proceeds thus:—

'Here then, sir, is proof abundant, that before the acknowledgment of American independence by *Great Britain*, we had a right to be considered as a nation; because on earth we had no common superior, to give a decision of the dispute between us and our sovereign. After declaring ourselves a sovereign people we had every right a nation can claim as an independent community. But the gentlemen on the other side greatly rely upon this principle, that a contract cannot be dissolved without the consent of all the contracting parties: the inference is, that the consent of the king of Great Britain was necessary to the dissolution of the government.

"Tyranny has too often and too successfully riveted its chains, to warrant a belief, that a tyrant will ever voluntarily release his subjects from the governmental compact. Rather might it be expected, that the last iota of human misery would be borne, and the oppression would descend from father to son, to the latest period of earthly existence. The despotism of our sovereign ought to be considered as an implied consent, on his part, to dissolve the compact between us; and he and his subjects must be considered as one—there can be no distinction. For, in any other view, his consent would not have been obtained without force. There is such a thing, indeed, as tyranny from free choice. Sweden not long ago surrendered its liberties in one day, as Denmark had done formerly; so that this branch of the human family is cut off from every possible enjoyment of human rights.

"But the right to resist oppression is not denied. The gentlemen's doctrine cannot therefore apply to national communities. If any additional force was wanting to confirm what I advance, it would be derived from the treaty of peace, which further proves, that we were entitled to all the privileges of independent nations. The consent of all the people of Europe said we were free. Our former master withheld his consent till a *few unlucky events* compelled him. And when he gave his *fiat*, it gave us, *by relation back to the time of the declaration of independence*, all the rights and privileges of a completely sovereign nation: our independence was acknowledged by him, previous to the completion of the treaty of peace. It was not a condition of the treaty, but was acknowledged, by his own overture, preparatory to it.

"View the consequences of their fatal doctrine. There would not only have been long arrears of debts to pay, but a long catalogue of crimes to be punished. If the ultimate acknowledgment of our independence by Great Britain had not relation back to the time of the declaration of independence, all the intermediate acts of legislation would be void—and every decision and act, consequent thereon, would be null. But, sir, we were a complete nation on every principle, according to the authorities I have already read; in addition to which I will refer your honours to Vattel, book iv. ch. vii. sec. 88, to show we were entitled to the benefits of national law, and to use all the resources of the community:

"'From the equality of all nations really sovereign and independent, it is a principle of the voluntary law of nations, that no nation can control another in its internal municipal legislation.' If we consider the business of confiscation according to the immemorial usages of Great Britain, we will find that the law and practice of that country support my position. In the wars which respect revolutions which have taken place in that island—life, fortune, goods, debts, and everything else were confiscated. The *crimen læsæ majestatis*, as it is called, involved everything. Every possible punishment has been inflicted on suffering humanity that it could endure, by the party which had the superiority in those wars, over the defeated party, which was charged with rebellion.

"What would have been the consequences, sir, if we had been conquered? Were we not fighting against that majesty? Would the justice of our opposition have been considered? The most horrid forfeitures, confiscations, and attainders, would have been pronounced against us. Consider their history, from the time of William the First till this day. Were not his *Normans* gratified with the confiscation of the richest estates in England? Read the excessive cruelties, attainders, and confiscations, of that reign. England depopulated—its inhabitants stripped of the dearest privileges of humanity—degraded with the most ignominious badges of bondage—and totally deprived of the power of resistance to usurpation and tyranny.

"This inability continued to the time of Henry the Eighth. In his reign, the business of confiscation and attainder, made considerable havoc. After his reign, some stop was put to that effusion of blood which preceded and happened under it. Recollect the sad and lamentable effects of the York and Lancastrian wars. Remember the rancorous hatred and inveterate detestations of contending factions—the distinction of the white and red roses. To come a little lower—what happened in that island in the rebellions of seventeen hundred and fifteen and seventeen hundred and forty-five? If we had been conquered, would not our men have shared the fate of the people of *Ireland?* A great part of that island was confiscated, though the *Irish* people thought themselves engaged in a laudable cause. What confiscation and punishments were inflicted in Scotland? The plains of *Culloden*, and the neighbouring gibbets, would show you. I thank Heaven that the spirit of liberty under the protection of the Almighty, saved, us from experiencing so hard a destiny.

"But had we been subdued, would not every right have been wrested from us? What right would have been saved? Would debts have been saved? Would it not be absurd to save debts, while they should burn, hang, and destroy? Before we can decide with precision, we are to consider the dangers we should have been exposed to, had we been subdued. After presenting to your view this true picture of what would have been our situation, had we been subjugated—surely a correspondent right will be found, growing out of the law of nations in our favour.

"Had our subjugation been effected, and we pleaded for pardon—represented that we defended the most valuable rights of human nature, and thought they were wrong—would our petition have availed? I feel myself impelled, from what has passed, to ask this question. I would not wish to have lived too see the sad scenes we should have experienced.

"Needy avarice, and savage cruelty, would have had full scope. Hungry *Germans*, blood-thirsty *Indians*, and nations of another colour, would have been let loose upon us. The sad effects of such warfare have had their full influence on a number of our fellow-citizens. Sir, if you had seen the sad scenes which I have known; if you had seen the simple but tranquil felicity of helpless and unoffending women and children, in little log huts on the frontiers, disturbed and destroyed by the sad effects of British warfare and Indian butchery, *your soul would have been struck with horror!* Even those helpless women and children were the objects of the most shocking barbarity.

"Give me leave again to refer to Vattel, p. 9:—'Nations being free, independent, and equal, and having a right to judge according to the dictates of conscience, of what is to be done in order to fulfil its duties; the effect of all this is, the producing, at least externally and among men, a perfect equality of rights between nations, in the administration of their affairs, and the pursuit of their pretensions, without regard to the intrinsic justice of their conduct, of which others have no right to form a definitive judgment: so that what is permitted in one, is also permitted in the other; and they ought to be considered in human society as having an equal right.'

"If it be allowed to the British nation to put to death, to forfeit and confiscate debts and everything else, may we not (having an equal right) confiscate—not life, for we never desire it—

but that which is the common object of confiscation—*property, goods*, and *debts*, which strengthen ourselves and weaken our enemies? I trust that this short recapitulation of events shows, that if there ever was in the history of man a case requiring the full use of all human means, it was our case in the late contest; and we were therefore warranted to confiscate the British debts."

He now takes another ground to establish the confiscation; I shall give his whole argument on this point in his own words:—

"I beg leave to add that these debts are lost on another principle. By the dissolution of the British government, America went into a state of nature—on the dissolution of that of which we had been members, there being no government antecedent, we went necessarily into a state of nature. To prove this, I need only refer to the Declaration of Independence, pronounced on the fourth day of July, seventeen hundred and seventy-six, and our state constitution."—Here Mr. Henry read part of the constitution.—"It recites many instances of *misrule* by the king of England—it asserts the right and expediency of dissolving the British government, and going into a state of nature; or, in other words, to establish a new government. The right of dissolving it and forming a new system, had preceded the fourth day of July, seventeen hundred and seventy six.

"A recapitulation of the events of the tyrannical acts of government, would demonstrate a right to dissolve it. But I may go farther, and even say, that the act of parliament which declared us out of the king's protection, dissolved it. For what is government? It is an express or implied compact between the rulers and ruled, stipulating reciprocal protection and obedience. That protection was withdrawn, solemnly withdrawn from us. Of consequence, obedience ceased to be due. Our municipal rights were taken away by one blow. Municipal obligations and government were also taken away by the same blow.

"Well, then, there being no antecedent government, we returned into a state of nature. Unless we did so, our new compact of government could only be a usurpation. In a state of nature there is no legal *lien* in the person or property of any one. If you are not clear of every antecedent engagement, what is the legality or strength of the present constitution of government? If any antecedent engagements are to bind, how far are they to reach? You had no right to form a new government, if the old system existed; and if it did not exist, you were necessarily and inevitably in a state of nature.

21*

"In my humble opinion, by giving validity to such claims, you destroy the very idea of the right to form a new government. Vattel calls government the totality of persons, estates, and effects, formed by every individual of the new society, and that totality represented by the governing power. How can the totality exist while an antecedent right exists elsewhere? See Grotius, page 4, which I have already read, and note 29: because the design and good of civil society necessarily require, that the natural and acquired rights of each member should admit of limitations several ways, and to a certain degree by the authority of him or them, in whose hands the sovereign authority is lodged. When we formed a new government, did there exist any authority that limited our rights? How can the totality exist, if any other person or persons have an existing claim upon you?

"It appears to me, that that equality which is involved in a state of nature cannot exist while such claim exists. The court will recollect what I have already read out of Vattel, in sections 15 and 18. The equality here ascribed to independent nations is equally ascribed to men in a state of nature. A moral society of persons cannot exist without this absolute equality. The existence of individuals in a state of nature, depends in like manner upon, and is inseparable from such equality.

"Rights, as before-mentioned, Vattel, pp. 8 and 9, are divided into *internal* and *external:* of *external* rights, he makes the distinction of perfect and imperfect. I beseech your honours to fix this distinction in your minds. The *perfect external* right only is accompanied with the right of constraint. The imperfect right loses that quality, and leaves it to the party to comply or not to comply with it. When the former government was dissolved, the American people became indebted to nobody. You either owe everything or nothing—and every contract and engagement must be done away, if any.

"In a state of nature you are free and equal. But how are you free, if another have a lien on your body? Where is your freedom, or your equality with that person, who has the right of constraining you? This right of constraint implies a complete authority over you, but not however to enslave you. This constraint is always adequate to the right or obligation. Where can you find the possibility of this equality which nature gives her sons, if we admit an existing right of constraint?

"If it be a fact, that on the dissolution of the government we did enter into a state of nature, (and that we did, I humbly judge, cannot be denied, as at that time no government existed at all,) it destroys all claim to one farthing. This will be found to be true, as well upon the ground of equity and good conscience as in law, when it is considered, that when we went into a state of nature, the means of paying debts were taken away from us by them; because, so far as they had power over us, they prevented us from getting money to pay debts. They interdicted us from the pursuit of profitable commerce; from getting gold and silver, the only things they would take—they unjustly drove us to this extremity. By the concession of the worthy gentlemen, their attack upon us was unjust.

"But then, debts are not subject to confiscation, say gentlemen, because there were no inquests, no office found for the commonwealth. Has a debt an ear-mark? Is it tangible or visible? Has it any discriminating quality? Unless tangible or visible, how is it to be ascertained or distinguished? What does an inquest mean? A solemn inquiry by a jury, by ocular examination, with other proofs. If an inquest of office were to be had of land, a jury could tell the lines and boundaries of it, because they may be distinguished from others, and its identity may thereby be ascertained. If a horse be the object of inquiry, he can be easily distinguished from any other horse.

"In like manner every other article of visible property may be subject to inquests; but such a thing as an inquest of a debt never existed, as far as my legal knowledge extends. What are to be the consequences, if this proceeding be requisite? You must set up a court of inquisition, summon the whole nation, and ask every man *how much do you owe?* This would be productive of endless confusion, perplexity and expense, without the desired effect. The laws of war and of nations require no more than that the sovereign power should openly signify its will, that the debts be forfeited. There is no particular forensic form necessary. The question here is not, whether this confiscation be traversed in all the forms of municipal regulations. There is a question between Great Britain and America similar to that between Alexander and the Thebans. *Has the sovereign signified his pleasure that debts be remitted?*

"A sign is completely sufficient, if it be understood by the people. There is a necessity of thus speaking the legislative will, that the other party may know it, and retaliate; for what is allowed to one, is to both parties. This was different from the nature of a solemn war. War is lawful or unlawful, according to the manner of conducting it. In the prosecution of a lawful solemn war, it is necessary that you do not depart from certain rules of moderation, honour, and humanity, but act according to the usual practice of belligerent powers. Did the mother-country conduct the war against us in this manner?

We did openly say, we mean to confiscate your debts, and modify them, because they have lost their perfect external quality—they are imperfect—we claim that right, as a sovereign people, over that species of your property.

"Sir, it was not done in a corner. It was understood by our enemies. They had a right to retaliate on any species of our property they could find. The right of retaliation, or just retortion, for equivalent damage on any part of an enemy's property, is permitted to every nation. What right has the British nation (for if the nation have not the right, none of its people have) to demand a breach of faith in the American government to its citizens? I have already mentioned the engagement of the government with its citizens respecting the paper money—*If you take it, it shall be money.* Shall it be judged now not to be money? Shall this compact be broken for the sake of the British nation? No, sir, the language of national law is otherwise.

"Sir, the laws of confiscation and paper-money made together one system, connected and sanctioned by the legislature, on which depended once the fate our country, and on which depend now the happiness, the ease, and comfort of thousands of your fellow-citizens. Will it not be a breach of the compact with your people, to say that the money is not to keep up its original standard in the quality given it by law? What were the effects of this system? What would have been the effects, had your citizens been apprized that British debts must be paid? Would they have taken the money? Would they have deposited the money in the loan-office if they had been warned by law, that they must deposite it, subject to the future regulations of peace; that it should not release them from the creditors?

"However right it may appear now to decry the paper-money, it would have been fatal then; for America might have perished, without the aid and effect of that medium. Your citizens, trusting to this compact, submitted to a number of things almost intolerable—impressments and violences on their property—it encouraged them to exert themselves in defence of their property against the enemy during the war. If the debt in the declaration mentioned be recovered, the compact is subverted, as respecting the paper-money. And this subversion is to take effect for the interest of those men, whom, by all laws human and divine, we were obliged to consider as enemies; men who were obliged to comply with the regulations and requisitions of their king; and our people will have been labouring, not for themselves, but for the benefit of the British subject.

"When a vessel is in danger in a storm, those who abide on

board of her, and encounter the dangers of the sea to save her, are allowed some little compensation for salvage, for their fidelity and gallantry in endeavouring to prevent her loss; while those who abandon her are entitled to nothing. But, in opposition to this wise and politic principle, we, who have withstood the storms and dangers, receive no compensation; but those who left the political ship, and joined those on the other side of the *water* who wished to sink her, and who caused her to fight eight long years for her preservation, shall come in at last, and get their full share of this vessel, and yet will have been exonerated from every charge.

"For whom, then, were the people of America engaged in war? Not for themselves, I am sure—the property that they saved will not be for themselves, but for those whom they had a right to call enemies. I am not willing to ascribe to the meanest American the love of money, or desire of eluding the payment of his debts, as the motive of engaging in the war. No, sir. He had nobler and better views. But he thinks himself well entitled to those debts, from the laws and usages of nations, as a compensation for the injuries he has sustained. There is a sad drawback on this property saved. A national debt for seventeen years, considerable taxes, which were profusely laid during the war on lands and slaves; and, since the peace, we have been loaded with a heavy taxation. I know that I advocate this cause on a very advantageous ground, when I speak of the right of salvage.

"The cargo on board the wrecked vessel belongs to the British, it will have been saved for them! but the salvage is due to us only. If you take it on the ground of interest—you may hold as a pledge—you may retain for salvage. If you take it on the scale of the common law, or of national law—you may oppose damages to debts—retain the debts, to retribute and compensate for the injuries they have done you. I have now got over and I trust established the first point; that is that debts in common wars are subject to forfeiture, and much more so in a revolution war like the American war."

These copious extracts from the report on Mr. Henry's first point are deemed necessary to give the reader an idea of his mode of argumentation, so far as it can be furnished by this report. It would be trespassing on the indulgence of the proprietor of the manuscript, (which has never been published,) and trespassing too, perhaps, on the patience of that portion of my readers who can find no enjoyment in legal discussion, to pursue any farther this extended mode of analysis. Having established his first position, he presents his next point thus:—

"My next point is, that the British debts being so forfeited (as

I conceive) can only be revived by the treaty; and unless they be so revived, they are gone for ever. I will then consider how this matter stands under the treaty."

He proceeds then to show by authority, the rules by which treaties are to be construed; and demonstrates, that a treaty can confer no benefit unless it be mutually observed with good faith; that perfidy on either side is a forfeiture of all its advantages; that the stipulations of a treaty are in the nature of conditions precedent; that a breach on either side dissolves the covenant altogether, and places the parties on the general ground which they occupied before the treaty; that Great Britain had violated the treaty, in the moment of its ratification, by carrying off our slaves, and detaining with an armed force those posts of which she had stipulated the immediate surrender; that the pretence of her having acted thus as a retaliatory measure for the non-payment of the debts, was an insult to common understanding, because she began her infractions before any experiment had been made of a recovery of the debts; that the notion of a reprisal, preceding any injury—and a retaliation, *in advance*, of any wrong on the opposite side, was so far from mitigating her offence, that it was a daring insult on the honour and good faith of this nation! Having, by a series of authorities directly in point, established the right of the American nation to regard the treaty as abolished by any perfidious infraction of it, on the part of Great Britain, he shows next, that those infractions were established by the pleadings in the cause; because the defendant, by his several pleas, had specified those infractions, and the plaintiff, by demurring tc the pleas, had admitted the truth of their averments.

Great Britain, then, *as a nation*, having by her own perfidy forfeited all right to insist upon the treaty, and that treaty, as *between the nations*, being annulled, the next question was, whether any individual of the British nation could claim any advantage under the treaty? This he shows could not be done, because in making the treaty, the sovereigns of the two nations acted for all the individuals of their respective nations; the individuals were bound by all the acts of those sovereigns, whether in making or abolishing a treaty. "Here," said he, "are two moral persons, Great Britain and America, making a contract.

The plaintiff claims and the defendant defends *under and through them;* and if either nation or moral person has no right to benefits from such contract, individuals *claiming under them* can have none. The plaintiff then *claims under his nation*, but if that nation have committed perfidy respecting the observance of the compact, no right can be carried therefrom to the plaintiff. It puts him back in the same situation he was in before the treaty."

He shows the absurdity of considering the treaty as annulled, in relation to *all* the individuals, in their collective character of a nation, and yet as in full force for the benefit of *each* individual separately; for if this plaintiff had a right to all the beneficial effects of the treaty, every man in England had the same right; and he cites and reads from Vattel, a conclusive authority, to show, that the conventional law of nations could take its effect only from universal right, extending equally to all the citizens or individuals of a nation.

But to say that America had a right to consider the treaty as void against all the individuals of the British nation, *collectively*, while each and every individual of that nation *separately*, could enforce it upon her, was to offer to the understanding a paradoxical absurdity, as insulting to common sense, as the conduct of Great Britain had been to the honour of the American nation.

He contended further on this point, that if the treaty had been observed by Great Britain, and were of consequence still obligatory, it did not and could not operate where moneys had been actually paid into the treasury under the laws of the state; for the provision of the treaty is, "that creditors on either side should meet with no lawful impediment to the recovery of all *bona fide debts* heretofore contracted." The defendant, he said, having paid the money into the treasury according to the act of assembly, and the truth of the payment being admitted in the record, this article of the treaty could not support the plaintiff's claim.

"To derive a benefit from the treaty, the plaintiff must demand a *bona fide* debt; that is, a debt *bona fide* due. The word *debt* implies that the thing is due; for if it be not *due*, how can it be a *debt?* To give to these words, *all debts heretofore contracted*, a strictly literal sense, would be to authorize a renewed demand for debts which had been actually paid off to the creditor; for these were certainly within *the words* of the treaty, being *debts heretofore* contracted:—to avoid this absurd and dishonest consequence, you must look at the intention of the thing; and the intention certainly was to embrace those cases where there had not been a *legal payment*. I ask," said he, "why a payment made in gold and silver is a *legal payment?* Because the coin of those metals is made current by the laws of this country. If paper be made current by the same authority, why should not a payment in *it* be equally valid?

"The British subject cannot demand payment, because I

confront his demand with a receipt. Why will a receipt dis charge in any instance?—because it is founded on the laws of the country. A receipt given in consequence of a payment in coin, is a legal discharge, *only because the laws of the country make it so.* I ask then, why a receipt given in consequence of a payment into the treasury, be not of equal validity, since it has precisely the same foundation? It is expressly constituted a *discharge* by a legislature having competent authority. This debt, therefore, having been *legally* paid by the contractor, was not *due* from him at the time of making the treaty, and therefore is not within the intention of that instrument.

"But, say the gentlemen on the other side, the one payment has the consent of the creditor, and the other has not: he who paid coin has the creditor's consent to the discharge, but he who paid money into the treasury wants it. Have we not satisfied this honourable court, that the governing power had a right to put itself in the place of the British subjects? Having had an unquestionable right to confiscate, sequester, or modify those debts as they pleased, they had an equally indubitable right to substitute themselves in the stead of the plaintiff, otherwise those authorities have been quoted in vain."

He then cites authorities to prove, that the law of the place governs the contract; and concludes that the payment into the treasury having in this instance been made in consequence of a law of this commonwealth, which was strictly consonant with the laws of nations, and which had declared that such payment *should operate as a complete and final discharge,* this was not a subsisting *debt*, within the contemplation of the treaty, and remained therefore, wholly unaffected by it.

"The next question was, whether *this court* could take notice of this infraction of the treaty, on the part of Great Britain, and found their judgment upon it. On this question he observes that the court were not called upon to step out of their appropriate sphere, in order to invade the province of the jury by trying facts; the facts were all agreed by the pleadings; the court were merely called upon to say what was the law arising on those facts.

"The existence or non-existence of the treaty, was a legal inference from the facts agreed; which the courts alone were competent to decide. The plaintiff himself had forced this question on the court, by relying in his replication on the treaty, as restoring his right to recover this debt. He sets up his right under this instrument expressly, and then questions the jurisdiction of the court to decide upon the instrument! The treaty, *quoad hoc*, is the covenant of the parties in this

ant: the question presented by the pleadings is, whether the plaintiff who, by that covenant, has taken upon himself the performance of a precedent condition, can claim any benefit under it, until he shall show that this precedent condition has been performed.

"On this question," said he, "the gentleman's argument is, that the court have no power to decide on the construction of the covenant, which he himself has brought before them; that they have nothing to do with the dependance or independence of the stipulations or the reciprocal rights of the parties, to claim under the covenant, without showing a previous performance on their respective parts!

"*He*, on the contrary, insisted that, under the constitution of the United States, the question belonged, *peculiarly and exclusively*, to the judicial department; that by the constitution it was expressly provided, that the judicial power should extend *to all cases arising under treaties;* that the law of treaties embraced the whole extent of natural and national law: that the constitution therefore, by referring all cases arising under treaties to the judiciary, had of necessity invested them with the power of appealing to that code of laws, by which alone the construction, the operation, the efficacy, the legal existence or non-existence of treaties, must be tested: and by this code they were told in the most emphatic terms, that he who violates one article of a treaty, releases the other party from the performance of any part of it: that the reference of all cases arising under treaties, to the judicial department, carried with it every power near or remote, direct or collateral which was essential to a fair and just decision of those cases that in every such case, the very first question was, *Is* there a treaty or not?—not whether there *has been* a treaty—but whether there *is* an *existing obligatory, operative treaty*.

"To decide this question, the court must bring the facts to the standard of the laws of nations; and by this standard it had been shown, that in the case at bar, there existed no treaty from which a British subject could claim any benefit. That if the judicial department had not the power of deciding this question, there was no department in the American government which did possess it: the state governments have nothing to do with it—congress cannot touch the subject—they may indeed declare war for a violation; but a nation was not to be forced to this extremity on every occasion; there were other modes of redress, short of a declaration of war, to which nations had a right to resort; and one of them, as he had shown, was the power of withholding from the perfidious violator of a treaty, those benefits which he claimed under it.

"Now congress could not by a law declare a treaty void—it is not among those grants of power which the constitution makes to them; they cannot, therefore, meddle with the subject in any other way than by a declaration of war; neither can the president and senate touch it. They can *make* treaties; but the constitution gives them no power to *expound* a treaty; much less to *declare it void;* they can only unite with the house of representatives, in punishing an infraction by a declaration of war. To the judiciary alone then, belongs this pacific power of withholding legal benefits, claimed under a treaty, because of the *mala fides* of the party claiming them.

"Now what will be the situation of this country, compared with that of Great Britain, if you deny this power to the judiciary? If you have not observed the treaty with good faith, and go to England, claiming any benefit under the treaty, there is a power there, called royal prerogative, which will tell you—no—go home and act honestly, and you shall have your rights under the treaty.

"Your breach of faith will not drive *them* to a declaration of war—there is a power there which obtains redress by withholding your rights, until you act with good faith: but where is the reciprocal and corresponding power in our government, if it be not in the judiciary? It is nowhere; we have no redress short of a declaration of war. Is this one of the precious fruits of the adoption of the federal constitution, to bind us hand and foot with the fetters of technicality, and leave us no way of bursting them asunder, but by a declaration of war, and the effusion of human blood! It was never intended. The wisdom and virtue which framed the constitution could never have intended to place the country in this humiliating and awful predicament."

"Give to this power of deciding on treaties, which is delegated to the federal judiciary, a liberal construction—give them all the incidental powers necessary to carry it into effect—open to them the whole region of natural and national law, which furnishes the only rule of expounding those national compacts, called treaties, and your government is unmutilated, its measure of power is full up to the exigences of the nation, and you treat on equal terms: but upon the opposite construction, much better would it be that America should have no treaties at all, than that having them, she should want those means of enforcement and redress which all other nations possess."

Having thus established that debts are subject to confiscation in common wars, and much more so in the war of the revolution—that Virginia was an independent nation, and as such, competent to the exercise of this right of eminent domain—of taking to herself the debts of her enemies—that she had in fact exercised this right, and that this debt had, under one of her laws of that character, been legally discharged—that the treaty had no effect in reviving the claim, because the treaty had been annulled by the infractions of it on the part of Great Britain—and because if it had not, this was not a subsisting debt, within the purview of the treaty—and finally, that the court's jurisdiction extended to every question touching the consequence or annulment of treaties.

He said he had now finished his own view of the subject, and should have taken his seat, but for the necessity of giving a *particular* answer to the various objections to these principles, which had been so ably urged by the counsel for the plaintiff.

In this part of his subject he shows the most masterly acuteness, address, and vigour. A gentleman who was present, (the late Mr. Hardin Burnley,) has described some of the circumstances of his manner, with a very interesting minuteness:—"Mr. Henry," he said, "had taken ample notes of the arguments of his adversaries: the people would give him his own time to examine his notes, and select the argument or remark that he meant to make the subject of his comments, observing in these pauses the most profound silence. If the answer he was about to give was a short one, he would give it without removing his spectacles from his nose—but if he was ever seen to give his spectacle a cant to the top of his wig, *it was a declaration of war*, and his adversaries must stand clear."

I propose to give a few specimens only of his mode of answering the arguments of the opposing counsel. It had been urged by them that the laws of nations had declared only the *estate* of an alien enemy liable to confiscation—but that debts were mere *rights—choses in action*—and therefore not of a confiscable character. His answer to this is a happy mixture of ridicule and argument. It is short, and I shall give it in his own words:—

"But a *chose* in action is not liable to forfeiture. Why? Because it is too terrible to be done. There is such a thing as *straining at a gnat and swallowing a camel*. Things much more terrible *have been done*—things, from which our nature, where it has any pretensions to be pure and correct, must recoil with horror. Show me those laws which forfeit your life, attaint your blood, and beggar your wife and children. Those sanguinary and inhuman laws, to which every thing valuable must yield, are to be found in the code of that people, under whom the plaintiff now claims.

"Is it so terrible to confiscate *debts*, when *they forfeit life*, and *corrupt* the very source of your blood? Though every other thing dear to humanity is forfeitable, yet *debts*, it seems, must be spared! Debts are too sacred to be touched? It is a mercantile idea that worships Mammon instead of God. A *chose* in action shall pass—it is without your reach. What authority can they adduce in support of such conclusive pre-eminence for debts? No political or human institution has placed them above other things. If debt be the most sacred of all earthly obligations, I am uninformed from whence it has derived that eminence. The principle is to be found in the day-books, journals and legers of merchants; not in the writings or reasonings of the wise and well-informed—the enlightened instructers of mankind.

"Can any gentlemen show me any instance, where the life or property of a gentleman or plebeian in England is forfeited, and yet his debts spared? The state can claim debts due to one guilty of high treason. Are they not subject to confiscation? I concur in that sound principle, that good faith is essential to the happiness of mankind; that its want stops all human intercourse, and renders us miserable. This principle is permanent, and universal. Look to what point of the compass you will, you will find it pervading all nations. Who does not set down its sacred influence as the only thing that comforts human life? *Does the plaintiff claim through good faith?* How does *he* derive his claim? *Through perfidy:* through a *polluted channel.* Everything of that kind would have come better from our side of the question, than from theirs."

Mr. Ronald had insisted strenuously, that there could be no forfeiture or escheat without the inquest of a jury; and that no act of the legislature had, in fact, directly forfeited these debts. In answer to this, Mr. Henry says, "but the gentleman has observed, that neither the declaration of the legislature, by the act of 1779, that the British subjects had become aliens, and their property vested in the commonwealth, nor any other act passed on the subject, could divest the debts out of the British creditors. It cannot be done without the solemnity of an inquiry by jury. The debt of A or B, cannot be given to C, without this solemnity.

"Is the little legality of forms, which are necessary when you speak of estates and titles, requisite on such mighty occasions as these? When the fate of a nation is concerned, you are to speak the language of nature. When your very existence is at stake, are you to speak the technical language of books, and to be confined to the limited rules of technical criticism? to those tricks and quirks—those little twists and twirls of low chicanery and sophistry, which are so beneficial to professional men? Alexander said, in the style of that mighty man, to the Thessalians, '*You are free from the Thebans*,' and the debts they owed them were thereby remitted.

"Every other sovereign has the same right to use the same natural, manly, and laconic language; not when he is victorious only, but in every situation, if he be in a state of hostility with other nations. The acts use not the language of technicality, they speak not of *releases, discharges* and *acquittances;* but they speak the legislative will, in simple speech, to the human understanding—a style better suited to the purpose, than the turgid and pompous phraseology of many great writers."

Mr. Ronald, who was a native of Scotland, and at the commencement of the revolutionary war at least, had been suspected of being not very warm in the American cause, had urged the objection to the national competency of Virginia, at the time of the passage of those laws of confiscation and forfeiture, on which the defendant relied; and in the course of his observations, had unfortunately used the remark, that Virginia was, at that time, nothing more than a *revolted colony.*

When Mr. Henry came to notice this remark, he gave his spectacles the *war cant*:—"But another observation," said he, "was made; that by the law of nations *we* had not a right to legislate on the subject of British debts—we were not an independent nation—and I thought," said he, raising himself aloft, while his frame dilated itself beyond the ordinary size, "that I heard the word—*revolt!*"

At this word, he turned upon Mr. Ronald his piercing eye, and knit his brows at him, with an expression of indignation and contempt, which seemed almost to annihilate him. It was like a stroke of lightning. Mr. Ronald shrunk from the withering look: and, pale and breathless, cast down his eyes, "seeming," says my informant, "to be in quest of an auger-hole, by which he might drop through the floor, and escape for ever from mortal sight."

Mr. Henry perceived his suffering, and his usual good-nature immediately returned to him. He raised his eyes gently toward the court, and shaking his head slowly, with an expression of regret, added, "I wish I had not heard it: for though innocently meant, (and I am sure that it was so, from the character of the gentleman who mentioned it,) yet the sound displeases me—it is unpleasant." Mr. Ronald breathed again, and looked up, and his generous adversary dismissed the topic, to resume it no more.

It may give the reader some idea of the amplitude of this

argument, when he is told that Mr. Henry was engaged three days successively in its delivery; and some faint conception of the enchantment which he threw over it, when he learns that although it turned entirely on questions of law, yet the audience, mixed as it was, seemed so far from being wearied, that they followed him throughout with increased enjoyment. The room continued full to the last; and such was the "listening silence" with which he was heard, that not a syllable that he uttered is believed to have been lost.

When he finally sat down, the concourse rose with a general murmur of admiration; the scene resembled the breaking up and dispersion of a great theatrical assembly, which had been enjoying for the first time, the exhibition of some new and splendid drama: the speaker of the house of delegates was at length able to command a *quorum* for business; and every quarter of the city, and, at length, every part of the state, was filled with the echoes of Mr. Henry's eloquent speech.

His practice during these last years, of which we are now speaking, was confined pretty generally to cases of consequence. He did not like the profession, and was not willing to embark in any case for the ordinary fees. I have an interesting sketch of him, in his professional character, during those years, from the same elegant pen, which in a former page, exhibits the parallel between him and Mr. Lee in 1784: it is as follows:—

"At the bar, Mr. Henry was eminently successful. When I saw him there, he must, from the course of his life, which had been chiefly political, have become somewhat rusty in the learning of his profession: yet I considered him as a good lawyer: he seemed to be well acquainted with the rules and canons of property. He would not, indeed, undergo the drudgery necessary for complicated business; yet I am told, that in the British debt cause, he astonished the public not less by the matter than the manner of his speech.

"It was however as a criminal lawyer that his eloquence had the fairest scope, and in that character I have seen him. He was perfect master of the passions of his auditory, whether in the tragic or comic line. The tones of his voice, to say nothing of his matter and gesture, were insinuated into the feelings of his hearers, in a manner that baffles all description. It seemed to operate by mere sympathy; and by his tones alone, it seemed to me, that he could make you cry or laugh at pleasure. I will endeavour to give you some account of this tragic and comic effect in two instances, which I witnessed.

"About the year 1792, one Holland killed a young man in Botetourt. The young man was popular, and lived, I think, with Mr. King, a wealthy merchant in Fincastle, who employed Mr. John Brackenridge to assist in the prosecution of Holland. This Holland had gone up from the county of Louisa as a schoolmaster, but had turned out badly, and was unpopular. The killing was in the night, and was generally believed to be *murder*. He was the son of one Doctor Holland, who was yet living in Louisa, and had been one of Mr. Henry's juvenile friends and acquaintances.

"It was chiefly at the instance of the father, and for a very moderate fee, that Mr. Henry undertook to go out to the district court of Greenbrier, to defend the prisoner. Such were the prejudices there, that the people had openly and repeatedly declared that even Patrick Henry need not come to defend Holland, unless he brought a jury with him. On the day of trial, the courthouse was crowded. I did not move from my seat for fourteen hours; and had no wish to do so. The examination of the witnesses took up great part of the time, and the lawyers were probably exhausted. Brackenridge was eloquent; but Henry left no dry eye in the courthouse.

"The case I believe was *murder;* though, *possibly, manslaughter only*. Mr. Henry laid hold of this possibility with such effect as to make all forget that Holland had killed the storekeeper at all; and presented the deplorable case of the jury killing Holland, an innocent man. By that force of description which he possessed in so wonderful a degree, he exhibited, as it were, at the clerk's table, old Holland and his wife, who were then in Louisa; but the drawing was so powerful, and so true to nature, that we seemed to see them before us, and to hear them asking of the jury, 'Where is our son? What have you done with him?'

"All this was done in a manner so solemn and touching, and a tone so irresistible, that it was impossible for the stoutest heart not to take sides with the criminal: as for the jury, they lost sight of the murder they were trying, and wept most profusely, with old Holland and his wife, whom Mr. Henry painted, and perhaps proved to be very respectable. During the examination of the evidence, the bloody clothes had been brought in. Mr. Henry objected to their exhibition, and applied most forcibly and pathetically Antony's remark on Cesar's wounds, on those *dumb mouths* which would raise the stones of Rome to mutiny.

"He urged that this sight would totally deprive the jury of their judgment, which would be merged in their *feelings*. The court were divided, and the motion fell. The result of the trial was, that after the retirement of a half or quarter of an hour, the jury brought in a verdict of *not guilty;* but on being reminded by the court that they might find a decree of homi cide, inferior to murder, they altered their verdict to *guilty of manslaughter.*"

"Mr. Henry was not less successful in the comic line, when it became necessary to resort to it. You have no doubt heard how he defeated John Hook, by raising the cry of *beef* against him. I will give you a similar instance. In the year 1792, there were many suits on the south side of James river, for inflicting Lynch's law; thirty-nine lashes, inflicted without trial or law, on a mere suspicion of guilt, which could not be regularly proved. This lawless practice, which, sometimes by the order of a magistrate, sometimes without, prevailed extensively in the upper counties on James river, took its name from the gentleman who set the first example of it.

"A verdict of five hundred pounds had been given in Prince Edward district court, in a case of this kind. This alarmed the defendant in the next case, who employed Mr. Henry to defend him. The case was, that a wagoner and the plaintiff were travelling to Richmond together, when the wagoner knocked down a turkey, and put it into his wagon. Complaint was made to the defendant, a justice of the peace; both the parties were taken up, and the wagoner agreed to take a whipping rather than be sent to jail: but the plaintiff refused: the justice, however, gave him also a small flagellation; and for this the suit was brought.

"The plaintiff, by way of taking off the force of the defence, insisted that he was wholly innocent of the act committed. Mr. Henry on the contrary contended, that he was a party present, aiding and assisting. In the course of his remarks, he expressed himself thus:—'But, gentlemen of the jury, the plaintiff tells you he had nothing to do with the turkey—I dare say, gentlemen, *not until it was roasted*,' &c. He pronounced this word *roasted* with such rotundity of voice, such a ludicrous whirl of the tongue, and in a manner so indescribably comical, that it threw every one into a fit of laughter *at the plaintiff*, who stood up in the place usually allotted to crimi nals; and the defendant was let off with little or no damages."

The case of John Hook, to which my correspondent alludes, is worthy of insertion. Hook was a Scotchman, a man of wealth, and suspected of being unfriendly to the American cause.. During the distresses of the American army, consequent on the joint invasion of Cornwallis and Phillips in seventeen hundred and eighty-one, a Mr. Venable, an army commissary had taken two of Hook's steers for the use of the troops.

The act had not been strictly legal; and on the establish

ment of peace, Hook, under the advice of Mr. Cowan, a gentleman of some distinction in the law, thought proper to bring an action of trespass against Mr. Venable, in the district court of New London. Mr. Henry appeared for the defendant, and is said to have disported himself in this cause to the infinite enjoyment of his hearers, the unfortunate Hook always excepted. After Mr. Henry became animated in the cause, says a correspondent, (Judge Stuart,) he appeared to have complete control over the passions of his audience: at one time he excited their indignation against Hook: vengeance was visible in every countenance: again when he chose to relax and ridicule him, the whole audience was in a roar of laughter.

He painted the distress of the American army, exposed almost naked to the rigour of a winter's sky, and marking the frozen ground over which they marched, with the blood of their unshod feet—"where was the man," he said, "who had an American heart in his bosom, who would not have thrown open his fields, his barns, his cellars, the doors of his house, the portals of his breast, to have received with open arms, the meanest soldier in that little band of famished patriots? Where is the man?—*There* he stands—but whether the heart of an American beats in his bosom, you, gentlemen, are to judge."

He then carried the jury, by the powers of his imagination, to the plains around York, the surrender of which had followed shortly after the act complained of: he depicted the surrender in the most glowing and noble colours of his eloquence—the audience saw before their eyes the humiliation and dejection of the British, as they marched out of their trenches—they saw the triumph which lighted up every patriot face, and heard the shouts of victory, and the cry of Washington and liberty as it rung and echoed through the American rank, and was reverberated from the hills and shores of the neighbouring river—"but hark! what notes of discord are these which disturb the general joy, and silence the acclamations of victory—they are the notes of *John Hook*, hoarsely brawling through the American camp, *beef! beef! beef!*"

The whole audience were convulsed: a particular incident will give a better idea of the effect, than any general description. The clerk of the court, unable to command himself, and unwilling to commit any breach of decorum in his place, rushed out of the courthouse, and threw himself on the grass, in the most violent paroxysm of laughter, where he was rolling, when Hook, with very different feelings, came out for relief into the yard also. "Jemmy Steptoe," said he to the clerk, "what the devil ails ye, mon?" Mr. Steptoe was only able to say, that *he could not help it*. "Never mind ye," said Hook, "wait till Billy Cowan gets up *he'll show* him the la'." Mr. Cowan, however, was so completely overwhelmned by the torrent which bore upon his client, that when he rose to reply to Mr. Henry, he was scarcely able to make an intelligible or audible remark.

The cause was decided almost by acclamation. The jury retired for form sake, and instantly returned with a verdict for the defendant. Nor did the effect of Mr. Henry's speech stop here. The people were so highly excited by the tory audacity of such a suit, that Hook began to hear around him a cry more terrible than that of *beef;* it was the cry of *tar and feathers:* from the application of which it is said, that nothing saved him but a precipitate flight and the speed of his horse.

I have not attempted, in the course of these sketches, to follow Mr. Henry through his professional career. I have no materials to justify such an attempt. It has been, indeed, stated to me in general, that he appeared in such and such a case, and that he shone with great lustre; but neither his speeches in those cases, nor any point of his argument, nor even any brilliant passage has been communicated, so that the sketch that could be given of them must be either confined to a meager catalogue of the causes, or the canvass must be filled up by my own fancy, which would at once be an act of injustice to Mr. Henry, and a departure from that historical veracity, which it has been my anxious study in every instance to observe.

I have been told, for example, that in the year seventeen hundred and seventy-four, Mr. Henry appeared at the bar of the general court, in defence of a married man by the name of Henry Bullard, indicted for the murder of a beautiful girl, who lived in his house, to whom he had unfortunately become attached, and whom in a moment of frantic despair, he sacrificed to his hopeless passion. The defence is said to have been placed on the ground of insanity; and it is easy to conceive, in general the figure which Mr. Henry must have made in such a course. Those pathetic powers of eloquence, in which he was so pre-eminently great, had ample scope for their exercise in this case; and we can credit, without difficulty, the assertion, that he deluged the house with tears, and effected the acquittal of his client. But this is all that we know of the case.*

* If this is the case of Henry Bullard, who was indicted at the April term of seventeen hundred and seventy-four, for the murder of Mary Pinner, this honour claimed by my correspondent for Mr. Henry, is not due; for the records of the general court show, that the indictment, although originally drawn for the charge of murder, was reduced to manslaughter by the grand jury; of which offence the prisoner was convicted. There is, probably, some mistake in the name.

So also I learn that, on the same occasion after the war, he appeared at the bar of the house of delegates, in support of a petition of the officers of the Virginia line, who sought to be placed on the footing of those who had been taken on continental establishment: and that, after having depicted their services and their sufferings in colours which filled every heart with sympathy and gratitude, he dropped on his knees at the bar of the house, and presented such an appeal as might almost have softened rocks, and bent the knotted oak. Yet no vestige of this splendid speech remains; nor have I been able, after the most diligent inquiries, to ascertain the year in which it occurred; similar petitions having been presented for several successive sessions.

It was in the year seventeen hundred and ninety-four, that he bade a final adieu to his profession, and retired to the bosom of his own family. He retired, loaded with honours, public and professional: and carried with him the admiration, the gratitude, the confidence, and the love of his country. No man had ever passed through so long a life of public service, with a reputation more perfectly unspotted.

Nor had Mr. Henry, on any occasion, sought security from censure, by that kind of prudent silence and temporizing neutrality, which politicians so frequently observe. On the contrary, his course had been uniformly active, bold, intrepid, and independent. On every great subject of public interest, the part which he had taken was open, decided, manly; his country saw his motives, heard his reasons, approved his conduct, rested upon his virtue and his vigour; and contemplated with amazement, the evolution and unremitted display of his transcendent talents.

For more than thirty years he had now stood before that country—open to the scrutiny and the censure of the invidious—yet he retired, not only without spot or blemish, but with all his laurels blooming full and fresh upon him—followed by the blessings of his almost adoring countrymen, and cheered by that most exquisite of all earthly possessions—the consciousness of having, in deed and in truth, *played well his part.* He had now, too, become disembarrassed of debt; his fortune was affluent; and he enjoyed in his retirement, that ease and dignity, which no man ever more richly deserved.

CHAPTER X.

Mr. Henry's Retirement—State of Politics—Letter to his Daughter—He is again elected Governor—Declines the Office—His Position in regard to the two great Political Parties—Presents himself as a Candidate for the House of Delegates—Speech before opening the Polls—Eminent Men arrayed against Him—His Death.

Whatever difference of opinion may exist as to other parts of his character, in *this* the concurrence is universal: that there never was a man better constituted than Mr. Henry to enjoy and adorn the retirement on which he had now entered. Nothing can be more amiable, notning more interesting and attaching, than those pictures which have been furnished from every quarter, without one dissentient stroke of the pencil, of this great and virtuous man in the bosom of private life.

Mr. Jefferson says, that "he was the best-humoured companion in the world." His disposition was indeed all sweetness—his affections were warm, kind, and social—his patience invincible—his temper ever unclouded, cheerful, and serene—his manners plain, open, familiar, and simple—his conversation easy, ingenuous, and unaffected, full of entertainment, full of instruction, and irradiated with all those light and softer graces which his genius threw without effort, over the most common subjects. It is said that there stood in the court, before his door, a large walnut-tree, under whose shade it was his delight to pass his summer evenings, surrounded by his affectionate and happy family, and by a circle of neighbours who loved him almost to idolatry. Here he would disport himself with all the careless gayety of infancy.

Here, too, he would sometimes warm the bosoms of the old, and strike fire from the eyes of his younger hearers, by recounting the tales of other times; by sketching with the boldness of a master's hand, those great historic incidents in which he had borne a part; and by drawing to the life, and placing before his audience, in colours as fresh and strong as those of nature, the many illustrious men in every quarter of the continent, with whom he had acted a part on the public stage. Here, too, he would occasionally discourse with all the wisdom and all the eloquence of a Grecian sage, of the various duties and offices of life; and pour forth those lessons of practical utility, with which long experience and observation had stored his mind.

Many were the visiters from a distance, old and young, who came on a kind of pious pilgrimage, to the retreat of the veteran patriot, and found him thus delightfully and usefully employed—the old to gaze upon him with long-remembered affection, and ancient gratitude—the young, the ardent, and the emulous, to behold and admire, with swimming eyes, the champion of other days, and to look with a sigh of generous regret, upon that height of glory which they could never hope to reach. Blessed be the shade of that venerable tree—ever hallowed the spot which his genius has consecrated!

Mr. Henry received these visits with all his characteristic plainness and modesty; and never failed to reward the fatigue of the journey by the warmest welcome, and by the unceremonious and fascinating familiarity, with which he would at once enter into conversation with his new guests, and cause them to forget that they were strangers, or abroad. Nor must the reader suppose that in these conversations he assumed any airs of superiority; much less that his conversation was, as in some of our conspicuous men, a continued, imperious, and didactic lecture. On the contrary, he carried into private life, all those principles of equality which had governed him in public.

That ascendancy, indeed, which proceeded from the superior energy of his mind, and the weight of his character, would manifest itself unavoidably, in the deference of his companions; but there was nothing in his manner which would have ever reminded them of it. On the contrary, it seemed to be his study to cause them to forget it, and to decoy them into a free and equal interchange of thought. If he took the lead in conversation, it was not because he sought it; but because it was forced upon him by that silent delight with which he perceived that his company preferred to listen to him.

But it was in the bosom of his own family, where the eye of every visiter and even every neighbour was shut out—where neither the love of fame, nor the fear of censure, could be suspected of throwing a false light upon his character—it was in that very scene, in which it has been said that "no man is a hero," that Mr. Henry's heroism shone with the most engaging beauty. It was to his wife, to his children, to his servants, that his true character was best known: to this grateful, devoted, happy circle, were best known the patient and tender forbearance, the kind indulgence, the forgiving mildness, and sweetness of his spirit, those pure and warm affections, which were always looking out for the means of improving their felicity, and that watchful prudence and circumspection, which guarded them from harm.

What can be more amiable than the playful tenderness with which he joined in the sports of his little children, and the boundless indulgence with which he received and returned their caresses? "His visiters," says one of my correspondents, "have not unfrequently caught him lying on the floor, with a group of these little ones, climbing over him in every direction, or dancing around him, with obstreperous mirth, to the tune of his violin, while the only contest seemed to be who should make the most noise." If there be any bachelor so cold of heart as to be offended at this anecdote, I can only remind him of the remark of the great Agesilaus to the friend who found him riding on a stick among *his* children: "*Don't mention it, till you are yourself a father!*"

Such were the scenes of domestic and social bliss, such the delicious tranquillity, in which Mr. Henry passed the first years of his retirement. Yet this retreat, which so well deserved to have been considered as sacred, was doomed in a few years to be disturbed by the bickerings of political party. Since Mr. Henry's retirement from public life, new parties had arisen in the United States, whose animosities had been carried to an alarming height.

The federalists, who supported the measures of the new government throughout, were accused by their adversaries of a disposition to strain the constructive powers of the constitution to their highest possible pitch; of a secret wish to convert the government, into a *substantial* monarchy at least; to which purpose, the assumption of state debts, the establishment of the funding system, and of the national bank, the alarming increase of the public debt, the imposition of a heavy load of internal taxes, the establishment of an army and a navy, with all their consequences of favouritism and extensive executive patronage, were alleged to have been introduced.

They were branded with the name of *aristocrats*, a name of reproach borrowed from the parties in France; and were charged with being inimical to the cause of human liberty, as was said to be proved by their hostility to the progress of the French revolution, as well as by the alarming character of those measures which they were pushing forward in America. They were suspected and accused of a preference for a government of ranks and orders, and a secret love of titles of nobility; of which it was said, one of their principal leaders had furnished a decisive proof, so far as he was concerned, by having proposed the introduction of titles in the continental convention which had framed the constitution.

The party which urged these charges, took the name of republicans and democrats; declared themselves the friends of liberty and the people, and the firm advocates of a government of the people by the people. They were devoted, with enthusiasm, to the cause of liberty in France: considered *man*, as the only title of nobility which ought to be admitted, and his freedom and happiness as the sole objects of government; this they contended, was the principle on which the American revolution had turned; that the great objects of the revolution could be no otherwise attained, than by a simple, pure, economical, and chaste administration of the federal government; and by restricting the several departments under the new constitution, to *the express letter* of the powers assigned to them by that instrument.

The federalists on the other hand, denied and repelled, with great acrimony and vehemence, the charges which had been urged against them by their adversaries. They contended that the measures complained of were warranted by the constitution, and were necessary to give to the federal government the effect which was intended by its adoption. They insisted that *they* were simply the friends of *order and good government;* and in their turn, branded their adversaries with the name of *Jacobins*, who having caught the *mania* from France, were for overturning all government and throwing everything into anarchy and uproar, in the hope of rising themselves to the top of the chaos.

They alleged that the opposition was formed of the dregs of the American people, headed and goaded on by a few designing men, and fermented into faction by the revolutionary elements thrown among them, from abroad, in the shape of French and Irish emigrants and convicts. They insisted that it was indispensably necessary to the peace and order of the American nation, that those foreign incendiaries should be driven out from the land, and that the licentious fury of our own populace should also be bridled. Under this impression, were passed those alien and sedition laws, which are supposed to have put an end to the federal power in America.

It is not my function to decide between these parties; nor do I feel myself qualified for such an office. I have lived too near the times, and am conscious of having been too strongly excited by the feelings of the day, to place myself in the chair of the arbiter. It would indeed, be no difficult task to present, under the engaging air of historic candour, the arguments on one side, in an attitude so bold and commanding; and to exhibit those on the other, under a form so faint and shadowy, as to beguile the reader into the adoption of my own opinions.

But this would be unjust to the opposite party, and a disingenuous abuse of the confidence of the reader. Let us then remit the question to the historian of future ages; who, if the particular memory of the past times shall not be lost in those great events which seem preparing for the nation, will probably decide, that, as in most family quarrels, both parties have been somewhat in the wrong.

For my purpose, it is sufficient to state the rise and existence of those parties, and the fact that their collision had convulsed the whole society. Mr. Henry, although removed from the immediate scene of contention, was still an object of too much consequence to be viewed with indifference. He had a weight of character which gave to his opinions a preponderating influence on every subject, and both parties were equally anxious to gain him to their cause. His expressions were watched with the most anxious attention, and it was not long before an alarm of his defection from the popular cause was given. The first occasion of it I discover, was the treaty of seventeen hundred and ninety-four, with Great Britain, commonly known by the name of Jay's treaty.

It will be remembered by the reader, that Mr. Henry had objected to the constitution on the ground that it gave to the president and senate the *whole* treaty-making power. This construction of the instrument was not denied in the state convention; but on the contrary, was at least impliedly admitted; and the provision was vindicated on the ground that the power of treating could be nowhere more safely and properly lodged.

"When, therefore, the republican leaders in the house of representatives claimed a right to participate in the ratification of Jay's treaty, Mr. Henry considered them as inconsistent with themselves, and as departing from their own construction of the constitution. This charge and the defence, have both been made known to me, by the following letter from Mr. Henry to his daughter, Mrs. Aylett:—

"Red Hill, *August* 20, 1796.

"My Dear Betsy: Mr. William Aylett's arrival here, with your letter, gave me the pleasure of hearing of your welfare, and to hear of that is highly gratifying to me, as I so seldom see you," &c. [The rest of this paragraph relates to family affairs.]

"As to the reports you have heard of my changing sides in politics, I can only say they are not true. I am too old to exchange my former opinions, which have grown up into fixed habits of thinking. True it is, I have condemned the conduct of our members in congress, because, in refusing to raise money for the purposes of the British treaty, they, in effect, would have surrendered our country, bound hand and foot, to the power of the British nation. This must have been the consequence, I think; but the reasons for thinking so are too tedious to trouble you with. The treaty is, in my opinion, a very bad one, indeed.

But what must I think of those men, whom I myself warned

of the danger of giving the power of making laws by means of a treaty, to the president and senate, when I see these same men denying the existence of that power, which they insisted, in our convention, ought properly to be exercised by the president and senate, and by none other? The policy of these men, both then and now, appears to me quite void of wisdom and foresight. These sentiments I did mention in conversation in Richmond, and perhaps others which I don't remember; but sure I am, my first principle is, that from the British we have everything to dread, when opportunities of oppressing us shall offer.

"It seems that every word was watched which I casually dropped, and wrested to answer party views. Who can have been so meanly employed, I know not—nor do I care; for I no longer consider myself as an actor on the stage of public life. It is time for me to retire; and I shall never more appear in a public character, unless some unlooked-for circumstance shall demand from me a transient effort, not inconsistent with private life—in which I have determined to continue.

I see with concern our old commander-in-chief most abusively treated—nor are his long and great services remembered, as any apology for his mistakes in an office to which he was totally unaccustomed. If he, whose character as our leader during the whole war was above all praise, is so roughly handled in his old age, what may be expected by men of the common standard of character? I ever wished he might keep himself clear of the office he bears, and its attendant difficulties—but I am sorry to see the gross abuse which is published of him. Thus, my dear daughter, have I pestered you with a long letter on politics, which is a subject little interesting to you, except as it may involve my reputation. I have long learned the little value which is to be placed on popularity, acquired by any other way than virtue; and I have also learned, that it is often obtained by other means.

The view which the rising greatness of our country presents to my eyes, is greatly tarnished by the general prevalence of deism; which, with me, is but another name for vice and depravity. I am, however, much consoled by reflecting, that the religion of Christ has, from its first appearance in the world, been attacked in vain, by all the wits, philosophers, and wise ones, aided by every power of man, and its triumph has been complete.

"What is there in the wit, or wisdom of the present deistical writers or professors, that can compare them with Hume, Shaftsbury, Bolingbroke, and others? and yet these have been confuted, and their fame decaying; insomuch, that the puny efforts of Paine are thrown in to prop their tottering fabric, whose foundations cannot stand the test of time.

"Among other strange things said of me, I hear it is said by the deists that I am one of the number; and, indeed, that some good people think I am no Christian. This thought gives me much more pain than the appellation of tory; because I think religion of infinitely higher importance than politics; and I find much cause to reproach myself, that I have lived so long, and have given no decided and public proofs of my being a Christian.

"But, indeed, my dear child, this is a character which I prize far above all this world has or can boast. And among all the handsome things I hear said of you, what gives me the greatest pleasure is, to be told of your piety and steady virtue. Be assured there is not one tittle, as to disposition or character, in which my parental affection for you would suffer a wish for your changing; and it flatters my pride to have you spoken of as you are.

"Perhaps Mr. Roane and Anne may have heard the reports you mention. If it will be any object with them to see what I write you, show them this. But my wish is to pass the rest of my days, as much as may be, unobserved by the critics of the world, who would show but little sympathy for the deficiencies to which old age is so liable. May God bless you, my dear Betsy, and your children. Give my love to Mr. Aylett,

"And believe me ever your affectionate father,

"P. Henry."

This charge, however, had not deprived Mr. Henry of the confidence of his country; for in the session of the legislature which followed the date of his letter, he was for the third time elected the governor of the state. The letter by which he declined the acceptance of that office is as follows:—

'*To the honourable the speaker of the house of delegates.*

"Charlotte County, *November* 29, 1796.

"Sir: I have just received the honour of yours, informing me of my appointment to the chief magistracy of the commonwealth. And I have to beg the favour of you, sir, to convey to the general assembly, my best acknowledgments, and warmest gratitude for the signal honour they have conferred on me. I should be happy if I could persuade myself, that my abilities were commensurate to the duties of that office; but my declining years warn me of my inability.

"I beg leave, therefore, to decline the appointment, and to hope and trust that the general assembly will be pleased to excuse me for doing so; as no doubt can be entertained that many of my fellow-citizens possess the requisite abilities for this high trust.

"With the highest regard, I am, sir,

"Your most obedient servant,

"P. Henry."

This was the last testimonial of public confidence which Mr. Henry received from his native state. The rumours of his political apostacy became strong and general. He was a prize worth contending for; and it is not wonderful, therefore, that the rival parties observed, with the most jealous distrust, every advance which was made toward him by the other, and interpreted such advances as so many stratagems to gain him over: nor is it wonderful, if, during the fever of that hot and violent struggle, many things were supposed to be seen, which did not in fact exist: and that those which did exist were sometimes seen under false shapes and colours.

It was reported at that day, that on Mr. Jefferson's resignation of the office of secretary of state, *that* office was offered to Mr. Henry, in the confidence, that while the offer would gratify him, he would nevertheless reject it: however this may be, it is certain that the embassy to Spain was offered to him, during the first administration; and that to France during the second.*

These offers were known at the time; and when compared with his advanced age—the large family with which he was encumbered—his settled and well-known purpose of retirement—and the consequent probability that these offers would not be accepted—and the sentiments which he afterward expressed, in favour of some of the measures of the administration, which were extremely obnoxious in Virginia—those offers were considered by the republicans, as so many strokes of political flattery, addressed to the vanity of an old man, and which had been but too successful in having won him to the federal ranks.

That he approved of the alien and sedition laws, as good measures, is undeniable; indeed, he was not a man who would deny any opinion that he held: and, however honest might have been his conviction, both of the constitutionality and expediency of these measures, it is equally undeniable, that his sentiments in relation to them, combined with the above causes, by which those sentiments were suspected of having been influenced, produced an extremely unpropitious effect on his popularity in Virginia.

* On the authority of Judge Winston.

The charge of apostacy, however, implies a previous commitment to the opposite side: but the evidence that Mr. Henry ever stood committed to the democratic or to any other party, (except the great American party of liberty and republican government,) has not yet been seen by the author of these sketches. At the time of his retirement, it is believed that the post-constitutional parties were not distinctly marked. He had no opportunity, after they were so marked, of expressing his opinion publicly in favour of the one side or the other.

It is highly probable, that his opinions did not coincide throughout with those of either side: and it would be rather rash to infer, from his disapprobation of one or more measures of the administration, or from his general love of liberty, that he must of necessity have been attached at first to the democratic side. Nor would it be more correct to infer, from his having resisted the adoption of the federal constitution, that he was therefore opposed to the measures of those who administered it; for the converse of this proposition, which must be equally true, would have thrown many more into the federal ranks than would have been willing to acknowledge the connexion. Mr. Henry had moreover declared, as we have seen, in the last speech which he made in the state convention, in opposition to the constitution, that if it should be adopted, he would be a peaceable citizen; that he would not go to violence, but that he would seek the correction of whatever he thought amiss, *by quiet means.*

Upon the whole, it would seem more liberal, more consonant to the high character of Mr. Henry's mind, with his time of life, and with that distant and feeble connexion which he now considered himself as holding with politics, and indeed with the world—to believe that he looked, without passion or prejudice of any kind, on the course of the administration, approving or condemning, according to his own judgment, without reference to the pleasure or opinions of either side: or if we *must* suppose him under personal influence of any kind, would it have been unpardonable in him, to have been influenced by the opinions of that man who had ever stood first both in his judgment and affections, and whom all America acknowledged as the father of his country? Other natural causes, too, may be fairly considered as having united their influence in producing this difference of political sentiment, between Mr. Henry and the majority of his state.

In the year seventeen hundred and ninety-seven, his health began to decline, and continued to sink gradually to the moment of his death.* He had now passed through a stormy life

* Judge Winston.

to his sixtieth year, and the vigour of his mind, exhausted more by past toils than by years, began to give way. Those energies which had enabled him to brave the power of Great Britain, and to push forward the glorious revolution which made us free, existed no longer in their original force.

The usual infirmities of age and disease began to press, sorely and heavily, upon his sinking spirits. He was startled by that clash of contending parties, which rang continually around him, and invaded, with perpetually increasing horror, the stillness of his retreat. His retirement cut him off, almost entirely, from all communication with those who were best able to explain the grounds, as well as the character and measure of opposition to the offensive measures, which was intended; and the spirit and views of that opposition were, no doubt, aggravated to him by report.

Acting as those things did on the mind of an infirm old man; worn out by the toils and troubles of the past revolution, and naturally wishing for repose; alarmed too, and agonized by the hideous scenes of that revolution which was then going on in France; and tortured by the apprehension that those scenes were about to be acted over again in his own country—it is not surprising, that he was dismayed by the vehemence of that political strife which then agitated the United States; nor would it be surprising, if his solicitude to allay the ferment and restore the peace of society, should, in some degree, have obscured the decisions of his mind; and placed him, rather by his fears than his judgment, in opposition to the forcible resistance, which he had been erroneously led to consider as meditated by the democratic party.

In a mind thus prepared, the strong and animated resolutions of the Virginia assembly, in seventeen hundred and ninety-eight, in relation to the alien and sedition laws, conjured up the most frightful visions of civil war, disunion, blood, and anarchy; and under the impulse of these phantoms, to make what *he* considered a virtuous effort for his country, he presented himself in Charlotte county, as a candidate for the house of delegates, at the spring election of seventeen hundred and ninety-nine.

On the day of the election, as soon as he appeared on the ground, he was surrounded by the admiring and adoring crowd, and whithersoever he moved, the concourse followed him. A preacher of the Baptist Church, whose piety was wounded by this homage paid to a mortal, asked the people aloud, "Why they thus followed Mr. Henry about?—Mr. Henry," said he, "is not a god!"

"No," said Mr. Henry, deeply affected both by the scene

and the remark: "no, indeed, my friend; I am but a poor worm of the dust—as fleeting and unsubstantial as the shadow of the cloud that flies over your fields, and is remembered no more." The tone with which this was uttered, and the look which accompanied it, affected every heart, and silenced every voice. Envy and opposition were disarmed by his humility; the recollection of his past services rushed upon every memory, and he "read his history" in their swimming eyes.

Before the polls were opened, he addressed the people of the county to the following effect:—"He told them that the late proceedings of the Virginian assembly had filled him with apprehensions and alarm; that they had planted thorns upon his pillow; that they had drawn him from that happy retirement which it had pleased a bountiful Providence to bestow, and in which he had hoped to pass, in quiet, the remainder of his days; that the state had quitted the sphere in which she had been placed by the constitution; and in daring to pronounce upon the validity of federal laws, had gone out of her jurisdiction in a manner not warranted by any authority, and in the highest degree alarming to every considerate man; that such opposition on the part of Virginia, to the acts of the general government, *must* beget their enforcement by military power; that this would probably produce civil war; civil war, foreign alliances; and that foreign alliances must necessarily end in subjugation to the powers called in.

"He conjured the people to pause and consider well, before they rushed into such a desperate condition, from which there could be no retreat. He painted to their imaginations, Washington, at the head of a numerous and well-appointed army, inflicting upon them military execution: 'And where (he asked) are our resources to meet such a conflict?—Where is the citizen of America who will dare to lift his hand against the father of his country?'

"A drunken man in the crowd threw up his arm, and exclaimed that 'he dared to do it.'—'No,' answered Mr. Henry, rising aloft in all his majesty: '*you dare not do it: in such a parricidal attempt, the steel would drop from your nerveless arm!*' 'The look and gesture at this moment, (says a correspondent,) gave to these words an energy on my mind unequalled by anything that I have ever witnessed.' Mr. Henry, proceeding in his address to the people, asked—'whether the county of Charlotte would have any authority to dispute an obedience to the laws of Virginia;' and he pronounced Virginia to be to the Union what the county of Charlotte was to *her*.

"Having denied the right of a state to decide upon the constitutionality of federal laws, he added, that perhaps it might be necessary to say something of the merits of the laws in question. His private opinion was, that they were *good* and *proper*. But, whatever might be their merits, it belonged to the people, who held the reins over the head of congress, and to them alone, to say whether they were acceptable or otherwise to Virginians; and that this must be done by way of petition. That congress were as much our representatives as the assembly, and had as good a right to our confidence.

"He had seen with regret, the unlimited power over the purse and sword consigned to the general government; but that he had been overruled, and it was now necessary to submit to the constitutional exercise of that power. 'If,' said he, 'I am asked what is to be done, when a people feel themselves intolerably oppressed, my answer is ready:—*Overturn the government*. But do not, I beseeech you, carry matters to this this length, without provocation. Wait at least until *some* infringement is made upon your rights, and which cannot otherwise be redressed; for if ever you recur to another change, you may bid adieu for ever to representative government.

"You can never exchange the present government but for a monarchy. If the administration have done wrong, let us all go wrong together, rather than split into factions, which must destroy that *union* upon which our existence hangs. Let us preserve our strength for the French, the English, the Germans, or whoever else shall dare to invade our territory, and not exhaust it in civil commotions and intestine wars.' He concluded, by declaring his design to exert himself in the endeavour to allay the heart-burnings and jealousies which had been fomented in the state legislature; and he fervently prayed, if *he* was deemed unworthy to effect it, that it might be reserved to some other and abler hand, to extend this blessing over the community."

This was *the substance* of the speech written down at the time by one of his hearers. "There was," says the writer, "an emphasis in his language, to which, like the force of his articulation, and the commanding expression of his eye, no representation *can* do justice; yet I am conscious of having given a correct transcript of his opinions, and in many instances, his very expression."

Such was the last effort of Mr. Henry's eloquence: the power of the noonday sun was gone; but its setting splendours were not less beautiful and touching. After this speech, the polls were opened; and he was elected by his usual commanding majority. His intention having been generally known for some time before the period of the state elections, the most formidable preparations were made to oppose him in the assembly.

Mr. Madison, (the late president of the United States,) Mr. Giles, of Amelia, Mr. Taylor, of Caroline, Mr. Nicholas of Albemarle, and a host of young men of shining talents from every part of the state, were arrayed in the adverse rank, and commanded a decided majority in the house. But Heaven, in its mercy, saved him from the unequal conflict. The disease which had been preying upon him for two years, now hastened to its crisis; and on the sixth day of June, seventeen hundred and ninety-nine, this friend of liberty and of man was no more!

Here let us pause. The storm of seventeen hundred and ninety-nine, thank Heaven! has passed away; and we again enjoy the calm and sunshine of domestic peace. We are able, now, to see with other eyes, and to feel with far different hearts. Who is there that, looking back upon the part he bore in those scenes, can say that *he* was at no time guilty of any fault of conduct, any error of opinion, or any vicious excess of feeling? The man who *can* say this, is either very much to be pitied, or most exceedingly to be envied.

But whatever we may be disposed to say or think of ourselves, there can be very little doubt, that that Being who is the searcher of hearts, sees very much during that period, to be forgiven in us all. It would, indeed, be presumptuous in the extreme, amid the universal admission which is made of the imperfections of human nature, in the happiest circumstances, to contend for its infallibility, while acting under the scourge of the most angry and vindictive passions.

Let it be admitted, then, that during the period of which we are speaking, Mr. Henry *was* guilty of a political aberration: but let all the peculiar circumstances of his case which have been enumerated, be taken into the account, and let it be farther remembered, that if he did go astray, as the majority of the state believe, he strayed in company with the father of his country—and where is the heart so cold and thankless, as to balance a mistake thus committed, against a long life of such solid, splendid, and glorious utility? Certainly not in Virginia—and it is to Virginians only that this appeal is made. The sentiments now so universally expressed, in relation to Mr. Henry, evince, that the age of party resentment has passed away, and that that of the noblest gratitude has taken its place. But let us return to our narrative.

At the session of the assembly immediately following Mr. Henry's death, before the spirit of party had time to relent, and give way to that generous feeling of grateful veneration for him, which now pervades the state, *a federal member* of the house moved the following resolution:—

"The general assembly of Virginia, as a testimonial of their veneration for the character of their late illustrious fellow-citizen, Patrick Henry, whose unrivalled eloquence and superior talents were, in times of peculiar peril and distress, so uniformly, so powerfully, and so successfully, devoted to the cause of freedom, and of his country—and, in order to invite the present and future generations to an imitation of his virtues, and an emulation of his fame—

"*Resolved*, That the executive be authorized and requested, to procure a marble bust of the said Patrick Henry, at the public expense, and to cause the same to be placed in one of the niches of the hall of the house of delegates."

Nothing could have been more unfortunate for the success of this resolution, than the time at which it was brought forward, and the mover by whom it was offered. The time, as we have seen, was during that paroxysm of displeasure against Mr. Henry, which even his death, although it had abated, had not entirely allayed: and the mover was a gentleman who had himself been recently counted on the republican side of the house, and was now also smarting under the charge of apostacy.

All the angry passions of the house immediately arose at such a proposition, from such a quarter. A republican member moved to lay the resolution on the table; the gentleman who offered it replied with warmth, that if it were so disposed of he would never call it up again. It was laid upon the table, and has been heard of no more.

Thus lived, and thus died, the celebrated Patrick Henry of Virginia; a man who justly deserves to be ranked among the highest ornaments and noblest benefactors of his country. Had his lot been cast in the republics of Greece or Rome, his name would have been enrolled by some immortal pen, among the expellers of tyrants and the champions of liberty: the proudest monuments of national gratitude would have risen to his honour, and handed down his memory to future generations.

As it is, his fame as yet, is left to rest upon tradition, and on that short notice which general history can take of him; while no memorial, no slab even, *raised by the hand of national gratitude*, points us to his grave, or tells where sleep the ashes of the patriot and the sage. May we not hope, that this reproach upon the state will soon be wiped away, and that ample atonement will be made for our past neglect?

CHAPTER XI.

Delineations of Mr. Henry's private Character—Anecdotes of Mr. Lee—of Mr. Gallatin—Mr. Henry's Political Foresight—Description of his Person—Further General View of his Character—Conclusion.

Mr. Henry, by his two marriages, was the father of fifteen children. By his first wife he had six, of whom two only survived him; by his last he had six sons and three daughters, all of whom, together with their mother, were living at his death.

He had been fortunate during the latter part of his life; and, chiefly by the means of judicious purchases of lands, had left his family, large as it was, not only independent, but rich.

In his habits of living, he was remarkably temperate and frugal. He seldom drank anything but water; and his table, though abundantly spread, was furnished only with the most simple viands. Necessity had imposed those habits upon him in the earlier part of his life; and use, as well as reason, now made them his choice.

His children were raised up with little or no restraint. He seems not to have thought very highly of early education. It is indeed probable, that his own success, which was attributable almost entirely to the natural powers of his mind, had diminished the importance of an extensive education in his view. But although they were suffered to run wild for some years, and, indeed, committed to the sole guidance of nature, to a much later period than usual, yet they were finally all well educated; and not only by the reflected worth of their father, but by their own merits, have always occupied a most respectable station in society.

Mr. Henry's conversation was remarkably pure and chaste. He never swore. He was never heard to take the name of his Maker in vain. He was a sincere Christian, though after a form of his own; for he was never attached to any particular religious society, and never, it is believed, communed with any church. A friend who visited him not long before his death, found him engaged in reading the Bible:—"Here," said he, holding it up, "is a book worth more than all the other books that were ever printed: yet it is my misfortune never to have found time to read it, with the proper attention and feeling, till lately. I trust in the mercy of Heaven that it is not yet too late."

He was much pleased with Soame Jenyns' view of the internal evidences of the Christian religion; so much so, that about the year seventeen hundred and ninety, he had an impression of it struck at his own expense, and distributed among the people. His other favourite works on the subject were Doddridge's "Rise and Progress of Religion in the Soul," and Butler's "Analogy of Religion, Natural and Revealed." This latter work, he used at one period of his life to style, by way of pre-eminence, *his Bible*. The selection proves not only the piety of his temper, but the correctness of his taste, and his relish for profound and vigorous disquisition.

His morals were strict. As a husband, a father, a master, he had no superior. He was kind and hospitable to the stranger, and most friendly and accommodating to his neighbours. In his dealings with the world, he was faithful to his promise, and punctual in his contracts, to the utmost of his power.

Yet we do not claim for him a total exemption from the failures of humanity. Moral perfection is not the property of man. The love of money is said to have been one of Mr. Henry's strongest passions. In his desire for accumulation, he was charged with wringing from the hands of his clients, and more particularly those of the criminals whom he defended, fees rather too exorbitant. He was censured too, for an attempt to locate the shores of the Chesapeake, which had heretofore been used as a public common, although there was, at that time, no law of the state which protected them from location.

In one of his earlier purchases of land, he was blamed also for having availed himself of the existing laws of the state, in paying for it in the depreciated paper currency of the country; nor was he free from censure on account of some participation which he is said to have had in the profits of the Yazoo trade. He was accused, too, of having been rather more vain of his wealth, toward the close of his life, than became a man so great in other respects. Let these things be admitted, and "let the man who is without fault cast the first stone."

In mitigation of these charges, if they be true, it ought to be considered that Mr. Henry, had been, during the greater part of his life, intolerably oppressed by poverty and all its distressing train of consequences; that the family for which he had to provide was very large; and that the bar, although it has been called the road to honour, was not in those days the road to wealth. With these considerations in view, charity may easily pardon him for having considered only *the legality* of the means which he used to acquire an independence; and she can easily excuse him too, for having felt the success of his endeavors a little more sensibly than might have been becoming.

He was certainly neither proud, nor hard-hearted nor penurious: if he was either, there can be no reliance on human testimony; which represents him as being, in his general intercourse with the world, not only rigidly honest, but one of the kindest, gentlest, and most indulgent of human beings.

While we are on this ungrateful subject of moral imperfection, the fidelity of history requires us to notice another charge against Mr. Henry. His passion for fame is said to have been too strong; he was accused of a wish to monopolize the public favour; and under the influence of this desire, to have felt no gratification in the rising fame of certain conspicuous characters; to have indulged himself in invidious and unmerited remarks upon them, and to have been at the bottom of a cabal against one of the most eminent. If these things were so —alas! poor human nature!

It is certain that these charges are very inconsistent with his general character. So far from being naturally envious, and disposed to keep back modest merit, one of the finest traits in his character was, the parental tenderness with which he took by the hand every young man of merit, covered him with his ægis in the legislature and led him forward at the bar. In relation to his first great rival in eloquence, Richard Henry Lee, he not only did ample justice to him on every occasion, in public, but defended his fame in private, with all the zeal of a brother; as is demonstrated by an original correspondence between those two eminent men, now in the hands of the author.

Of Colonel Innis, his next great rival, he entertained, and uniformly expressed, the most exalted opinion; and in the convention of 1788, as will be remembered, paid a compliment to his eloquence, at once so splendid, so happy, and so just, that it will live for ever. The debates of that convention abound with the most unequivocal and ardent declarations of his respect, for the talents and virtues of the other eminent gentlemen who were arrayed against him—Mr. Madison—Mr. Pendleton—Mr. Randolph.

Even the justly great and overshadowing fame of Mr. Jefferson never extorted from him, in public at least, one invidious remark; on the contrary, the name of that gentleman, who was then in France, having been introduced into the debates of the convention, for the purpose of borrowing the weight of his opinion, Mr. Henry spoke of him in the strongest and warmest terms, not only of admiration, but of affection—styling him "*our illustrions fellow-citizen*,"—"*our enlightened and worthy countryman*,"—"*our common friend*."

The inordinate love of money and of fame, are, certainly,

base and degrading passions. They have sometimes tarnished characters otherwise the most bright; but they will find no advocate or apologist in any virtuous bosom. In relation to Mr. Henry, however, we may be permitted to doubt whether the facts on which these censures (so inconsistent with his general character) are grounded, have not been misconceived; and whether so much of them as is really true, may not be fairly charged to the common account of human imperfection.

Mr. Henry's great intellectual defect was his indolence. To this it was owing, that he never possessed that admirable alertness and vigouros versatility of mind, which turns promptly to everything, attends to everything, arranges everything, and by systematizing its operations, despatches each in its proper time, and place and manner. To the same cause it is to be ascribed, that he never possessed that patient drudgery, and that ready, neat, copious, and masterly command of details, which forms so essential a part of the duties both of the statesman and the lawyer.

Hence, too, he did not avail himself of the progress of science and literature, in his age. He had not, as he might have done, amassed those ample stores of various, useful, and curious knowledge, which are so naturally expected to be found in a great man. His library (of which an inventory has been furnished to the author) was extremely small; composed not only of a very few books, but those, too, commonly odd volumes. Of science and literature, he knew little or nothing more than was occasionly gleaned from conversation. It is not easy to conceive, what a mind like his might have achieved in either, or both of these walks, had it been properly trained at first, or industriously occupied in those long intervals of leisure which he threw away.

One thing, however, may be safely pronounced; that had that mind of Herculean strength been either so trained, or so occupied, he would have left behind him some written monument, compared with which, even statutes and pillars would have been but the ephemeræ of a day. But he seems to have been of Hobbes's opinion, who is reported to have said of himself, that "if he had read as much as other men, he should have been as ignorant as they were."* Mr. Henry's book was the great volume of human nature. In this, he was more deeply read than any of his countrymen. He knew *men* thoroughly; and hence arose his great power of persuasion.†

* Bayle: article Hobbes.

† "It is in vain," says the Chancellor D'Aguesseau, "that the orator flatters himself with having the talent to persuade men, if he has not acquired that of knowing them." Discourse i., p. 1.

His preference of this study, is manifested by the following incident:—he met once, in a bookstore, with the late Mr. Ralph Wormley, who, although a great bookworm, was infinitely more remarkable for his ignorance of men, than Mr. Henry was for that of books.—"What, Mr. Wormley," said he, "still buying books?" "Yes," said Mr. Wormley, "I have just heard of a new work, which I am extremely anxious to peruse." "Take my word for it," said he, "Mr. Wormley, "*we are too old to read books: read men*—they are the only volumes that *we* can peruse to advantage." But Mr. Henry might have perused both with infinite advantage, not only to himself, but to his country, and to the world; and that he did not do it, may, it is believed, be fairly ascribed, rather to the indolence of his temper, than the deliberate decision of his judgment.

Judge Winston says, that "he was, *throughout life*, negligent of his dress:" but this, it is apprehended, applied rather to his habits in the country, than to his appearance in public. At the bar of the general court, he always appeared in a full suit of black cloth, or velvet, and a tie wig, which was dressed and powdered in the highest style of forensic fashion; in the winter season, too, according to the *costume* of the day, he wore over his other apparel an ample cloak of scarlet cloth; and thus attired, made a figure bordering on grandeur. While he filled the executive chair, he is said to have been justly attentive to his dress, and appearance; "not being disposed to afford the occasion of humiliating comparisons between the past and present government."

He had long since, too, laid aside the offensive rusticity of his juvenile manners. His manners, indeed, were still unostentatious, frank, and simple; but they had all that natural ease and unaffected gracefulness, which distinguish the circles of the polite and wellbred. On occasions, too, where state and ceremony were expected, there was no man who could act better his part. I have had a description of Mr. Henry, entering, in the full dress which I have mentioned, the hall of delegates, at whose bar he was about to appear as an advocate, and saluting the house, all around, with a dignity and even majesty, that would have done honour to the most polished courtier in Europe.

This, however, was only on extraordinary occasions, when such a deportment was expected, and was properly in its place. In general, his manners were those of the plain Virginian gentleman—kind—open—candid—and conciliating—warm without insincerity, and polite without pomp—neither chilling by his reserve, nor fatiguing by his loquacity—but adapting himself, without an effort, to the character of his company. "He would be pleased and cheerful," says a correspondent, "with persons of any class or condition, vicious and abandoned persons only excepted; he preferred those of character and talents, but would be amused with any who could contribute to his amusement."

He had himself a vein of pleasantry, which was extremely amusing, without detracting from his dignity. His companions, although perfectly at their ease with him, were never known to treat him with degrading familiarities. Their love and their respect for him equally forbade it. Nor had they any dread of an assault upon their feelings; for their was nothing cruel in his wit.

The tomahawk and scalping-knife were no part of his colloquial apparatus. He felt no pleasure in seeing the victim writhe under his stroke. The benignity of his spirit could not have borne such a sight without torture. He found himself happiest in communicating happiness to others. His conversation was instructive and delightful; stately where it should be so, but in general, easy, familiar, sprightly, and entertaining; always, however, good-humoured, and calculated to amuse without wounding.

As a specimen of this light and good-natured pleasantry, the following anedote has been furnished: Mr. Henry, together with Mr. Richard H. Lee, and several other conspicuous members of the assembly, were invited to pass the evening and night at the house of Mr. Edmund Randolph, in the neighbourhood of Richmond. Mr. Lee, who was as brilliant and copious in conversation as in debate, had amused the company to a very late hour, by descanting on the genius of Cervantes, particularly as exhibited in his *chef d' œuvre*, Don Quixote.

The dissertation had been continued rather too long: the company began to yawn, when Mr. Henry, who had observed it, although Mr. Lee had not, rose slowly from his chair, and remarked as he walked across the room, that Don Quixote was certainly a most excellent work, and most skilfully adapted to the purpose of the author: "but," said he, "Mr. Lee," stopping before him, with a most significant archness of look, "you have overlooked in your eulogy, one of the finest things in the book." "What is *that?*" asked Mr. Lee. "It is," said Mr. Henry, "that divine exclamation of Sancho, '*Blessed be the man that first invented sleep: it covers one all over, like a cloak.*'" Mr. Lee took the hint; and the company broke up in good humour.

His quick and true discernment of characters, and his prescience of political events, were very much admired. The following examples of each, have been furnished by Mr. Pope:—

Mr. Gallatin came to Virginia when a very young man: he was obscure and unknown, and spoke the English language so badly, that it was with difficulty he could be understood. He was engaged in some agency which made it necessary to present a petition to the assembly, and endeavoured to interest the leading members in its fate, by attempting to explain, out of doors, its merits and justice. But they could not understand him well enough to feel any interest either for him or his petition. In this hopeless condition he waited on Mr. Henry, and soon felt that he was in different hands.

Mr. Henry, on his part, was so delighted with the interview, that he spoke of Mr. Gallatin everywhere in raptures—"he declared him, without hesitation or doubt, to be the most sensible and best informed man he had ever conversed with—*he is to be sure*," said he, "*a most astonishing man!*" The reader well knows how eminently Mr. Gallatin has since fulfilled this character; and considering the very disadvantageous circumstances under which he was seen by Mr. Henry, is certainly a striking proof of the superior sagacity of the observer.

In relation to his political foresight, the following anecdote is in Mr. Pope's own words:—"In the year 1798, after Bonaparte had annihilated five Austrian armies, and, flushed with victory, was carrying away everything before him, I heard Mr. Henry in a public company observe, (shaking his head after his impressive manner)—'It won't *all* do! the present generation in France is so debased by a long despotism, they possess so few of the virtues that constitute the life and soul of republicanism, that they are incapable of forming a correct and just estimate of *rational* liberty.

"'Their revolution will terminate differently from what you expect—their state of anarchy will be succeeded by despotism; and I should not be surprised, if *the very man* at whose victories you now rejoice, should, Cesar-like, subvert the liberties of his country. All who know me,' continued Mr. Henry, 'know that I am a firm advocate for liberty and republicanism; I believe I have given *some* evidences of this. I wish it may not be so, but I am afraid the event will justify this prediction.'"

The following is the fullest description which the author has been able to procure of Mr. Henry's person. He was nearly six feet high; spare, and what may be called rawboned, with a slight stoop of the shoulders—his complexion was dark, sunburnt, and sallow, without any appearance of blood in his cheeks—his countenance grave, thoughtful, penetrating, and strongly marked with the lineaments of deep reflection—the earnestness of his manner, united with an habitual contraction or knitting of his brows, and those lines of thought with which his face was profusely furrowed, gave to his countenance, at some times, the appearance of severity—yet such was the power which he had over its expression, that he could shake off from it in an instant, all the sternness of winter, and robe it in the brightest smiles of spring.

His forehead was high and straight; yet forming a sufficient angle with the lower part of his face—his nose somewhat of the Roman stamp, though like that which we see in the bust of Cicero, it was rather long, than remarkable for its Cesarean form. Of the colour of his eyes, the accounts are almost as various as those which we have of the colour of the chameleon—they are said to have been blue, gray, what Lavater calls green, hazel, brown, and black—the fact seems to have been that they were of a bluish-gray, not large; and being deeply fixed in his head, overhung by dark, long, and full eyebrows, and farther shaded by lashes that were both long and black, their apparent colour was as variable as the lights in which they were seen—but all concur in saying that they were, unquestionably, the finest feature in his face—brilliant—full of spirit, and capable of the most rapidly-shifting and powerful expression—at one time piercing and terrible as those of Mars, and then again soft and tender as those of Pity herself—his cheeks were hollow—his chin long, but well formed, and rounded at the end, so as to form a proper counterpart to the upper part of his face.

"I find it difficult," says the correspondent from whom I have borrowed this portrait, "to describe his mouth; in which there was nothing remarkable, except when about to express a modest dissent from some opinion on which he was commenting—he then had a sort of half-smile, in which *the want of conviction* was *perhaps* more strongly expressed, than the satirical emotion, which probably prompted it. His manner and address to the court and jury might be deemed the excess of humility, diffidence, and modesty.

"If, as rarely happened, he had occasion to answer any remark from the bench, it was impossible for Meekness herself to assume a manner less presumptuous—but in the *smile* of which I have been speaking, you might anticipate the want of conviction, expressed in his answer, at the moment that he submitted to the *superior wisdom* of the court, with a grace that would have done honour to Westminster hall. In his reply to counsel, his remarks on the evidence, and on the conduct of the parties, he preserved the same distinguished deference and politeness, still accompanied, however, by the *never-failing index of this skeptical smile*, where the occasion prompted."

In short, his features were manly, bold, and well-proportioned, full of intelligence, and adapting themselves intuitively to every sentiment of his mind, and every feeling of his heart. His voice was not remarkable for its sweetness; but it was firm, of full volume, and rather melodious than otherwise. Its charms consisted in the mellowness and fulness of its note, the ease and variety of its inflections, the distinctness of its articulation, the fine effect of its emphasis, the felicity with which it attuned itself to every emotion, and the vast compass which enabled it to range through the whole empire of human passion, from the deep and tragic half whisper of horror, to the wildest exclamation of overwhelming rage.

In mild persuasion, it was as soft and gentle as the zephyr of spring; while in rousing his countrymen to arms, the winter storm that roars along the troubled Baltic, was not more awfully sublime. It was at all times perfectly under his command; or rather, indeed, it seemed to command itself and to modulate its notes, most happily to the sentiment he was uttering. It never exceeded, or fell short of the occasion. There was none of that long-continued and deafening vociferation, which always takes place, when an ardent speaker has lost possession of himself—no monotonous clangour, no discordant shriek.

Without being strained, it had that body and enunciation which filled the most distant ear, without distressing those which were nearest him: hence it never became cracked or hoarse, even in his longest speeches, but retained to the last all its clearness and fulness of intonation, all the delicacy of its inflection, all the charms of its emphasis, and enchanting variety of its cadence.

His delivery was perfectly natural and well timed. It has indeed been said, that, on his first rising, there was a species of *sub-cantus* very observable by a stranger, and rather disagreeable to him; but that in a very few moments even this itself became agreeable, and seemed, indeed, indispensable to the full effect of his peculiar diction and conceptions. In point of time, he was very happy: there was no slow and heavy dragging, no quaint and measured drawling, with equidistant pace, no stumbling and floundering among the fractured members of deranged and broken periods, no undignified hurry and trepidation, no recalling and recasting of sentences as he went along, no retraction of one word and substitution of another not better, and none of those affected bursts of almost inarticulate impetuosity, which betray the rhetorician rather than display the orator.

On the contrary, ever self-collected, deliberate and dignified, he seemed to have looked through the whole period before he commenced its delivery; and hence his delivery was smooth, and firm, and well accented; slow enough to take along with him the dullest hearer, and yet so commanding, that the quick had neither the power nor the disposition to get the start of him. Thus he gave to every thought its full and appropriate force; and to every image all its radiance and beauty.

No speaker ever understood better than Mr. Henry the true use and power of the *pause:* and no one ever practised it with happier effect. His pauses were never resorted to for the purpose of investing an insignificant thought with false importance; much less were they ever resorted to as a *finesse* to gain time for thinking. The hearer was never disposed to ask, "why that pause?" nor to measure its duration by a reference to his watch. On the contrary, it always came at the very moment when he would himself have wished it, in order to weigh the striking and important thought which had just been uttered; and the interval was always filled by the speaker with a matchless energy of look, which drove the thought home through the mind and through the heart.

His gesture, and this varying play of his features and voice, were so excellent, so exquisite that many have referred his power as an orator principally to that cause; yet this was all his own, and his gesture, particularly, of so peculiar a cast, that it is said it would have become no other man. I do not learn that it was very abundant; for there was no trash about it; none of those false motions to which undisciplined speakers are so generally addicted; no chopping nor sawing of the air; no thumping of the bar to express an earnestness, which was much more powerfully, as well as more elegantly expressed by his eye and countenance. Whenever he moved his arm, or his hand, or even his finger, or changed the position of his body, it was always to some purpose; nothing was inefficient; everything told; every gesture, every attitude, every look was emphatic; all was animation, energy, and dignity.

Its great advantage consisted in this—that various, bold, and original as it was, it never appeared to be studied, affected, or theatrical, or "to overstep," in the smallest degree, "the modesty of nature;" for he never made a gesture, or assumed an attitude, which did not seem imperiously demanded by the occasion. Every look, every motion, every pause, every start was completely filled and dilated by the thought which he was uttering, and seemed indeed to form a part of the thought itself. His action, however strong, was never vehement. He was never seen rushing forward, shoulder foremost, fury in his countenance, and phrensy in his voice, as if to overturn the bar, and charge his audience sword in hand. His judgment was too manly and too solid, and his taste too true, to permit him to indulge in any such extravagance.

His good sense and his self-possession never deserted him. In the loudest storm of declamation, in the fiercest blaze of passion, there was a dignity and temperance which gave it seeming. He had the rare faculty of imparting to his hearers all the excess of his own feelings, and all the violence and tumult of his emotions, all the dauntless spirit of his resolution, and all the energy of his soul, without any sacrifice of his own personal dignity, and without treating his hearers otherwise than as rational beings. He was not the orator of a day; and therefore sought not to build his fame on the sandy basis of a false taste, fostered, if not created, by himself. He spoke for immortality; and therefore raised the pillars of his glory on the only solid foundation—the rock of Nature.

So much has been already said, incidentally, of his attainments, and the character of his mind, both as a statesman and an orator, that little remains to be added in a general way. As a statesman, the quality which strikes us most is his political intrepidity: and yet it has sometimes been objected to him, that he waited on every occasion, to see which way the popular current was sitting, when he would artfully throw himself into it, and seem to guide its course. Nothing can be more incorrect: it would be easy to multiply proofs to refute the charge; but I shall content myself with a few which are of general notoriety.

1. The American revolution is universally admitted to have begun in the upper circles of society. It turned on principles too remote and abtruse for vulgar apprehension or consideration. Had it depended on the unenlightened mass of the community, no doubt can be entertained at this day, that the tax imposed by parliament would have been paid without a question. Since, then, the upper circle of society did not take its impulse from the people, the only remaining inquiry is, who gave the revolutionary impulse to that circle itself? It was unquestionably Patrick Henry.

This is affirmed by Mr. Jefferson; it is demonstrated by the resistance given to Mr. Henry's measures, by those who were afterward the stanchest friends of the revolution; it is farther proved, by the sentiment before noticed, with which Doctor Franklin (who was then considered as the first American statesman) dismissed Mr. Ingersoll on his departure from London; a sentiment, which evinces beyond doubt, that Doctor Franklin considered resistance to the British power to be, at that time, premature; and finally, this honour is assigned to Mr. Henry, I perceive, by a late interesting historian of Massachusets, the only state which has ever pretended to dispute the palm with Virginia.

The historian to whom I allude, is Mrs. Mercy Warren, who is said to be the widow of the celebrated General Warren, the hero of Bunker's Hill. These are her words:—"The house of burgesses of Virginia were the first who formally resolved against the encroachments of power, and the unwarrantable designs of the British parliament. The novelty of their procedure, and the boldness of spirit that marked the resolutions of that assembly, at once astonished and disconcerted the officers of the crown, and the supporters of the measures of administration. These resolutions were ushered into the house on the thirtieth of May, one thousand seven hundred and sixty-five, by Patrick Henry, Esq., a young gentleman of the law, till then unknown in political life. He was a man possessed of strong powers, much professional knowledge, and of such abilities as qualified him for the exigences of the day. Fearless of the cry of *treason*, echoed against him from several quarters, he justified the measure and supported the resolves, in a speech that did honour both to his understanding and his patriotism," &c. MRS. WARREN'S *History of the American Revolution*, vol. i., p. 28.

On this great occasion, then, it is manifest, that he did not wait for the popular current; but on the contrary, that it was he alone, who, by his single power moved the mighty mass of stagnant waters, and changed the silent lake into a roaring torrent. When it is remembered too, that he was then young and obscure, and of course without personal influence—that this step was the result of his own solitary reflection, and that he was perfectly aware of the personal danger which must attend it—we can require nothing farther to satisfy us, that he was a bold, original, independent politician, who thought for himself, and pursued the dictates of his own judgment, wholly regardless of personal consequences.

2. Again, in the spring of 1775, that upper circle, which still headed the revolution, were disposed to acquiesce in the plunder of the magazine, and exerted their utmost efforts to allay the ferment which it had excited. They had, in fact succeeded; and the people were everywhere composed, save within the immediate sphere of Mr. Henry's influence. The reader has already seen, that it was he who on that occasion excited the people, not who was excited by them; that he put them into motion, and avowed to his confidential friends, at the time, the motives of policy by which he was actuated; that he placed himself at the head of an armed band, which he had himself convened for the purpose; and in spite of the entreaties and supplications

of the patriots at Williamsburgh, and in defiance of the threats of Dunmore and his myrmidons, pressed firmly and intrepidly on, until the object of his expedition was completely obtained.

3. So also in the state convention, the same year, the old patriotic leaders were disposed still to rely on the efficacy of petitions, memorials, and remonstrances; it was Mr. Henry who proposed, and in spite of their opposition (which was of so strenuous and serious a character, that one of them in making it, is said to have shed tears most profusely) carried the bold measure of arming the militia. This was not dictated by the people.

The fact was, that at that day, the people placed themselves in the hands of their more enlightened friends; they never ventured to prescribe either the time, the manner, or the measure of resistance; and there can be no room for a candid doubt that, but for the bold spirit and overpowering eloquence of Patrick Henry, the people would have followed the pacific counsels of Mr. Randolph, Mr. Nicholas, Mr. Pendleton, Mr. Wythe, and other men of acknowledged talents and virtue.

It was Mr. Henry, therefore, who led both the people and their former leaders. The latter, indeed came on so reluctantly *at first*, that they may be said to have been rather dragged along than led; they did come, however, and acquiring warmth by their motion, made ample amends thereafter for their early hesitation.

The author has no intention, by these remarks, to impair in the smallest degree, the well-earned reputation of those veteran statesmen. They had commenced the opposition to the stamp act, and the other obnoxious acts of the British parliament, before Mr. Henry made his appearance as a politician; they had commenced it too, on the same grounds, and would, probably, at some later period, have been wrought up by their own principles and feelings, to a forcible resistance to those measures.

But the statements above are unquestionably correct; *they did not approve of the immediate application of force;* Mr. Henry's policy was condemned by them as *rash and precipitate*. The author is in possession of an original letter from one of these statements, in which Mr. Henry is expressly and directly accused of having precipitated the revolution, against the judgment of the older and cooler patriots. "Events, however," as we have seen, "favoured the bolder measures of Mr. Henry," and proved his policy to be the best.

4. Abou the close of the war, again, when he proposed to permit the return of that obnoxious class of men called *British refugees* and *Scotch tories*, did he follow the popular cur-

rent? So far from it, that he stemmed the current, and turned back its course, by the power of his resistance.

5. So in the case of the federal constitution, whither did the current of the American people tend? Most certainly to its adoption, yet Mr. Henry, to use his own language, "with manly firmness, and in spite of an erring world," with the revered Washington at their head, opposed its adoption with all the powers of his eloquence.

The truth seems to be, that this charge is only a variation of that conveyed by the opprobrious epithets of demagogue and factious tribune, which we have seen that his rival long since sought to fasten upon him; and there can be little doubt, that it proceeded from the writhings and contortions of the same agonized envy. That a poor young man, issuing from his native woods, unknown, unfriended, and comparatively unlettered, should have been able, by the mere force of unassisted nature, to break to pieces the strong political confederacy which then ruled the country, to annihilate all the arts and *finesse* of parliamentary intrigue; to eclipse by his sagacity, the experience of age; and, by the sole strength of his native genius, to throw into the shade all the hard-earned attainments of literature and science, was entirely too humiliating to be borne in silence.

It was necessary, therefore, to resort to some solution of this phenomenon which should at once reduce the honours of this plebeian up-start, and sooth the wounded feelings of those whose pride he had brought down. Hence it became fashionable, in the higher circles, to speak of Mr. Henry as a *designing demagogue, a factious tribune*, who carried his points not by fair and open debate, but by violent and inflammatory appeals to the worst passions of the multitude; and who frequently gave himself the air of leading the people, when in truth he was merely following their own blind lead.

This cant has had its day, and its propagators. Truth has set the subject to rights. Mr. Henry is alleged, by those who had the best opportunities of knowing him, to have been not inferior, either in public or private virtue, to any patriot of the revolution: and he was confessedly superior to them all, in that combination of bold, hardy, adventurous, splendid, and solid qualifications, which are so peculiarly fitted to revolutionary times.

"He left," says Judge Winston, "no manuscripts." This was to have been expected. We have seen that he could not bear the labour of writing; nor, indeed, of that long-continued, coherent, and methodical thinking, without which, no successful composition, of any extent, can be produced. He thought, indeed, a great deal; but his thinking was too desultory and irregular to take the form of composition.

His mind had never been disciplined to wait upon his pen—it still moved on—and its prismatic beauties were as evanescent as they were beautiful. His imagination "bodied forth the forms of things" much more rapidly than his unpractised pen could "turn them to shapes;" and it is not improbable, that his own observation of the difference between the vigour with which he thought, and the comparative decrepitude with which he wrote, disgusted him with his first attempts, and prevented their repetition.

Yet this habit which he had of thinking for himself, and looking directly at every subject, with the natural eyes of his understanding, without using what has been called the *spectacles of books*, was perhaps of advantage to him, both as a statesman and an orator: as a statesman, it possibly exempted him from that common error of scientific theorists, of forcing resemblances between the present and some past historical era, and accommodating their measures to this imaginary identity; by *his* mode of considering subjects, no circumstance was either sunk or magnified, or distorted, in order to bend the case to a fanciful hypothesis; nor, in deciding what was proper to be done in America, did he look to see what had been found expedient at Athens or Rome.

On the contrary, knowing well the people with whom he had to deal, of what they were capable, and what was necessary to their happiness, how much they could bear, and how much achieve, and looking immediately at the subject, (whatever it might be,) with that piercing vision, that solid judgment and ready resource, which characterized his mind—he seemed to seize in every case, rather "luckily than laboriously," the course which of all others was surest of success.

In short, this habit made him an original, sound and practical statesman, instead of being a learned, dreaming, and visionary theorist. Not that Mr. Henry was deficient in historical knowledge; he had enough of it for all the useful purposes either of analogy or illustration; but he never permitted it to intercept his proper view of the subject, or to take the lead in suggesting what was fit to be done. This he chose rather to derive from the nature of the case itself, and the character of the people among whom that case occurred.

This habit of relying more on his own meditations than on books, was, also, perhaps, a service to him as an orator: for by this course, he avoided the beaten paths and roads of thought; and instead of exhibiting in his speeches old ideas newly vamped up, and ancient beauties tricked off in mod ern tinsel, his arguments, sentiments, and figures, had all that freshness and novelty which are so universally captivating.

In what did his peculiar excellence as an orator consist? in what consisted that unrivalled power of speaking, which all who ever heard him admit him to have possessed? The reader is already apprized, that the author of these sketches never had the advantage of hearing Mr. Henry, and that no entire speech of his was ever extant, either in print or writing: hence, there are no materials for minute and exact analysis. This inquiry, however, is natural, and has been directed, without success, to many of the most discriminating of Mr. Henry's admirers. Their answers are as various as the complexion of their own characters; each preferring that property from which he had himself derived the most enjoyment. Some ascribe his excellence wholly to his manner; others, in great part, to the originality and soundness of his matter. And among the admirers, in both classes, there are not two who concur in assigning the pre-eminence to the same quality.

Of his matter, one will admire the plainness and strength of his reasoning; another, the concentrated spirit of his aphorisms; a third, his wit; a fourth, his pathos; a fifth, the intrinsic beauty of his imagination: so in regard to his manner, one will place his excellence in his articulation and emphasis; a second, in the magic power with which he infused the tones of his voice into the nerves of his hearers, and riveted their attention. The truth therefore, probably is, that it was not in any singular charm, either of matter or manner, that we are to look for the secret of his power; but that like Pope's definition of beauty, it was "the joint force and full result of all."

If, however, we are to consider as really and entirely his, those speeches which have already been given in his name to the public, or are now prepared for them, there can be no difficulty in deciding, that his power must have consisted principally in his delivery. We know what extraordinary effects have been produced by the mere manner of an orator, without any uncommon weight or worth of matter.

"Friar Narni, a capuchin, was so remarkable for his eloquence, that his hearers, after a sermon, cried out *mercy* in the streets, as he passed home: and thirty bishops, starting up under a discourse, hurried home to their respective dioceses: yet, when his sermons came to be published, they were thought to be unworthy of his reputation; which shows how much depends on action; and how correct the saying of Demosthenes was on that subject."—BAYLE. Article Narni.

We have the authority, however, of those who heard the identical speeches now professed to be given as his, for decharing, that they are an extremely imperfect representation of them; and their ability to correct them so frequently from memory, establishes the fact, that it was not the charm of delivery merely, which constituted the difference between the report and the original.

This is not the only instance in which a great orator has been injured, by imperfect attempts to represent him: for (to say nothing of those modern proofs, which will easily occur to the reader) we are told that the great Pericles himself met with a similar fate. "Some harangues of Pericles were still extant in Quintilian's time; but that learned rhetorician, finding them disproportioned to the high reputation of this great man, approved the opinion of those who looked upon them as a supposititious work. An indifferent harangue, however, being recited by an excellent orator, may charm the hearers. *Action is almost all!*" Article Pericles.

Candour and justice, however, require us to repeat, that Mr. Robertson's reports are unquestionable, in point of good faith; and that they are highly valuable, on account of the accuracy and fidelity with which they are believed to have preserved the substance of the debates. It is with extreme regret that the author has made a single comment to their disadvantage; but justice to Mr. Henry has made it indispensable.

The basis of Mr. Henry's intellectual character was *strong natural sense*. His knowledge of human nature was, as we have seen, consummate. His wisdom was that of observation, rather than of reading. His fancy, although sufficiently pregnant to furnish supplies for the occasion, was not so exuberant as to oppress him with its productions. He was never guilty of the fault, with which Corinna is said to have reproached her rival Pindar, of pouring his vase of flowers all at once upon the ground; on the contrary, their beauty and their excellence were fully observed, from their rarity, and the happiness with which they were distributed through his speeches.

His feelings were strong, yet completely under his command; they rose up to the occasion, but were never suffered to overflow it; his language was often careless, sometimes incorrect; yet upon the whole it was pure and perspicuous, giving out his thoughts in full and clear proportion; free from affectation, and frequently beautiful; strong without effort, and adapted to the occasion; nervous in argument, burning in passion, and capable of matching the loftiest flights of his genius.

It may perhaps assist the reader's conception of Mr. Henry's peculiar cast of eloquence, to state the points in which he differed from some other orators. Those which distinguished him from Mr. Lee have been already exhibited. Colonel Innis's manner was also very different. *His* habitual indolence followed him into debate; he generally contented himself with a single view of his subject; but that was given with irresistible power.

His eloquence was indeed a mighty and a roaring torrent; it had not, however, that property of Horace's stream, *labitur et labetur, in omne volubilis ævum*—on the contrary, it commonly ran by in half an hour. But it bore a striking resemblance to the eloquence of Lord Chatham; it was a short but bold and most terrible assault—a vehement, impetuous and overwhelming burst—a magnificent meteor, which shot majestically across the heavens, from pole to pole, and straight expired in a glorious blaze.

Mr. Henry, on the contrary, however indolent in his general life, was never so in debate, where the occasion called for exertion. He rose against the pressure, with the most unconquerable perseverance. He held his subject up in every light in which it could be placed; yet always with so much power, and so much beauty, as never to weary his audience, but on the contrary to delight them. He had more art than Colonel Innis: he appealed to every motive of interest—urged every argument that could convince—pressed every theme of persuasion—awakened every feeling, and roused every passion to his aid. He had more variety, too, in his manner; sometimes he was very little above the tone of conversation; at others in the highest strain of epic sublimity.

His course was of longer continuance—his flights better sustained, and more diversified, both in their direction, and velocity. He rose like the thunder-bearer of Jove, when he mounts on strong and untiring wing, to sport in fearless majesty over the troubled deep—now sweeping in immense and rapid circles—then suddenly arresting his grand career, and hovering aloft in tremulous and terrible suspense—at one instant, plunged amid the foaming waves—at the next, reascending on high, to play undaunted among the lightnings of heaven, or soar toward the sun.

He differed too, from those orators of Great Britain, with whom we have become acquainted by their printed speeches. He had not the close method and high polish of those of England; nor the exuberant imagery which distinguishes those of Ireland. On the contrary, he was loose, irregular, desultory—sometimes rough and abrupt—careless in connecting the parts of his discourse, but grasping whatever he touched with gigantic strength. In short, he was the ORATOR OF NATURE; and such a one as Nature might not blush to avow.

If the reader shall still demand how he acquired those wonderful powers of speaking which have been assigned to him, we can only answer, with Gray, that they were the gift of Heaven—the birthright of genius.

> "Thine too, these keys, immortal boy!
> *This* can unlock the gates of joy;
> Of horror, *that*, and thrilling fears,
> Or ope the sacred source of sympathetic tears."

It has been said of Mr. Henry, by Mr. John Randolph, of Roanoke, with inimitable felicity, that "he was SHAKSPEARE and GARRICK COMBINED!" Let the reader then imagine the wonderful talents of those two men united in the same individual, and transferred from scenes of fiction to the business of real life, and he will have formed some conception of the eloquence of Patrick Henry. In a word, he was one of those perfect prodigies of Nature, of whom very few have been produced since the foundations of the earth were laid; and of *him* may it be said, as truly as of any one that ever existed:—

> "He was a man, take him for all in all,
> *We ne'er shall look upon his like again.*"

APPENDIX.

NOTE A.

It appears by the journals of the house of burgesses, of the 14th November, seventeen hundred and sixty-four, (page 38,) that a committee was appointed to draw up the following address, memorial, and remonstrance; which committee was composed of the following persons, to wit: Mr. Attorney, (Peyton Randolph,) Mr. Richard Henry Lee, Mr. Landon Carter, Mr. Wythe, Mr. Edmund Pendleton, Mr. Benjamin Harrison, Mr. Cary, and Mr. Fleming, to whom, afterward, Mr. Bland was added. The address to the king is from the pen of the attorney.*

"*To the king's most excellent Majesty.*

"Most Gracious Sovereign,

"We, your majesty's dutiful and loyal subjects, the council and burgesses of your ancient colony and dominion of *Virginia*, now met in general assembly, beg leave to assure your majesty of our firm and inviolable attachment to your sacred person and government; and as your faithful subjects here have at all times been zealous to demonstrate this truth, by a ready compliance with the royal requisitions during the late war, by which a heavy and oppressive debt of near half a million had been incurred, so at this time they implore permission to approach the throne with humble confidence, and to entreat that your majesty will be graciously pleased to protect our people of this colony in the enjoyment of their ancient and inestimable right of being governed by such laws, respecting their internal polity and taxation, as are derived from their own consent, with the approbation of their sovereign or his substitute: a right which, as men, and descendants of *Britons*, they have ever quietly possessed, since, first by royal permission and encouragement, they left the mother kingdom to extend its commerce and dominion.

"Your majesty's dutiful subjects of *Virginia* most humbly and unanimously hope, that this invaluable birthright, descended to them from their ancestors, and in which they have been protected by your royal predecessors, will not be suffered to receive an injury under the reign of your sacred majesty, already so illustriously distinguished by your gracious attention to the liberties of the people.

"That your majesty may long live to make nations happy, is the ardent prayer of your faithful subjects, the council and burgesses of *Virginia*."

The author cannot learn who drew the following memorial; but from the style of the composition, compared with the members of the committee, and the distribution of its other labours, he thinks it probable that it was Mr. Pendleton; possibly Mr. Bland.

U

* On the authority of Mr. Jefferson.

"To the Right Honourable the Lords Spiritual and Temporal, in Parliament assembled:—

"*The Memorial of the Council and Burgesses of Virginia, now met in General Assembly,*

"HUMBLY REPRESENTS,

"That your memorialists hope an application to your lordships, the fixed and hereditary guardians of *British* liberty, will not be thought improper at this time, when measures are proposed, subversive, as they conceive, of that freedom, which all men, especially those who derive their constitution from *Britain*, have a right to enjoy; and they flatter themselves that your lordships will not look upon them as objects so unworthy your attention, as to regard any impropriety in the form or manner of their application, for your lordships' protection, of their just and undoubted rights as *Britons*.

"It cannot be presumption in your memorialists to call themselves by this distinguished name, since they are descended from *Britons*, who left their native country to extend its territory and dominion, and who, happily for *Britain*, and as your memorialists once thought, for themselves too, effected this purpose. As our ancestors brought with them every right and privilege they could with justice claim in their mother kingdom, their descendants may conclude, they cannot be deprived of those rights without injustice.

"Your memorialists conceive it to be a fundamental principle of the *British* constitution, without which freedom can nowhere exist, that the people are not subject to any taxes but such as are laid on them by their own consent or by those who are legally appointed to represent them: property must become too precarious for the genius of a free people which can be taken from them at the will of others, who cannot know what taxes such people can bear, or the easiest mode of raising them; and who are [illegible] that restraint, which is the greatest security against a burdensome taxation, when the representatives themselves must be affected by every tax imposed on the people.

"Your memorialists are therefore led into an humble confidence, that your lordships will not think any reason sufficient to support such a power, in the *British* parliament, where the colonies cannot be represented: a power never before constitutionally assumed, and which, if they have a right to exercise on any occasion, must necessarily establish this melancholy truth, that the inhabitants of the colonies are the slaves of *Britons* from whom they are descended: and from whom they might expect every indulgence that the obligations of interest and affection can entitle them to.

"Your memorialists have been invested with the right of taxing their own people from the first establishment of a regular government in the colony, and requisitions have been constantly made to them by their sovereigns, on all occasions when the assistance of the colony was thought necessary to preserve the *British* interest in *America*; from whence they must conclude they cannot now be deprived of a right they have so long enjoyed, and which they have never forfeited.

"The expenses incurred during the last war, in compliance with the demands on this colony by our late and present most gracious sovereigns, have involved us in a debt of near half a million, a debt not likely to decrease under the continued expense we are at, in providing for the security of the people against the incursions of our savage neighbours; at a time when the low state of our staple commodity, the total want of specie, and the late restrictions upon the trade of the colonies, render the circumstances of the people extremely distressful; and which, if taxes are accumulated upon them by the *British* parliament, will make them truly deplorable.

"Your memorialists cannot suggest to themselves any reason why they should not still be trusted with the property of their people, with whose abilities, and the least burdensome mode of taxing, (with great deference to the superior wisdom of parliament,) they must be best acquainted.

"Your memorialists hope they shall not be suspected of being actuated, on this occasion, by any principles but those of the purest loyalty and affection, as they always endeavoured by their conduct to demonstrate, that they consider their connexion with *Great Britain*, the seat of liberty, as their greatest happiness.

"The duty they owe to themselves and their posterity, lays your memorialists under the necessity of endeavouring to establish their constitution upon its proper foundation; and they do most humbly pray your lordships to take this subject into your consideration with the attention that is due to the well-being of the colonies, on which the prosperity of *Great Britain* does, in a great measure, depend."

Mr. Wythe was the author of the following remonstrance. "It was done with so much freedom, that, as he told me himself, his colleagues of the committee shrunk from it as wearing the aspect of treason, and smoothed its features to its present form."*

"To the Honourable the Knights, Citizens, and Burgesses of *Great Britain*, in Parliament assembled:—

"*The Remonstrance of the Council and Burgesses of* Virginia.

"It appearing, by the printed votes of the house of commons of *Great Britain* in parliament assembled, that in a committee of the whole house the seventeenth day of *March*, last, it was resolved, that toward defending, protecting, and securing the *British* colonies and plantations in *America*, it may be proper to charge certain stamp duties in the said colonies and plantations; and it being apprehended that the same subject, which was then declined, may be resumed and further pursued in a succeeding session, the council and burgesses of *Virginia*, met in general assembly, judge it their indispensable duty, in a respectful manner, but with decent firmness, to remonstrate against such a measure; that at least a cession of those rights, which in their opinion must be infringed by that procedure, may not be inferred from their silence, at so important a crisis.

"They conceive it is essential to *British* liberty, that laws, imposing taxes on the people, ought not to be made without the consent of representatives chosen by themselves; who, at the same time that they are acquainted with the circumstances of their constituents, sustain a portion of the burden laid on them. The privileges, inherent in the persons who discovered and settled these regions, could not be renounced or forfeited by their removal hither, not as vagabonds or fugitives, but licensed and encouraged by their prince, and animated with a laudable desire of enlarging the *British* dominion, and extending its commerce: on the contrary, it was secured to them and their descendants, with all other rights and immunities of British subjects, by a royal charter, which hath been invariably recognised and confirmed by his majesty and his predecessors, in their commissions to the several governors, granting a power, and prescribing a form of legislation; according to which, laws for the administration of justice, and for the welfare and good government of the colony, have been hitherto enacted by the governor, council, and general assembly; and to them, requisitions and applications for supplies have been directed by the crown. As an instance of the opinion which former sovereigns entertained of these rights and privileges, we beg leave to refer to three acts

* Mr. Jefferson.

of the general assembly, passed in the thirty-second year of the reign of King *Charles* II. (one of which is entitled '*An act for raising a public revenue for the better support of the government of his majesty's colony of Virginia,*' imposing several duties for that purpose,) which being thought absolutely necessary, were prepared in *England*, and sent over by their then governor, the lord *Culpepper*, to be passed by the general assembly, with a full power to give the royal assent thereto; and which were accordingly passed, after several amendments were made to them here; thus tender was his majesty of the rights of his *American* subjects; and the remonstrants do not discern by what distinction they can be deprived of that sacred birthright and most valuable inheritance by their fellow-subjects, nor with what propriety they can be taxed or affected in their estates, by the parliament, wherein they are not, and indeed cannot constitutionally, be represented.

"And if it were proper for the parliament to impose taxes on the colonies at all, which the remonstrants take leave to think would be inconsistent with the fundamental principles of the constitution, the exercise of that power, at this time, would be ruinous to *Virginia*, who exerted herself in the late war, it is feared beyond her strength, insomuch that to redeem the money granted for that exigence, her people are taxed for several years to come; this, with the larger expenses incurred for defending the frontiers against the restless *Indians*, who have infested her as much since the peace as before, is so grievous, that an increase of the burthen would be intolerable; especially as the people are very greatly distressed already from the scarcity of circulating cash among them, and from the little value of their staple at the *British* markets.

"And it is presumed, that adding to that load which the colony now labours under, will not be more oppressive to her people than destructive of the interests of *Great Britain*: for the plantation trade, confined as it is to the mother-country, hath been a principal means of multiplying and enriching her inhabitants; and, if not too much discouraged, may prove an inexhaustible source of treasure to the nation. For satisfaction in this point, let the present state of the *British* fleets and trade be compared with what they were before the settlement of the colonies; and let it be considered, that while property in land may be acquired on very easy terms, in the vast uncultivated territory of *North America*, the colonists will be mostly, if not wholly, employed in agriculture; whereby the exportation of their commodities to *Great Britain*, and the consumption of manufactures supplied from thence, will be daily increasing. But this most desirable connexion between *Great Britain* and her colonies, supported by such a happy intercourse of reciprocal benefits as is continually advancing the prosperity of both, must be interrupted, if the people of the latter, reduced to extreme poverty, should be compelled to manufacture those articles they have been hitherto furnished with from the former.

"From these considerations, it is hoped that the honourable house of commons will not prosecute a measure which those who may suffer under it cannot but look upon as fitter for exiles driven from their native country, after ignominiously forfeiting her favours and protection, than for the posterity of *Britons*, who have at all times been forward to demonstrate all due reverence to the mother-kingdom; and are so instrumental in promoting her glory and felicity; and that *British* patriots will never consent to the exercise of any anti-constitutional power which, even in this remote corner, may be dangerous in its example to the interior parts of the *British* empire, and will certainly be detrimental to its commerce."

NOTE B.

Council Chamber, October 17th, 1785.

SIR—Since the last session of assembly, I have received sundry acts, resolutions, and other communications from congress, which I transmit to the general assembly, marked No. 1, and which will claim the attention of the legislature, according to their nature and importance, respectively.

The execution of the militia law hath caused much embarrassment to the executive. Compelled to name all the field officers throughout the state, and possessing sufficient information as to the fitness of individuals for these offices in a few counties only, they were constrained to search out proper persons, by such means as accident furnished, and by letters addressed to the several counties. In some instances, the gentleman to whom they were addressed, refused to give any information. In many others, the answers came too late to avail; the law directing the commissions to issue the first of April. In this situation, the business has been conducted: and from a partial knowledge of characters in some counties, and a total ignorance of them in others, I am sensible many who are worthy of command have been passed by, and others less fit for office may have been commissioned. And notwithstanding a close attention has been given to this business, many of the counties have not yet been officered, for want of the recommendations of captains and subalterns.

Finding that the arms and ammunition directed to be purchased, could not be procured except from beyond the sea, application has been made by me to Mr. Jefferson and the Marquis de la Fayette, requesting their assistance to Mr. Barclay, (who was commissioned to make the purchase,) in accomplishing this important work; and I have the satisfaction to find, that the affair is in such a train as to promise the speedy arrival of these much-wanted articles. For more full information respecting this transaction, I send you sundry letters, (No. 2,) by one of which you will see that our noble friend the marquis offers us his services, if there shall be occasion for them.

I transmit, herewith, a letter from the honourable Mr. Hardy, covering a memorial to congress from sundry inhabitants of Washington county, praying the establishment of an independent state, to be bounded as is therein expressed. The proposed limits include a vast extent of country in which we have numerous and very respectable settlements, which, in their growth, will form an invaluable barrier between this country and those who, in the course of events, may occupy the vast plains westward of the mountains, some of whom may have views incompatible with our safety. Already the militia of that part of the state is among the most respectable we have: and by these means it is, that the neighbouring Indians are awed into professions of friendship. But a circumstance has lately happened, which renders the possession of that territory, at the present time, indispensable to the peace and safety of Virginia: I mean the assumption of sovereign power by the western inhabitants of North Carolina. If these people, who, without consulting their own safety or any other authority known in the American constitution, have assumed government, and while unallied to us, and under no engagements to pursue the objects of the federal government, they shall be strengthened by the accession of so great a part of our country, consequences fatal to our repose will probably follow. It is to be observed, that the settlements of this new society stretch on to great extent in contact with ours in Washington county, and thereby expose our citizens to the contagion of that example, which bids fair to destroy the peace of North Carolina.

In this state of things it is, that variety of informations have come to me, stating that several persons, but especially Col. Arthur Campbell, have used their utmost endeavours, and with some success, to persuade the citizens in that quarter to break off from this commonwealth, and attach themselves to the newly-assumed government, or erect one distinct from it. And in order to effect this purpose, the equity and authority of the laws have been arraigned, the collection of the taxes impeded, and our national character impeached. But as I send you the several papers I have received on that subject, I need not enlarge further than remark that if this most important part of our territory be lopped off, we lose that barrier for which our people have long and often fought, that nursery of soldiers from which future armies may be levied, and through which it will be almost impossible for our enemies to penetrate: we shall aggrandize the new state, whose connexions, views, and designs we know not; shall cease to be formidable to our savage neighbours, or respectable to our western settlements, at present and in future.

While these and many other matters were contemplated by the executive, it is natural to suppose, the attempt for separation was discouraged by every lawful means; the chief of which was, displacing such of the field officers of militia, in Washington county, as were active partisans for separation, in order to prevent the weight of office being cast in the scale against this state: to this end a proclamation was issued, declaring the militia law of the last session in force in that county, and appointments of officers were made agreeable to it.

I hope to be excused for expressing a wish, that the assembly, in deliberating on this affair, will prefer lenient measures in order to reclaim our erring fellow-citizens. Their taxes have run into three years' arrear, and, thereby, grown to an amount beyond the ability of many to discharge, while the system of our trade has been such, as to render their agriculture unproductive of money; and I cannot but suppose, that if even the warmest supporters of separation had seen the mischievous consequences of it, they would have retracted; and condemned that intemperance in their own proceedings, which opposition in sentiments is too apt to produce.

A letter from the countess of Huntingdon, and another from Sir James Jay, expressing her intentions to attempt the civilization of the Indians, are also sent you. It will rest with the assembly to decide upon the means for executing this laudable design, that reflects so much honour on that worthy lady.

By a resolution of the last assembly, the auditors were prevented from liquidating the claims of the officers and soldiers, after the first day of May last. Although the wisdom of such a measure must be admitted, yet several cases have come to my knowledge where claims, founded upon the clearest principles of justice, have been rejected by reason of that restriction: and when I consider that the claimants will be found to consist, in considerable degree, of widows, orphans, and those who have been taken prisoners, I am persuaded the assembly will think that a rigorous adherence to the forementioned resolution is improper, and that justice will be done to the claims of those few, whose poverty, ignorance, or other misfortunes, prevented earlier applications.

By Mr. Ross's letter No. 5, the assembly will observe his demand against the state, and that it can be properly discussed only by the legislature. Although the post at Point of Fork has been long occupied, I cannot discover the least trace of title to the ground vested in the public, or any previous stipulation with the proprietor for the temporary possession of it. While the assembly are considering of a proper satisfaction to the owner for the time past, I trust provision will be made to secure a permanent repository for the public arms and military stores, at that or some other place most proper for the purpose.

The honourable William Nelson hath resigned his office as a member of the council, as appears by his letter, No. 6.

The honourable Henry Tazewell, esq., has been appointed a judge of the general court in the room of the honourable B. Danbridge, esq., deceased, until the assembly shall signify their pleasure.

The honourable George Muter, esq., has been appointed a judge of the general court in Kentucky, in the room of Cyrus Griffin, esq., who resigned his appointment.

Thomas Massie, esq., having resigned his appointment for opening a road on the northwestern frontier, Joseph Neville, esq., has been appointed in his room.

The report of the commissioners for disposing of the Gosport lands, No. 9, will explain to the assembly their transactions in that business.

Mr. René Rapicault, of New Orleans, exhibited an account against this commonwealth for a considerable sum of money which appears to be due to him. But as it will be found by reference to his papers, No. 10, that this debt, however just, cannot be paid from any fund now existing, it is submitted to the legislature to make such provision for its payment, as to them shall seem proper.

The report of the commissioners for extending the boundary line between Virginia and Pennsylvania, No. 11, will explain the manner in which that business has been executed.

By Mr. Jefferson's letters it appears, that the original sum granted to procure a statue of General Washington will be deficient. The further sum wanting, together with the reasons for increasing the expense of the work, will appear by Mr. Jefferson's correspondence, No. 12.

The crews of the boats Liberty and Patriot were ordered to be enlisted for twelve months from August last, unless sooner discharged. This was done in order that the assembly might, if they judged proper, determine to discontinue them, or if they are retained, make suitable provision for their support: hitherto, that has been defrayed out of the contingent fund. But the great variety of expenses charged on that fund, make it necessary, in future, to provide some other mode of support for them. The assembly will, no doubt, observe in the course of their deliberations on the subject of revenue, that it is necessary for the executive to commission the officers. The officer commanding one of these boats has detected several persons attempting to evade the payment of duty, and in compliance with the law, as he supposes, took bonds for the payments of the penalties imposed for making false entries. But it seems there are great difficulties in recovering judgment on these bonds, owing to ambiguity in the law respecting the subject. The assembly will apply such remedy for this evil as they think proper.

Application hath been made to the executive, on the subject of paying into the continental treasury, warrants for interest due on loan-office certificates, and other liquidated claims against the continent. And although there can be no doubt that payments made by the treasurer to the continental receiver, may include the proportion of warrants specified by congress in their acts of the twenty-eighth of April, seventeen hundred and eighty-four, yet the receiver, when possessed of the cash, although it was unaccompanied by any warrants, does not conceive himself justified in parting with any money in exchange for them. So that until the assembly shall interpose, by making these warrants receivable at the treasury, our citizens will suffer great injury, and be deprived of a facility enjoyed by the citizens of the other states.

The sum of money allowed by the assembly in their resolution of the thirteenth of June, seventeen hundred and eighty-three, for compiling, printing, and binding the laws, has proved inadequate to the purpose; five hundred pounds having been expended in the printing, and two hundred and fifty engaged to be divided among the gentlemen who made the compilation; so that nothing is left to pay for the binding.

I cannot forbear informing the assembly, that many county courts have failed to recommend sheriffs in the months of June and July. In consequence of this, many of the counties will be without sheriffs, inasmuch as the executive think they have no power to issue commissions in such cases. As this evil threatens so many parts of the state with anarchy, I have no doubt of the legislature remedying it with all possible despatch.

I have the honour to be, with great regard,
Your most obedient, humble servant,
P. HENRY.

The Honourable the Speaker of the House of Delegates.

NOTE C.

Judge Tucker, in his edition of Blackstone, having fallen into Mr. Randolph's mistake, in regard to the case of Josiah Philips, the following note has been furnished to the author by the gentleman who was the chairman of the committee:—

"The case of Josiah Philips, I find strangely represented by Judge Tucker and Mr. Edmund Randolph, and very negligently vindicated by Mr. Henry. That case is personally known to me, because I was of the legislature at the time, was one of those consulted by Mr. Henry, and had my share in the passage of the bill. I never before saw the observation of those gentlemen, which you quote on this case, and will now, therefore, briefly make some strictures on them.

"Judge Tucker, instead of a definition of the functions of bills of attainder, has given a just diatribe against their abuse. The occasion and proper office of a bill of attainder is this; when a person charged with a crime withdraws from justice, or resists it by force, either in his own or a foreign country, no other means of bringing him to trial or punishment being practicable, a special act is passed by the legislature, adapted to the particular case; this prescribes to him a sufficient term to appear and submit to a trial by his peers, declares that his refusal to appear shall be taken as a confession of guilt, as in the ordinary case of an offender at the bar refusing to plead, and pronounces the sentence which would have been rendered on his confession or conviction in a court of law. No doubt that these acts of attainder have been abused in England as instruments of vengeance by a successful over a defeated party, but what institution is insusceptible of abuse, in wicked hands?

"Again, the judge says, 'the court refused to pass sentence of execution pursuant to the directions of the act.' The court could not refuse this, because it was never proposed to them, and my authority for this assertion shall be presently given.

"For the perversion of a fact so intimately known to himself, Mr. Randolph can be excused only by our indulgence for orators who, pressed by a powerful adversary, lose sight, in the ardour of conflict, of the rigorous accuracies of fact, and permit their imagination to distort and colour them to the views of the moment. He was attorney-general at the time, and told me himself, the first time I saw him after the trial of Philips, that when taken and delivered up to justice, he had thought it best to make no use of the act of attainder, and to take no measure under it; and that he had indicted him, at the common law, either for murder or robbery, (I forget which, and whether for both,) that he was tried on this indictment in the ordinary way, found guilty by the jury, sentenced and executed under the common law; a course which every one approved, because the first object of the act of attainder was, to bring him to a fair trial. Whether Mr. Randolph was right in this information to me, or, when in the debate with Mr. Henry, he represents this atrocious offender as sentenced and executed under the act of attainder, let the record of the case decide.

"'Without being confronted with his accusers and witnesses, without the privilege of calling for evidence in his behalf, he was sentenced to death, and afterward actually executed.' I appeal to the universe to produce one single instance from the first establishment of government in this state to the present day, where, in a trial at bar, a criminal has been refused confrontation with his accusers and witnesses, or denied the privilege of calling for evidence in his behalf. Had it been done in this case, I would have asked of the attorney-general, why he proposed or permitted it? But, without having seen the record, I will venture, on the character of our courts, to deny that it was done. But if Mr. Randolph meant, only, that Philips had not these advantages, on the passage of the bill of attainder, how idle to charge the legislature with omitting to confront the culprit with his witnesses, when he was standing out in arms, and in defiance of their authority; and their sentence was to take effect, only on his own refusal to come in and be confronted. We must either, therefore, consider this as a mere hyperbolism of imagination, in the heat of debate, or, what I should rather believe, a defective statement by the reporter of Mr. Randolph's argument. I suspect this last the rather, because this point in the charge of Mr. Randolph is equally omitted in the defence of Mr. Henry. This gentleman must have known that Philips was tried and executed under the common law, and yet, according to this report, he rests his defence on a justification of the attainder only. But all who knew Mr. Henry, know, that when at ease in argument, he was sometimes careless, not giving himself the trouble of ransacking either his memory or imagination for all the topics of his subject, or his audience that of hearing them. No man on earth knew better when he had said enough for his hearers.

"Mr. Randolph charges us with having read the bill three times in the same day. I do not remember the fact, nor whether this was enforced on us by the urgency of the ravages of Philips, or of the time at which the bill was introduced. I have some idea it was at or near the close of the session. The journals, which I have not, will ascertain this fact."

The following proceedings against Josiah Philips and his associates, are extracted from the records of the general court; and are followed by the notice of the execution of these men, from the public prints of the day: which, it is hoped, will put a final end to this mistake, so little to the honour of our revolution.

"Virginia, to wit:—

"The jurors for the commonwealth, upon their oath present: That Josiah Philips, late of the parish of Lynhaven, in the county of Princess Ann, labourer, on the ninth day of May, in the year of our Lord one thousand seven hundred and seventy-eight, with force and arms, at the parish aforesaid, in the county aforesaid, in the highway of the commonwealth there, in and upon one James Hargrove, in the peace of God and of the commonwealth, then and there being, feloniously did make an assault, and him, the said James Hargrove, in bodily fear and danger of his life, in the highway aforesaid, then and there feloniously did put, and twenty-eight men's felt hats of the value of twenty shillings each, and five pounds of twine of the value of five shillings each pound, of the goods and chattels of the same James Hargrove, from the person and against the will of the said James Hargrove, in the highway aforesaid, then and there feloniously and violently did steal, take and carry away, against the peace and dignity of the commonwealth.

"Witness.—James Hargrove, Benjamin Griffin, William Lovett, Polly Davis, Horatio Davis, and John Matthias. Sworn in court, Oct. 20th, 1778.

John May."

The above endictment is thus endorsed:—

"An endictment against Josiah Philips for robbery," (in Mr. Randolph's hand-writing.) "A true bill. Wm. Holt, foreman."

"VIRGINIA,

"In the General Court, 20th October, 1778.

"Josiah Philips, late of the parish of Lynhaven, in the county of Princess Ann, labourer, who stands *endicted for robbery*, was led to the bar in custody of the keeper of the public jail, and was thereof arraigned, and pleaded not guilty to the endictment, and for his trial put himself upon God and his country. Whereupon came a jury, to wit: James Letate, Thomas Stanley, Gilliam Booth, Stapleton Crutchfield, John Tankerley, John Draper, Leonard Henley, Micajah Chiles, Richard Swepson, William James Lewis, Thomas Cowles, and Ambrose Raines, who, being elected, tried and sworn the truth of, and upon premises to speak, and having heard the evidence, upon their oath to say, that the said Josiah Philips is guilty of the robbery aforesaid in manner and form as in the endictment against him is alleged, and that he had neither lands nor tenements, goods nor chattels at the time of committing the said robbery, nor at any time since, to their knowledge; and thereupon he is remanded to jail.

"October the 27th, 1778.

"Josiah Philips, late of the parish of Lynhaven, in the county of Princess Ann, labourer, who stands *convicted of robbery*, was again led to the bar in custody of the keeper of the public jail, and thereupon it being demanded of him if any thing he had or knew to say for himself, why the court, here, to judgment and execution of and upon the premises, should not proceed, he said he had nothing but what he had before said. Therefore, it is considered by the court, that he be hanged by the neck until he be dead.

"October 28, 1778.

"John Lowry, John Reizen, and Charles Bowman, for murder, *Josiah Philips*, James Hodges, Henry M'Lalen, and Robert Hodges, *for robbery*, James Randolph for horse-stealing, Joseph Turner, otherwise called Josiah Blankenship, for Burglary, and John Highwarden, for grand larceny, being under sentence of death by the judgment of the court yesterday passed against them for their said offence: It is awarded that execution of the said sentence be severally made and done upon them the said John Lowry, John Reizen, Charles Bowman, *Josiah Philips*, James Hodges, Henry M'Lalen, Robert Hodges, James Randolph, Joseph Turner, otherwise called Josiah Blankenship, and John Highwarden, by the sheriff of York county, on Friday the fourth day of December next, between the hours of ten and twelve in the forenoon, at the usual place of execution.

"Copies—Teste,

"PEYTON DREW, C. G. C."

Extract from Dixon and Hunter's paper of October 30th, 1778.

"WILLIAMSBURGH—At a general court, begun and held at the capitol the 10th instant, the following criminals were condemned to suffer death: Charles Bowman, from Prince George, for murder; John Lowry, from Bedford, for ditto; *Josiah Philips, James Hodges, Robert Hodges, and Henry M'Lalen, from Princess Ann, for robbery*: John Highwarden, from Fauquier, for grand larceny; Joseph Turner, alias Josiah Blankenship, from Albemarle, for burglary; and James Randolph, from Culpeper, for horse-stealing."

Extract from Dixon and Hunter's paper of December 4, 1778.

"WILLIAMSBURGH—This day were executed, at the gallows near this city, pursuant to their sentence, the following criminals, viz.: *Josiah Philips*, Henry M'Lalen, Robert Hodges, John Reizen and Josiah Blankenship."

CPSIA information can be obtained
at www.ICGtesting.com
Printed in the USA
BVHW061027240920
589464BV00002B/176